STOP!

This is the back of the book. You wouldn't want to spoil a great ending!

This book is printed "manga-style," in the authentic Japanese right-to-left format. Since none of the artwork has been flipped or altered, readers get to experience the story just as the creator intended. You've been asking for it, so TOKYOPOP® delivered: authentic, hot-off-the-press, and far more fun!

DIRECTIONS

If this is your first time reading manga-style, here's a quick guide to help you understand how it works.

It's easy... just start in the top right panel and follow the numbers. Have fun, and look for more 100% authentic manga from TOKYOPOP®!

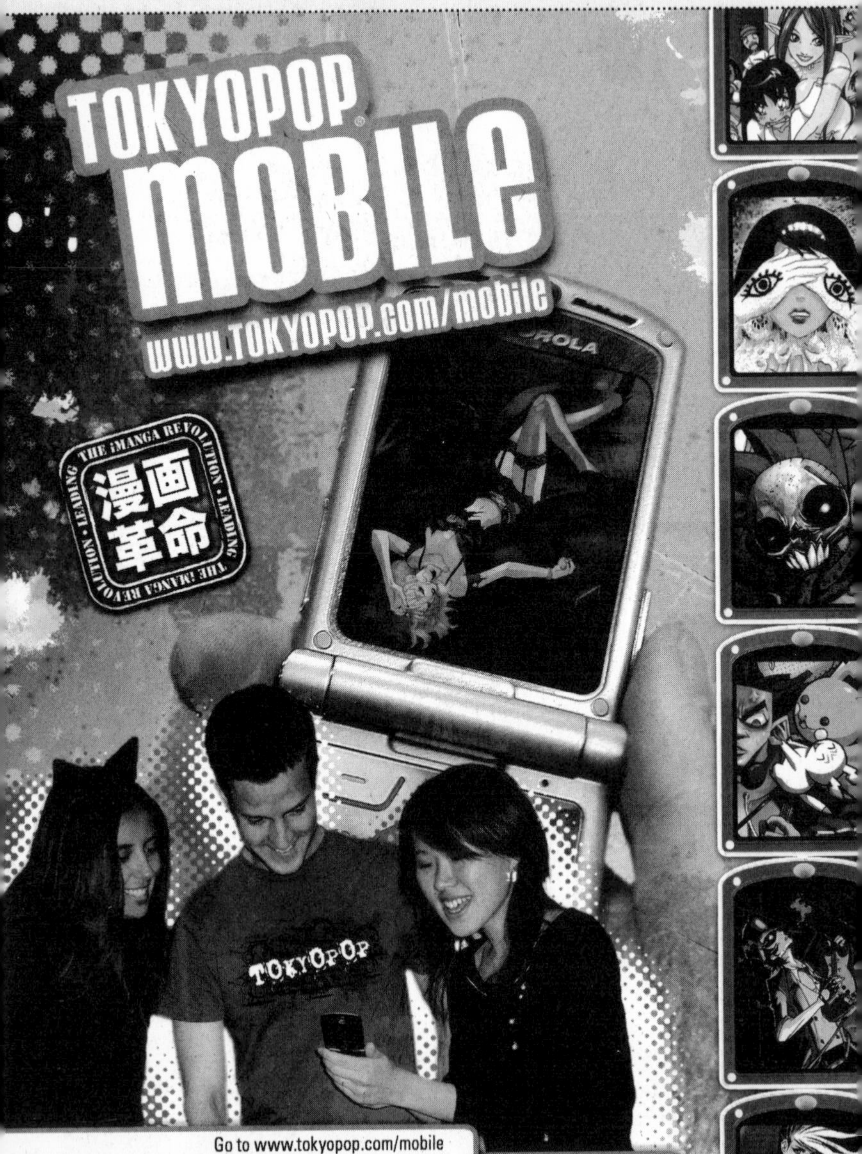
TOKYOPOP MOBILE
www.TOKYOPOP.com/mobile
THE MANGA REVOLUTION · LEADING
漫画
革命
TOKYOPOP
Go to www.tokyopop.com/mobile
for wallpapers, ringtones and more!
www.TOKYOPOP.com

CHARACTERS PROFILE

ME & MY BROTHERS

🍓 **SAKURA MIYASHITA:**
THE YOUNGEST.
IN 8TH GRADE. THE ONLY GIRL
IN THE MIYASHITA FAMILY.
SHE IS NOT BLOOD RELATED
TO HER FOUR BROTHERS.

🍓 **MASASHI MIYASHITA:**
THE ELDEST.
ROMANCE NOVELIST. ACCORDING
TO HIM, HE SOUNDS LIKE A
WOMAN BECAUSE OF HIS
JOB. HE'S THE LEADER OF THE
FOUR SAKURA-SPOILERS.

🍓 **TAKASHI MIYASHITA:**
THE 2ND BROTHER.
TEACHER. HE TEACHES
JAPANESE AT SAKURA'S
SCHOOL. HE'S A GENTLEMAN.

🍓 **TSUYOSHI MIYASHITA:**
THE 3RD BROTHER.
FULL-TIME PART-TIMER.
HE HAS A DIRTY MOUTH,
BUT IS ACTUALLY SHY.

🍓 **TAKESHI MIYASHITA:**
THE 4TH BROTHER.
IN 11TH GRADE. HE LOOKS OLD,
BUT HE'S THE YOUNGEST OF
FOUR BROTHERS. HE'S QUIET
AND LOVES PLANTS.

🍓 **NAKA-CHAN:**
SAKURA'S BEST FRIEND.
HER FAMILY NAME IS TANAKA.
A CHEERFUL GIRL.

🍓 **SUZUKI-KUN:**
SAKURA'S CLASSMATE.
DOES HE HAVE A
CRUSH ON SAKURA?

STORY

SAKURA LOST HER PARENTS WHEN SHE WAS
THREE AND WAS RAISED BY HER GRANDMOTHER.
THEN, WHEN SAKURA WAS 14, HER
GRANDMOTHER PASSED AWAY. SHE WAS ALL
ALONE UNTIL FOUR STEPBROTHERS SHOWED UP
WHILE HER STEPBROTHER'S FATHER HAD RAISED
SAKURA AS HIS OWN, SAKURA'S BIRTH FATHER
IS ACTUALLY HER MOTHER'S EX-BOYFRIEND.
EVEN THOUGH THE BROTHERS HAVE NO BLOOD
CONNECTION TO SAKURA, AFTER 11 YEARS OF
SEPARATION, THEY STARTED TO LIVE TOGETHER.
NOW THEIR HOUSE IS LIVELY EVERYDAY...

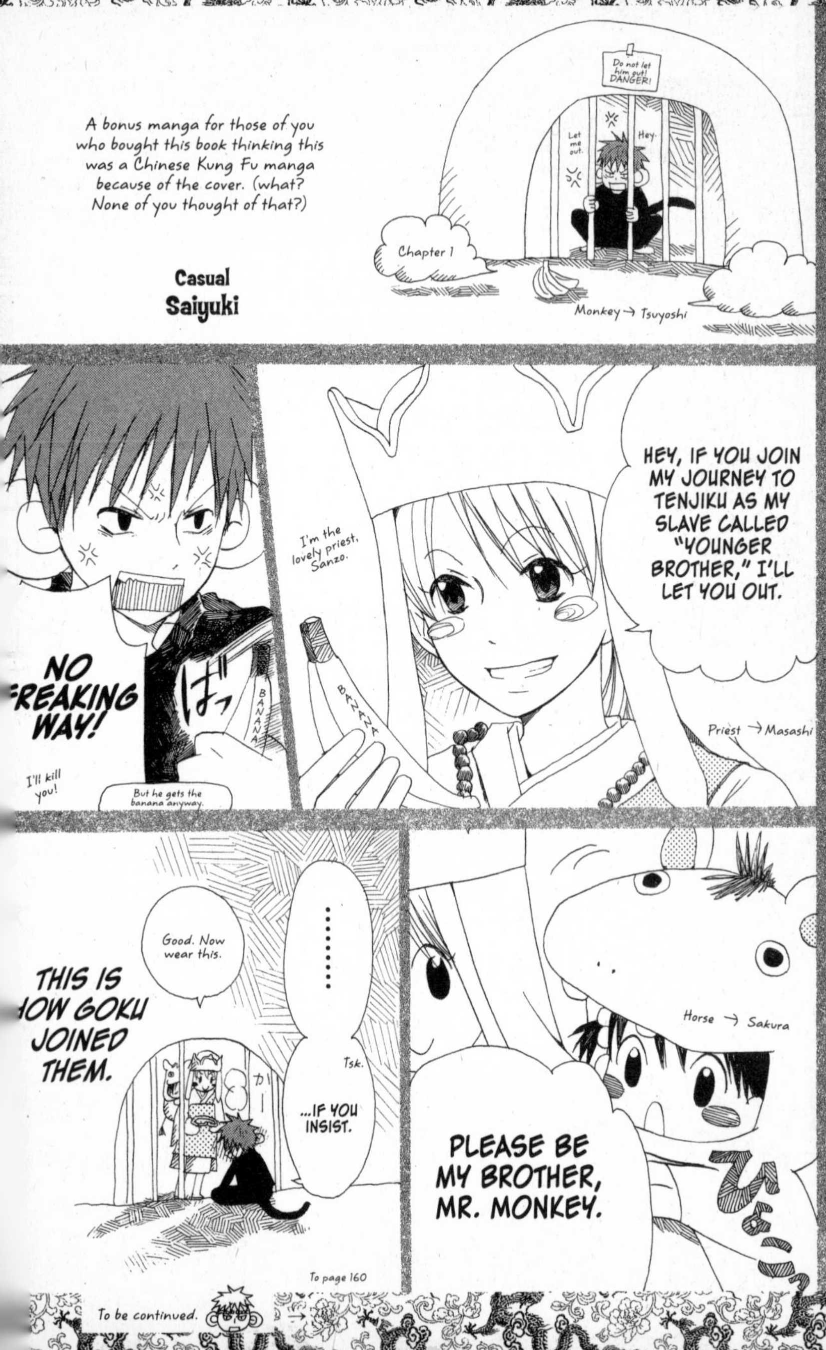
Do not let him out! DANGER!
Hey.
Let me out.
Chapter 1
Monkey → Tsuyoshi
A bonus manga for those of you who bought this book thinking this was a Chinese Kung Fu manga because of the cover. (what? None of you thought of that?)
Casual Saiyuki
HEY, IF YOU JOIN MY JOURNEY TO TENJIKU AS MY SLAVE CALLED "YOUNGER BROTHER," I'LL LET YOU OUT.
I'm the lovely priest, Sanzo.
BANANA
Priest → Masashi
NO FREAKING WAY!
BANANA
I'll kill you!
But he gets the banana anyway.
Horse → Sakura
PLEASE BE MY BROTHER, MR. MONKEY.
....
Tsk.
...IF YOU INSIST.
Good. Now wear this.
THIS IS HOW GOKU JOINED THEM.
To page 160
To be continued.

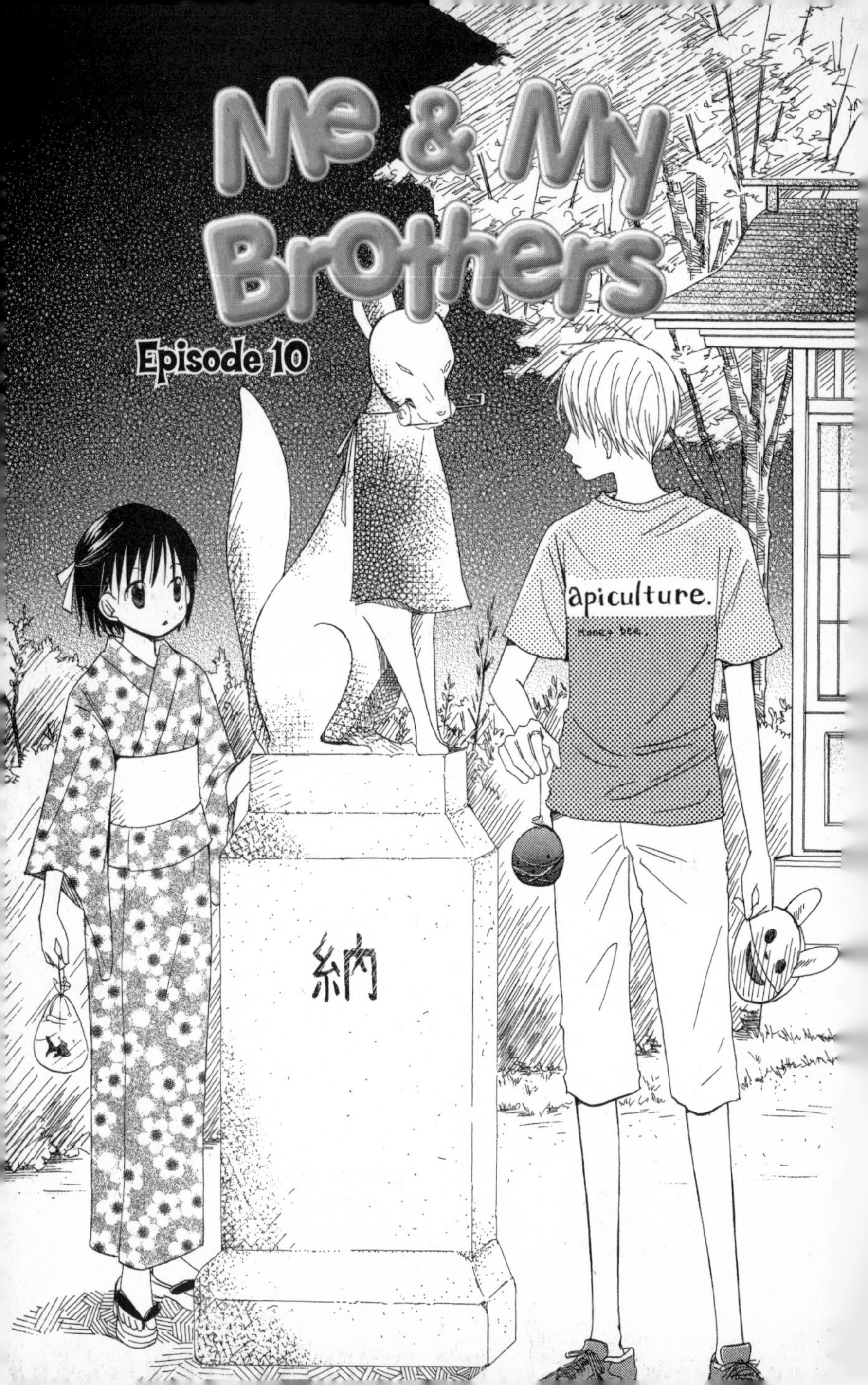
Me & My Brothers
Episode 10
apiculture.
納

WHY?

WHY IS THERE...

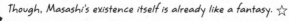

CAUTION!!

 Episode 10 takes you into a fantasy world.

Though, Masashi's existence itself is already like a fantasy. ☆

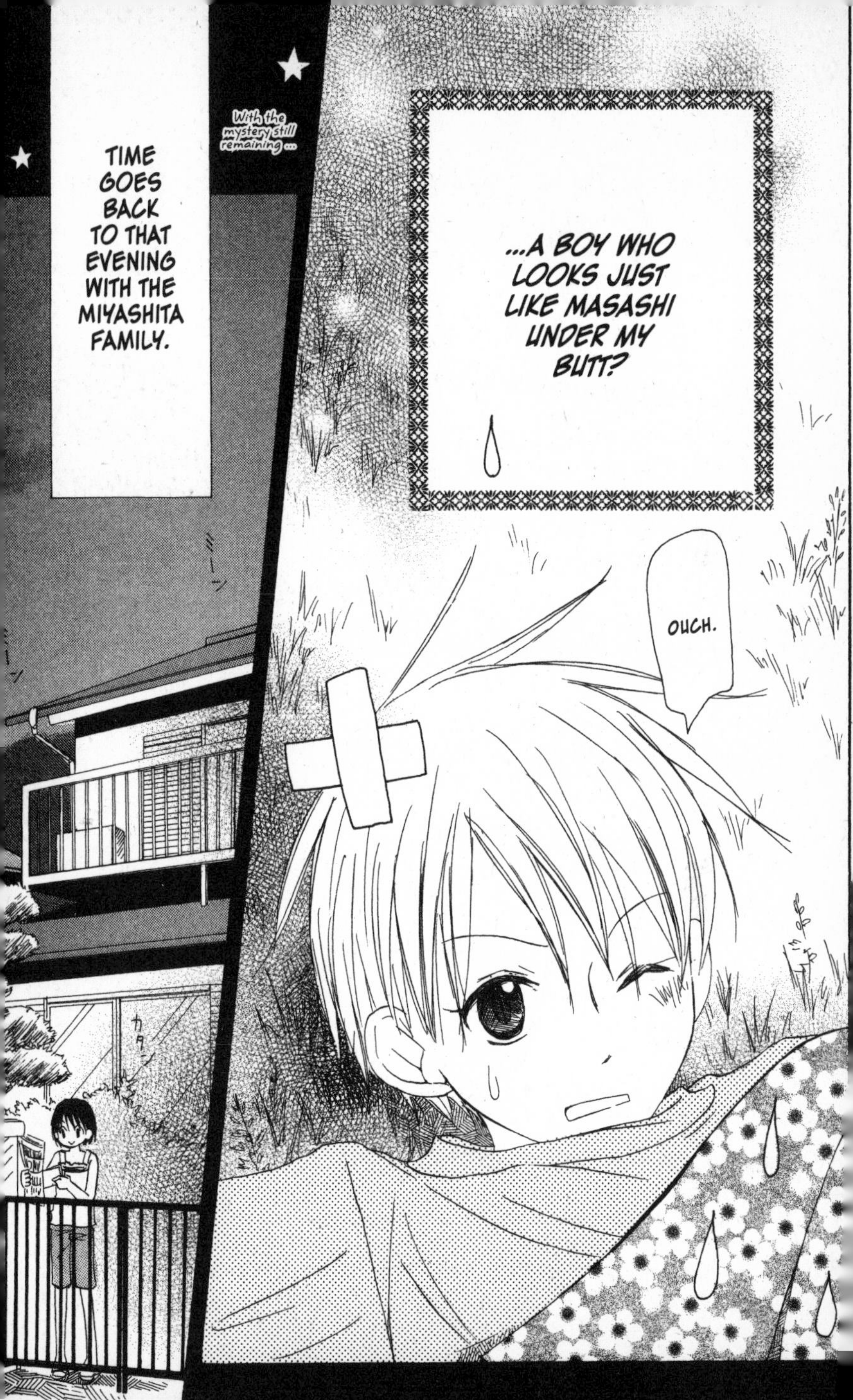
...A BOY WHO LOOKS JUST LIKE MASASHI UNDER MY BUTT?
OUCH.
With the mystery still remaining...
TIME GOES BACK TO THAT EVENING WITH THE MIYASHITA FAMILY.

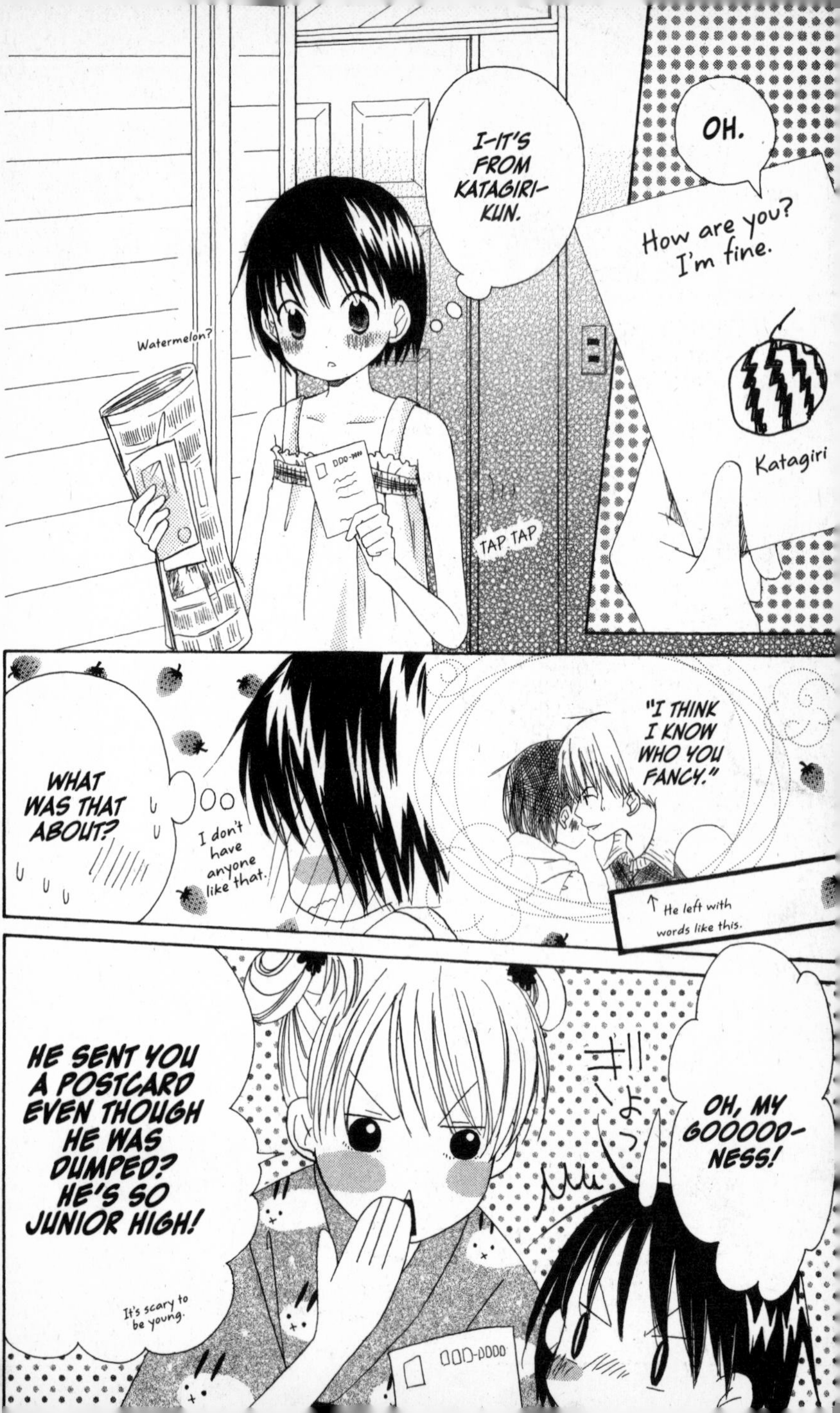
OH.
How are you? I'm fine.
Katagiri
I-IT'S FROM KATAGIRI-KUN.
TAP TAP
Watermelon?
"I THINK I KNOW WHO YOU FANCY."
He left with words like this.
WHAT WAS THAT ABOUT?
I don't have anyone like that.
OH, MY GOOOOOD-NESS!
HE SENT YOU A POSTCARD EVEN THOUGH HE WAS DUMPED? HE'S SO JUNIOR HIGH!
It's scary to be young.

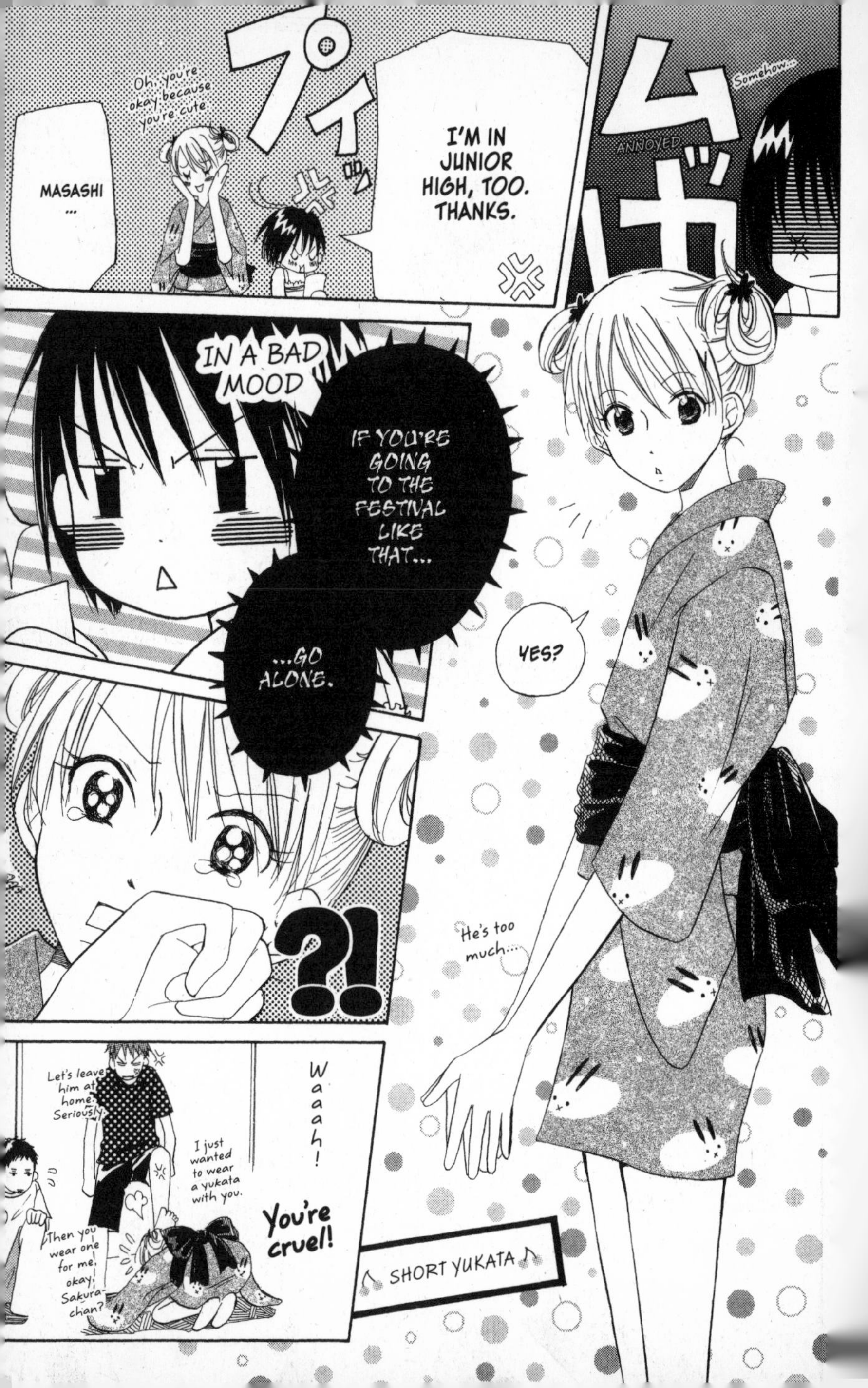
Somehow...
ANNOYED
I'M IN JUNIOR HIGH, TOO. THANKS.
Oh, you're okay because you're cute.
MASASHI ...
YES?
He's too much...
SHORT YUKATA
IN A BAD MOOD
IF YOU'RE GOING TO THE FESTIVAL LIKE THAT...
...GO ALONE.
?!
Waaaah!
You're cruel!
I just wanted to wear a yukata with you.
Let's leave him at home. Seriously.
Then you wear one for me, okay! Sakura-chan?

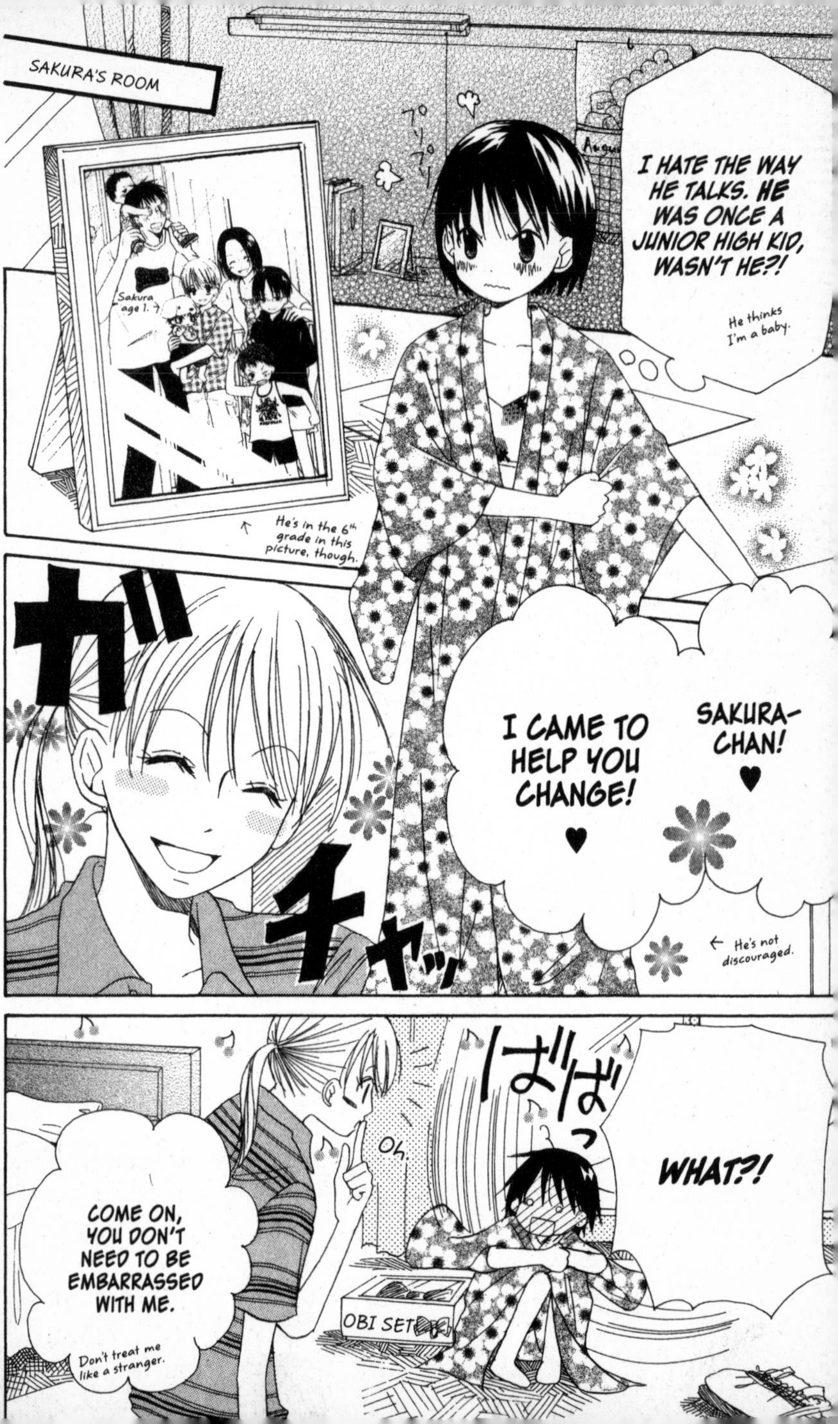
SAKURA'S ROOM
I HATE THE WAY HE TALKS. HE WAS ONCE A JUNIOR HIGH KID, WASN'T HE?!
He thinks I'm a baby.
プリプリ
Sakura age 1.
He's in the 6th grade in this picture, though.
SAKURA-CHAN!
I CAME TO HELP YOU CHANGE!
ガチャッ
He's not discouraged.
WHAT?!
ばばっ
Oh.
COME ON, YOU DON'T NEED TO BE EMBARRASSED WITH ME.
Don't treat me like a stranger.
OBI SET

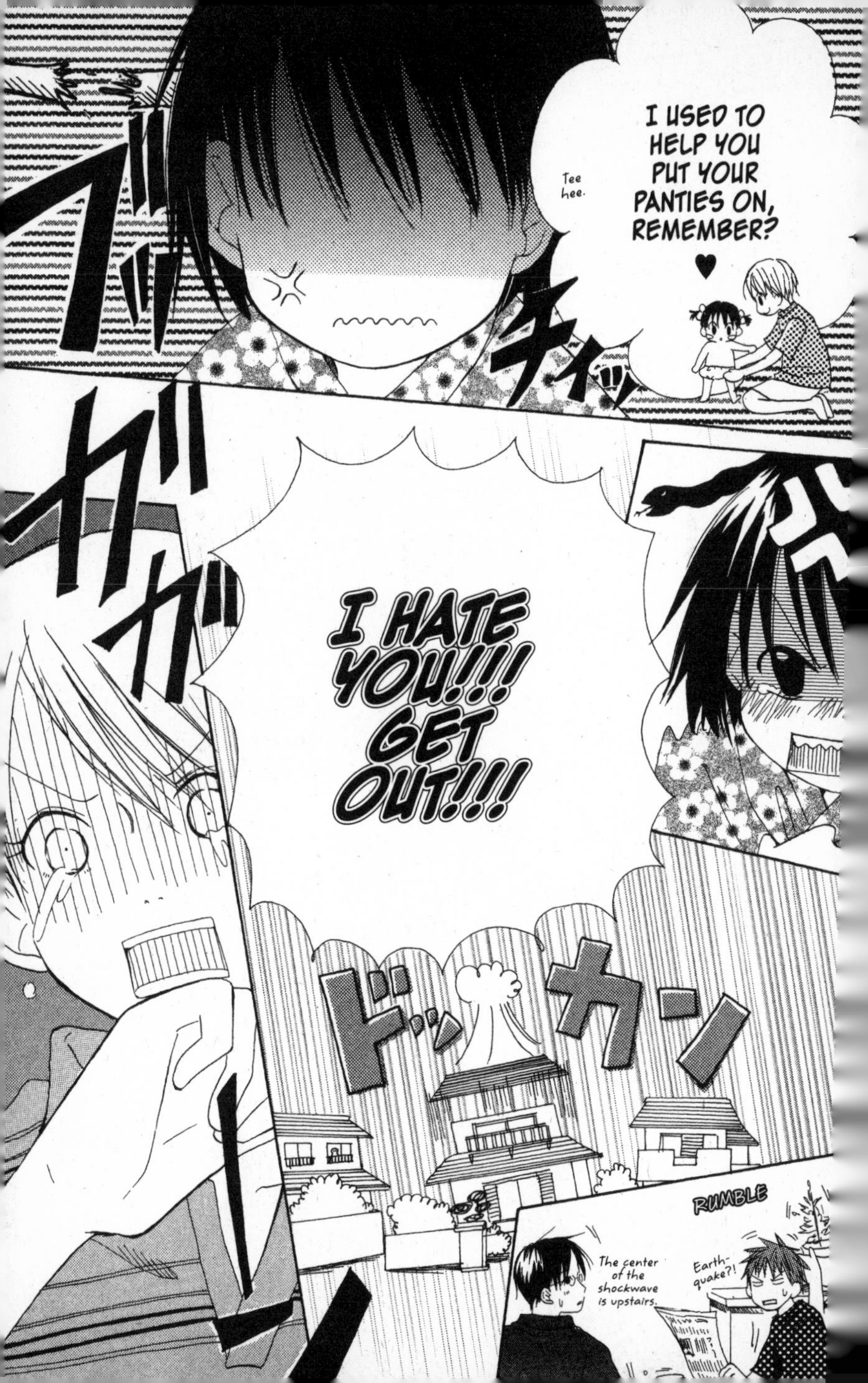
I USED TO HELP YOU PUT YOUR PANTIES ON, REMEMBER? ♥
Tee hee.
I HATE YOU!!! GET OUT!!!
RUMBLE
Earth-quake?!
The center of the shockwave is upstairs.

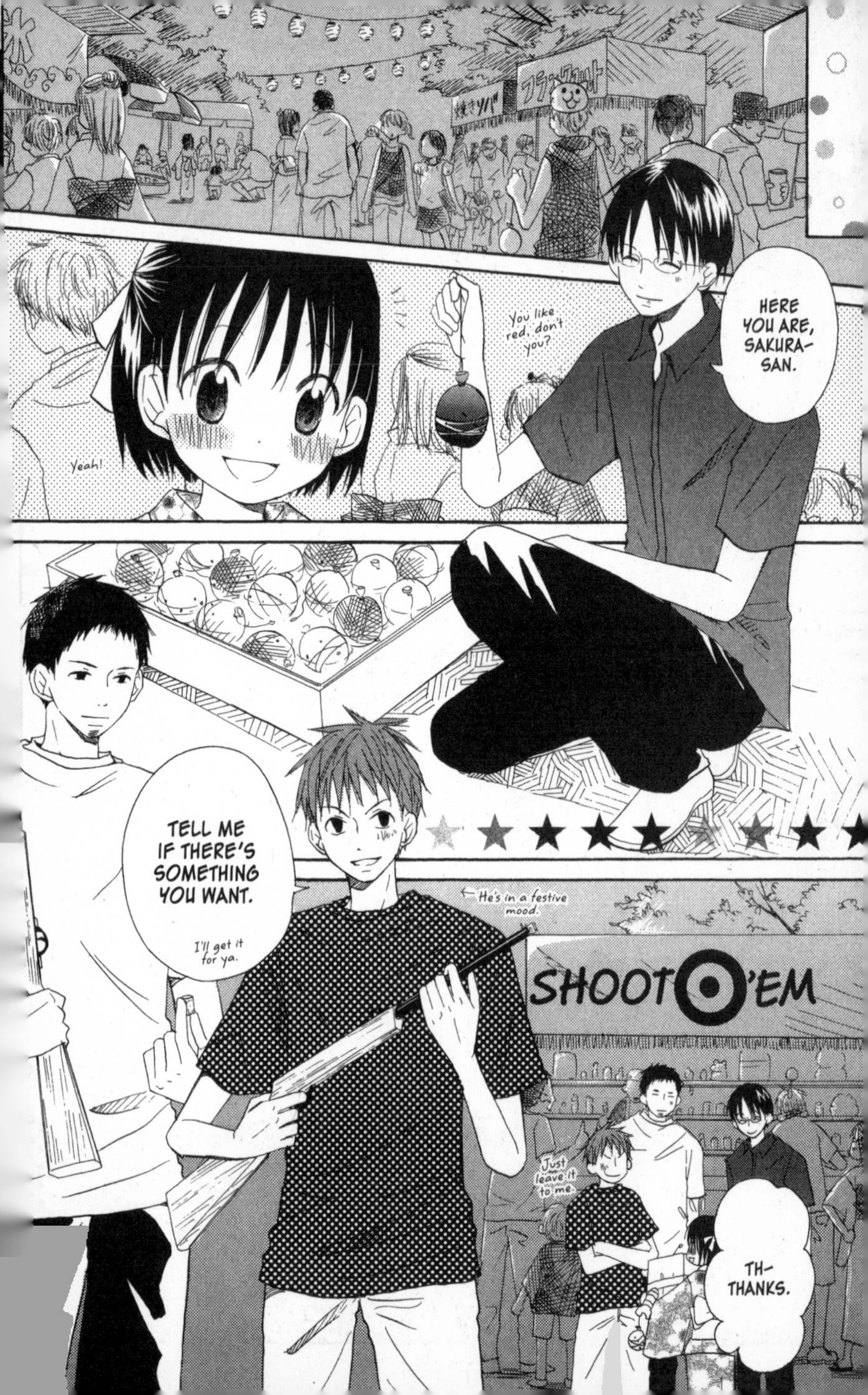
HERE YOU ARE, SAKURA-SAN.
You like red, don't you?
Yeah!
TELL ME IF THERE'S SOMETHING YOU WANT.
I'll get it for ya.
← He's in a festive mood.
SHOOT 'EM
Just leave it to me.
TH-THANKS.

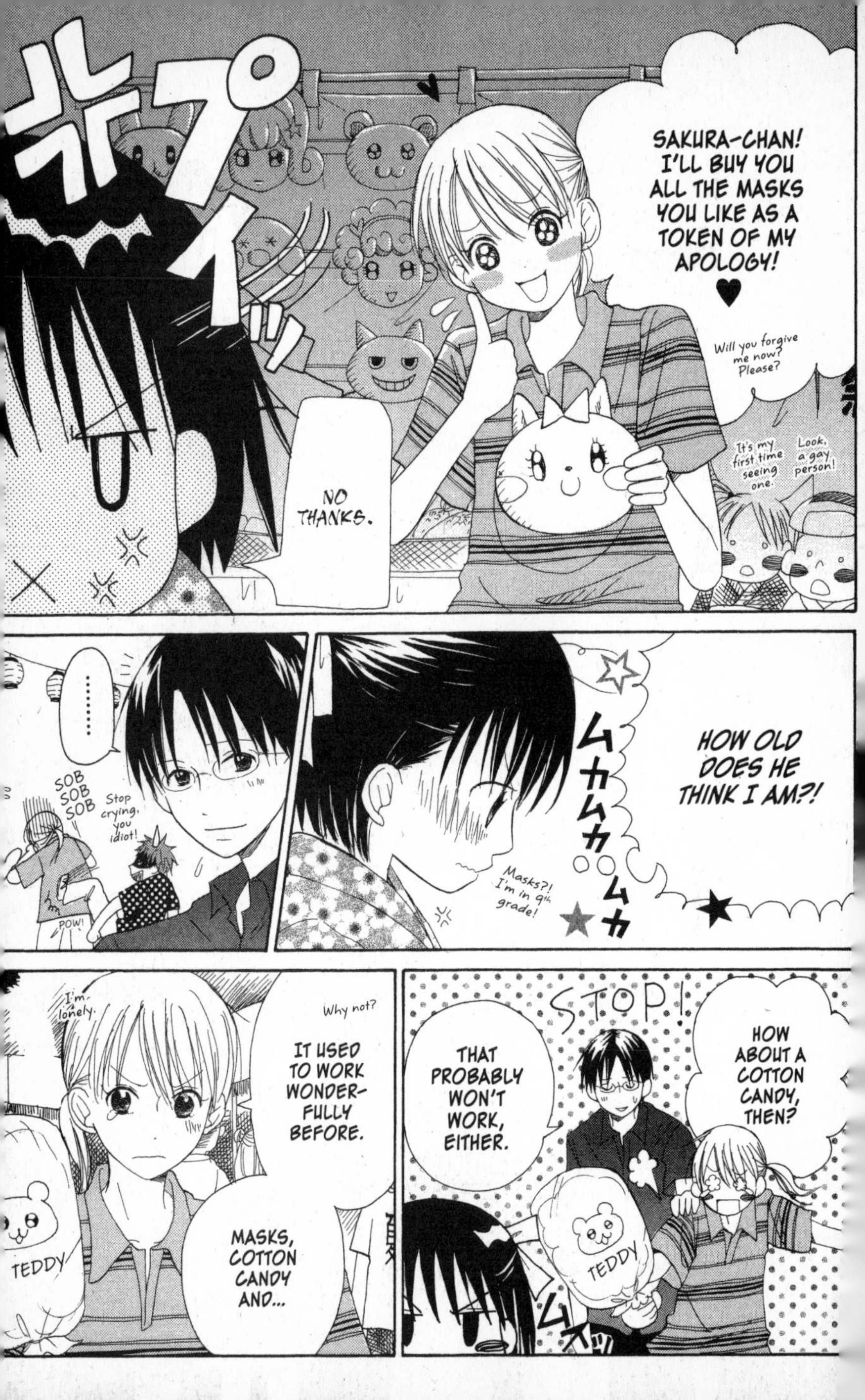
SAKURA-CHAN! I'LL BUY YOU ALL THE MASKS YOU LIKE AS A TOKEN OF MY APOLOGY! ♥
Will you forgive me now? Please?
Look, a gay person!
It's my first time seeing one.
NO THANKS.
HOW OLD DOES HE THINK I AM?!
Masks?! I'm in 9th grade!
......
SOB SOB SOB
Stop crying, you idiot!
POW!
STOP!
HOW ABOUT A COTTON CANDY, THEN?
THAT PROBABLY WON'T WORK, EITHER.
TEDDY
Why not?
IT USED TO WORK WONDERFULLY BEFORE.
I'm lonely.
MASKS, COTTON CANDY AND...
TEDDY

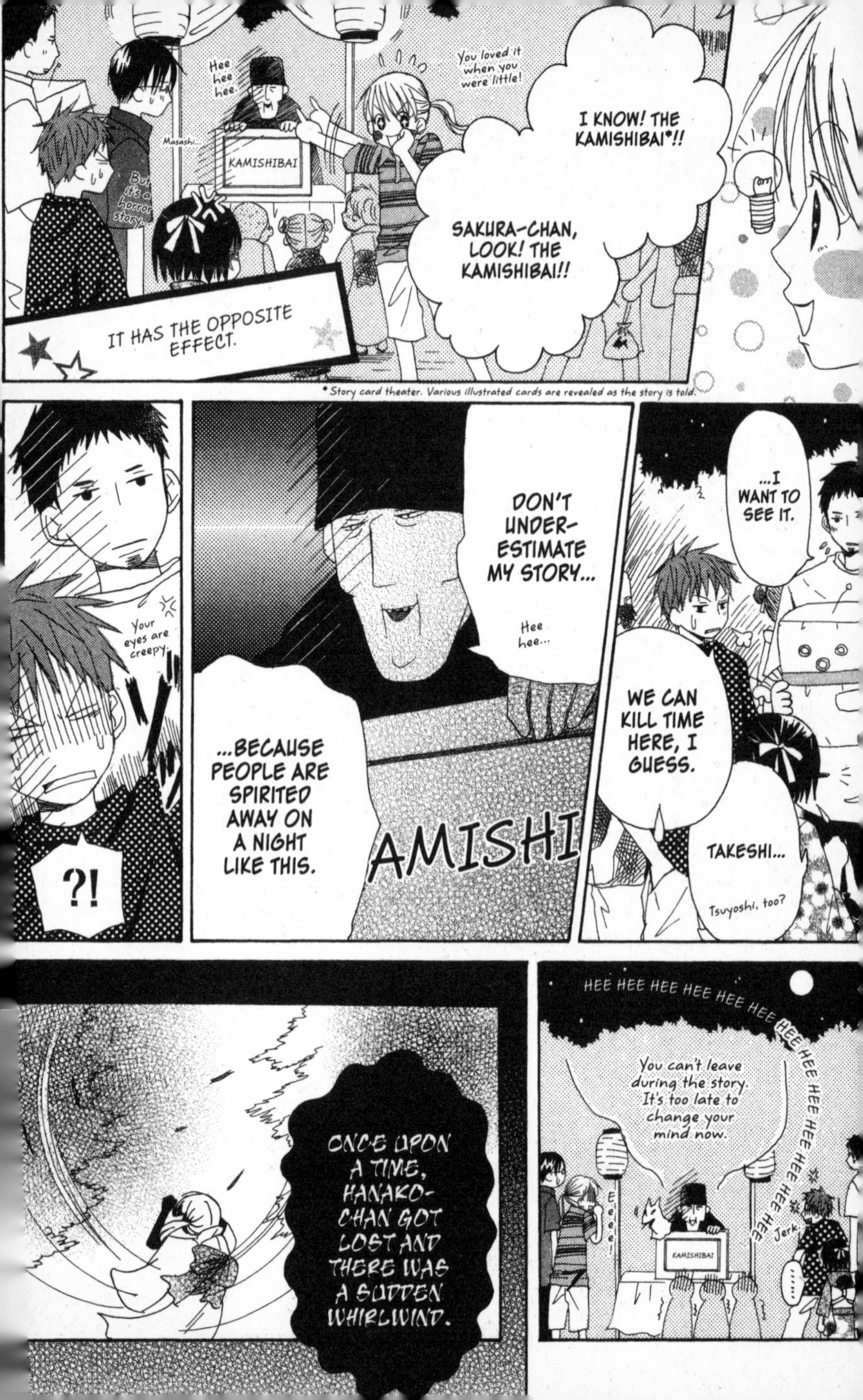
I KNOW! THE KAMISHIBAI*!!
You loved it when you were little!
SAKURA-CHAN, LOOK! THE KAMISHIBAI!!
Hee hee hee.
KAMISHIBAI
Masashi...
But it's a horror story...
IT HAS THE OPPOSITE EFFECT.
...I WANT TO SEE IT.
WE CAN KILL TIME HERE, I GUESS.
TAKESHI...
Tsuyoshi, too?
DON'T UNDER-ESTIMATE MY STORY...
Hee hee...
...BECAUSE PEOPLE ARE SPIRITED AWAY ON A NIGHT LIKE THIS.
AMISHI
Your eyes are creepy.
?!
HEE HEE HEE HEE HEE HEE HEE HEE HEE HEE HEE HEE HEE HEE
You can't leave during the story. It's too late to change your mind now.
Eeee!
KAMISHIBAI
Jerk.
......
ONCE UPON A TIME, HANAKO-CHAN GOT LOST AND THERE WAS A SUDDEN WHIRLWIND.

* Story card theater. Various illustrated cards are revealed as the story is told.

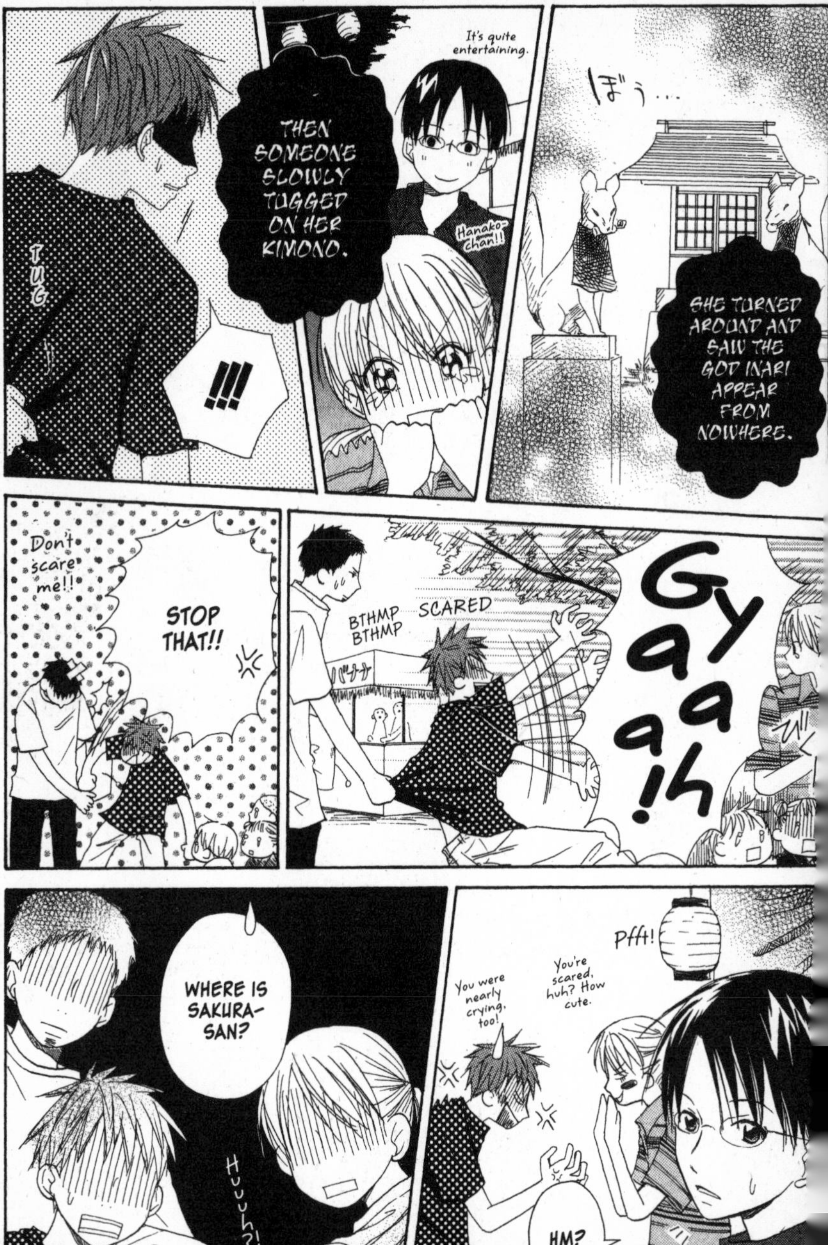
ぼう…
SHE TURNED AROUND AND SAW THE GOD INARI APPEAR FROM NOWHERE.
It's quite entertaining.
THEN SOMEONE SLOWLY TUGGED ON HER KIMONO.
Hanako-chan!!
TUG
!!!
Gyaaaah!
SCARED
BTHMP BTHMP
STOP THAT!!
Don't scare me!!
Pfft!
You're scared, huh? How cute.
You were nearly crying, too!
HM?
WHERE IS SAKURA-SAN?
Huuuh?!

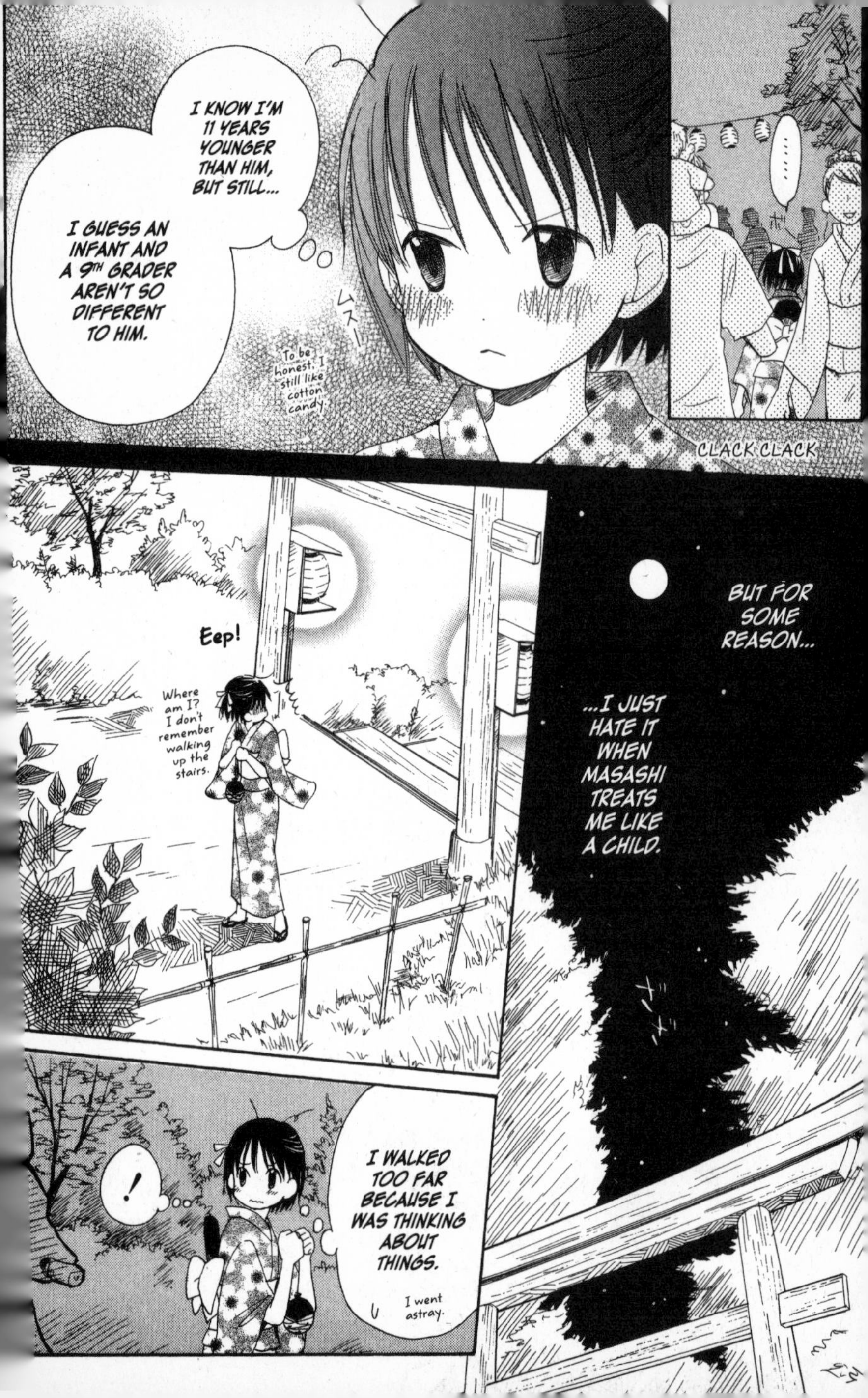
......
CLACK CLACK
I KNOW I'M 11 YEARS YOUNGER THAN HIM, BUT STILL...
I GUESS AN INFANT AND A 9TH GRADER AREN'T SO DIFFERENT TO HIM.
To be honest, I still like cotton candy.
BUT FOR SOME REASON...
...I JUST HATE IT WHEN MASASHI TREATS ME LIKE A CHILD.
Eep!
Where am I? I don't remember walking up the stairs.
!
I WALKED TOO FAR BECAUSE I WAS THINKING ABOUT THINGS.
I went astray.

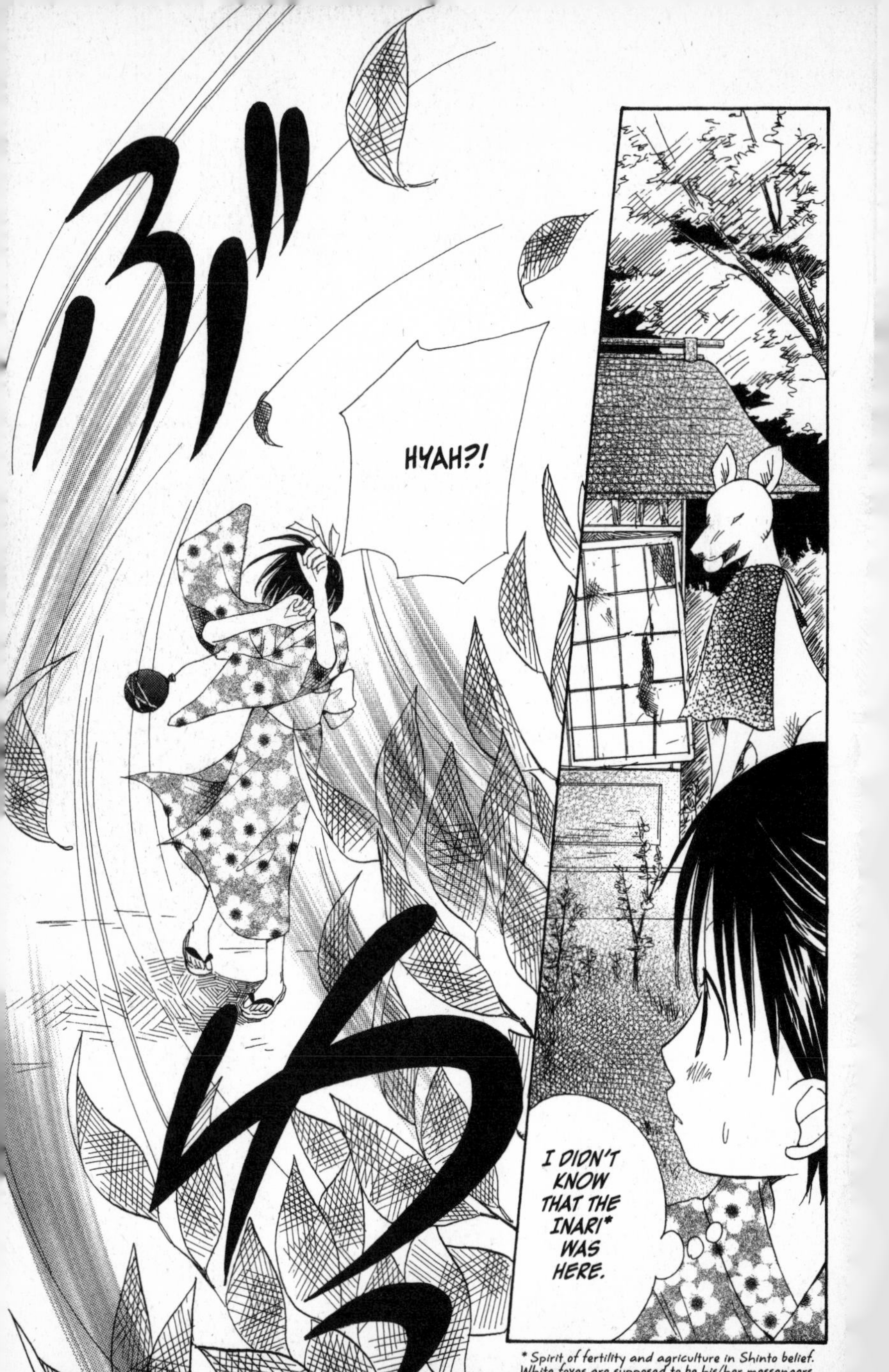
I DIDN'T KNOW THAT THE INARI* WAS HERE.
HYAH?!

* Spirit of fertility and agriculture in Shinto belief. White foxes are supposed to be his/her messengers.

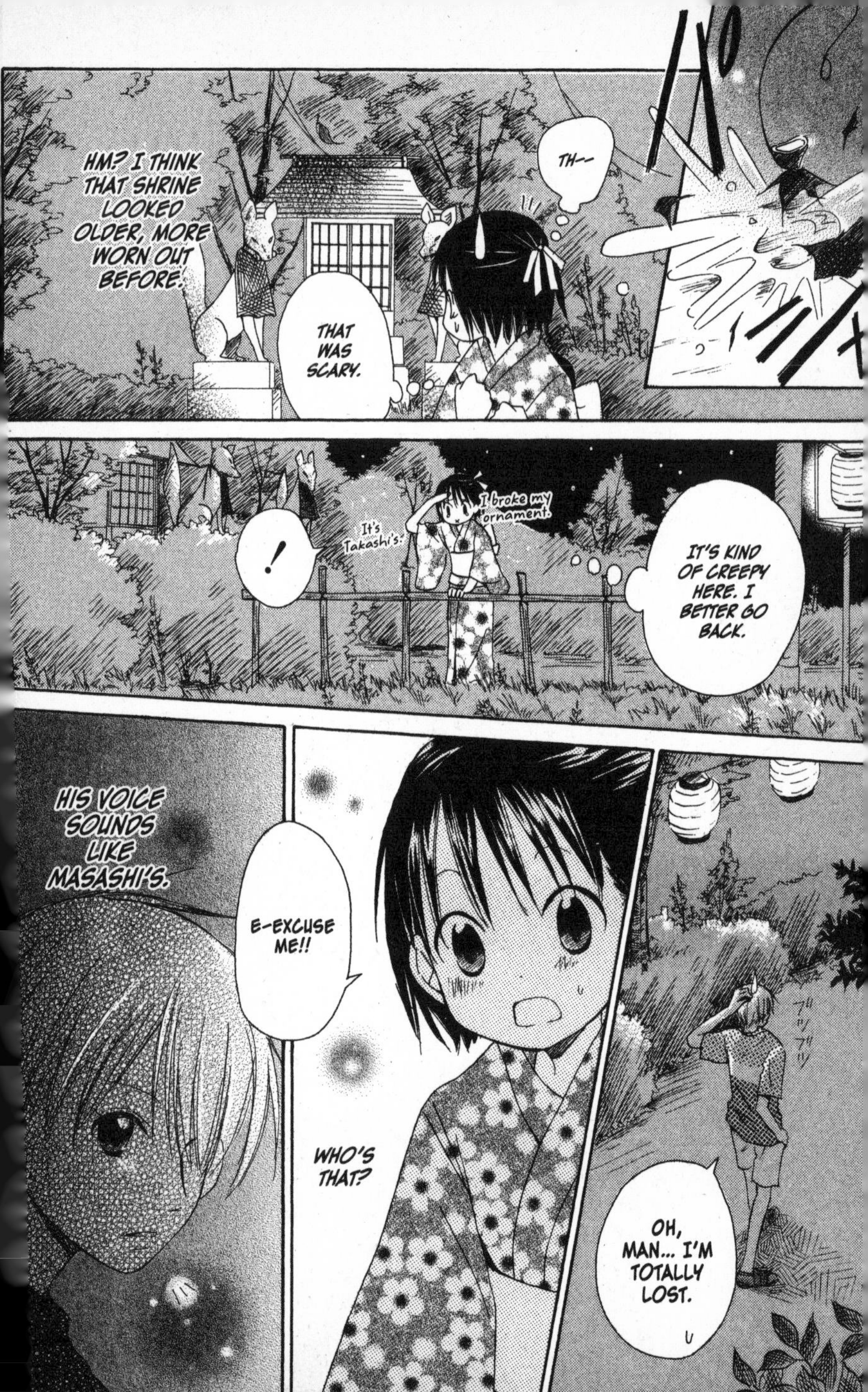
TH--
HM? I THINK THAT SHRINE LOOKED OLDER, MORE WORN OUT BEFORE.
THAT WAS SCARY.
IT'S KIND OF CREEPY HERE. I BETTER GO BACK.
I broke my ornament.
It's Takashi's.
!
OH, MAN... I'M TOTALLY LOST.
E-EXCUSE ME!!
WHO'S THAT?
HIS VOICE SOUNDS LIKE MASASHI'S.

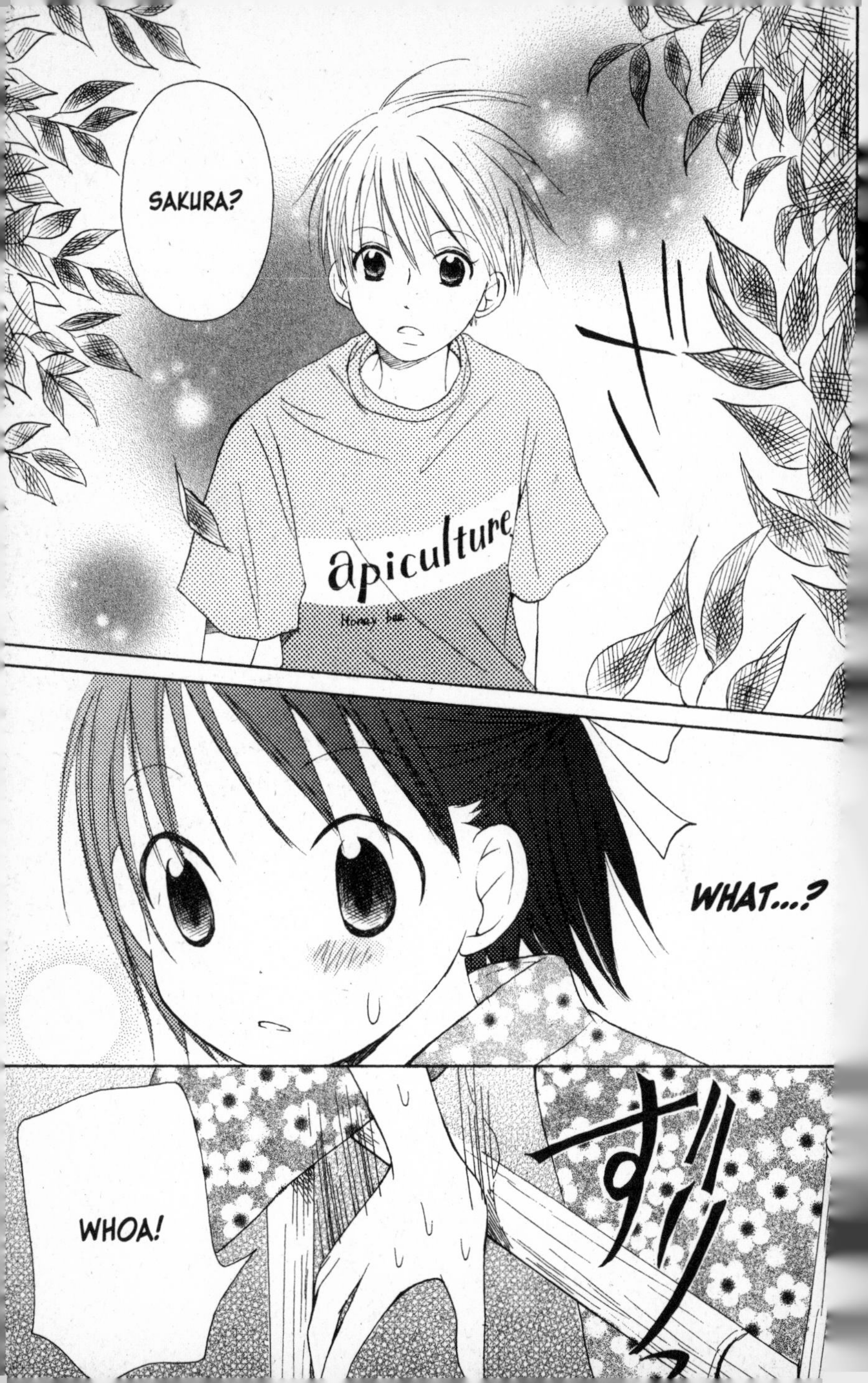
SAKURA?
apiculture
WHAT...?
WHOA!

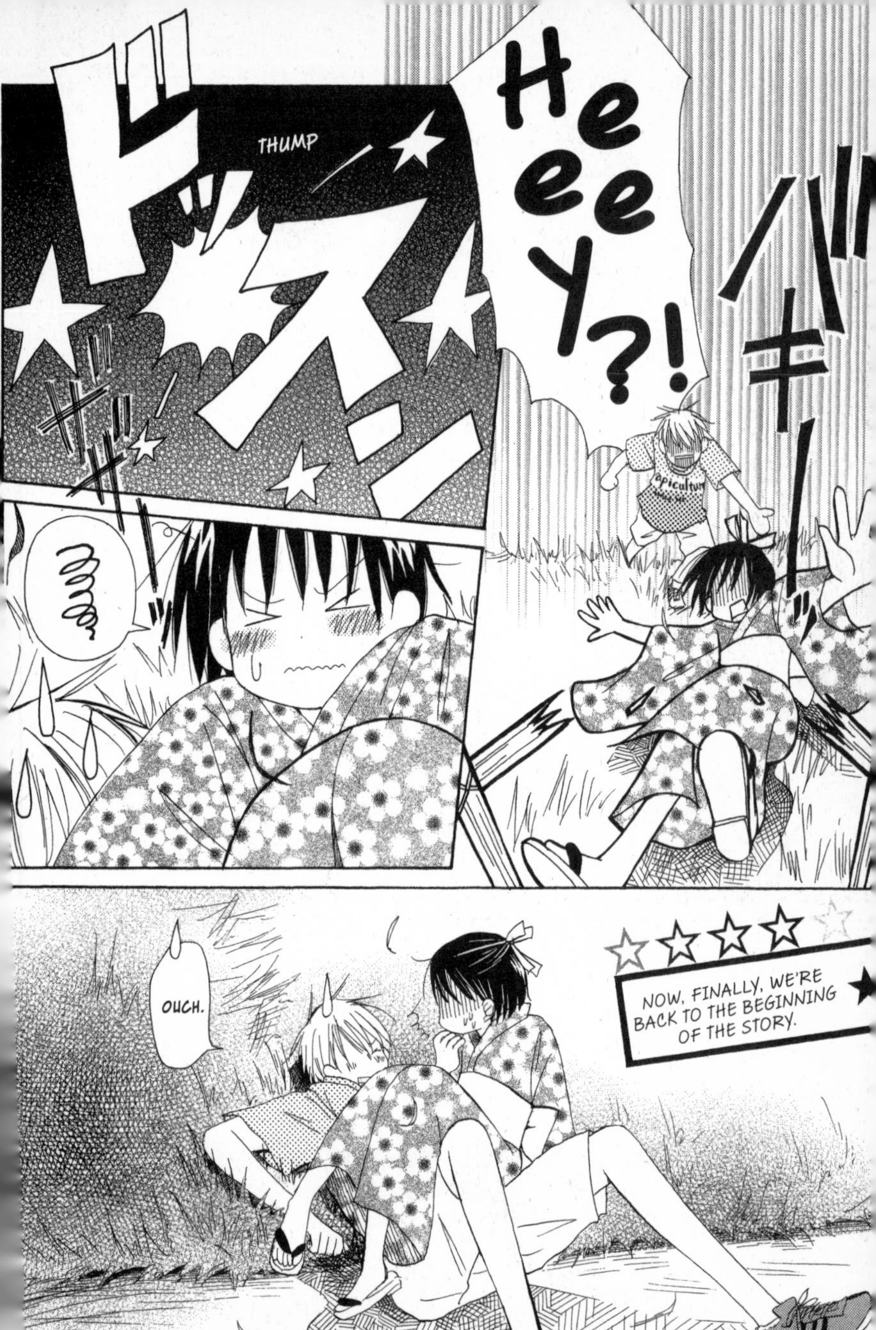
Heeey?!
THUMP
NOW, FINALLY, WE'RE BACK TO THE BEGINNING OF THE STORY.
OUCH.

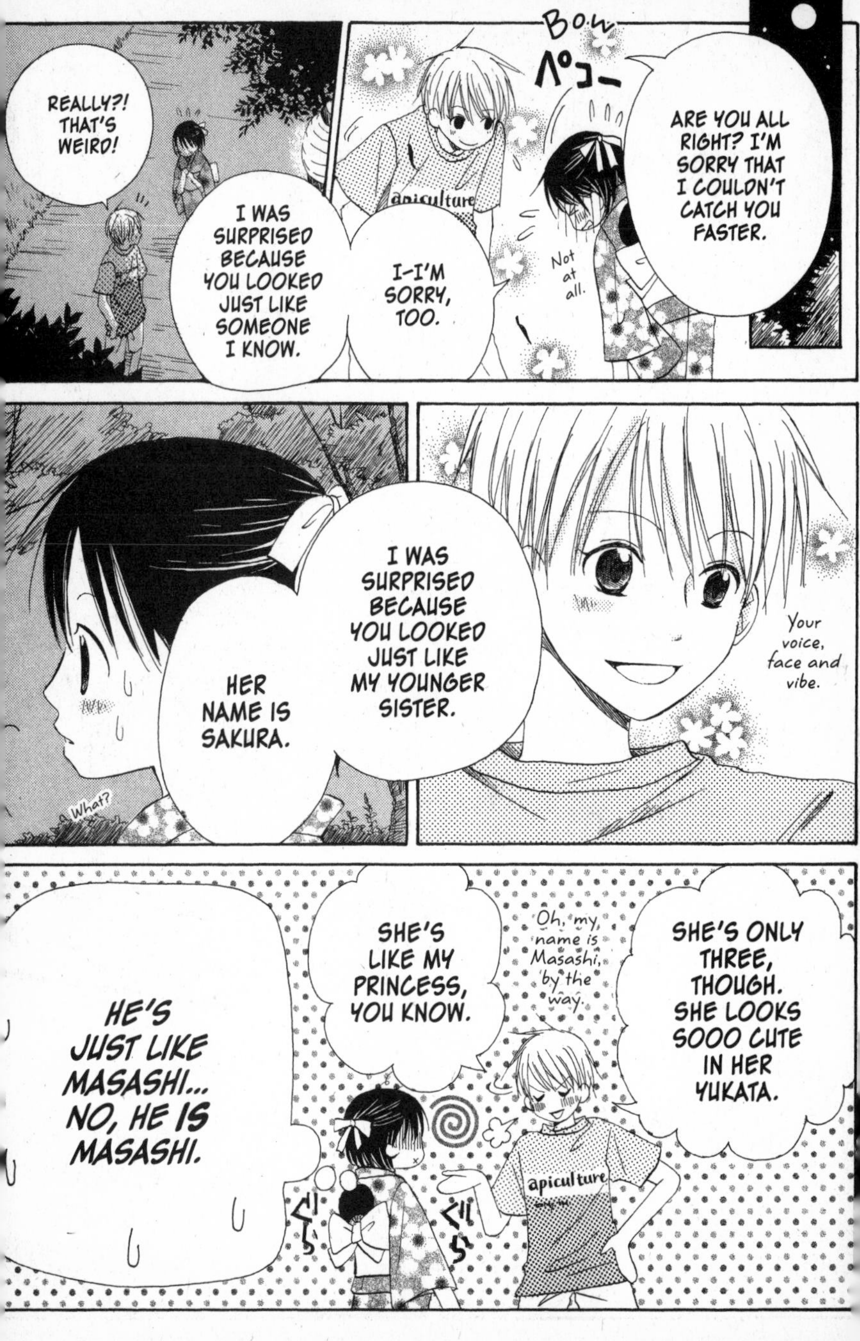
Bow
ペコー
ARE YOU ALL RIGHT? I'M SORRY THAT I COULDN'T CATCH YOU FASTER.
Not at all.
I-I'M SORRY, TOO.
I WAS SURPRISED BECAUSE YOU LOOKED JUST LIKE SOMEONE I KNOW.
apiculture
REALLY?! THAT'S WEIRD!
I WAS SURPRISED BECAUSE YOU LOOKED JUST LIKE MY YOUNGER SISTER.
Your voice, face and vibe.
HER NAME IS SAKURA.
What?
SHE'S ONLY THREE, THOUGH. SHE LOOKS SOOO CUTE IN HER YUKATA.
Oh, my name is Masashi, by the way.
SHE'S LIKE MY PRINCESS, YOU KNOW.
apiculture
HE'S JUST LIKE MASASHI... NO, HE IS MASASHI.

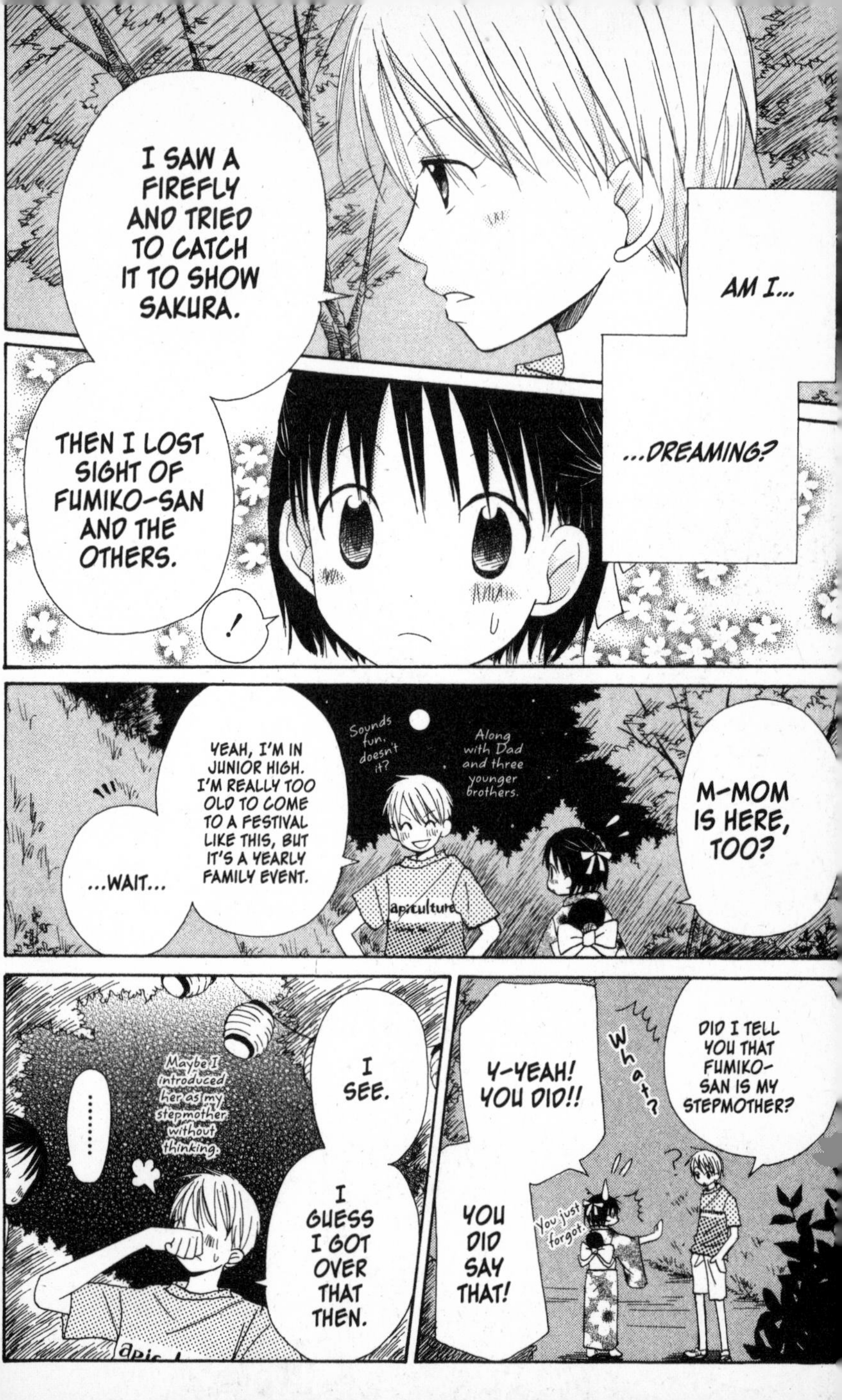
AM I...
...DREAMING?
I SAW A FIREFLY AND TRIED TO CATCH IT TO SHOW SAKURA.
THEN I LOST SIGHT OF FUMIKO-SAN AND THE OTHERS.
!
M-MOM IS HERE, TOO?
Along with Dad and three younger brothers.
Sounds fun, doesn't it?
YEAH, I'M IN JUNIOR HIGH. I'M REALLY TOO OLD TO COME TO A FESTIVAL LIKE THIS, BUT IT'S A YEARLY FAMILY EVENT.
...WAIT...
apiculture
DID I TELL YOU THAT FUMIKO-SAN IS MY STEPMOTHER?
What?
Y-YEAH! YOU DID!!
YOU DID SAY THAT!
You just forgot.
I SEE.
I GUESS I GOT OVER THAT THEN.
Maybe I introduced her as my stepmother without thinking.
....

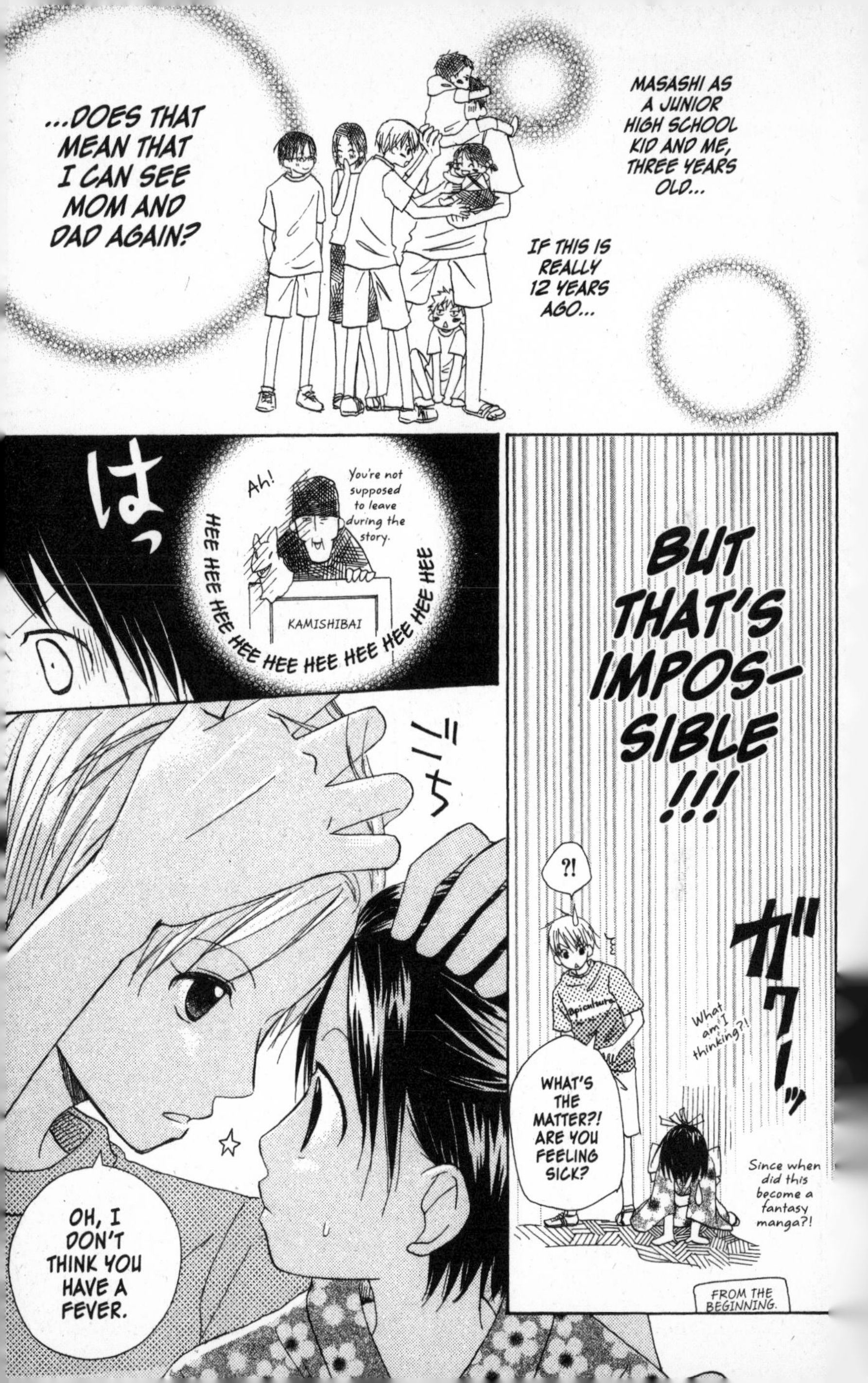
MASASHI AS A JUNIOR HIGH SCHOOL KID AND ME, THREE YEARS OLD...
IF THIS IS REALLY 12 YEARS AGO...
...DOES THAT MEAN THAT I CAN SEE MOM AND DAD AGAIN?
BUT THAT'S IMPOSSIBLE!!!
?!
What am I thinking?!
ガクーッ
WHAT'S THE MATTER?! ARE YOU FEELING SICK?
Since when did this become a fantasy manga?!
FROM THE BEGINNING.
はっ
Ah!
You're not supposed to leave during the story.
HEE HEE HEE HEE HEE HEE HEE HEE HEE
KAMISHIBAI
OH, I DON'T THINK YOU HAVE A FEVER.

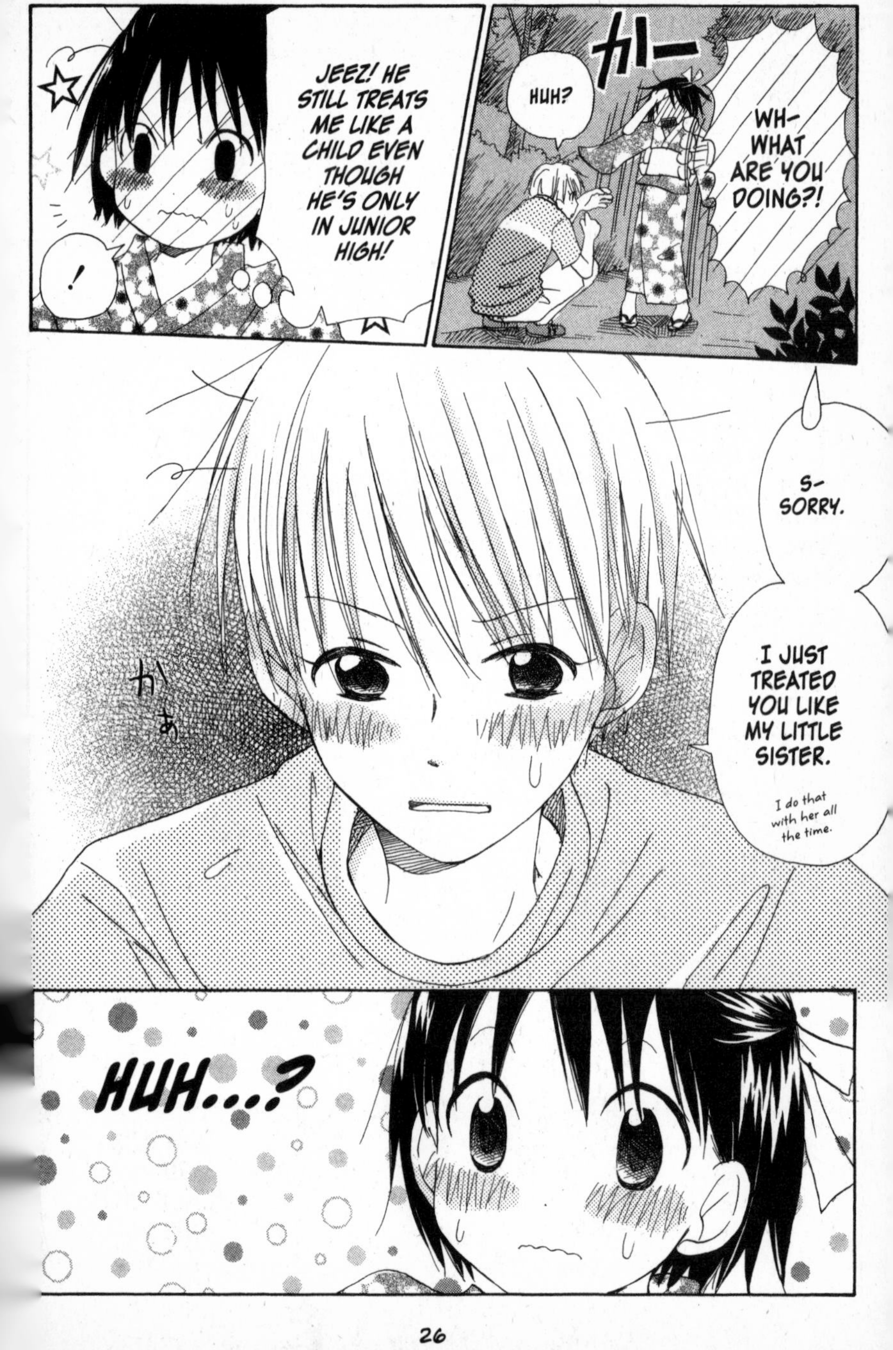
カー
WH- WHAT ARE YOU DOING?!
HUH?
JEEZ! HE STILL TREATS ME LIKE A CHILD EVEN THOUGH HE'S ONLY IN JUNIOR HIGH!
!
S- SORRY.
I JUST TREATED YOU LIKE MY LITTLE SISTER.
I do that with her all the time.
かぁ
HUH...?

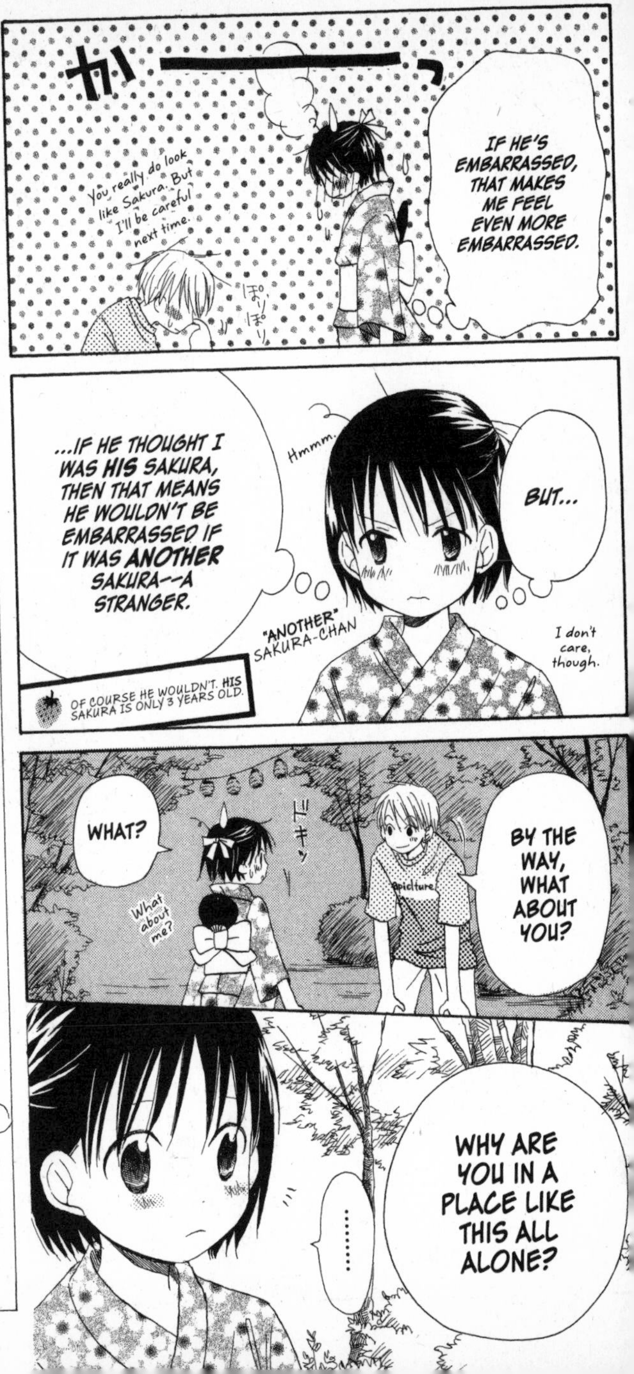
かーーーっ
IF HE'S EMBARRASSED, THAT MAKES ME FEEL EVEN MORE EMBARRASSED.
You really do look like Sakura. But I'll be careful next time.
ぽりぽり
BUT...
Hmmm.
...IF HE THOUGHT I WAS HIS SAKURA, THEN THAT MEANS HE WOULDN'T BE EMBARRASSED IF IT WAS ANOTHER SAKURA--A STRANGER.
I don't care, though.
"ANOTHER" SAKURA-CHAN
OF COURSE HE WOULDN'T. HIS SAKURA IS ONLY 3 YEARS OLD.
BY THE WAY, WHAT ABOUT YOU?
ドキッ
WHAT?
What about me?
WHY ARE YOU IN A PLACE LIKE THIS ALL ALONE?
......

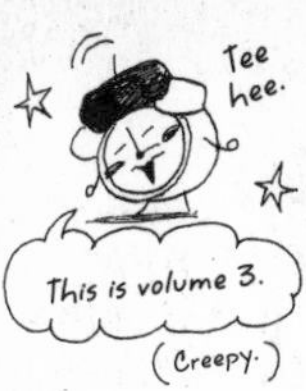
Tee hee.
This is volume 3.
(Creepy.)

Sorry, am I creeping you out? Although, actually, I'm happy I'm creepy! This is like a dream. No, this must be a dream. I'm scared that I might wake up from it soon. Anyway, if this is not a dream, this is volume 3!! I hope you'll enjoy it.

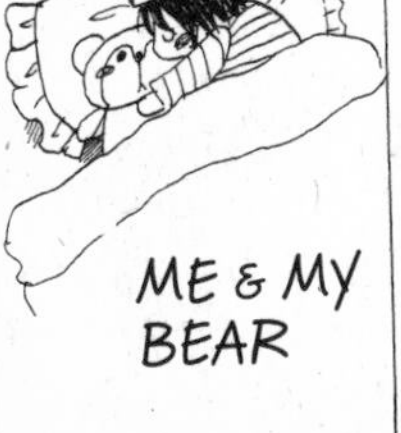

ME & MY BEAR

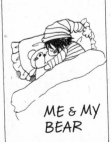

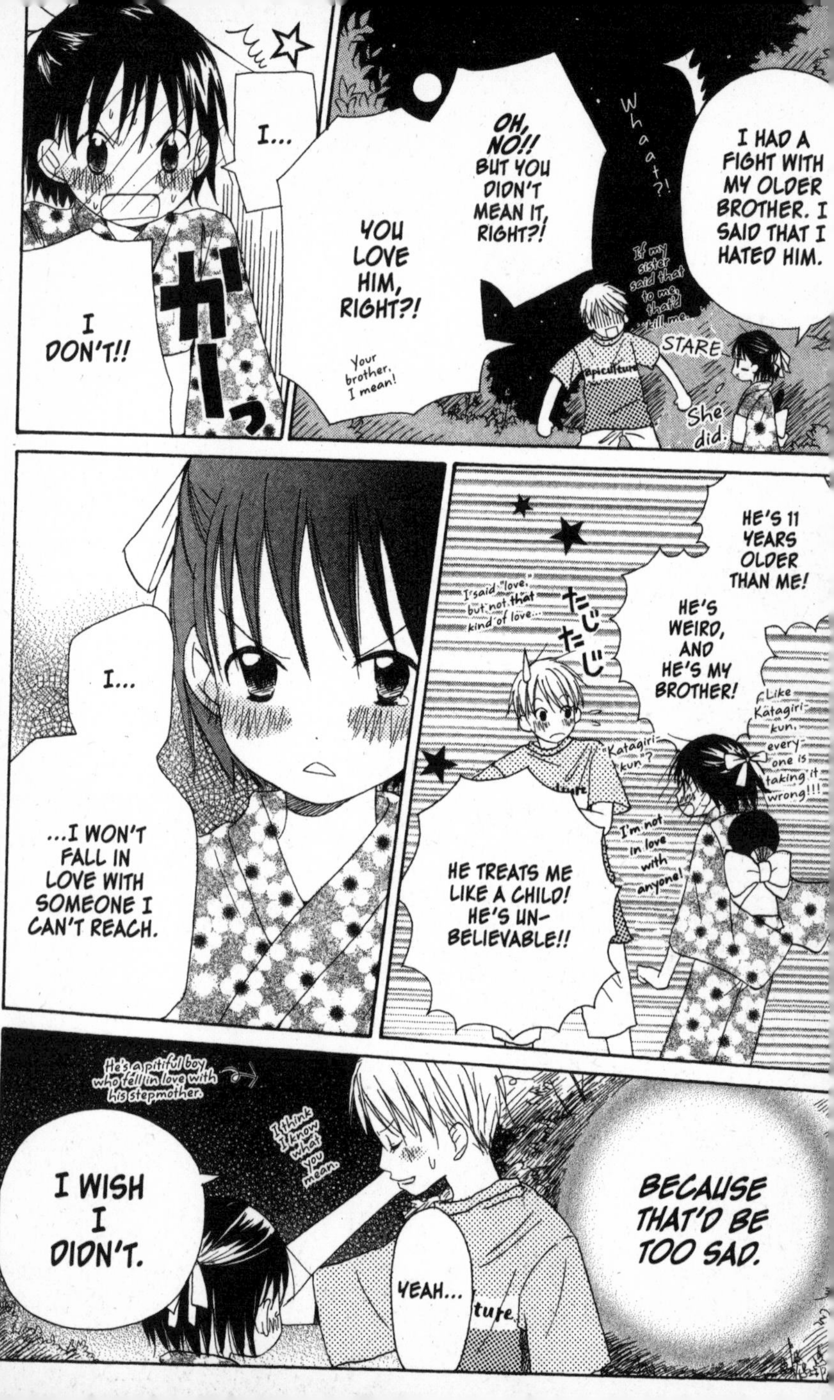
I HAD A FIGHT WITH MY OLDER BROTHER. I SAID THAT I HATED HIM.
Whaaat?!
If my sister said that to me, that'd kill me.
STARE
apiculture
She did.
OH, NO!! BUT YOU DIDN'T MEAN IT, RIGHT?!
YOU LOVE HIM, RIGHT?!
Your brother, I mean!
I...
ガーッ
I DON'T!!
HE'S 11 YEARS OLDER THAN ME!
HE'S WEIRD, AND HE'S MY BROTHER!
Like Katagiri-kun, every-one is taking it wrong!!!
"Katagiri-kun"?
I'm not in love with anyone!
I said "love," but not that kind of love...
たじたじ
HE TREATS ME LIKE A CHILD! HE'S UN-BELIEVABLE!!
I...
...I WON'T FALL IN LOVE WITH SOMEONE I CAN'T REACH.
BECAUSE THAT'D BE TOO SAD.
YEAH...
I think I know what you mean.
He's a pitiful boy who fell in love with his stepmother.
I WISH I DIDN'T.

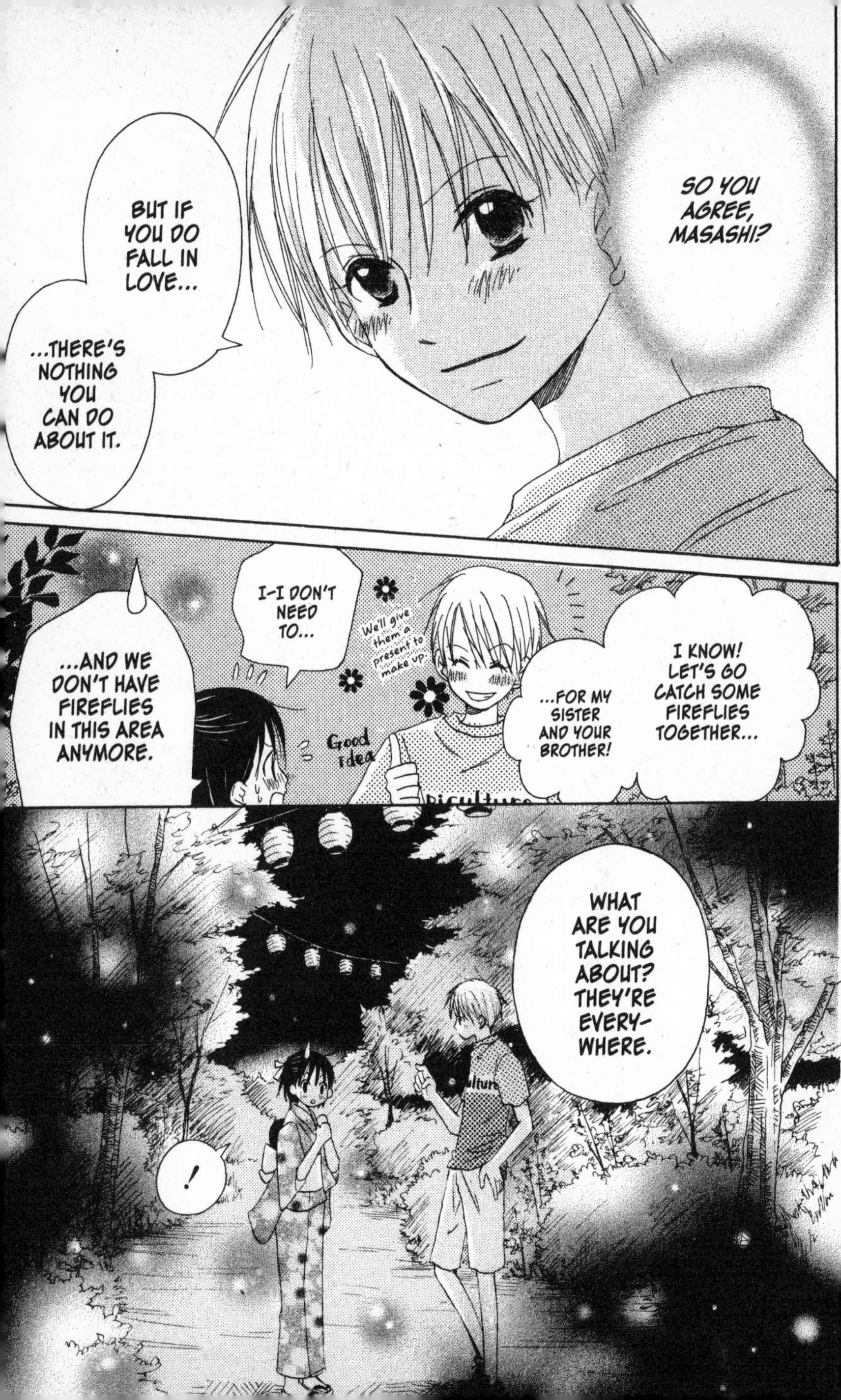
SO YOU AGREE, MASASHI?
BUT IF YOU DO FALL IN LOVE...
...THERE'S NOTHING YOU CAN DO ABOUT IT.
I KNOW! LET'S GO CATCH SOME FIREFLIES TOGETHER...
...FOR MY SISTER AND YOUR BROTHER!
We'll give them a present to make up.
Good idea
I-I DON'T NEED TO...
...AND WE DON'T HAVE FIREFLIES IN THIS AREA ANYMORE.
WHAT ARE YOU TALKING ABOUT? THEY'RE EVERY-WHERE.
!

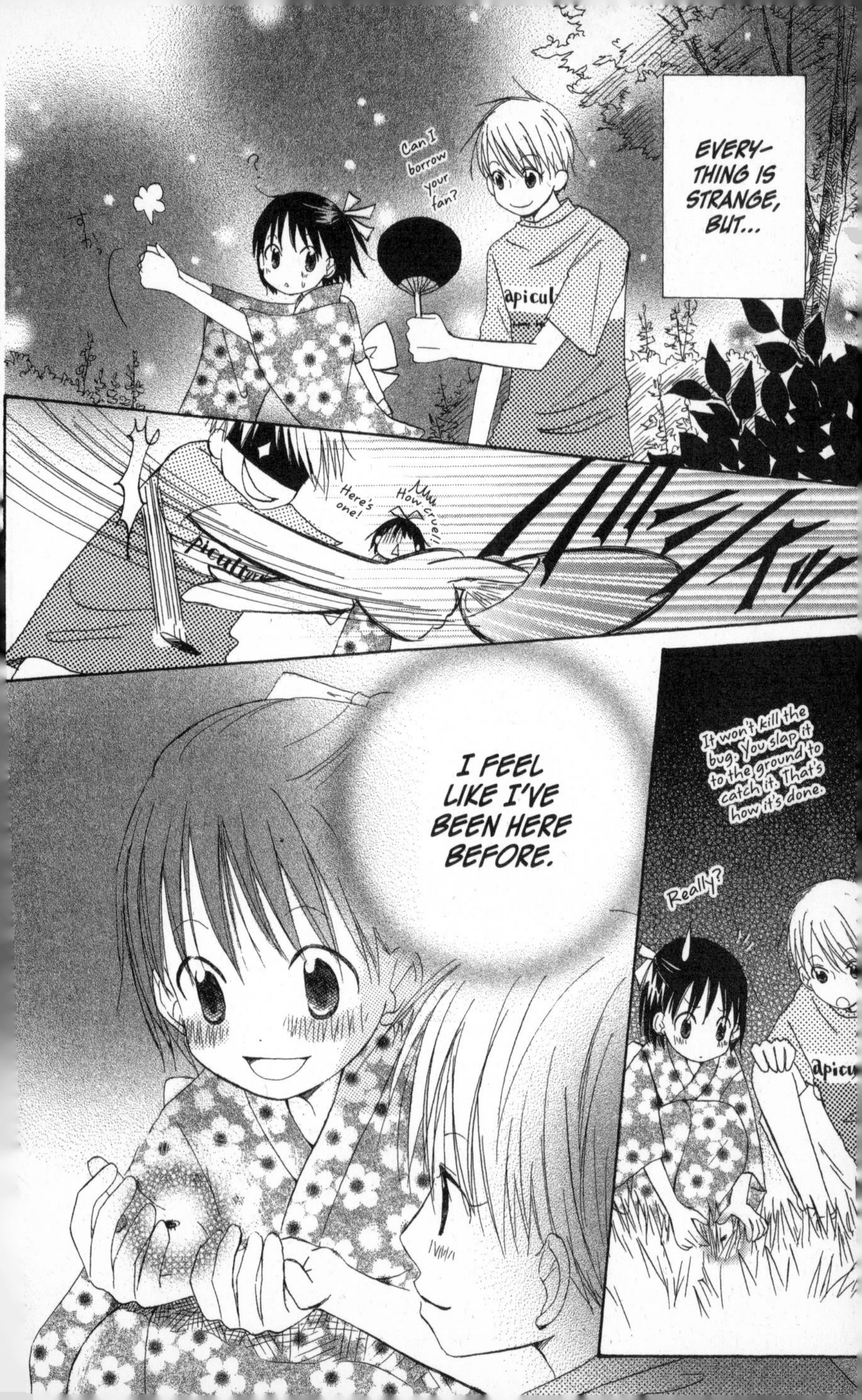
EVERYTHING IS STRANGE, BUT...
Can I borrow your fan?
Here's one!
How cruel!!
It won't kill the bug. You slap it to the ground to catch it. That's how it's done.
Really?
I FEEL LIKE I'VE BEEN HERE BEFORE.

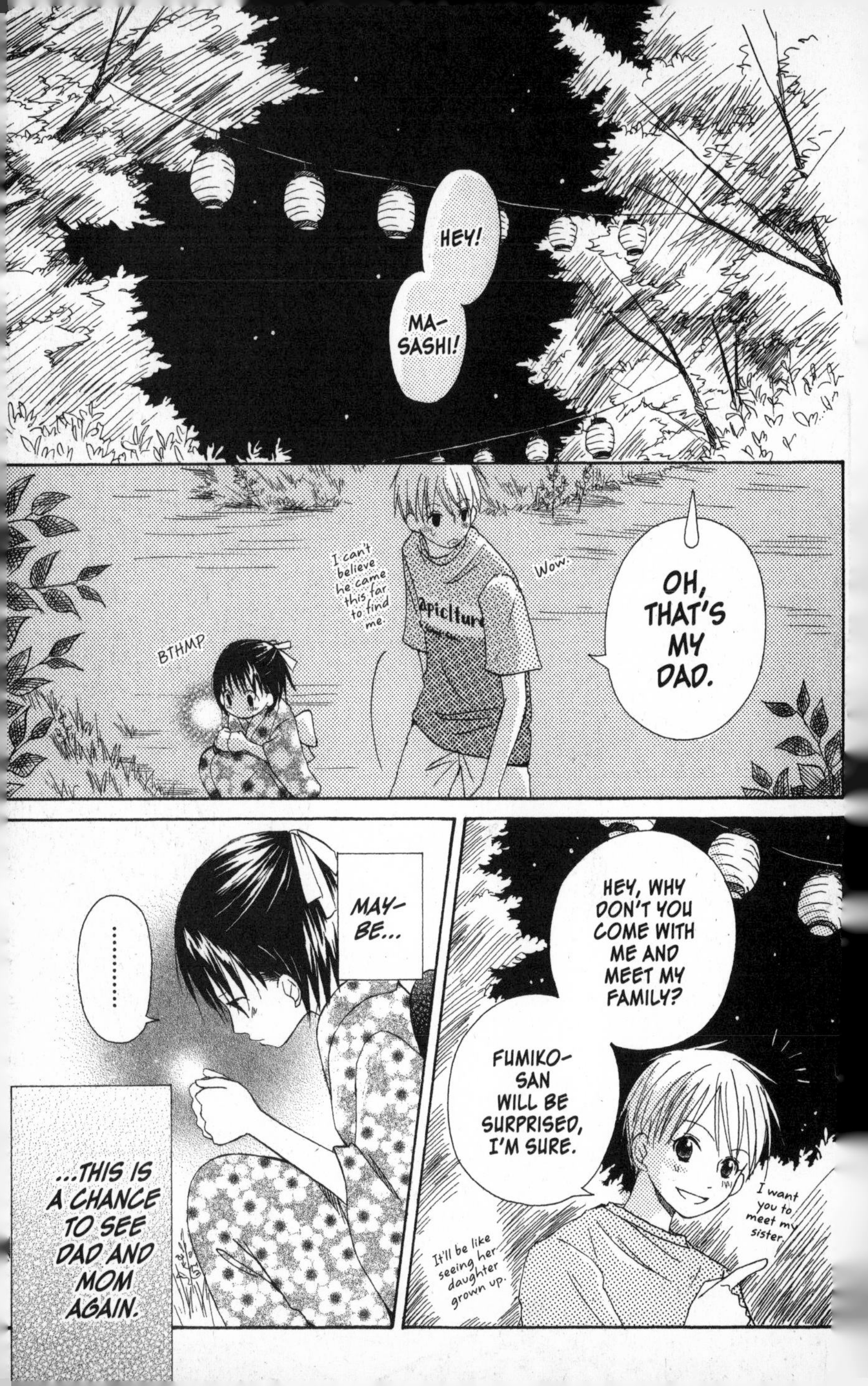
HEY!
MA-SASHI!
OH, THAT'S MY DAD.
Wow.
I can't believe he came this far to find me.
BTHMP
HEY, WHY DON'T YOU COME WITH ME AND MEET MY FAMILY?
FUMIKO-SAN WILL BE SURPRISED, I'M SURE.
I want you to meet my sister.
It'll be like seeing her daughter grown up.
MAY-BE...
......
...THIS IS A CHANCE TO SEE DAD AND MOM AGAIN.

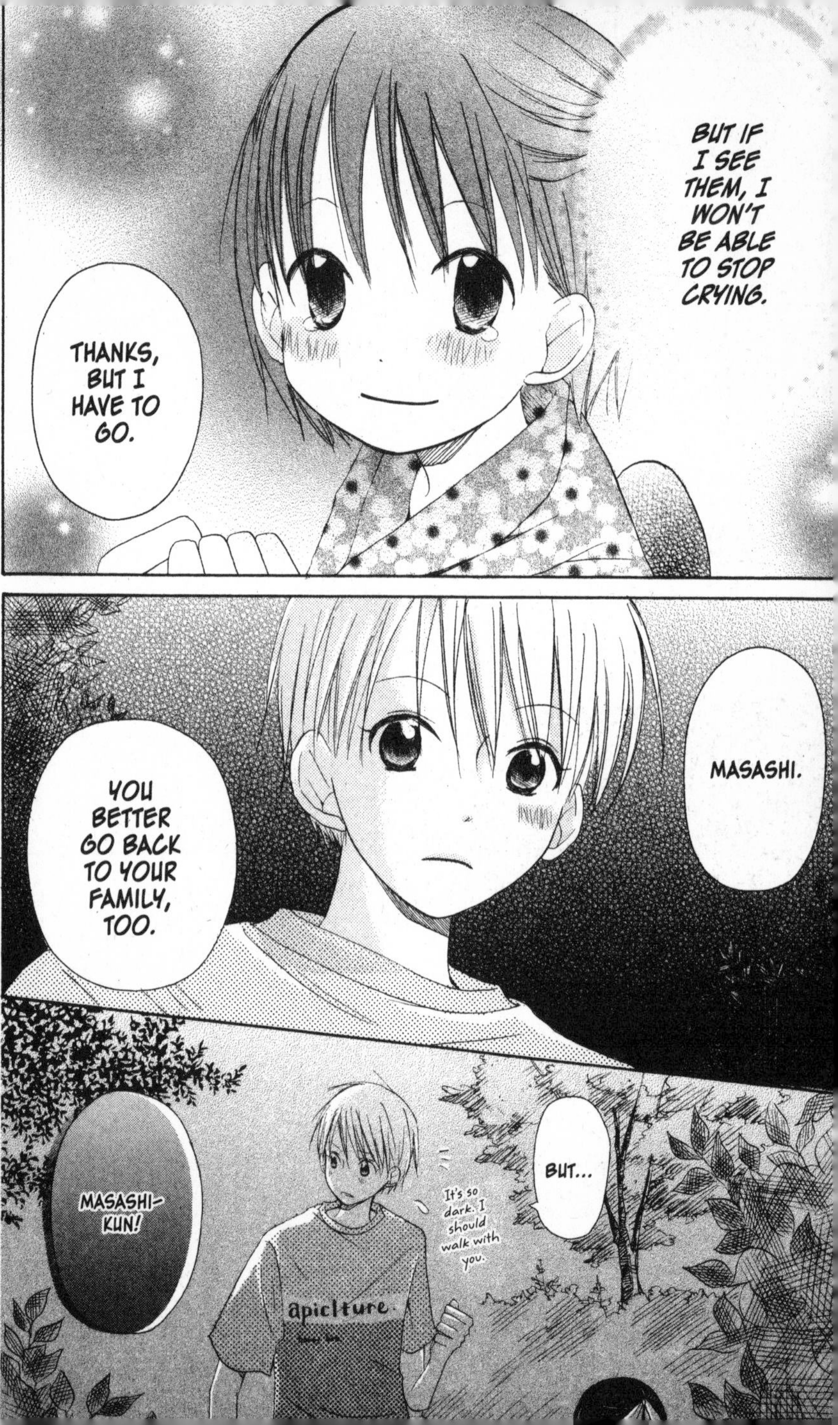
BUT IF I SEE THEM, I WON'T BE ABLE TO STOP CRYING.
THANKS, BUT I HAVE TO GO.
MASASHI.
YOU BETTER GO BACK TO YOUR FAMILY, TOO.
BUT...
It's so dark. I should walk with you.
apiclture
MASASHI-KUN!

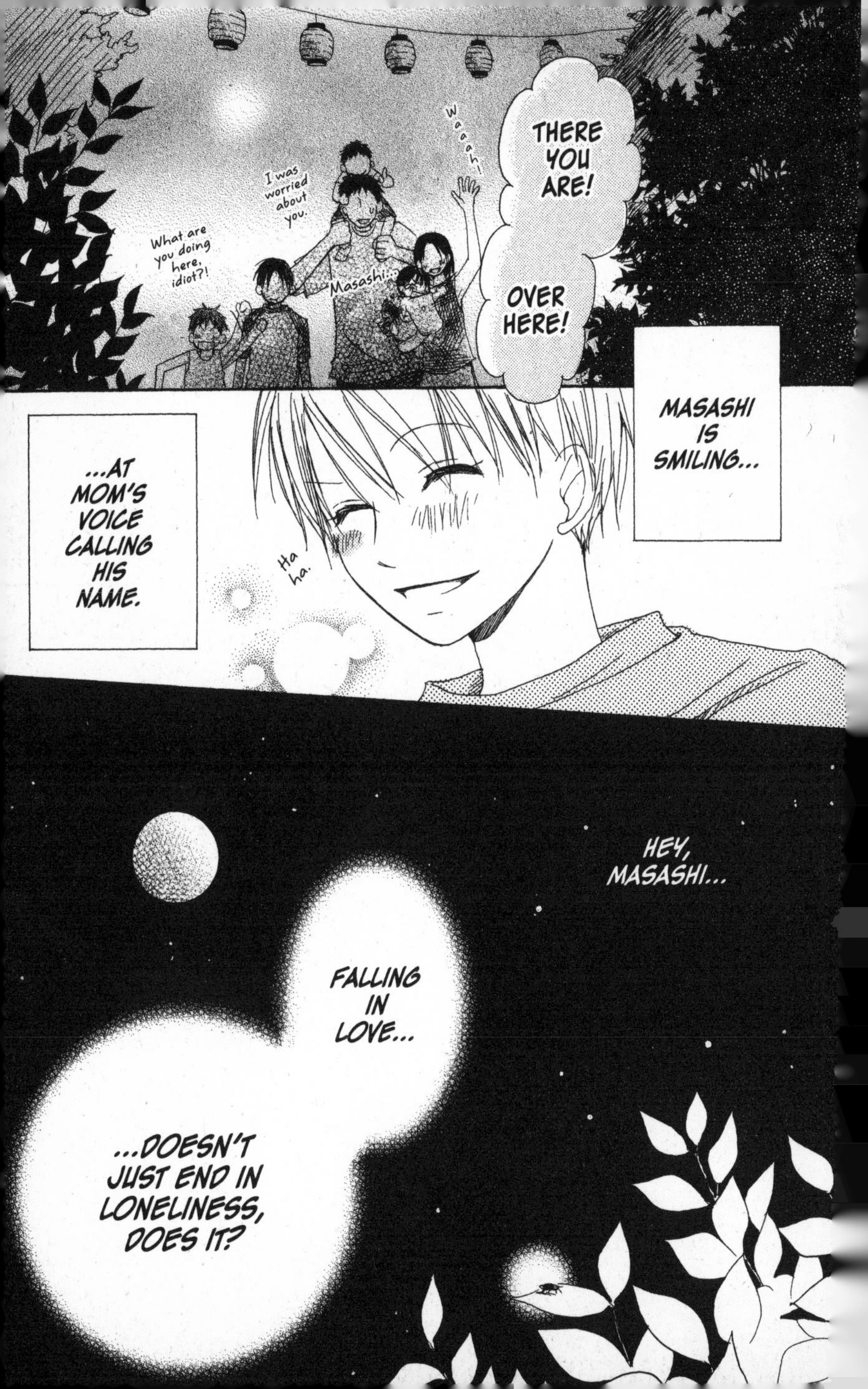
THERE YOU ARE!
OVER HERE!
Waaaah!
I was worried about you.
Masashi...
What are you doing here, idiot?!
MASASHI IS SMILING...
Ha ha.
...AT MOM'S VOICE CALLING HIS NAME.
HEY, MASASHI...
FALLING IN LOVE...
...DOESN'T JUST END IN LONELINESS, DOES IT?

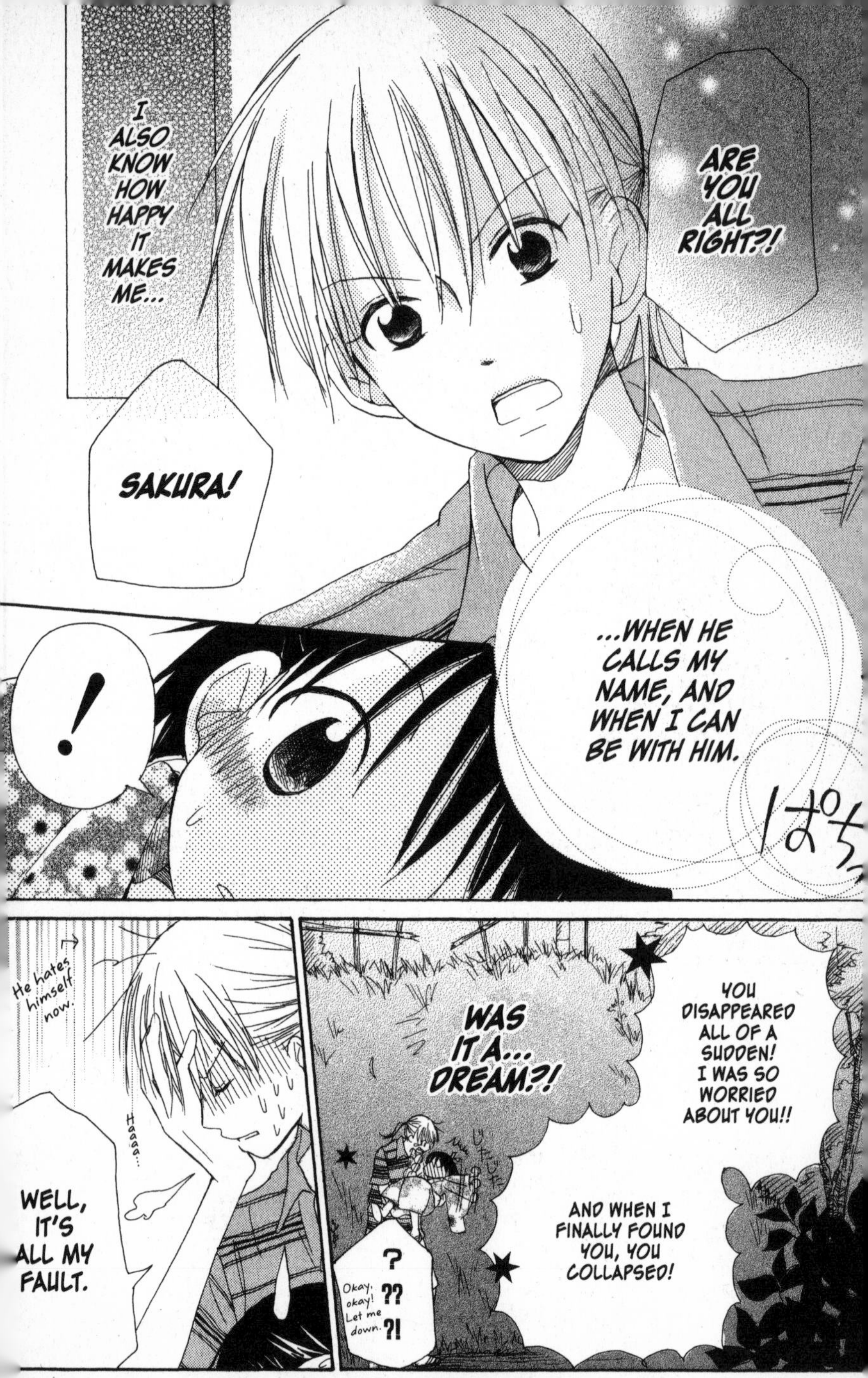
ARE YOU ALL RIGHT?!
I ALSO KNOW HOW HAPPY IT MAKES ME...
SAKURA!
...WHEN HE CALLS MY NAME, AND WHEN I CAN BE WITH HIM.
ぱち
!
YOU DISAPPEARED ALL OF A SUDDEN! I WAS SO WORRIED ABOUT YOU!!
WAS IT A... DREAM?!
AND WHEN I FINALLY FOUND YOU, YOU COLLAPSED!
?
??
?!
Okay, okay! Let me down.
He hates himself now.
Haaaa...
WELL, IT'S ALL MY FAULT.

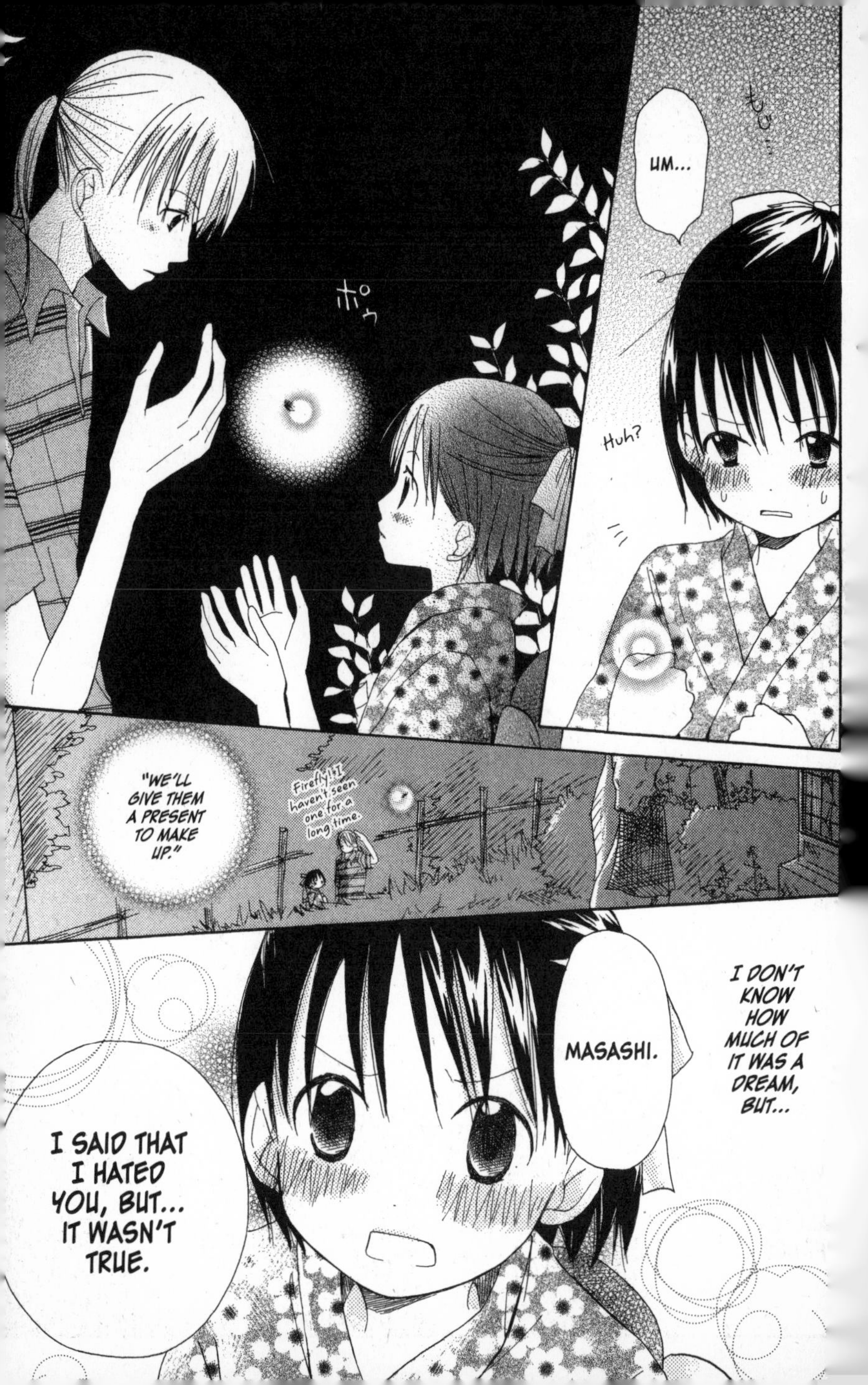
UM...
Huh?
"WE'LL GIVE THEM A PRESENT TO MAKE UP."
Firefly!! I haven't seen one for a long time.
I DON'T KNOW HOW MUCH OF IT WAS A DREAM, BUT...
MASASHI.
I SAID THAT I HATED YOU, BUT... IT WASN'T TRUE.

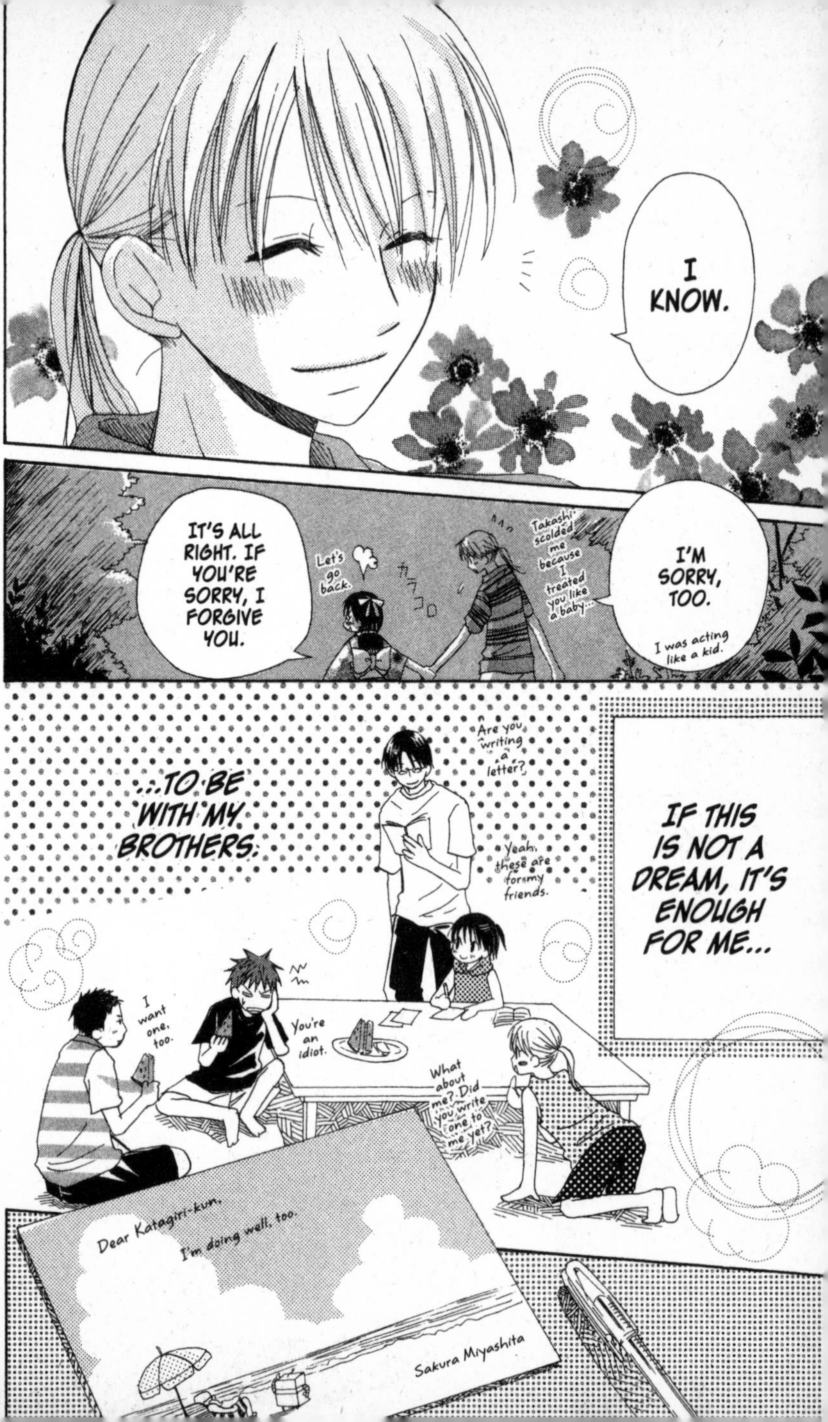

I KNOW.
I'M SORRY, TOO.
I was acting like a kid.
Takashi scolded me because I treated you like a baby...
カラコロ
Let's go back.
IT'S ALL RIGHT. IF YOU'RE SORRY, I FORGIVE YOU.
IF THIS IS NOT A DREAM, IT'S ENOUGH FOR ME...
...TO BE WITH MY BROTHERS.
Are you writing a letter?
Yeah, these are for my friends.
What about me? Did you write one to me yet?
You're an idiot.
I want one, too.
Dear Katagiri-kun,
I'm doing well, too.
Sakura Miyashita

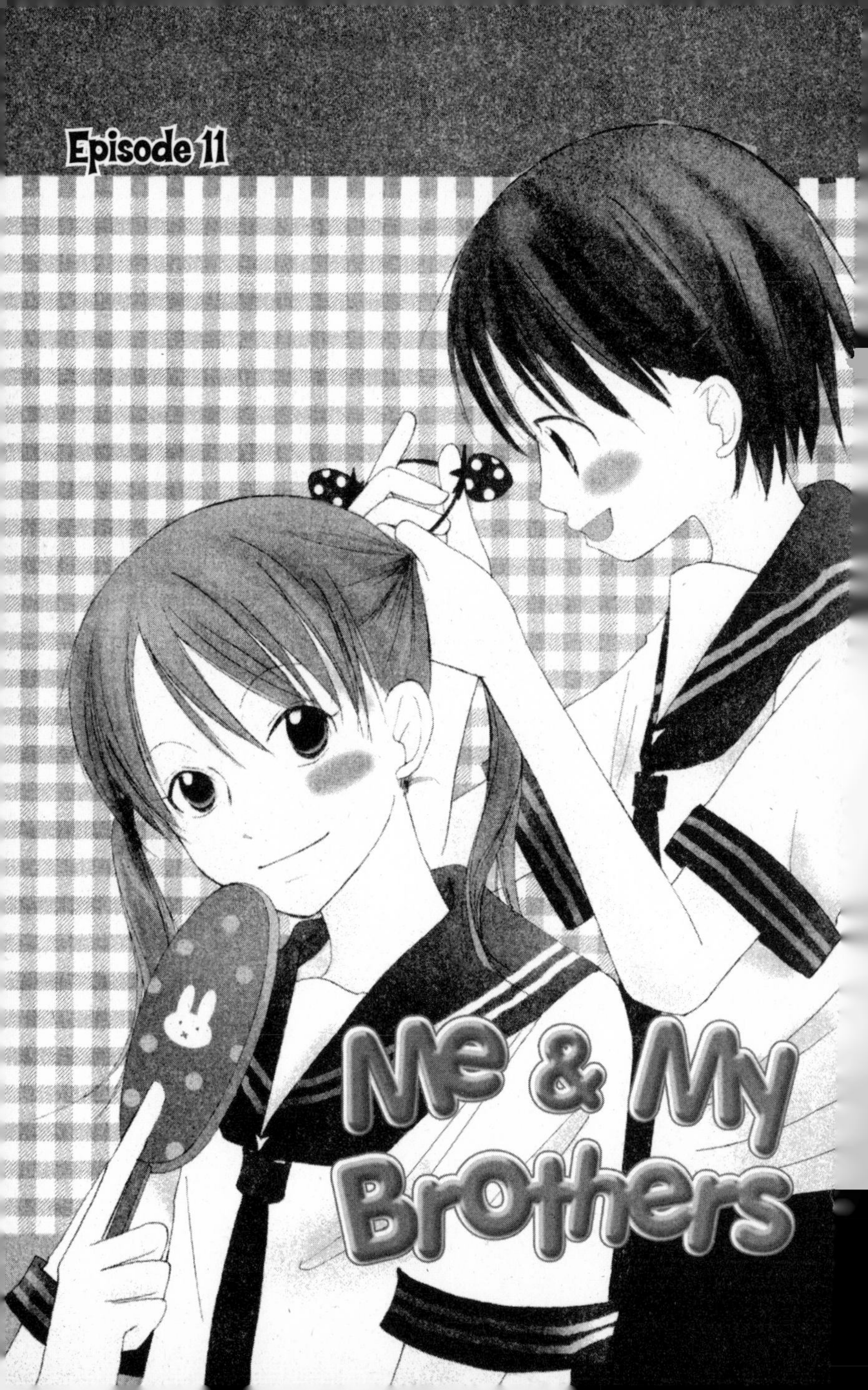
Episode 11
Me & My Brothers

☆I'll still write the character profiles.☆

'sup.

Tsuyoshi Miyashita

Date of Birth:
Jan. 30th, 1984
(Aquarius)

Blood type: B

Height: 172cm

Hobby: Part-time jobs (?)
and watching K-1

Likes:
Wrestling
masks

Hates:
Spinach,
dogs and
many more
things,
I'm sure.

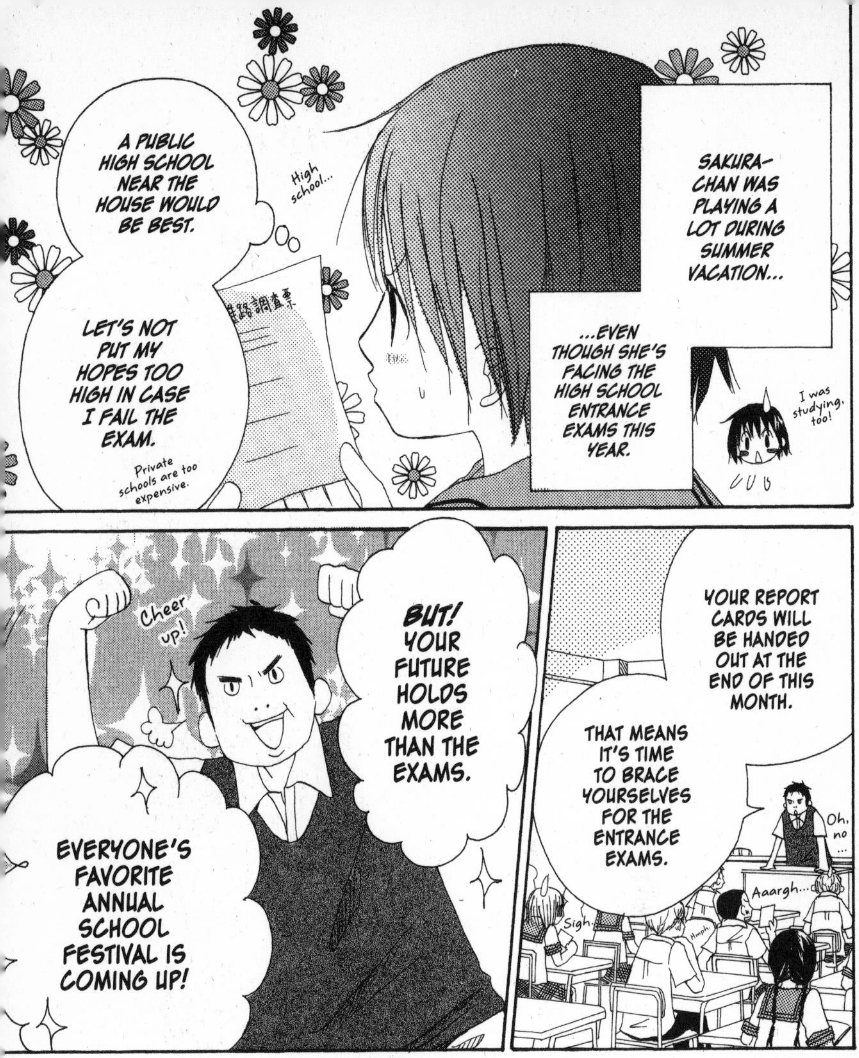
SAKURA-CHAN WAS PLAYING A LOT DURING SUMMER VACATION...
...EVEN THOUGH SHE'S FACING THE HIGH SCHOOL ENTRANCE EXAMS THIS YEAR.
I was studying, too!
A PUBLIC HIGH SCHOOL NEAR THE HOUSE WOULD BE BEST.
High school...
LET'S NOT PUT MY HOPES TOO HIGH IN CASE I FAIL THE EXAM.
Private schools are too expensive.
YOUR REPORT CARDS WILL BE HANDED OUT AT THE END OF THIS MONTH.
THAT MEANS IT'S TIME TO BRACE YOURSELVES FOR THE ENTRANCE EXAMS.
Oh, no...
Aaargh...
Hmph.
Sigh.
BUT! YOUR FUTURE HOLDS MORE THAN THE EXAMS.
Cheer up!
EVERYONE'S FAVORITE ANNUAL SCHOOL FESTIVAL IS COMING UP!

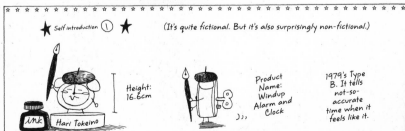

★ Self introduction ① ★

(It's quite fictional. But it's also surprisingly non-fictional.)

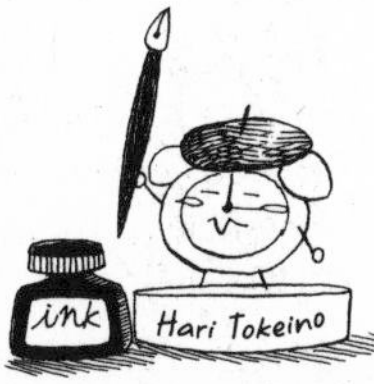
ink
Hari Tokeino

Height: 16.6cm

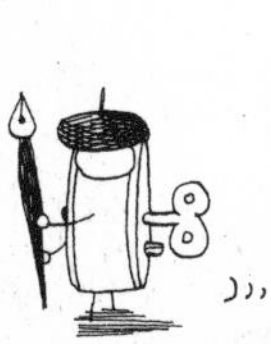

Product Name: Windup Alarm and Clock

1979's Type B. It tells not-so-accurate time when it feels like it.

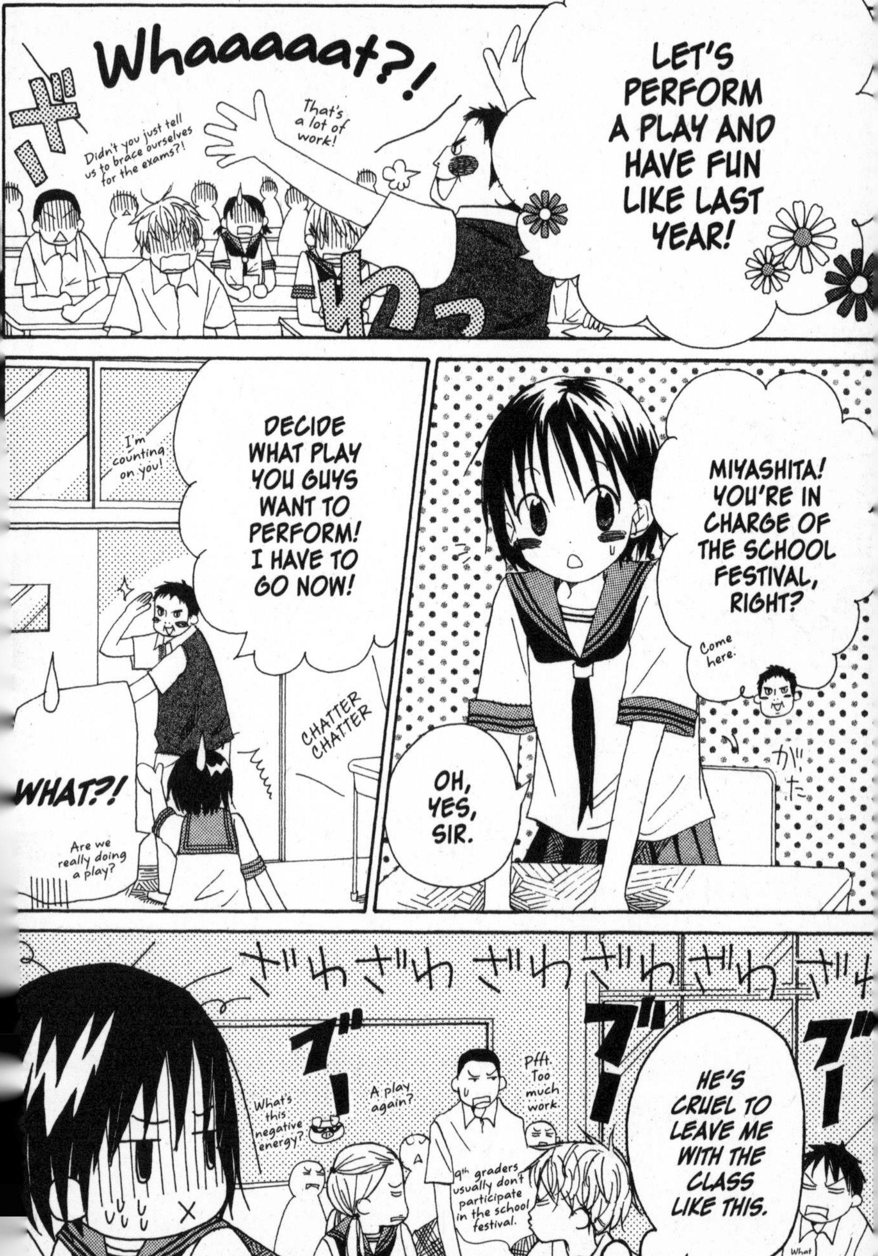
LET'S PERFORM A PLAY AND HAVE FUN LIKE LAST YEAR!
Whaaaaat?!
That's a lot of work!
Didn't you just tell us to brace ourselves for the exams?!
MIYASHITA! YOU'RE IN CHARGE OF THE SCHOOL FESTIVAL, RIGHT?
Come here.
OH, YES, SIR.
DECIDE WHAT PLAY YOU GUYS WANT TO PERFORM! I HAVE TO GO NOW!
I'm counting on you!
CHATTER CHATTER
WHAT?!
Are we really doing a play?
HE'S CRUEL TO LEAVE ME WITH THE CLASS LIKE THIS.
What is he thinking?
Pfft. Too much work.
9th graders usually don't participate in the school festival.
A play again?
What's this negative energy?

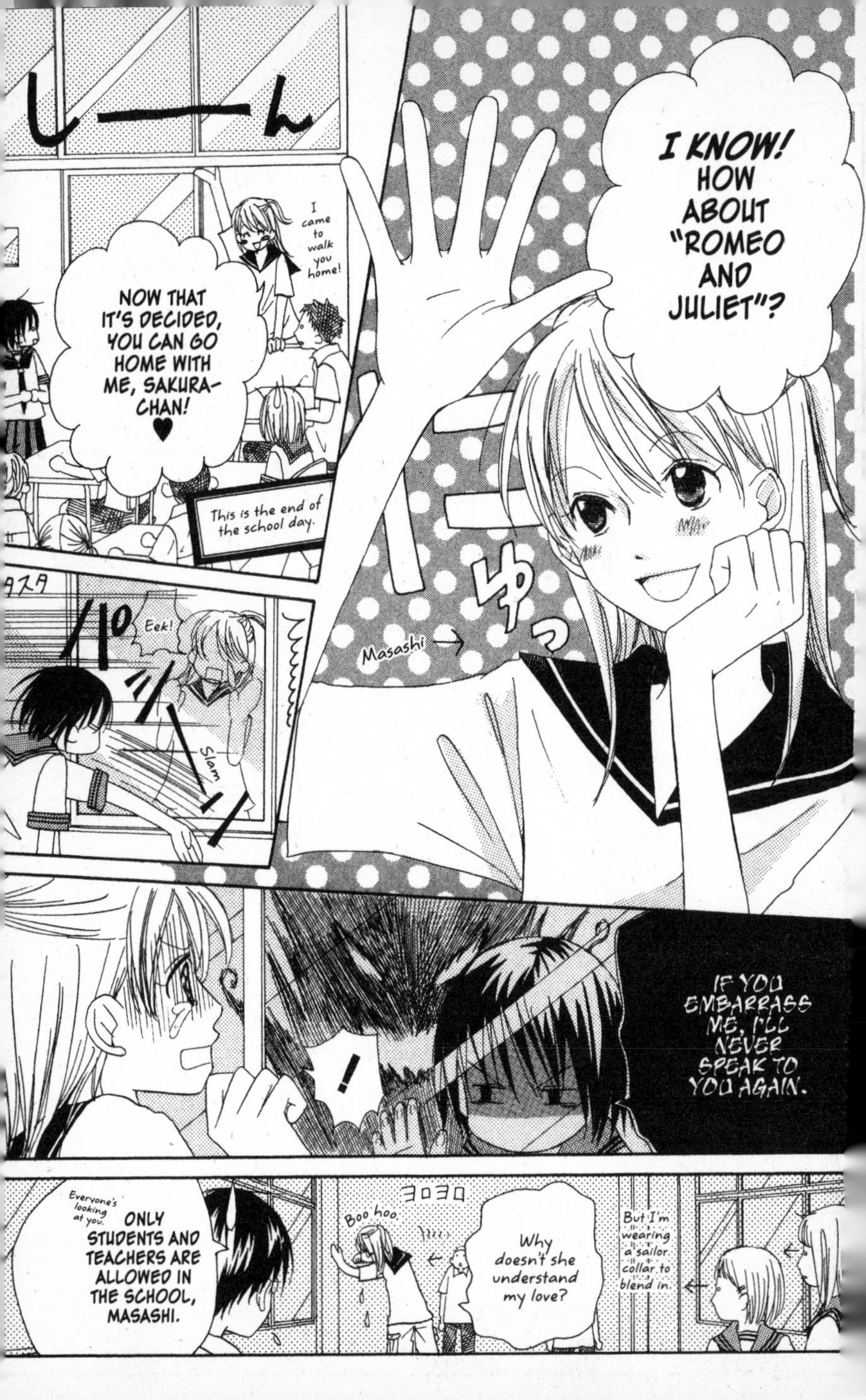
I KNOW! HOW ABOUT "ROMEO AND JULIET"?
ゆっ
Masashi
しーん
I came to walk you home!
NOW THAT IT'S DECIDED, YOU CAN GO HOME WITH ME, SAKURA-CHAN! ♥
This is the end of the school day.
Eek!
Slam
IF YOU EMBARRASS ME, I'LL NEVER SPEAK TO YOU AGAIN.
!
But I'm wearing a sailor collar to blend in.
Why doesn't she understand my love?
ヨロヨロ
Boo hoo.
Everyone's looking at you.
ONLY STUDENTS AND TEACHERS ARE ALLOWED IN THE SCHOOL, MASASHI.

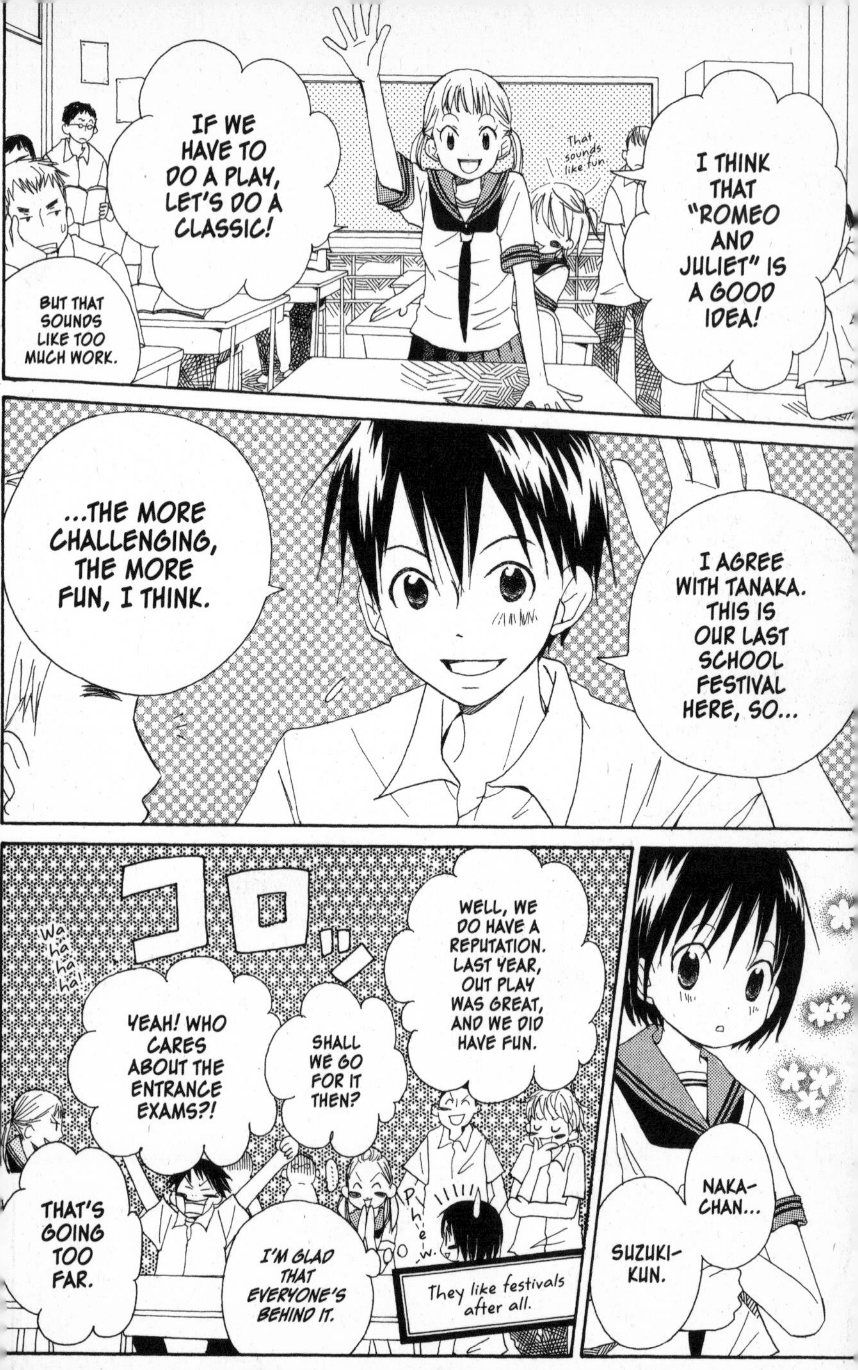
I THINK THAT "ROMEO AND JULIET" IS A GOOD IDEA!
That sounds like fun.
IF WE HAVE TO DO A PLAY, LET'S DO A CLASSIC!
BUT THAT SOUNDS LIKE TOO MUCH WORK.
I AGREE WITH TANAKA. THIS IS OUR LAST SCHOOL FESTIVAL HERE, SO...
...THE MORE CHALLENGING, THE MORE FUN, I THINK.
NAKA-CHAN...
SUZUKI-KUN.
WELL, WE DO HAVE A REPUTATION. LAST YEAR, OUT PLAY WAS GREAT, AND WE DID HAVE FUN.
コロッ
SHALL WE GO FOR IT THEN?
YEAH! WHO CARES ABOUT THE ENTRANCE EXAMS?!
Wa ha ha ha!
Phew.
They like festivals after all.
I'M GLAD THAT EVERYONE'S BEHIND IT.
THAT'S GOING TOO FAR.

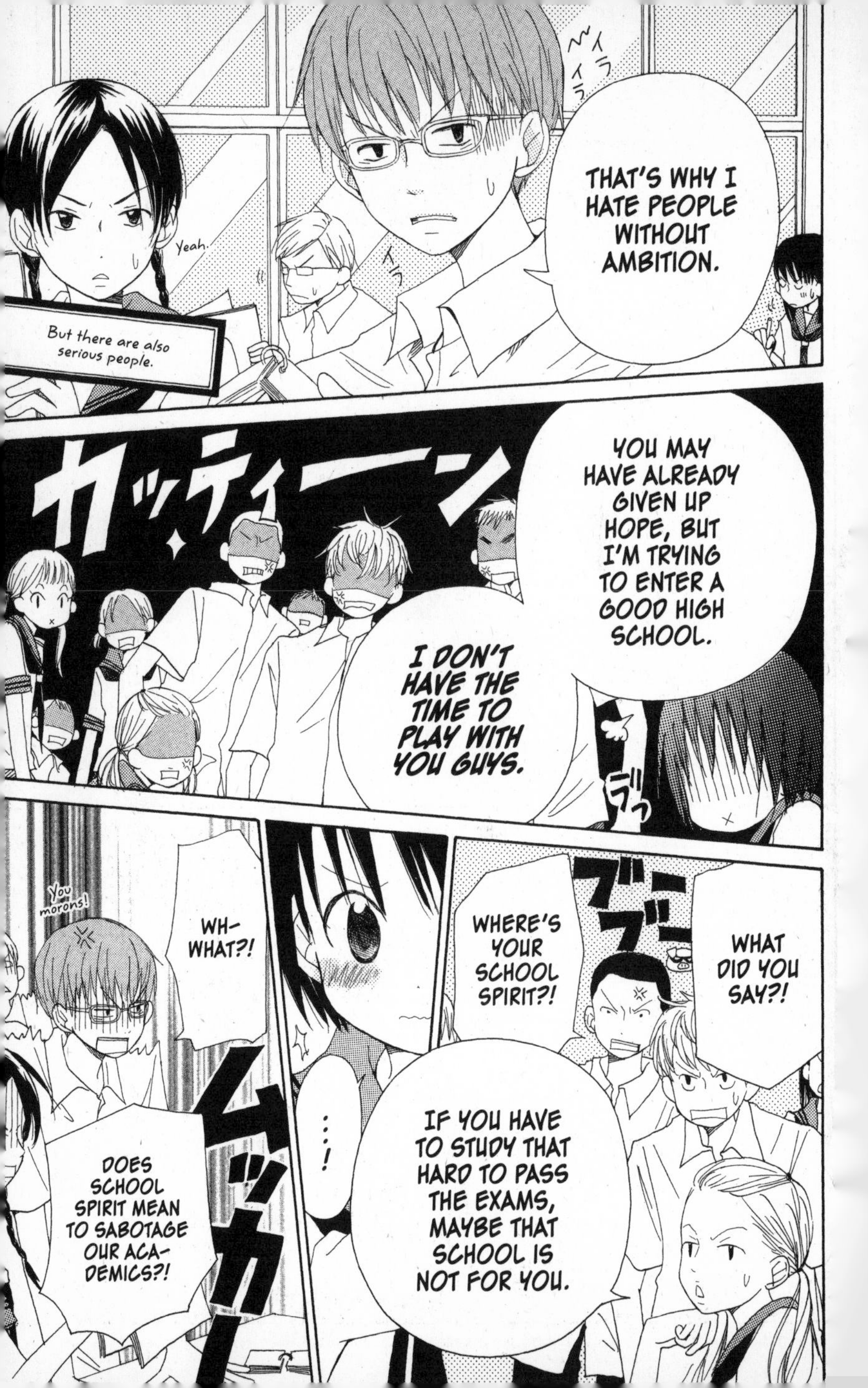
THAT'S WHY I HATE PEOPLE WITHOUT AMBITION.
Yeah.
But there are also serious people.
YOU MAY HAVE ALREADY GIVEN UP HOPE, BUT I'M TRYING TO ENTER A GOOD HIGH SCHOOL.
I DON'T HAVE THE TIME TO PLAY WITH YOU GUYS.
WHAT DID YOU SAY?!
WHERE'S YOUR SCHOOL SPIRIT?!
IF YOU HAVE TO STUDY THAT HARD TO PASS THE EXAMS, MAYBE THAT SCHOOL IS NOT FOR YOU.
...!
You morons!
WH- WHAT?!
DOES SCHOOL SPIRIT MEAN TO SABOTAGE OUR ACA- DEMICS?!

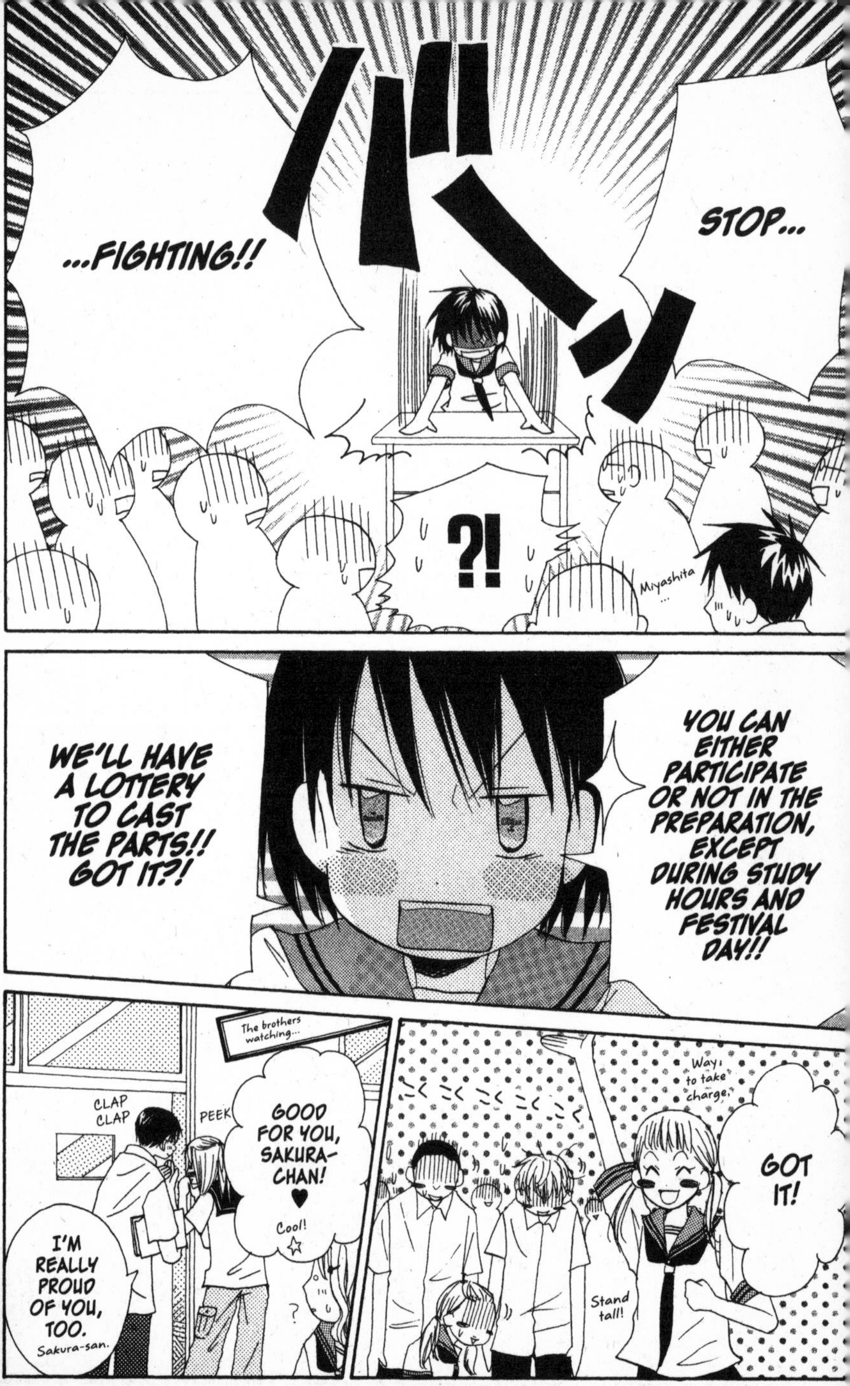
STOP...
バーンッ
...FIGHTING!!
?!
Miyashita...
YOU CAN EITHER PARTICIPATE OR NOT IN THE PREPARATION, EXCEPT DURING STUDY HOURS AND FESTIVAL DAY!!
WE'LL HAVE A LOTTERY TO CAST THE PARTS!! GOT IT?!
Way to take charge,
GOT IT!
こく こく こく こく こく
Stand tall!
The brothers watching...
GOOD FOR YOU, SAKURA-CHAN! ♥
Cool! ☆
PEEK
CLAP CLAP
I'M REALLY PROUD OF YOU, TOO. Sakura-san.

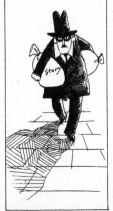

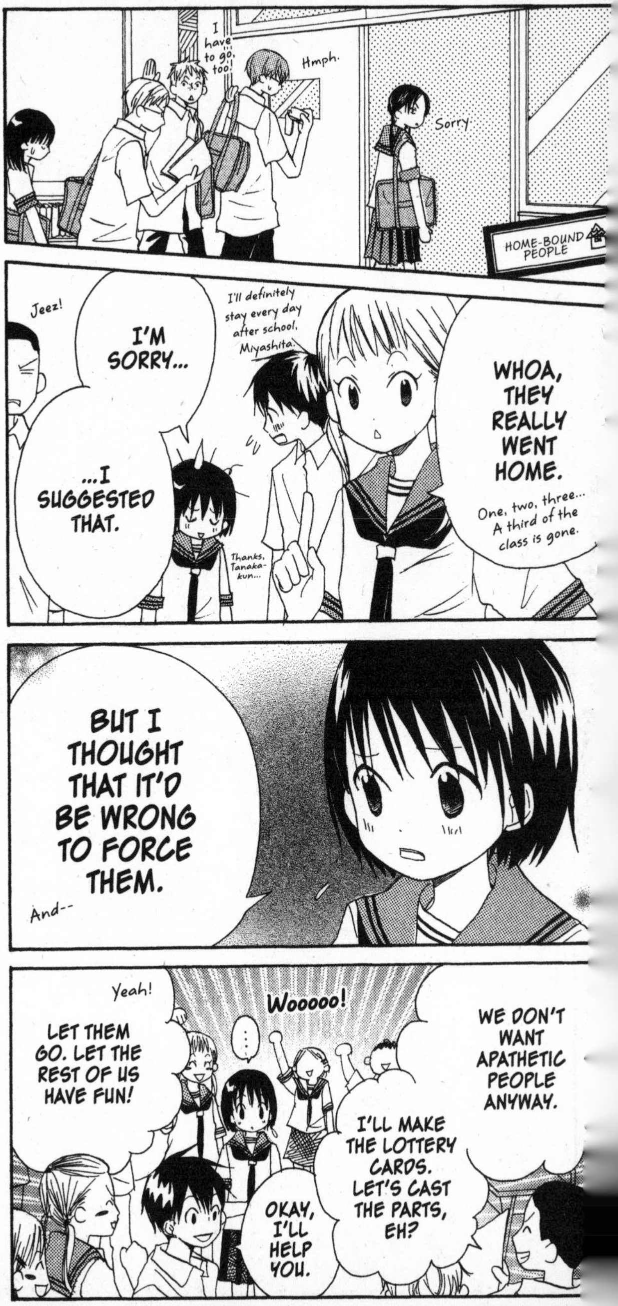
Sorry
HOME-BOUND PEOPLE
Hmph.
I have to go, too!
WHOA, THEY REALLY WENT HOME.
One, two, three... A third of the class is gone.
I'll definitely stay every day after school, Miyashita.
Thanks, Tanaka-kun...
I'M SORRY...
...I SUGGESTED THAT.
Jeez!
BUT I THOUGHT THAT IT'D BE WRONG TO FORCE THEM.
And--
WE DON'T WANT APATHETIC PEOPLE ANYWAY.
I'LL MAKE THE LOTTERY CARDS. LET'S CAST THE PARTS, EH?
OKAY, I'LL HELP YOU.
Wooooo!
...
Yeah!
LET THEM GO. LET THE REST OF US HAVE FUN!

☆2☆

About the profile... I did the two that I gave up on before.

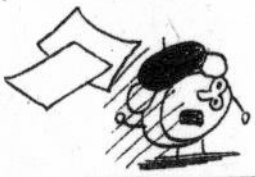

ME GIVING UP.

I make up the story as I go, so I'd be in trouble if I made up their profiles now.

I hope someday I'll be able to decide the characters' personalities, how the story goes, etc., beforehand.

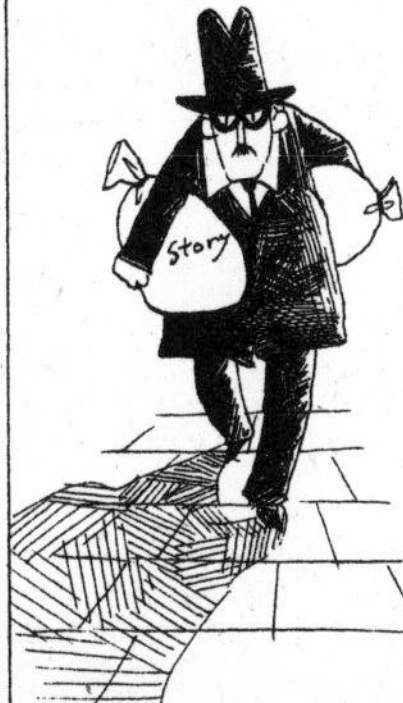
Story

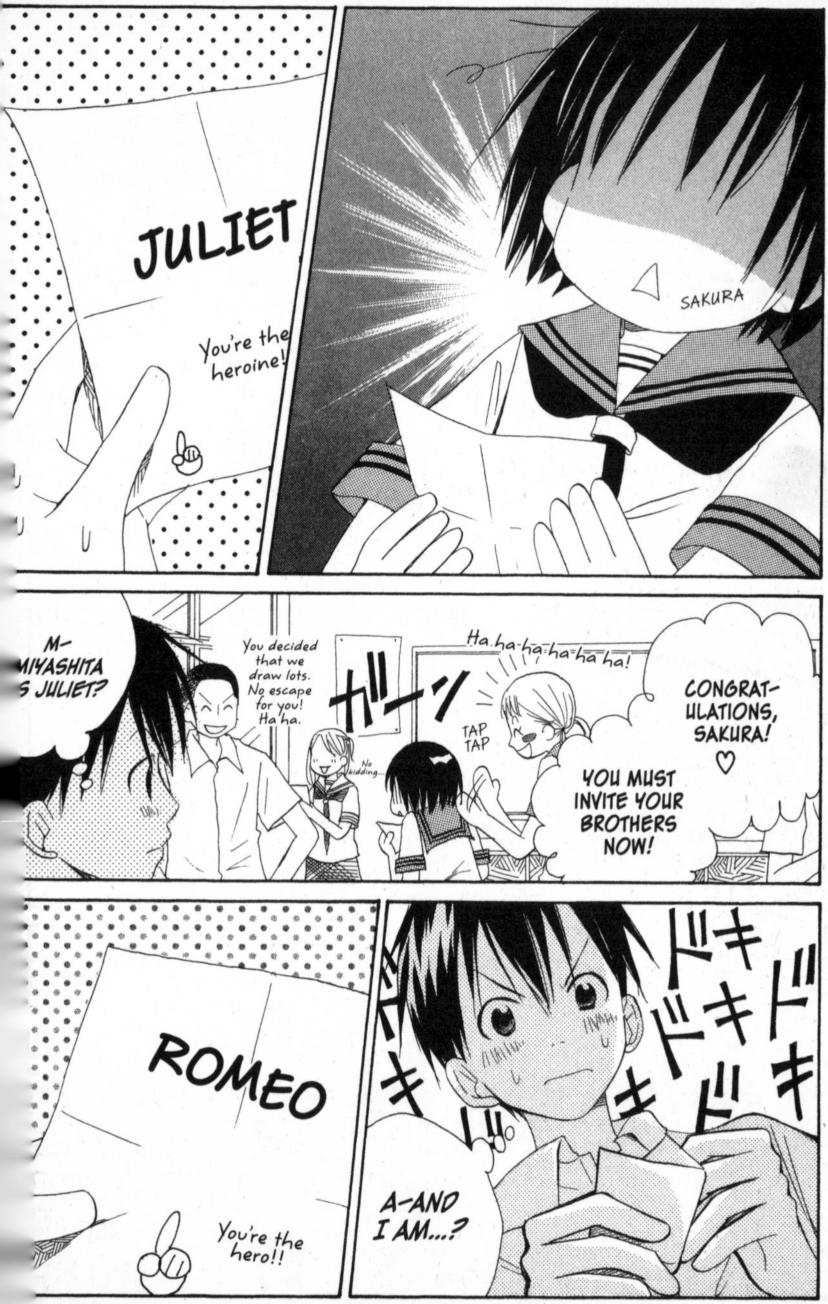
SAKURA
JULIET
You're the heroine!
Ha ha-ha-ha-ha ha!
CONGRATULATIONS, SAKURA! ♡
YOU MUST INVITE YOUR BROTHERS NOW!
TAP TAP
ガーン
No kidding...
You decided that we draw lots. No escape for you! Ha ha.
M-MIYASHITA S JULIET?
ドキ ドキ ドキ ドキ
A-AND I AM...?
ROMEO
You're the hero!!

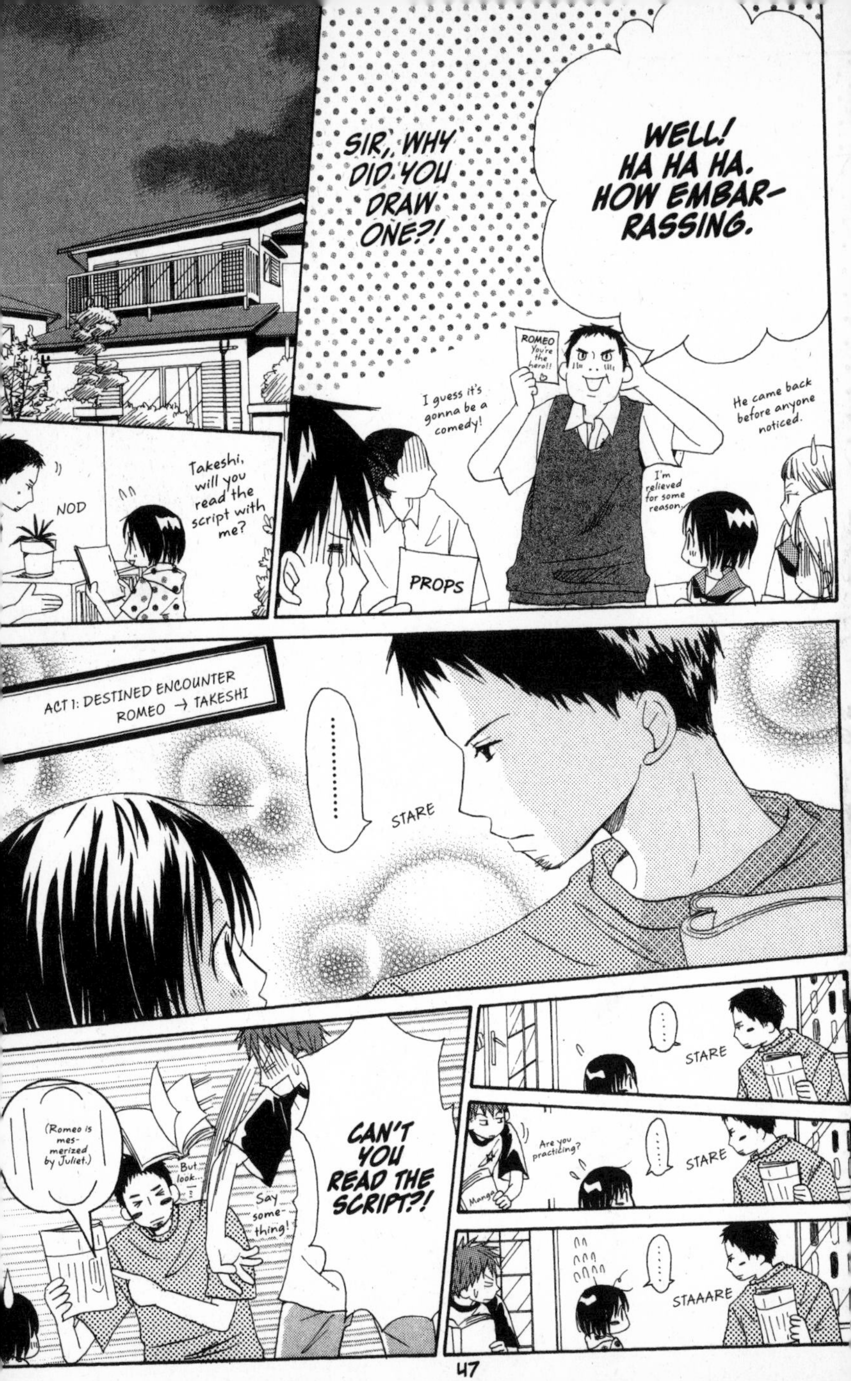
WELL! HA HA HA. HOW EMBAR-RASSING.
SIR, WHY DID YOU DRAW ONE?!
ROMEO You're the hero!!
He came back before anyone noticed.
I guess it's gonna be a comedy!
I'm relieved for some reason.
PROPS
Takeshi, will you read the script with me?
NOD
ACT 1: DESTINED ENCOUNTER
ROMEO → TAKESHI
......
STARE
...
STARE
Are you practicing?
...
STARE
Manga
...
STAAARE
CAN'T YOU READ THE SCRIPT?!
Say some-thing!
But look...
(Romeo is mes-merized by Juliet.)

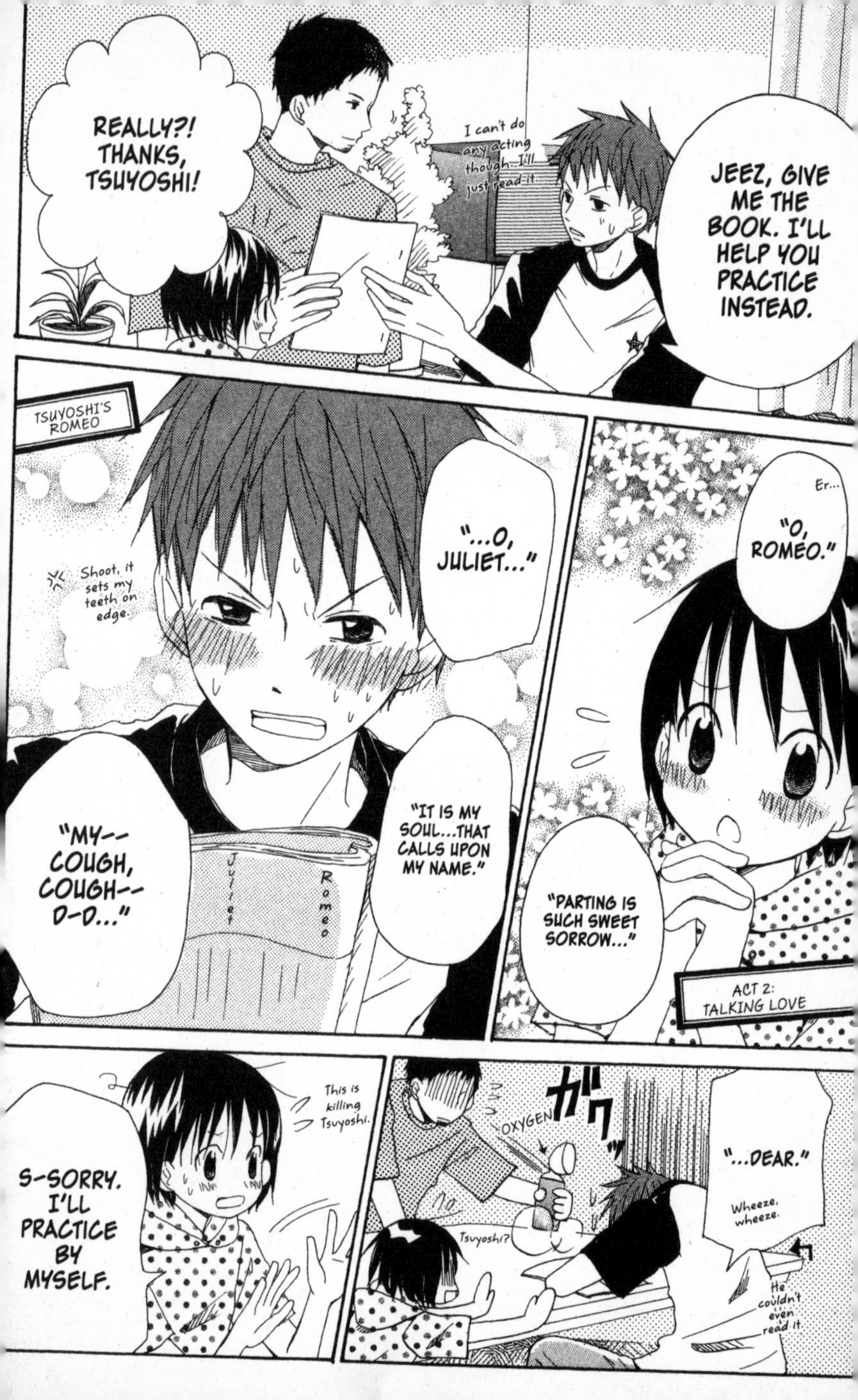
JEEZ, GIVE ME THE BOOK. I'LL HELP YOU PRACTICE INSTEAD.
I can't do any acting though. I'll just read it.
REALLY?! THANKS, TSUYOSHI!
Er...
"O, ROMEO."
"PARTING IS SUCH SWEET SORROW..."
ACT 2: TALKING LOVE
TSUYOSHI'S ROMEO
"...O, JULIET..."
Shoot, it sets my teeth on edge.
"IT IS MY SOUL...THAT CALLS UPON MY NAME."
Romeo
Juliet
"MY--COUGH, COUGH--D-D..."
"...DEAR."
Wheeze, wheeze.
OXYGEN
Tsuyoshi?
He couldn't even read it.
This is killing Tsuyoshi.
S-SORRY. I'LL PRACTICE BY MYSELF.

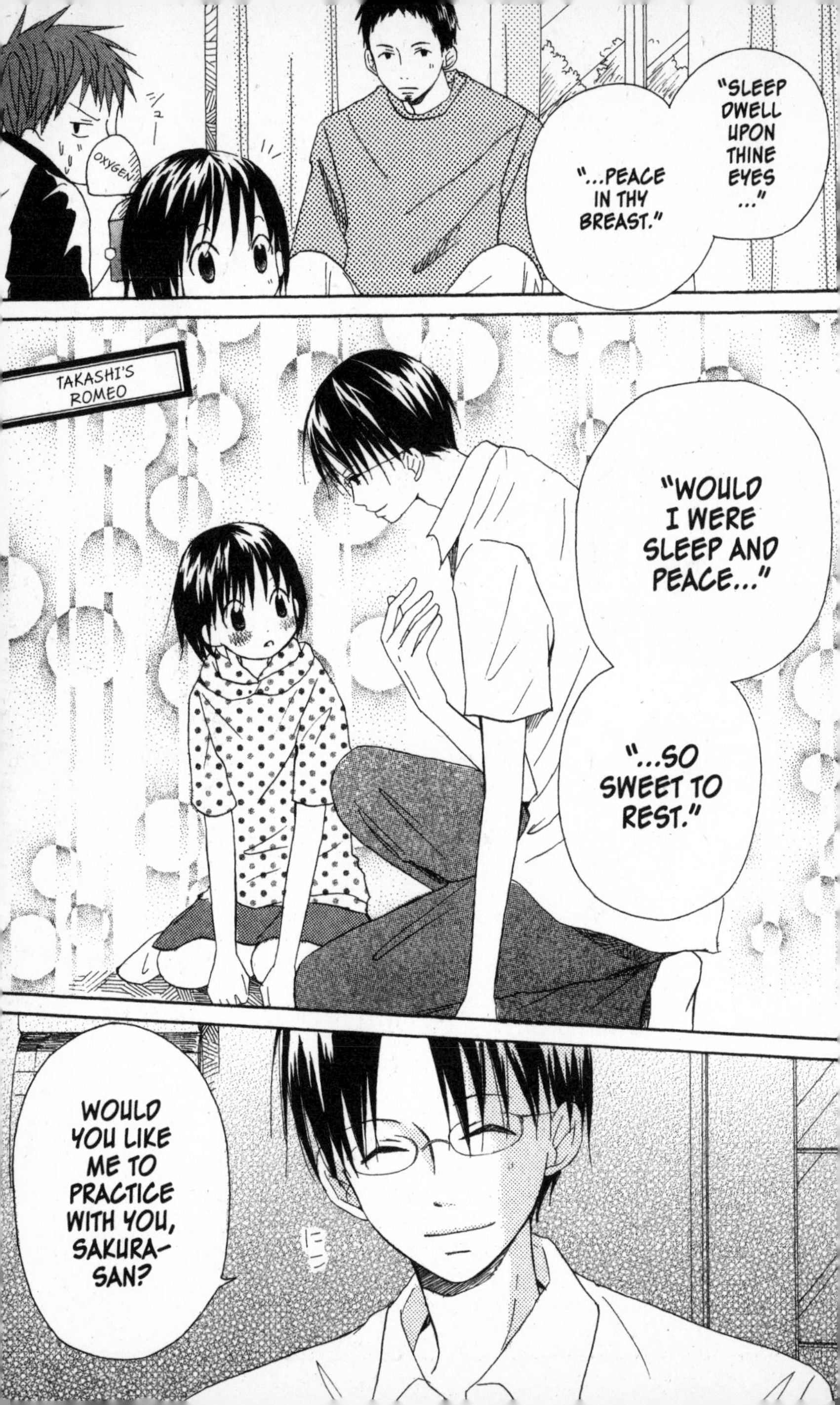
"SLEEP DWELL UPON THINE EYES ..."
"...PEACE IN THY BREAST."
OXYGEN
"WOULD I WERE SLEEP AND PEACE..."
"...SO SWEET TO REST."
TAKASHI'S ROMEO
WOULD YOU LIKE ME TO PRACTICE WITH YOU, SAKURA-SAN?

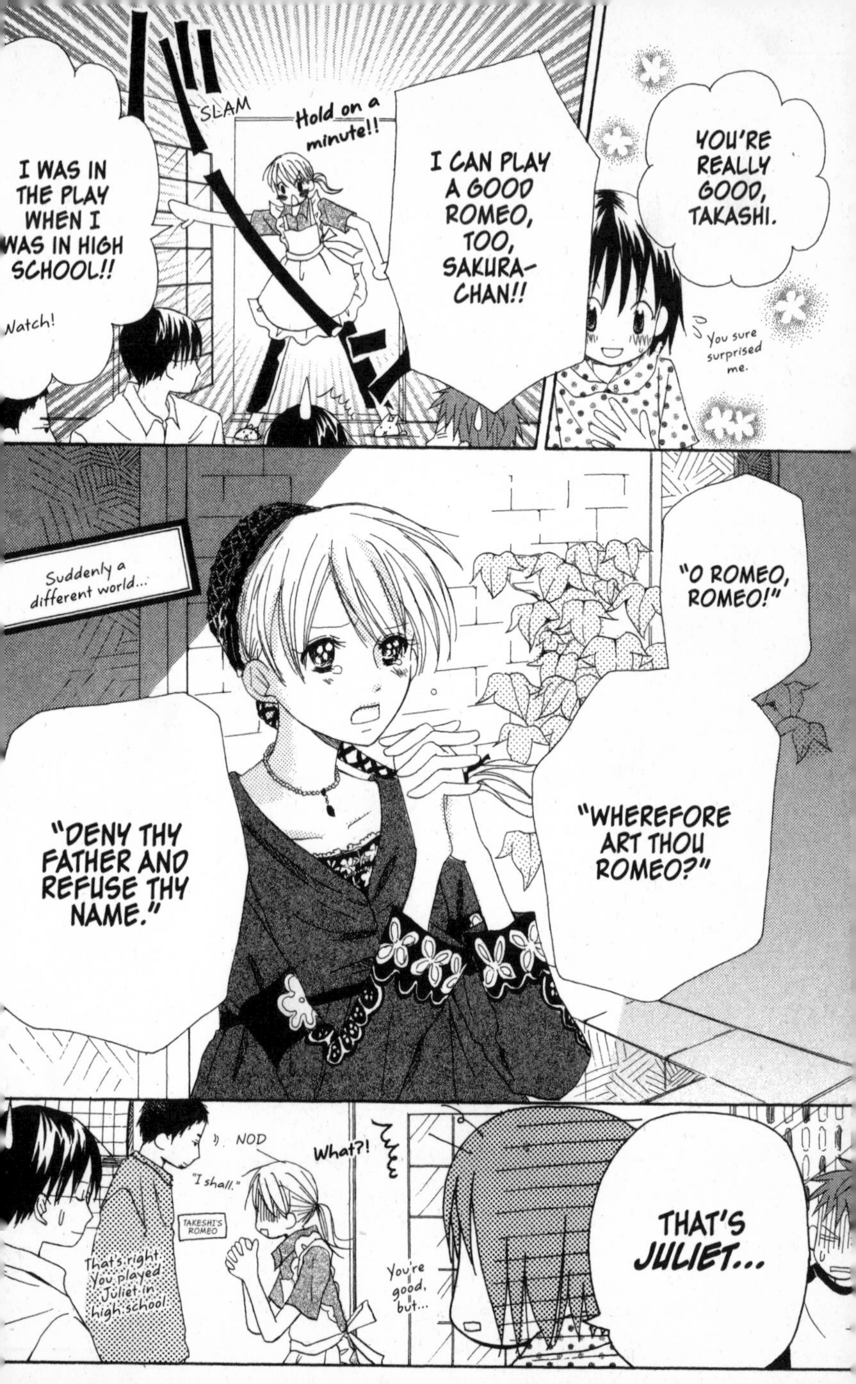
YOU'RE REALLY GOOD, TAKASHI.
You sure surprised me.
I CAN PLAY A GOOD ROMEO, TOO, SAKURA-CHAN!!
Hold on a minute!!
SLAM
I WAS IN THE PLAY WHEN I WAS IN HIGH SCHOOL!!
Watch!
"O ROMEO, ROMEO!"
"WHEREFORE ART THOU ROMEO?"
Suddenly a different world...
"DENY THY FATHER AND REFUSE THY NAME."
THAT'S JULIET...
You're good, but...
What?!
NOD
"I shall."
TAKESHI'S ROMEO
That's right. You played Juliet in high school.

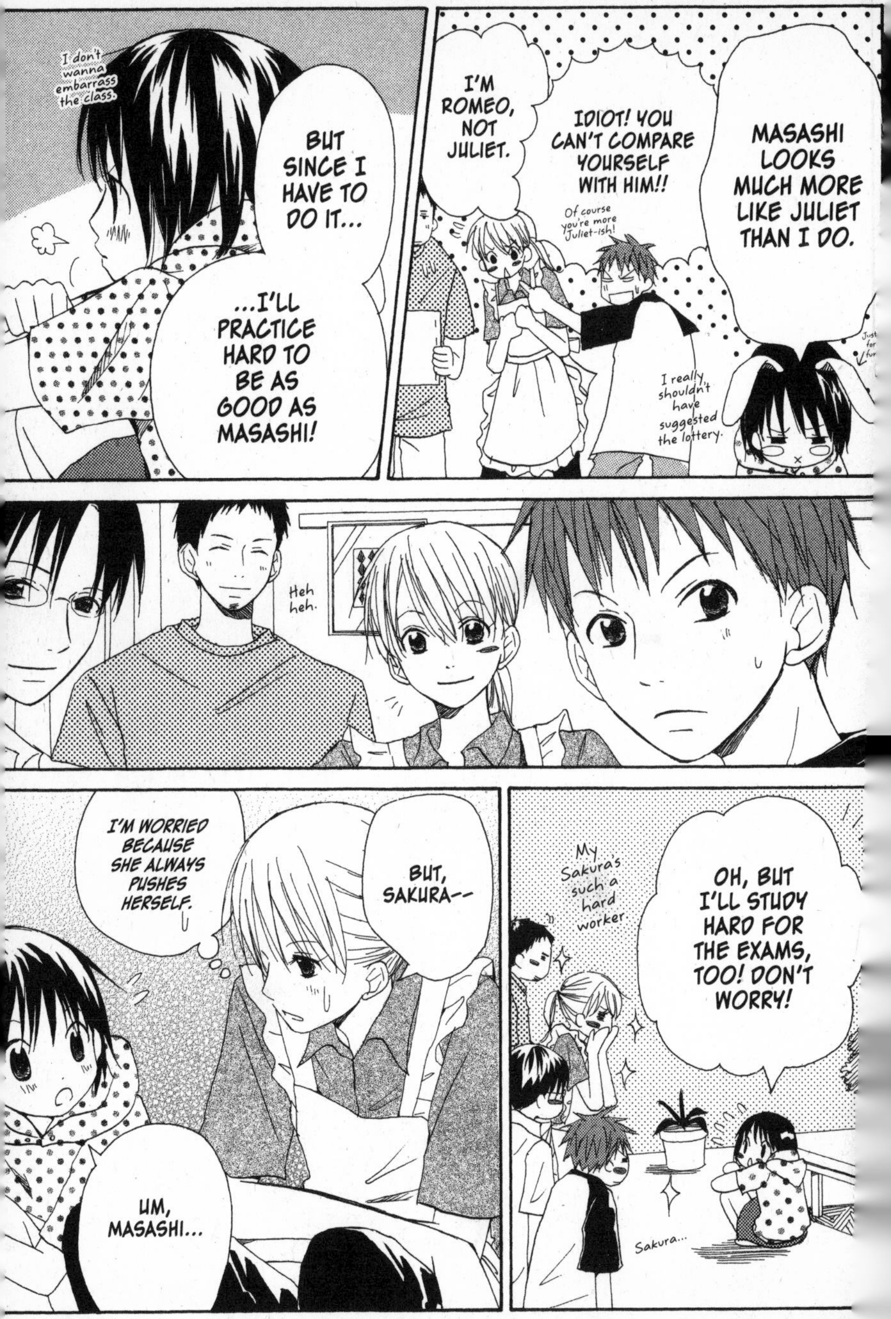
MASASHI LOOKS MUCH MORE LIKE JULIET THAN I DO.
Just for
IDIOT! YOU CAN'T COMPARE YOURSELF WITH HIM!!
Of course you're more Juliet-ish!
I'M ROMEO, NOT JULIET.
I really shouldn't have suggested the lottery.
BUT SINCE I HAVE TO DO IT...
I don't wanna embarrass the class.
...I'LL PRACTICE HARD TO BE AS GOOD AS MASASHI!
Heh heh.
OH, BUT I'LL STUDY HARD FOR THE EXAMS, TOO! DON'T WORRY!
My Sakura's such a hard worker
Sakura...
BUT, SAKURA--
I'M WORRIED BECAUSE SHE ALWAYS PUSHES HERSELF.
UM, MASASHI...

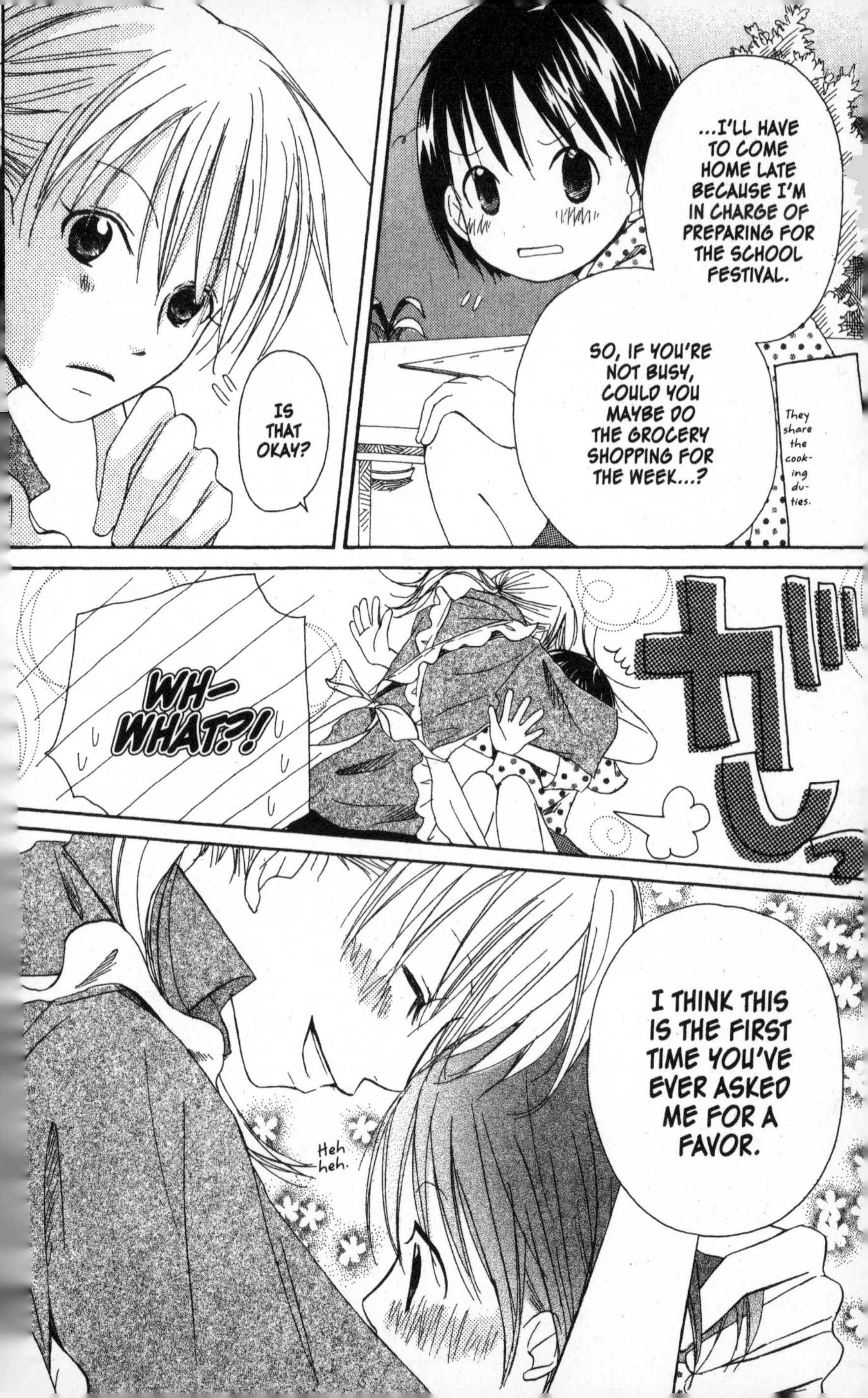
...I'LL HAVE TO COME HOME LATE BECAUSE I'M IN CHARGE OF PREPARING FOR THE SCHOOL FESTIVAL.
SO, IF YOU'RE NOT BUSY, COULD YOU MAYBE DO THE GROCERY SHOPPING FOR THE WEEK...?
They share the cooking duties.
IS THAT OKAY?
ガしっ
WH-WHAT?!
I THINK THIS IS THE FIRST TIME YOU'VE EVER ASKED ME FOR A FAVOR.
Heh heh.

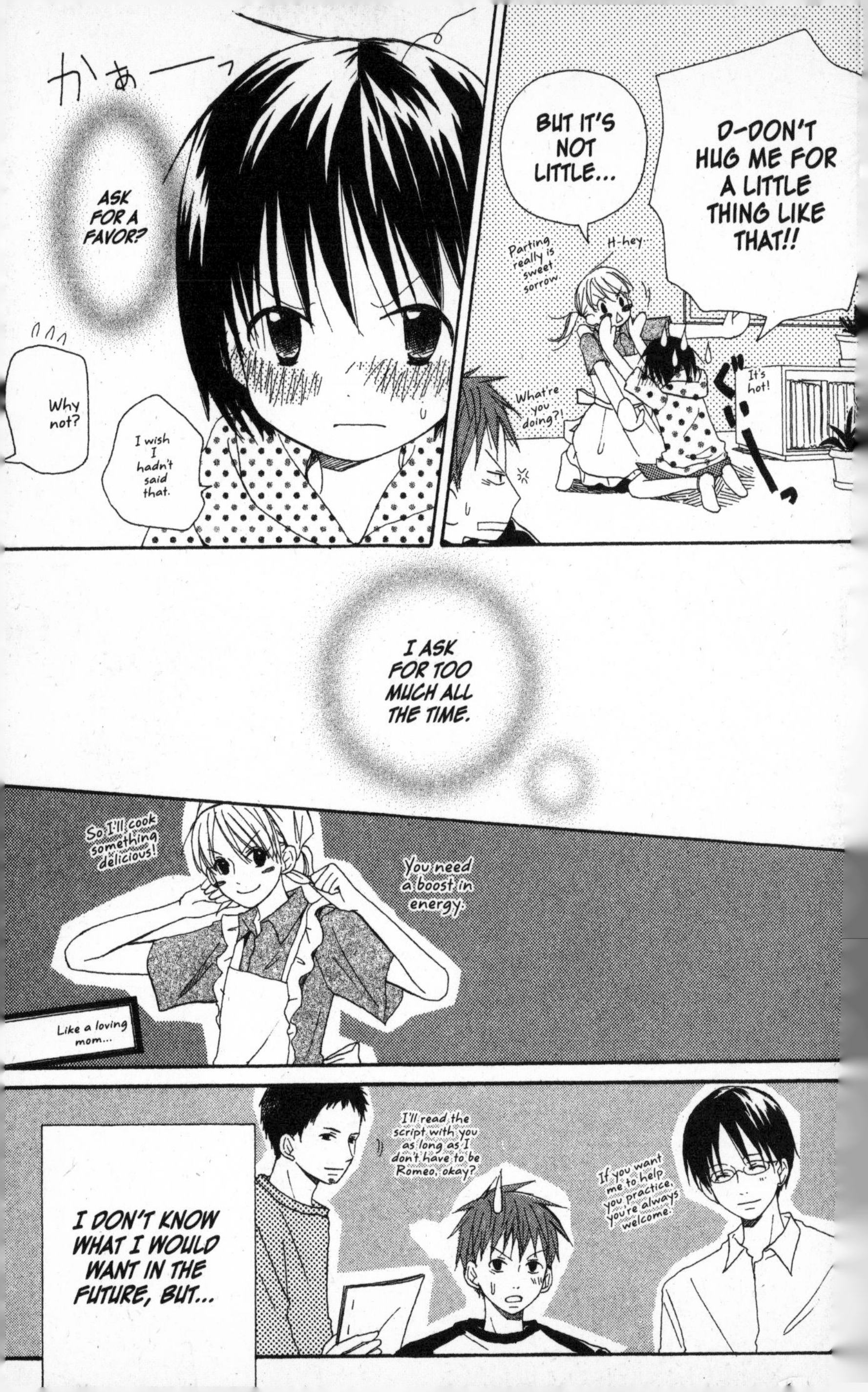
D-DON'T HUG ME FOR A LITTLE THING LIKE THAT!!
BUT IT'S NOT LITTLE...
H-hey
Parting really is sweet sorrow.
It's hot!
What're you doing?!
かぁーっ
ASK FOR A FAVOR?
Why not?
I wish I hadn't said that.
I ASK FOR TOO MUCH ALL THE TIME.
You need a boost in energy.
So I'll cook something delicious!
Like a loving mom...
If you want me to help you practice, you're always welcome.
I'll read the script with you as long as I don't have to be Romeo, okay?
I DON'T KNOW WHAT I WOULD WANT IN THE FUTURE, BUT...

PLAY REHEARSAL

You're overdoing it, Miyashita.

How energetic. Very good.

"O Romeo!!"

...I WANT TO DO MY BEST WITH THIS.

CLASS

REHEARSAL AT SCHOOL

Stage order.

REHEARSAL AT HOME

NOD

"A thousand times good-night!"

"Madam!"

NURSE

Just go make our dinner, all right?

Hmph.

I wanna help her study, too.

STUDY AT HOME

Sakura, try on the costume.

I went online and did some research on Juliet's balcony for this.

We can stick these to the desk and...

SCHOOL-FESTIVAL COMMITTEE

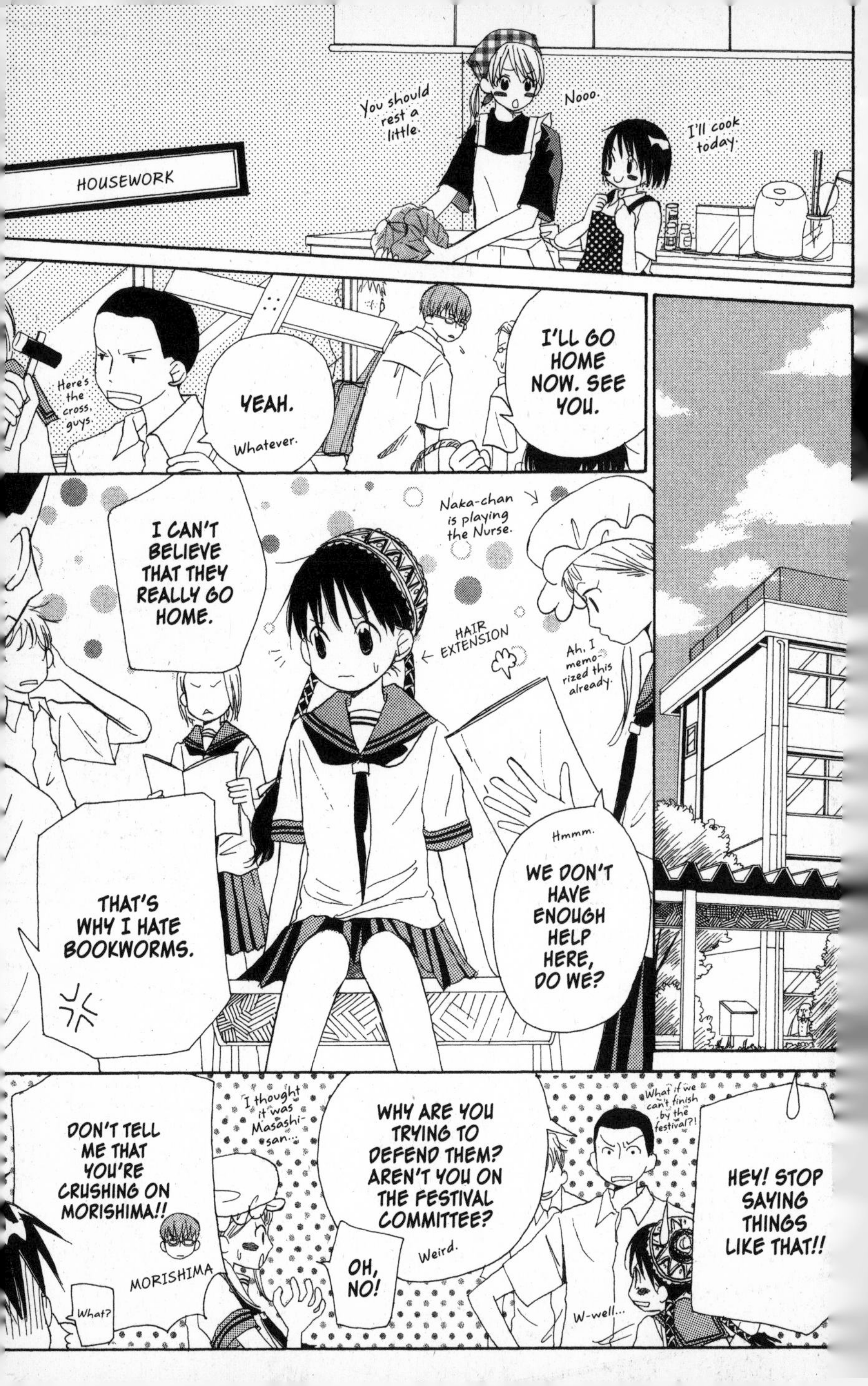
Nooo.
I'll cook today.
You should rest a little.
HOUSEWORK
I'LL GO HOME NOW. SEE YOU.
YEAH.
Whatever.
Here's the cross, guys.
Naka-chan is playing the Nurse.
I CAN'T BELIEVE THAT THEY REALLY GO HOME.
HAIR EXTENSION
Ah, I memorized this already.
Hmmm.
WE DON'T HAVE ENOUGH HELP HERE, DO WE?
THAT'S WHY I HATE BOOKWORMS.
HEY! STOP SAYING THINGS LIKE THAT!!
What if we can't finish by the festival?!
W-well...
WHY ARE YOU TRYING TO DEFEND THEM? AREN'T YOU ON THE FESTIVAL COMMITTEE?
Weird.
I thought it was Masashi-san...
OH, NO!
DON'T TELL ME THAT YOU'RE CRUSHING ON MORISHIMA!!
MORISHIMA
What?

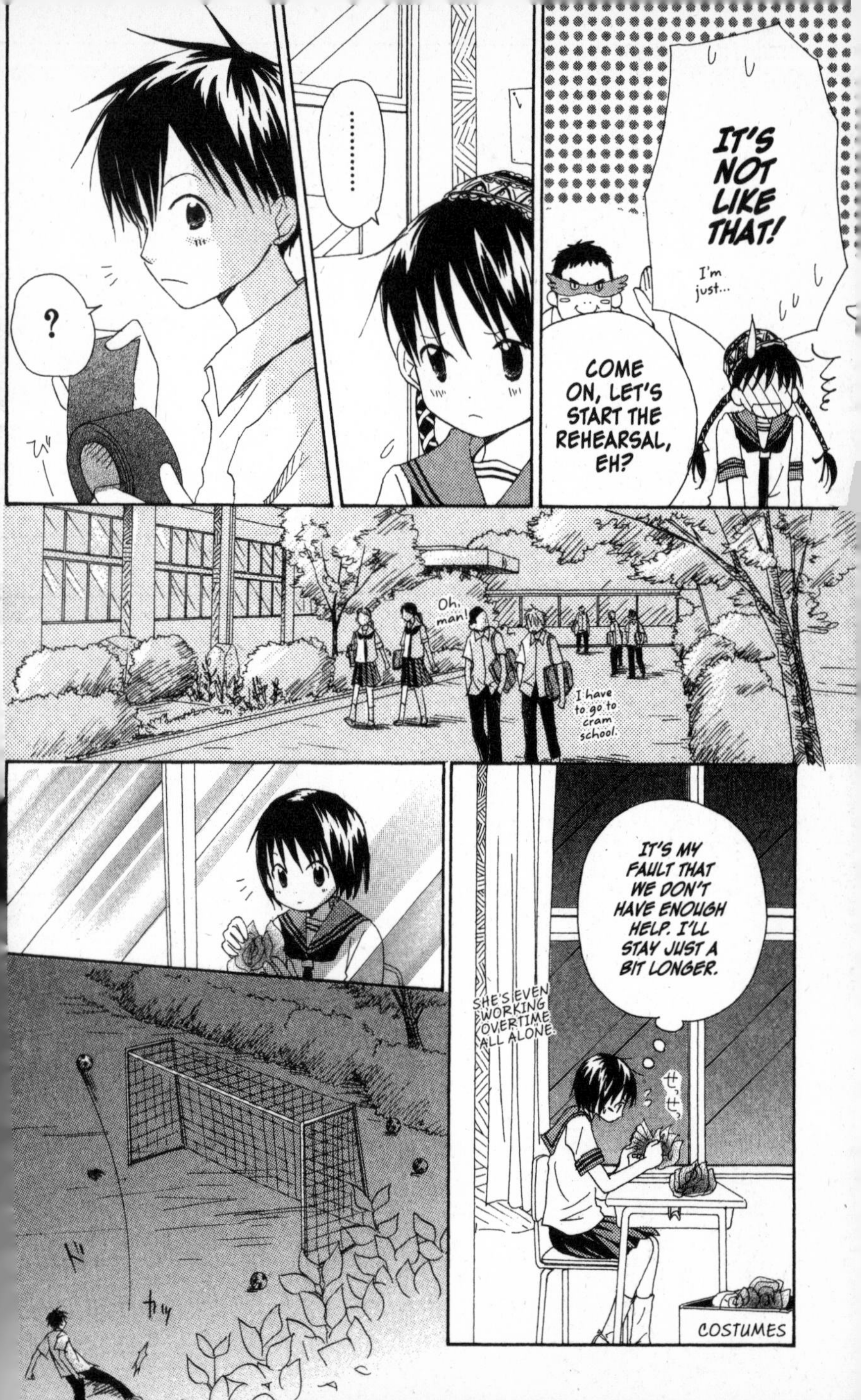
IT'S NOT LIKE THAT!
I'm just...
COME ON, LET'S START THE REHEARSAL, EH?
......
?
Oh, man!
I have to go to cram school.
IT'S MY FAULT THAT WE DON'T HAVE ENOUGH HELP. I'LL STAY JUST A BIT LONGER.
SHE'S EVEN WORKING OVERTIME ALL ALONE.
COSTUMES

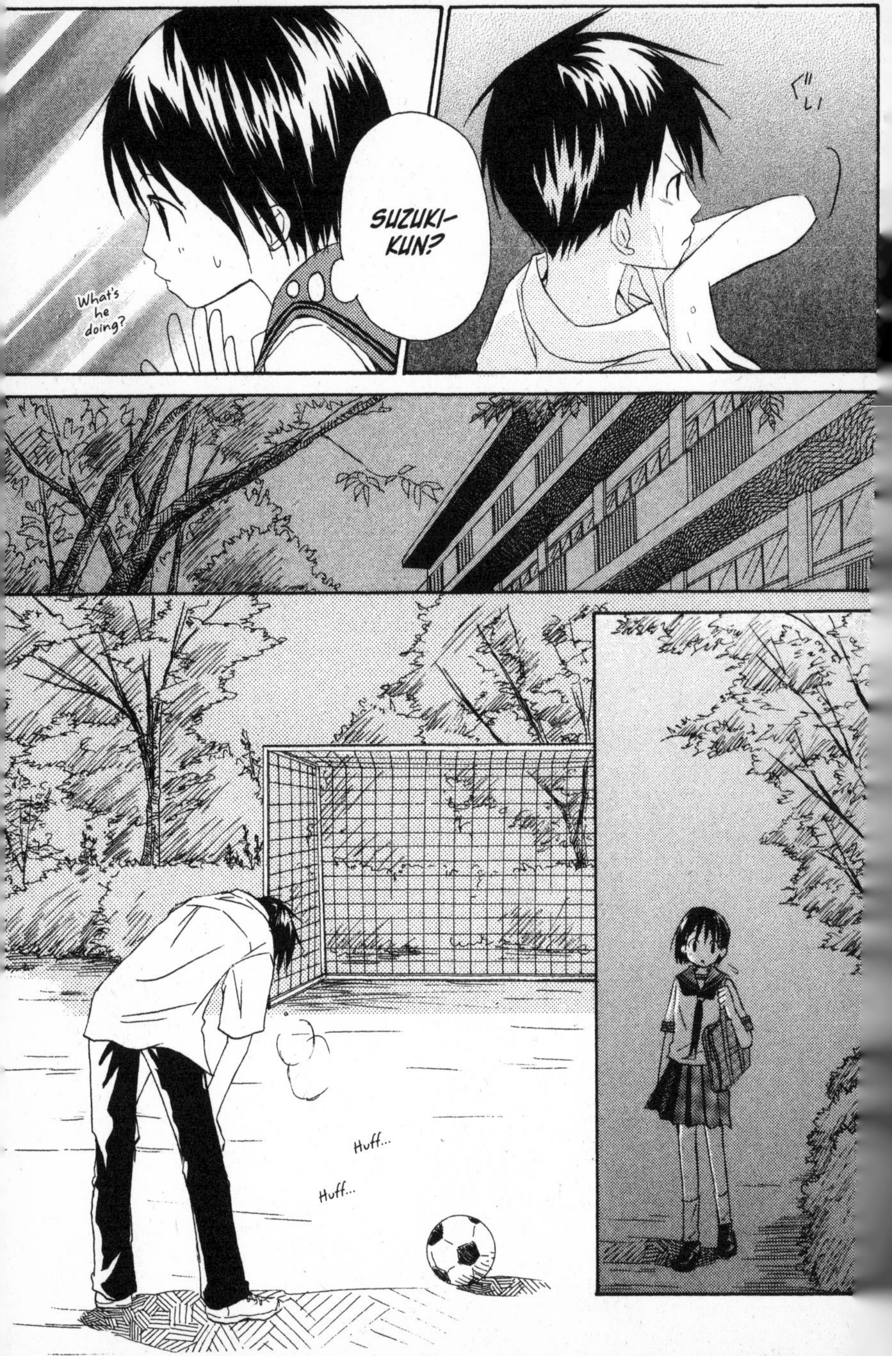
ぐい
SUZUKI-KUN?
What's he doing?
Huff...
Huff...

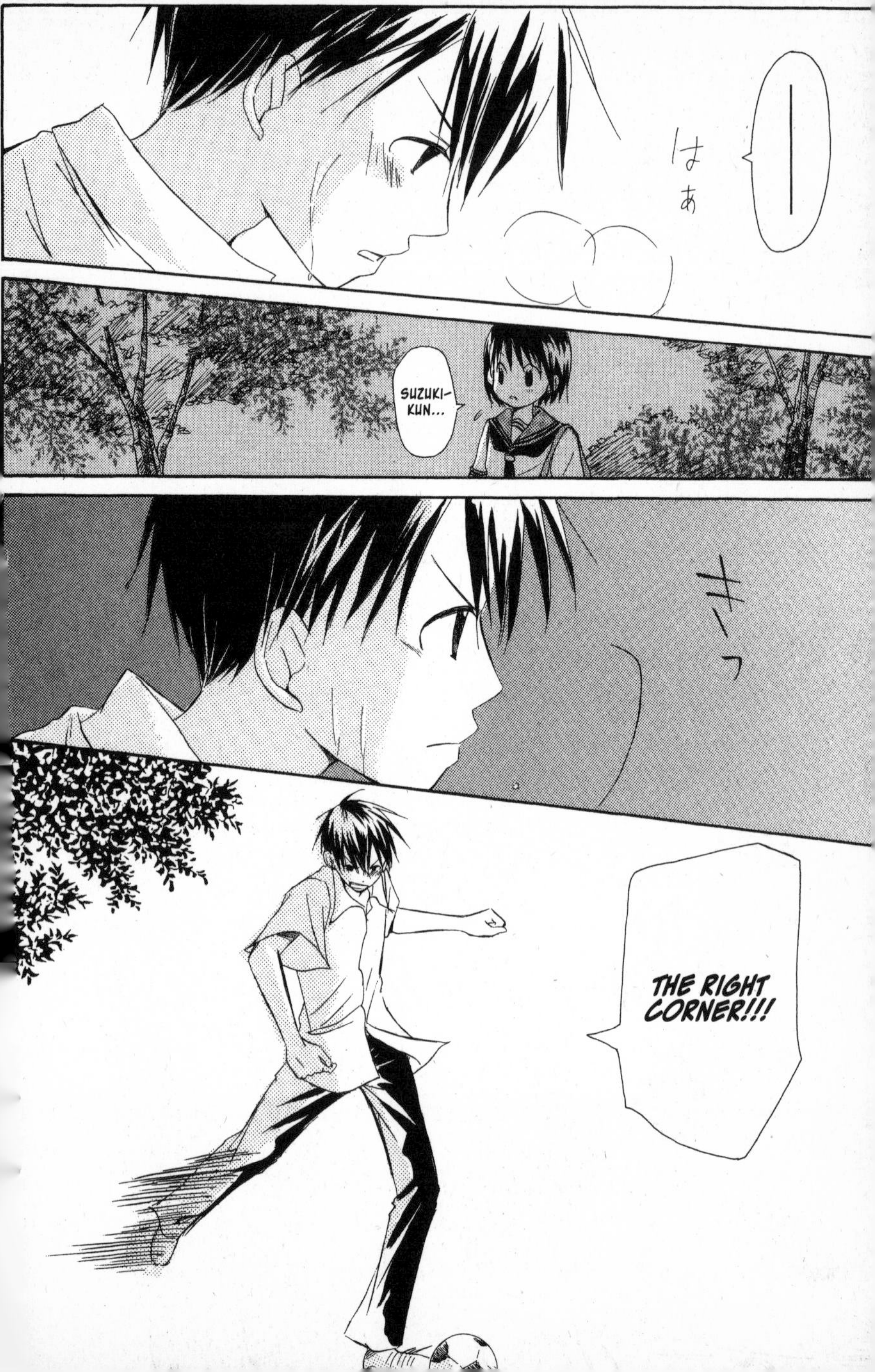
はあ
SUZUKI-KUN...
キッ
THE RIGHT CORNER!!!

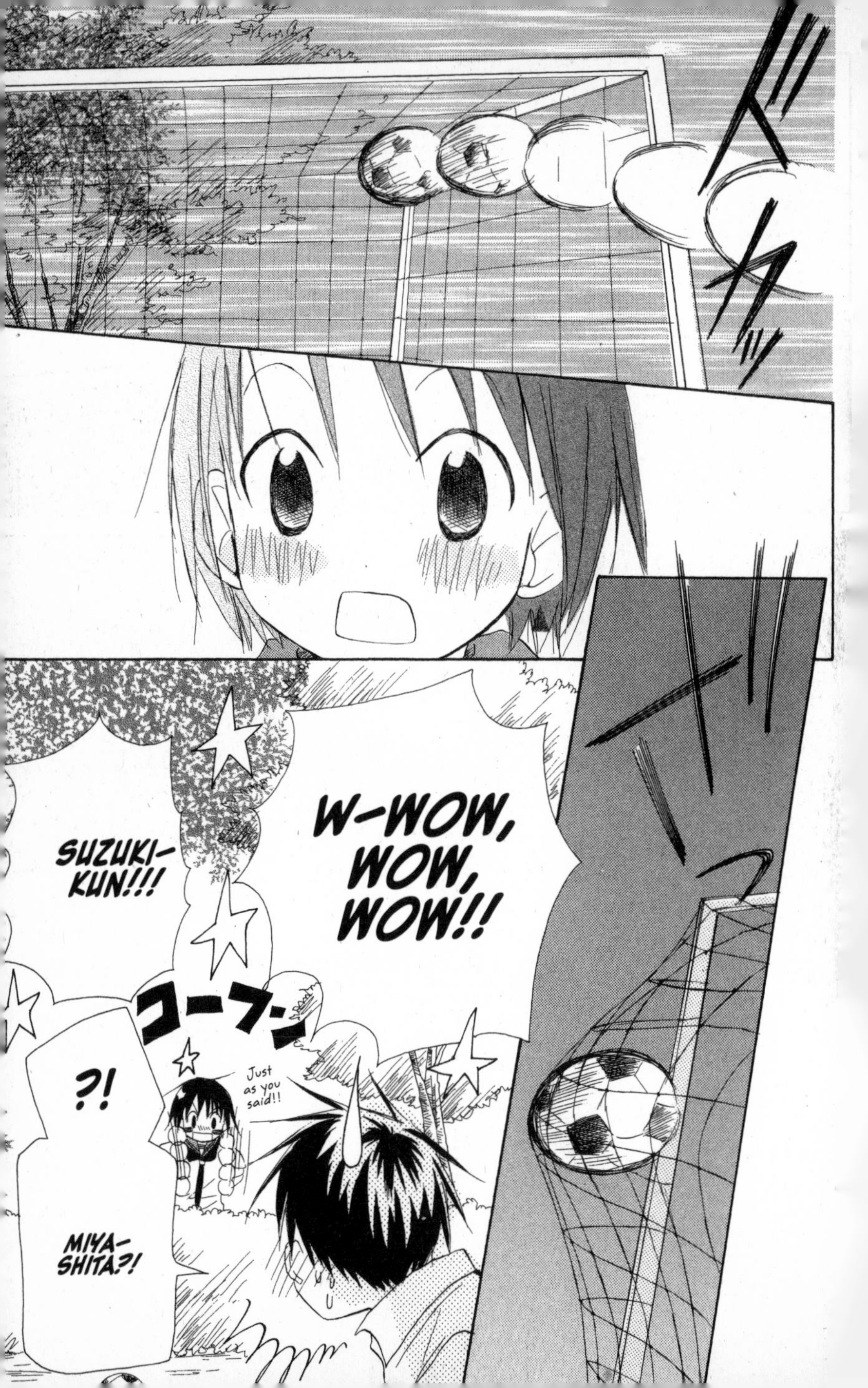
ドバッ
W-WOW, WOW, WOW!!
SUZUKI-KUN!!!
コーフン
Just as you said!!
?!
MIYA-SHITA?!

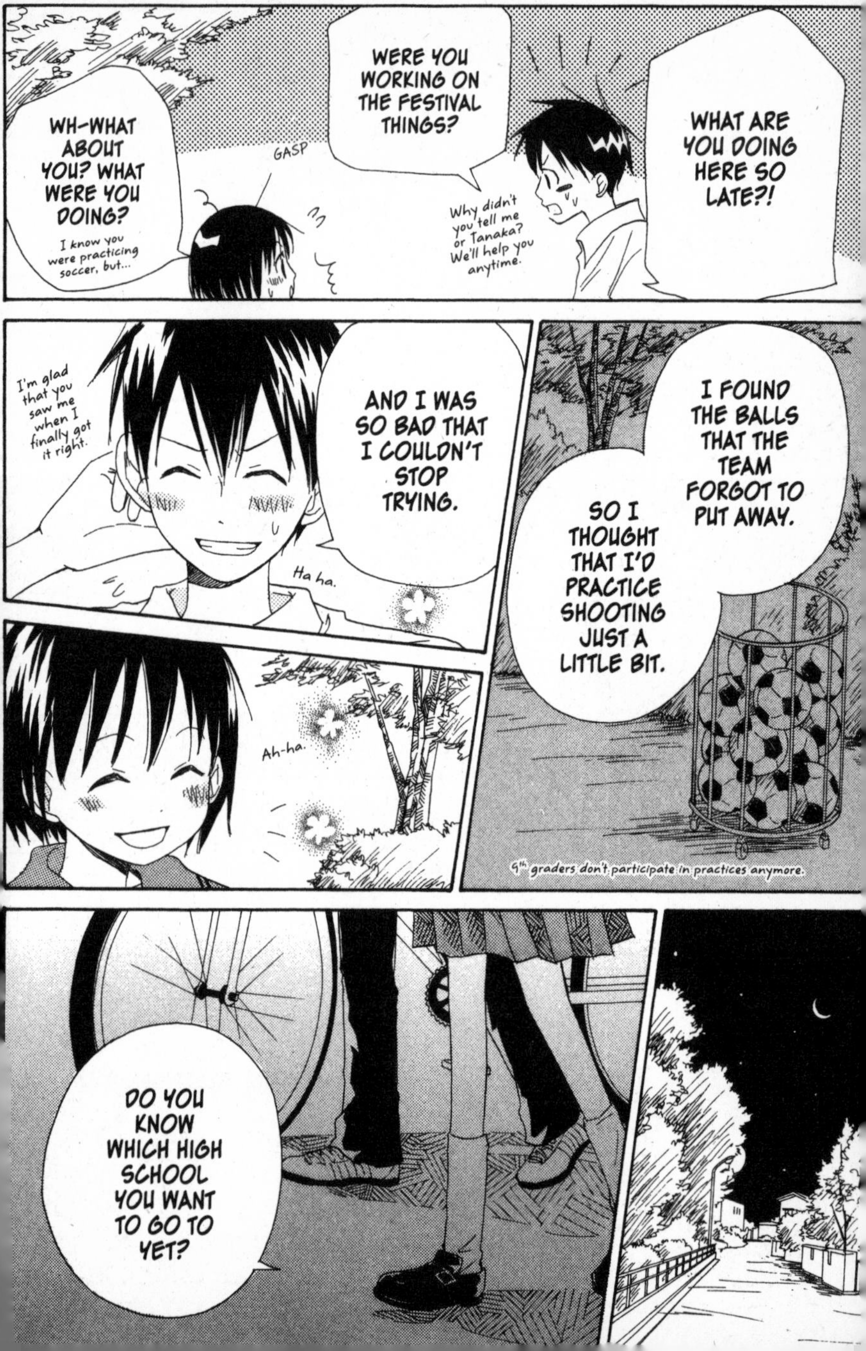
WHAT ARE YOU DOING HERE SO LATE?!
Why didn't you tell me or Tanaka? We'll help you anytime.
WERE YOU WORKING ON THE FESTIVAL THINGS?
GASP
WH-WHAT ABOUT YOU? WHAT WERE YOU DOING?
I know you were practicing soccer, but...
I FOUND THE BALLS THAT THE TEAM FORGOT TO PUT AWAY.
SO I THOUGHT THAT I'D PRACTICE SHOOTING JUST A LITTLE BIT.
9th graders don't participate in practices anymore.
AND I WAS SO BAD THAT I COULDN'T STOP TRYING.
Ha ha.
I'm glad that you saw me when I finally got it right.
Ah-ha.
DO YOU KNOW WHICH HIGH SCHOOL YOU WANT TO GO TO YET?

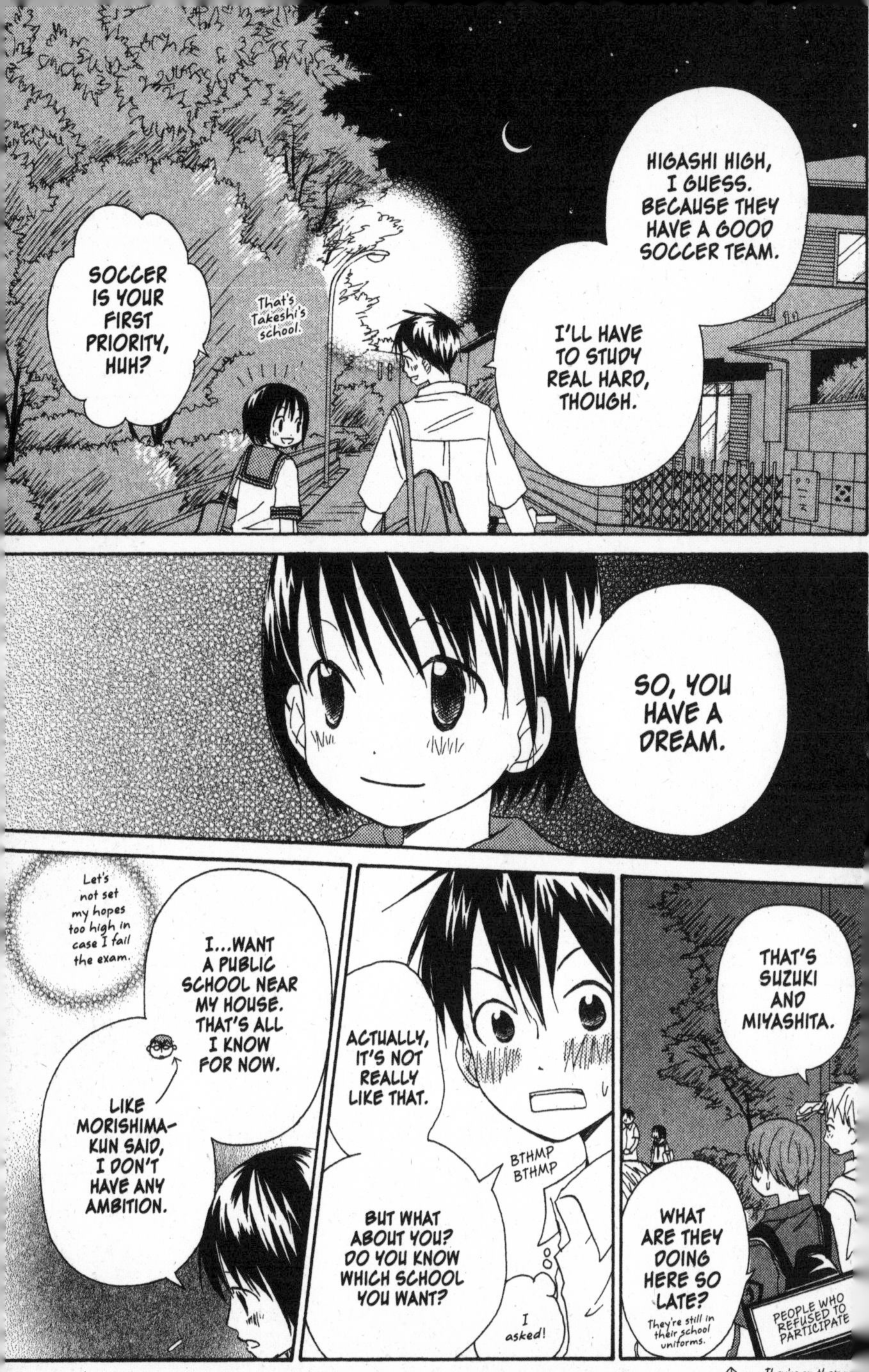

HIGASHI HIGH, I GUESS. BECAUSE THEY HAVE A GOOD SOCCER TEAM.
I'LL HAVE TO STUDY REAL HARD, THOUGH.
That's Takeshi's school.
SOCCER IS YOUR FIRST PRIORITY, HUH?
SO, YOU HAVE A DREAM.
THAT'S SUZUKI AND MIYASHITA.
WHAT ARE THEY DOING HERE SO LATE?
They're still in their school uniforms.
PEOPLE WHO REFUSED TO PARTICIPATE
ACTUALLY, IT'S NOT REALLY LIKE THAT.
BTHMP BTHMP
BUT WHAT ABOUT YOU? DO YOU KNOW WHICH SCHOOL YOU WANT?
I asked!
Let's not set my hopes too high in case I fail the exam.
I...WANT A PUBLIC SCHOOL NEAR MY HOUSE. THAT'S ALL I KNOW FOR NOW.
LIKE MORISHIMA-KUN SAID, I DON'T HAVE ANY AMBITION.

↑ They're on their w
to cram schools

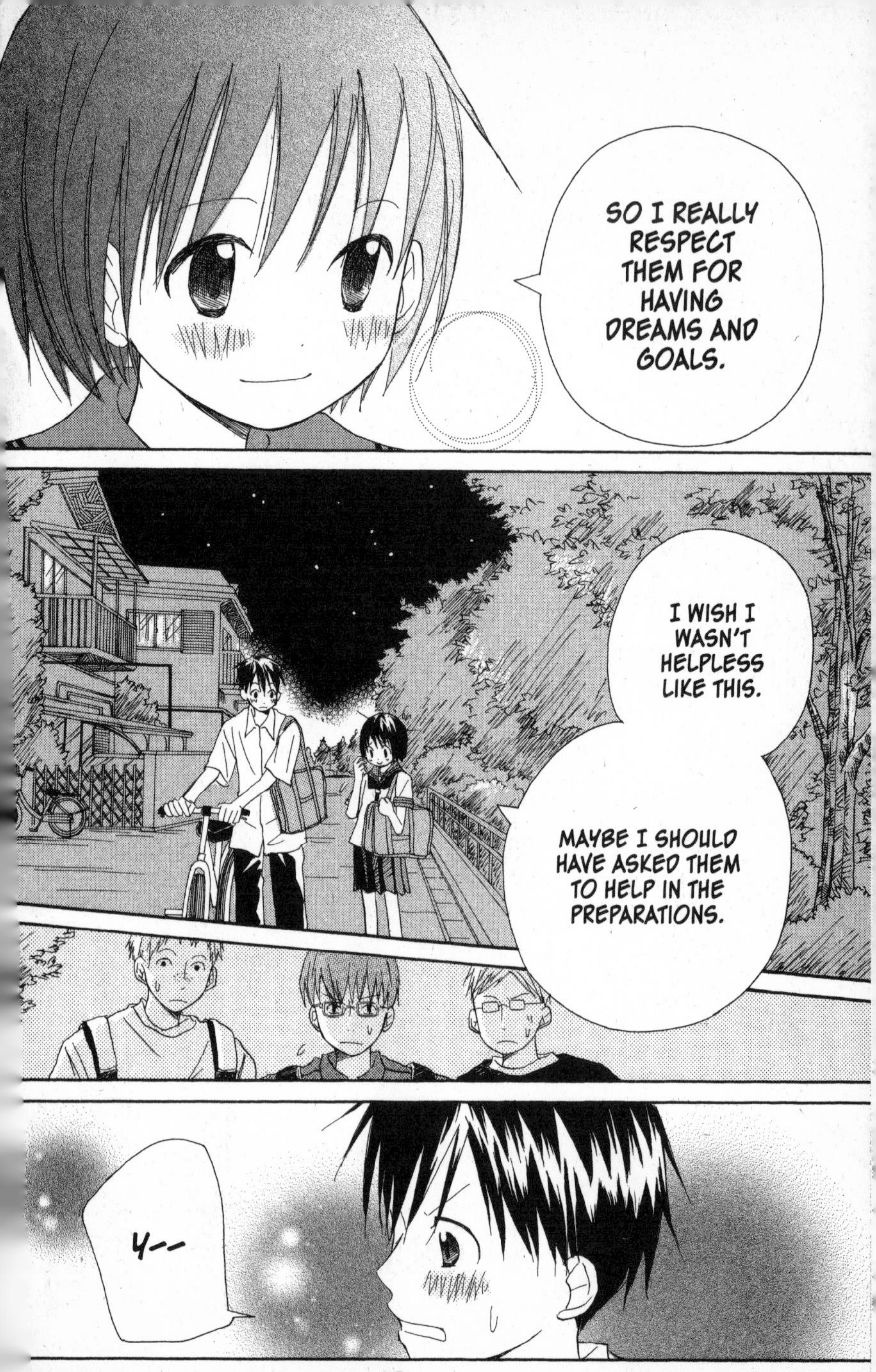
SO I REALLY RESPECT THEM FOR HAVING DREAMS AND GOALS.
I WISH I WASN'T HELPLESS LIKE THIS.
MAYBE I SHOULD HAVE ASKED THEM TO HELP IN THE PREPARATIONS.
Y--

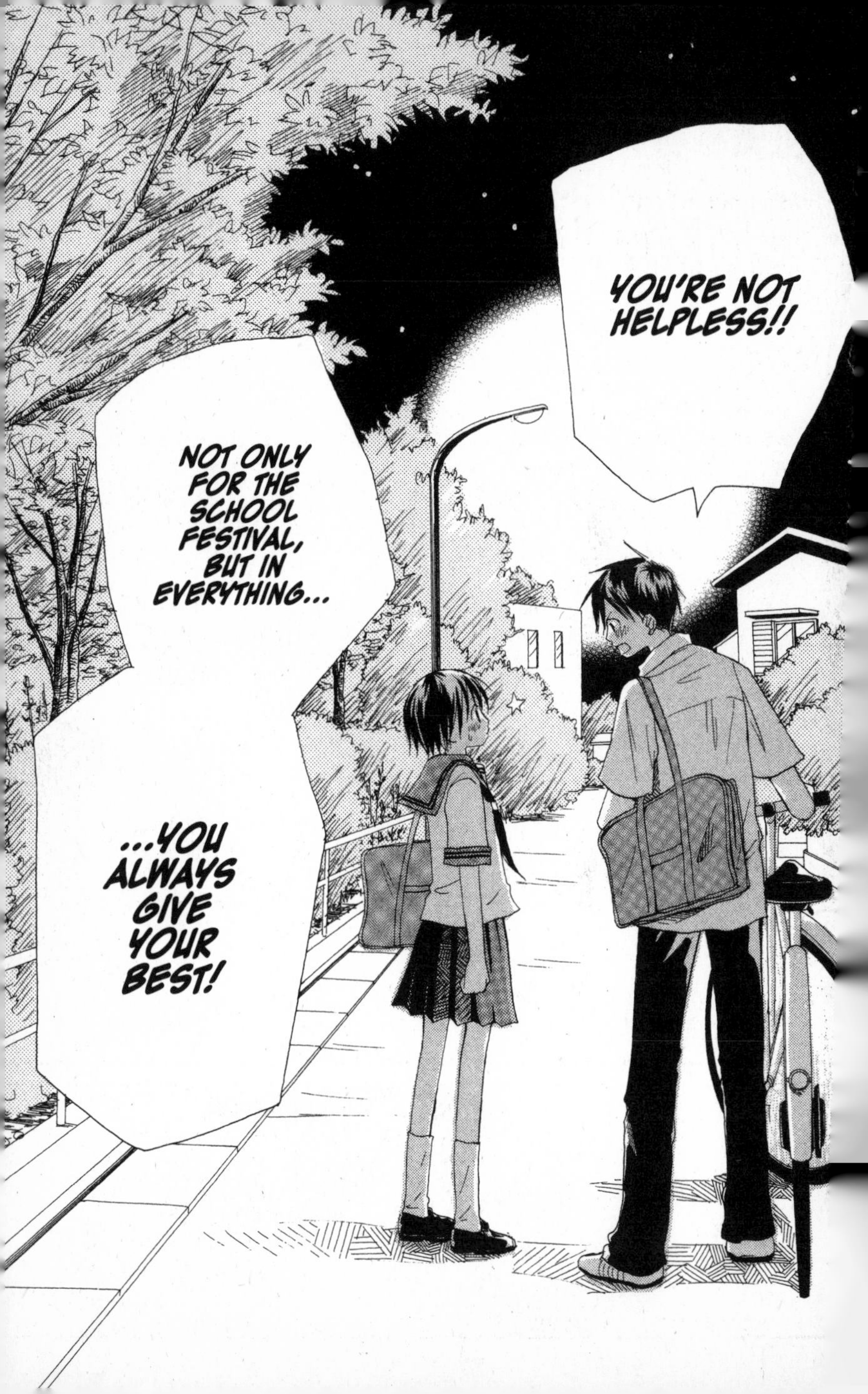
YOU'RE NOT HELPLESS!!
NOT ONLY FOR THE SCHOOL FESTIVAL, BUT IN EVERYTHING...
...YOU ALWAYS GIVE YOUR BEST!

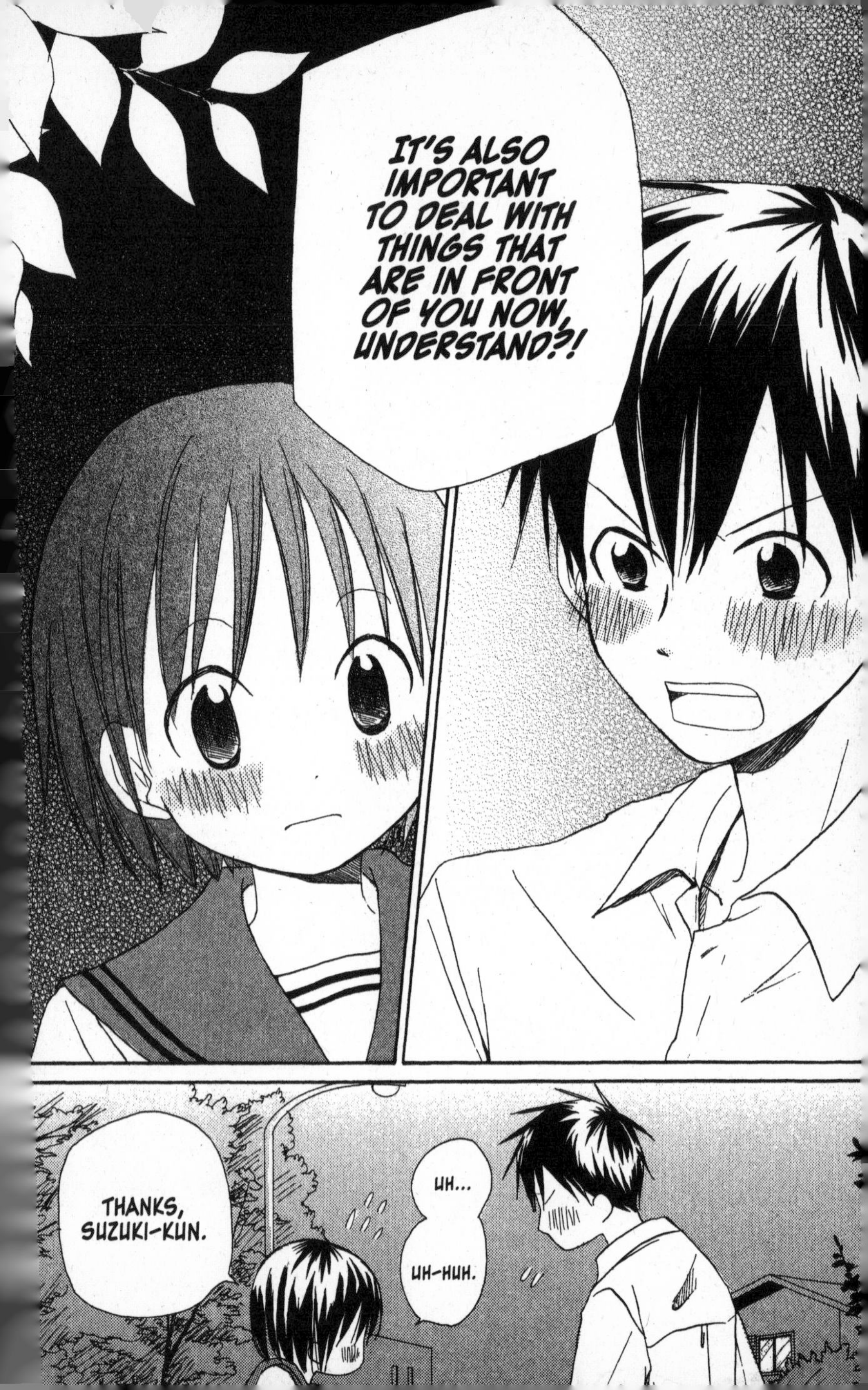
IT'S ALSO IMPORTANT TO DEAL WITH THINGS THAT ARE IN FRONT OF YOU NOW, UNDERSTAND?!
UH... UH-HUH.
THANKS, SUZUKI-KUN.

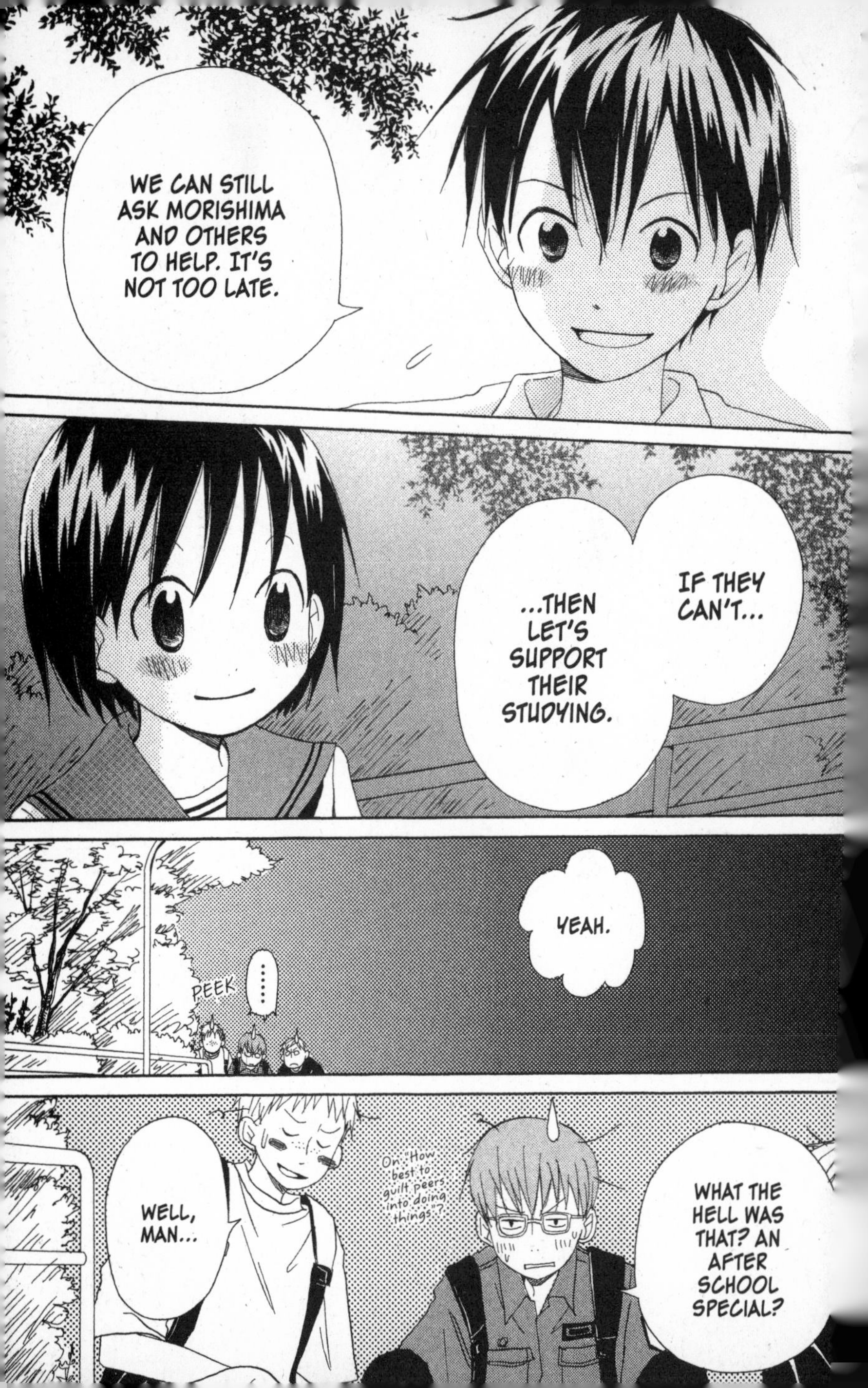
WE CAN STILL ASK MORISHIMA AND OTHERS TO HELP. IT'S NOT TOO LATE.
IF THEY CAN'T...
...THEN LET'S SUPPORT THEIR STUDYING.
YEAH.
......
PEEK
WHAT THE HELL WAS THAT? AN AFTER SCHOOL SPECIAL?
On "How best to guilt peers into doing things"?
WELL, MAN...

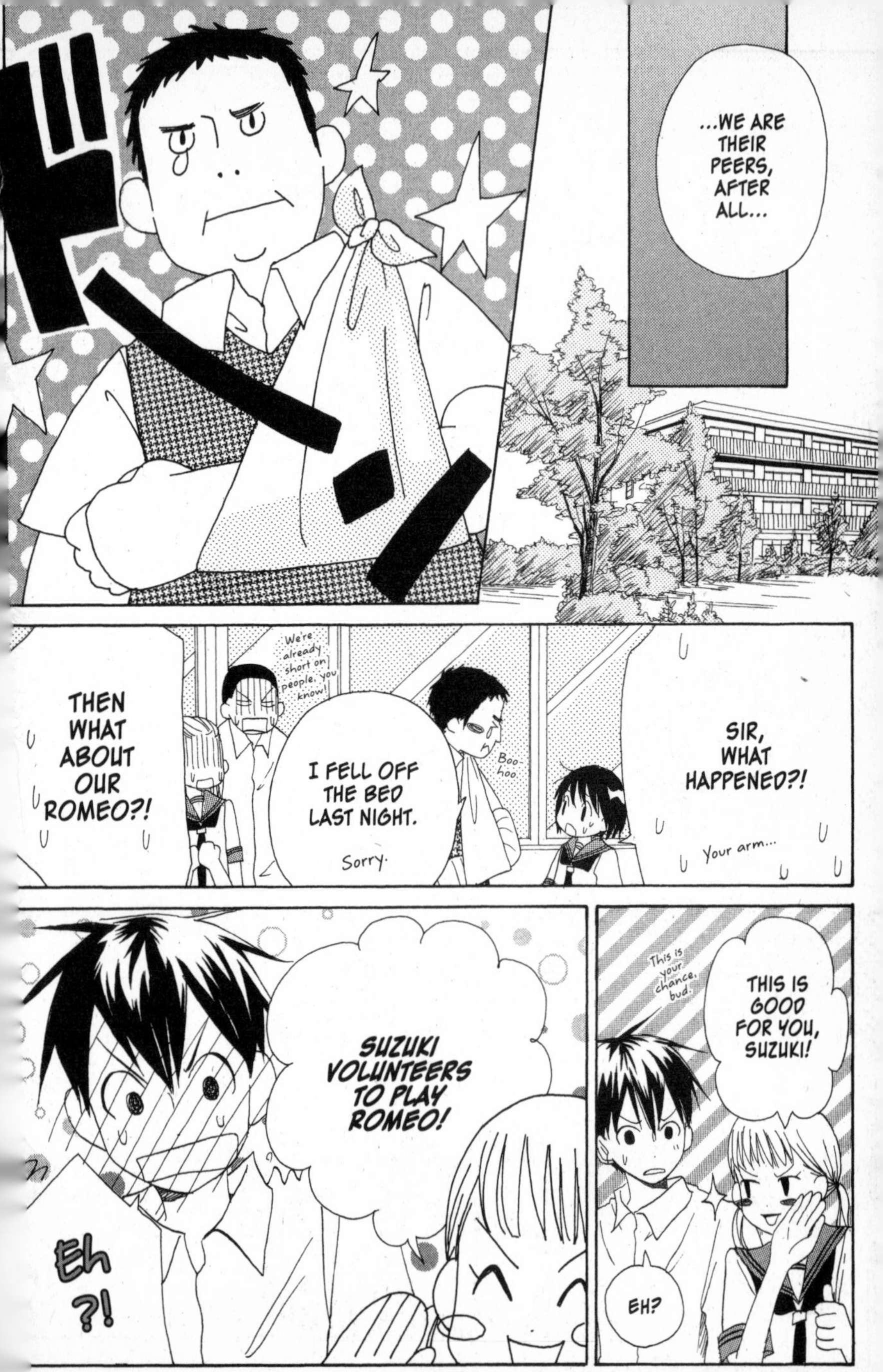
...WE ARE THEIR PEERS, AFTER ALL...
SIR, WHAT HAPPENED?!
Your arm...
Boo-hoo.
I FELL OFF THE BED LAST NIGHT.
Sorry.
We're already short on people, you know!
THEN WHAT ABOUT OUR ROMEO?!
THIS IS GOOD FOR YOU, SUZUKI!
This is your chance, bud.
EH?
SUZUKI VOLUNTEERS TO PLAY ROMEO!
Eh ?!

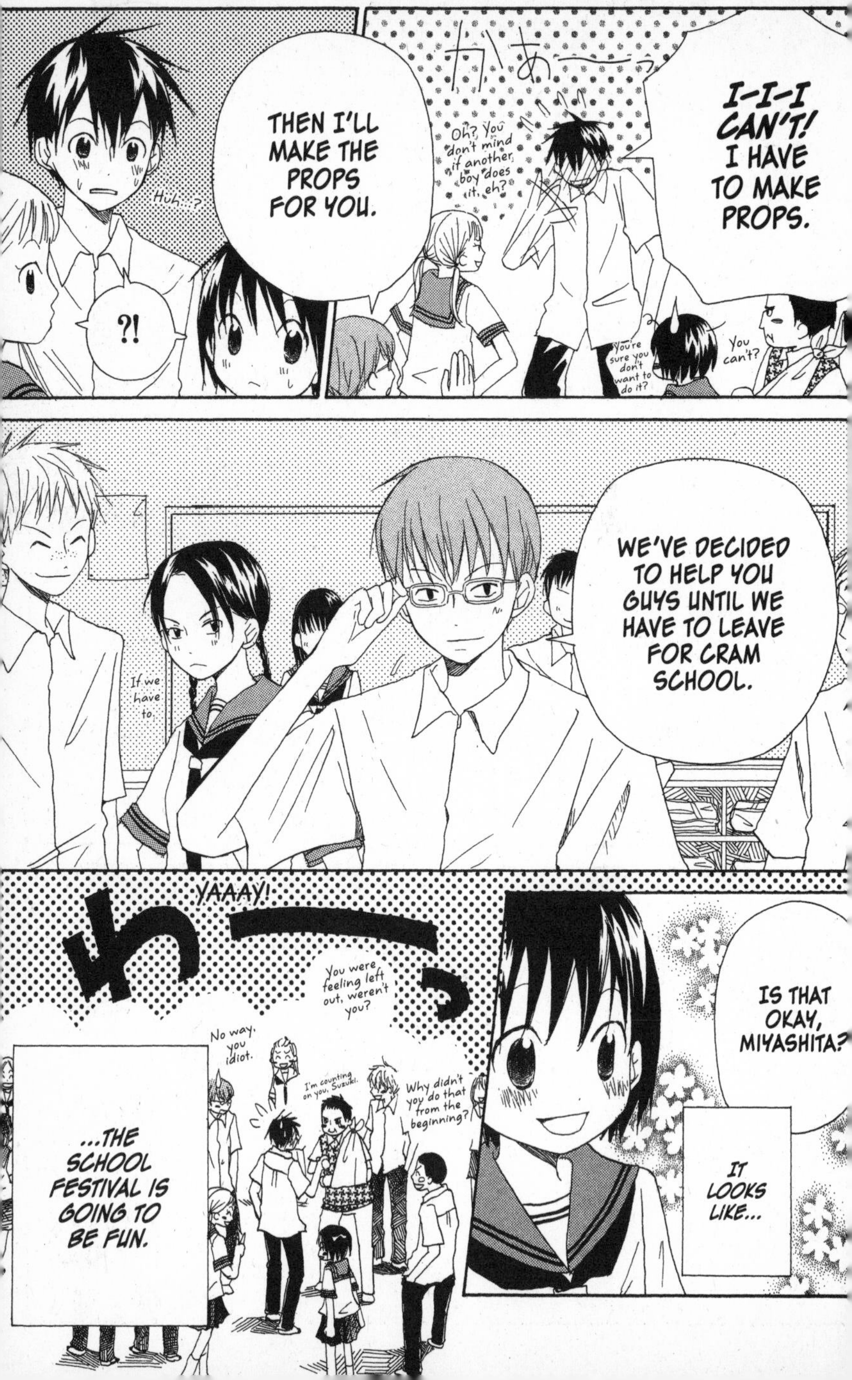
I-I-I CAN'T! I HAVE TO MAKE PROPS.
You can't?
You're sure you don't want to do it?
Oh? You don't mind if another boy does it, eh?
THEN I'LL MAKE THE PROPS FOR YOU.
Huh...?
?!
WE'VE DECIDED TO HELP YOU GUYS UNTIL WE HAVE TO LEAVE FOR CRAM SCHOOL.
If we have to.
IS THAT OKAY, MIYASHITA?
IT LOOKS LIKE...
YAAAY!
You were feeling left out, weren't you?
Why didn't you do that from the beginning?
I'm counting on you, Suzuki.
No way, you idiot.
...THE SCHOOL FESTIVAL IS GOING TO BE FUN.

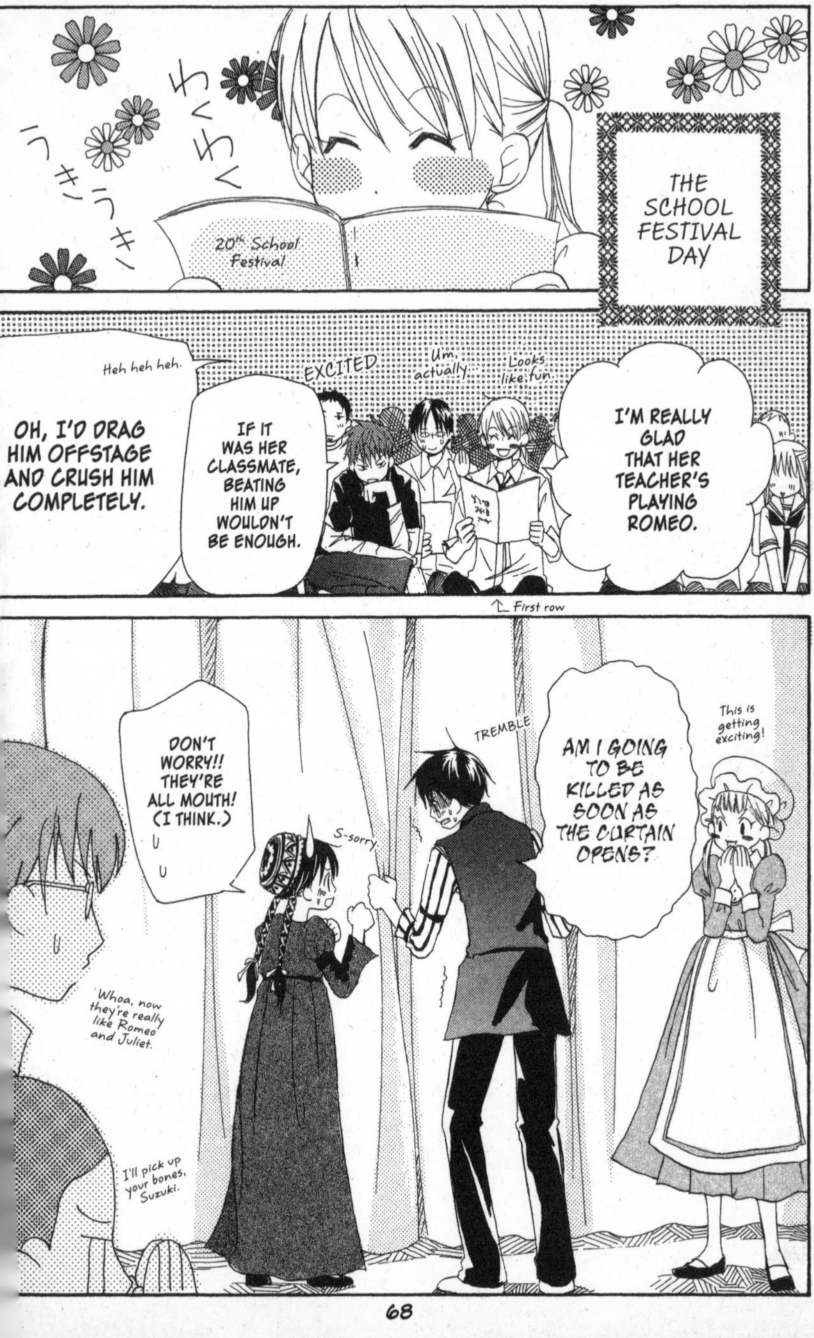
THE SCHOOL FESTIVAL DAY
わくわく
ウキウキ
20th School Festival
I'M REALLY GLAD THAT HER TEACHER'S PLAYING ROMEO.
Looks like fun.
Um, actually...
EXCITED
IF IT WAS HER CLASSMATE, BEATING HIM UP WOULDN'T BE ENOUGH.
Heh heh heh.
OH, I'D DRAG HIM OFFSTAGE AND CRUSH HIM COMPLETELY.
First row
This is getting exciting!
AM I GOING TO BE KILLED AS SOON AS THE CURTAIN OPENS?
TREMBLE
S-sorry
DON'T WORRY!! THEY'RE ALL MOUTH! (I THINK.)
Whoa, now they're really like Romeo and Juliet.
I'll pick up your bones, Suzuki.

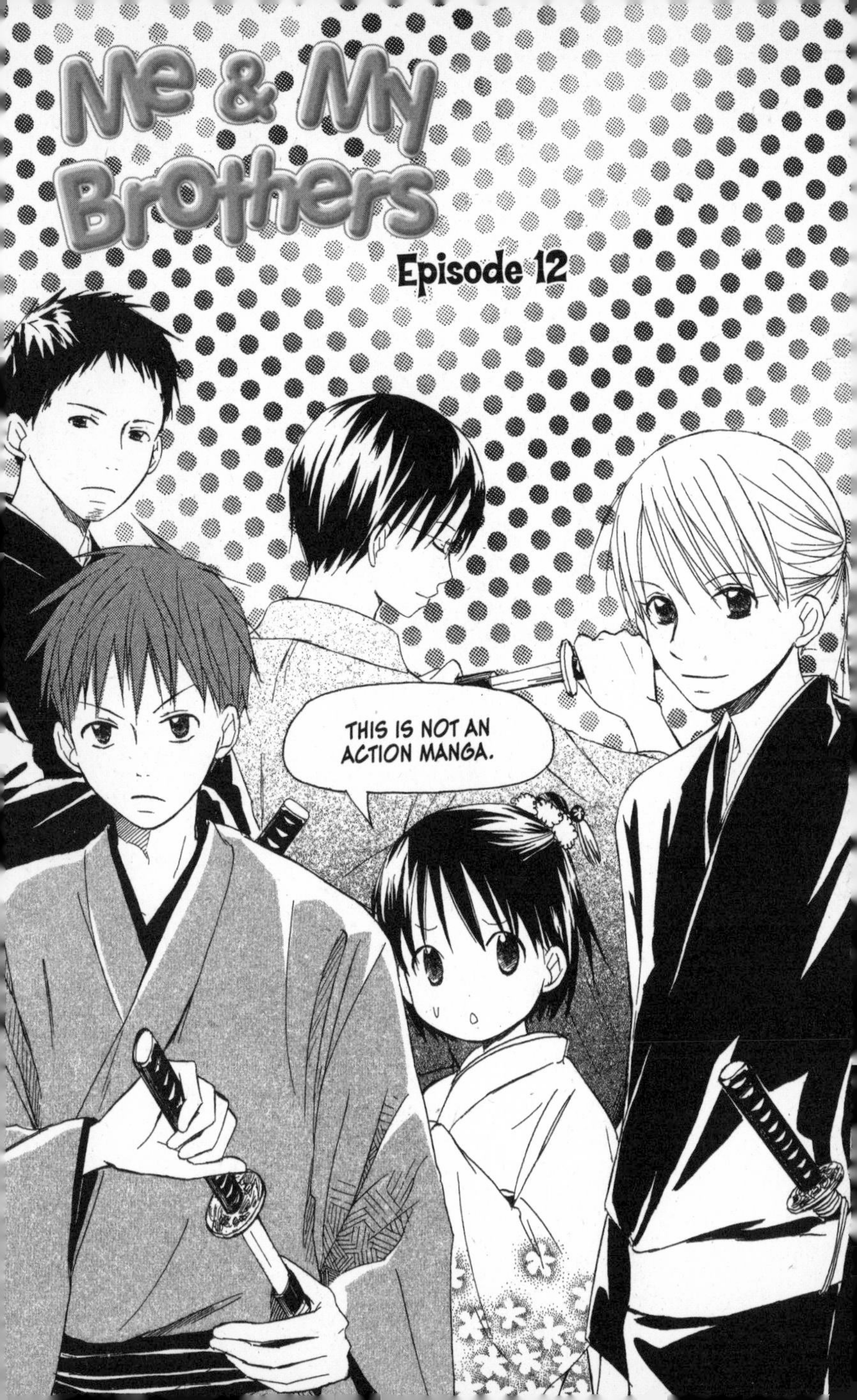
Me & My Brothers
Episode 12
THIS IS NOT AN ACTION MANGA.

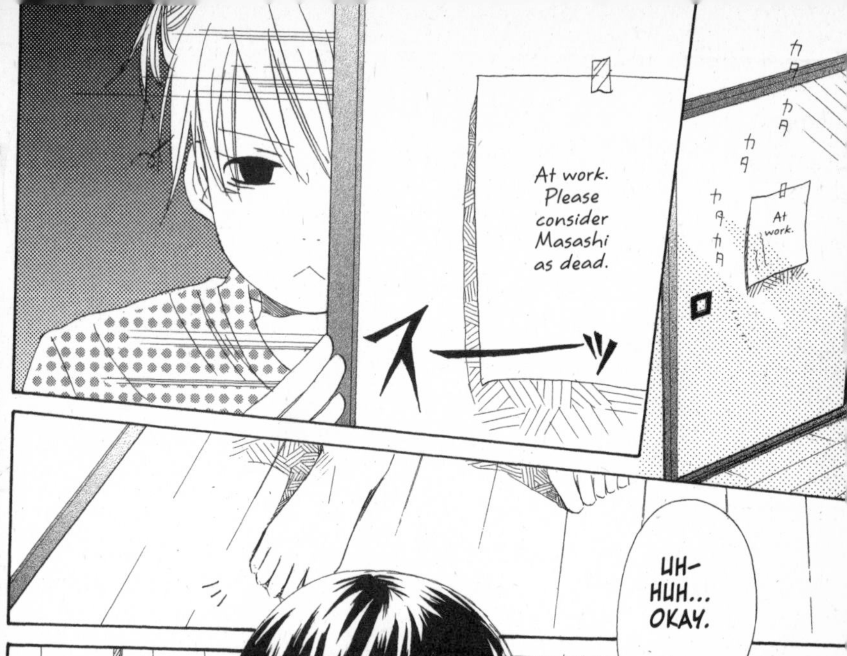
カタ
カタ
カタ
カタカタ
At work. Please consider Masashi as dead.
At work.
スーッ
UH-HUH... OKAY.
THEN I'LL SEE YOU IN FRONT OF SUNFLOWER PARK ON SUNDAY.

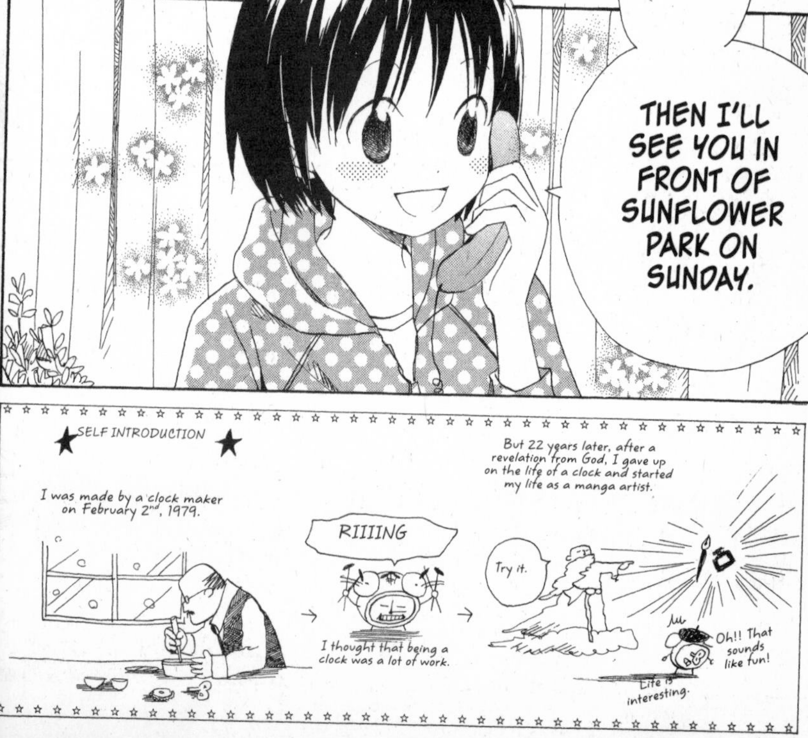
★SELF INTRODUCTION★
I was made by a clock maker on February 2nd, 1979.
RIIIING
I thought that being a clock was a lot of work.
But 22 years later, after a revelation from God, I gave up on the life of a clock and started my life as a manga artist.
Try it.
Oh!! That sounds like fun!
Life is interesting.

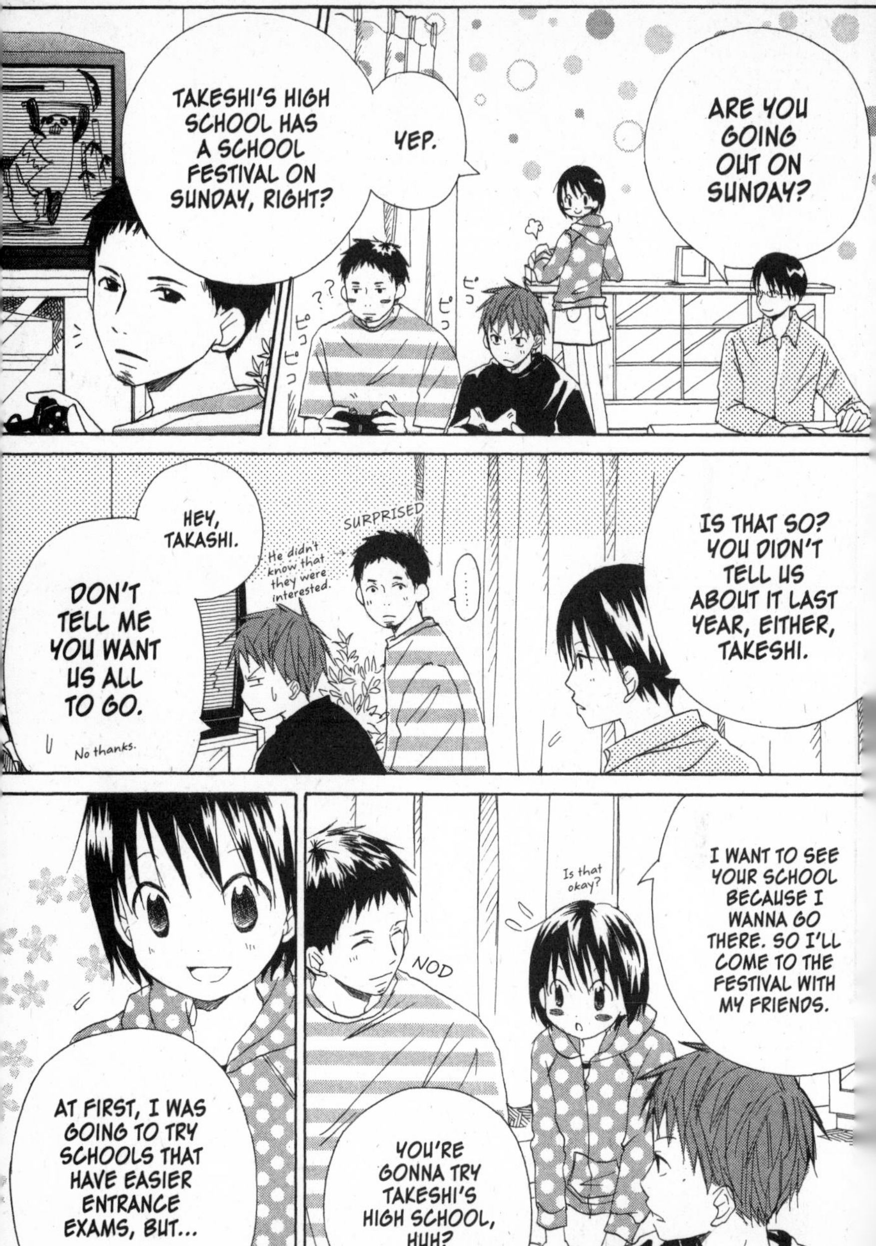
ARE YOU GOING OUT ON SUNDAY?
TAKESHI'S HIGH SCHOOL HAS A SCHOOL FESTIVAL ON SUNDAY, RIGHT?
YEP.
ピコ ピコ
ピコ ピコ
IS THAT SO? YOU DIDN'T TELL US ABOUT IT LAST YEAR, EITHER, TAKESHI.
SURPRISED
......
He didn't know that they were interested.
HEY, TAKASHI.
DON'T TELL ME YOU WANT US ALL TO GO.
No thanks.
I WANT TO SEE YOUR SCHOOL BECAUSE I WANNA GO THERE. SO I'LL COME TO THE FESTIVAL WITH MY FRIENDS.
Is that okay?
NOD
YOU'RE GONNA TRY TAKESHI'S HIGH SCHOOL, HUH?
AT FIRST, I WAS GOING TO TRY SCHOOLS THAT HAVE EASIER ENTRANCE EXAMS, BUT...

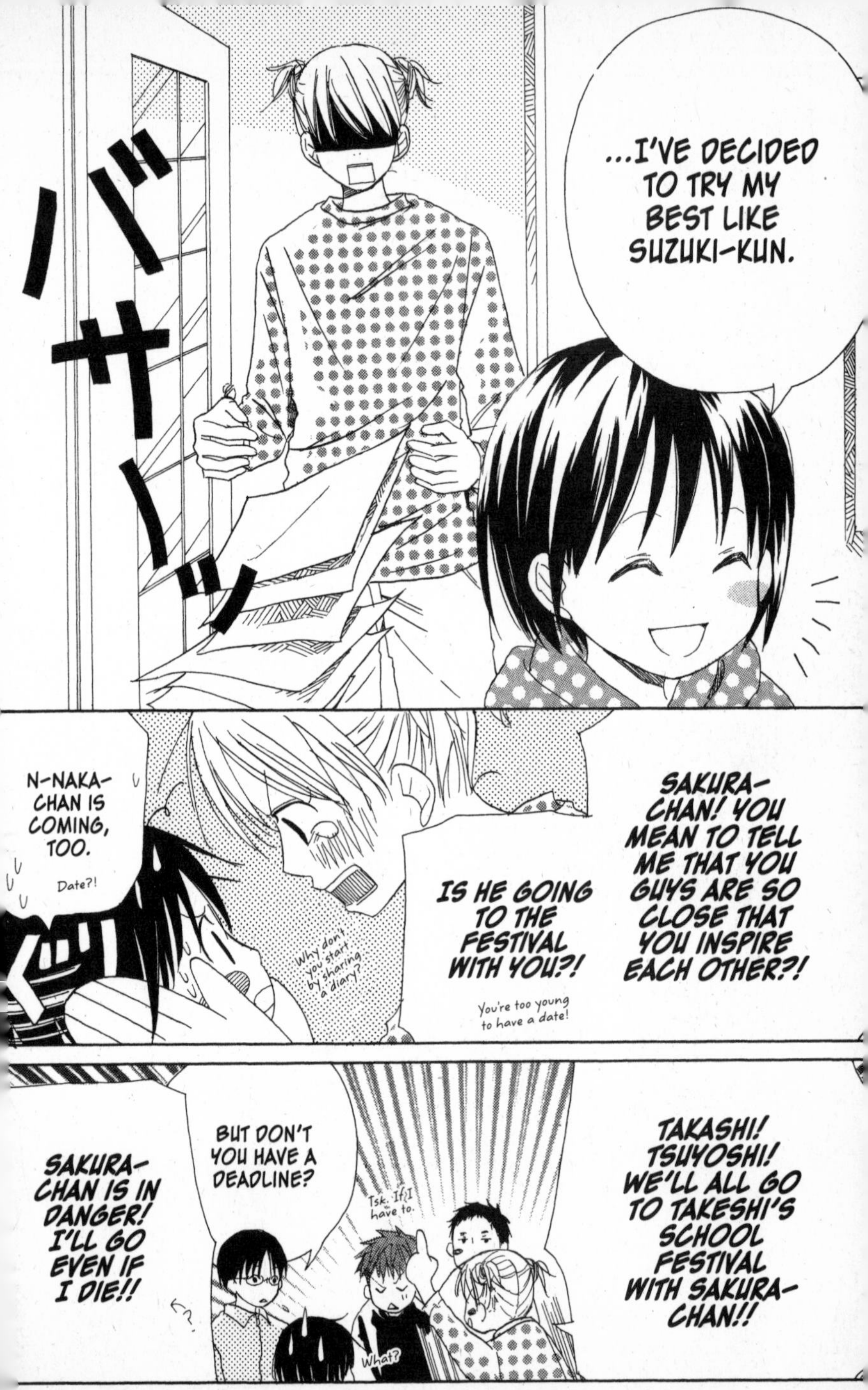
...I'VE DECIDED TO TRY MY BEST LIKE SUZUKI-KUN.
バサーッ
SAKURA-CHAN! YOU MEAN TO TELL ME THAT YOU GUYS ARE SO CLOSE THAT YOU INSPIRE EACH OTHER?!
IS HE GOING TO THE FESTIVAL WITH YOU?!
You're too young to have a date!
Why don't you start by sharing a diary?
N-NAKA-CHAN IS COMING, TOO.
Date?!
TAKASHI! TSUYOSHI! WE'LL ALL GO TO TAKESHI'S SCHOOL FESTIVAL WITH SAKURA-CHAN!!
Tsk. If I have to.
BUT DON'T YOU HAVE A DEADLINE?
What?
SAKURA-CHAN IS IN DANGER! I'LL GO EVEN IF I DIE!!

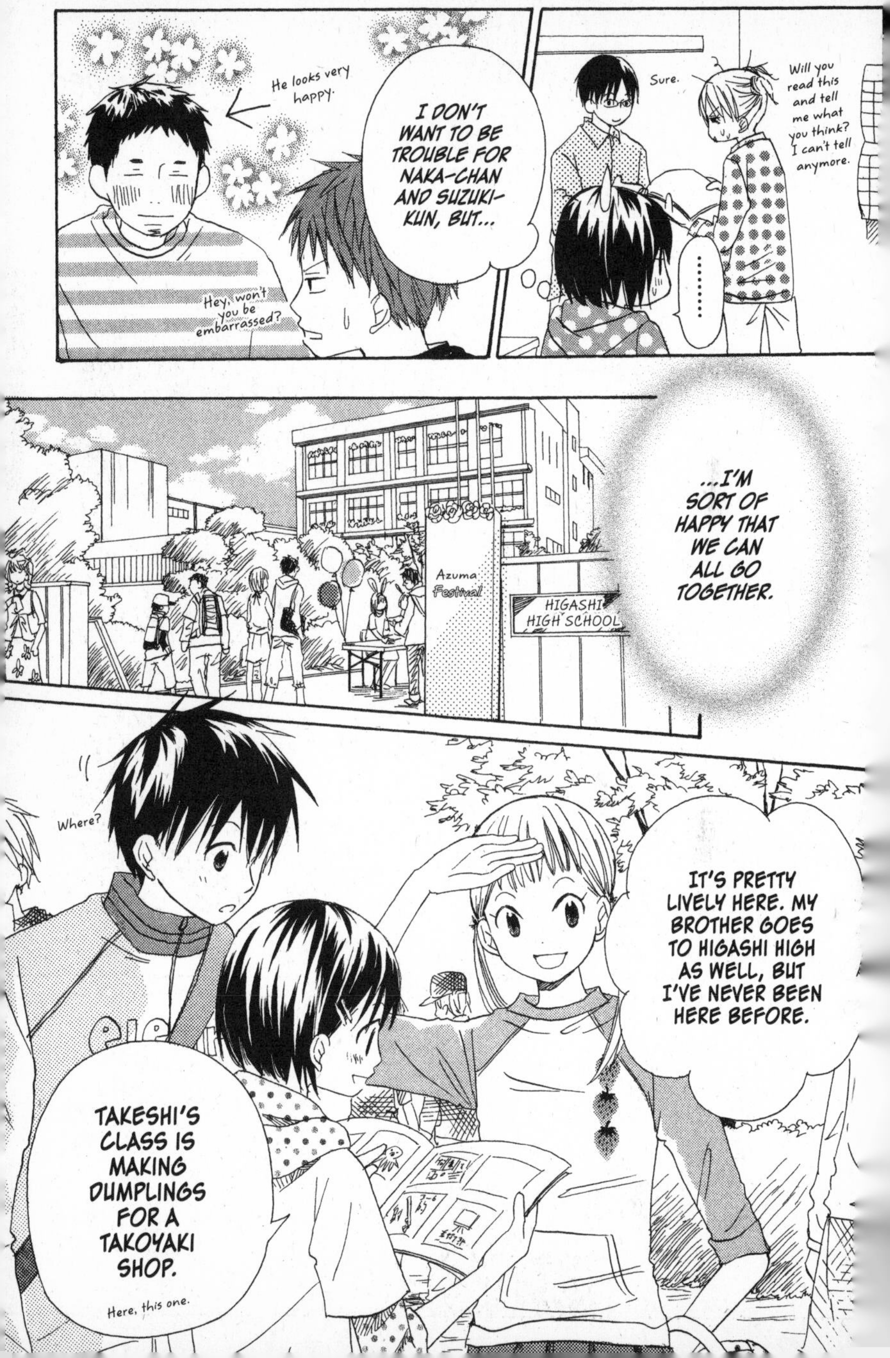
Will you read this and tell me what you think? I can't tell anymore.
Sure.
......
I DON'T WANT TO BE TROUBLE FOR NAKA-CHAN AND SUZUKI-KUN, BUT...
He looks very happy.
Hey, won't you be embarrassed?
...I'M SORT OF HAPPY THAT WE CAN ALL GO TOGETHER.
HIGASHI HIGH SCHOOL
Azuma Festival
IT'S PRETTY LIVELY HERE. MY BROTHER GOES TO HIGASHI HIGH AS WELL, BUT I'VE NEVER BEEN HERE BEFORE.
Where?
TAKESHI'S CLASS IS MAKING DUMPLINGS FOR A TAKOYAKI SHOP.
Here, this one.

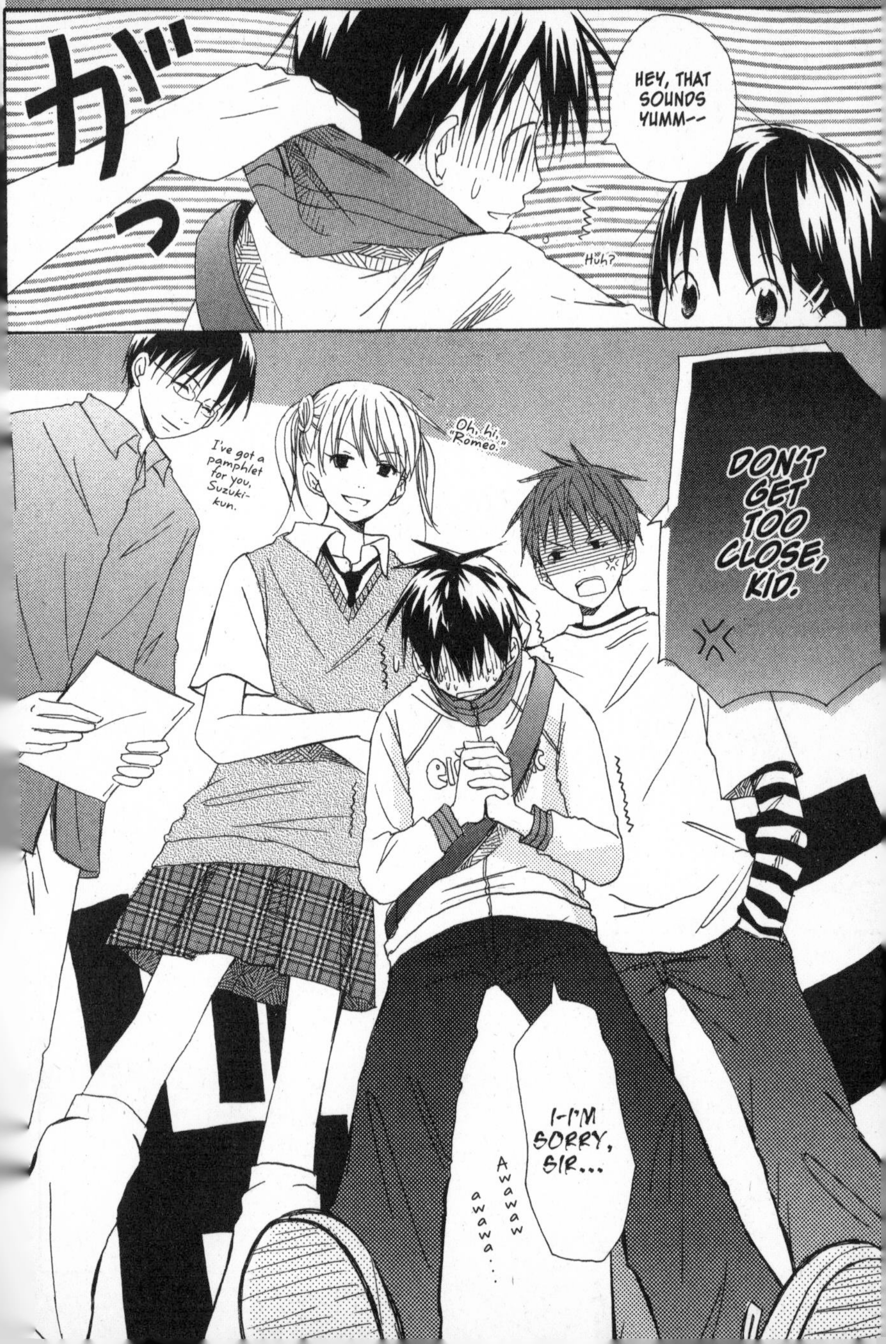
HEY, THAT SOUNDS YUMM--
Huh?
ガッ
DON'T GET TOO CLOSE, KID.
Oh, hi, "Romeo."
I've got a pamphlet for you, Suzuki-kun.
I-I'M SORRY, SIR...
Awawaw awawa...

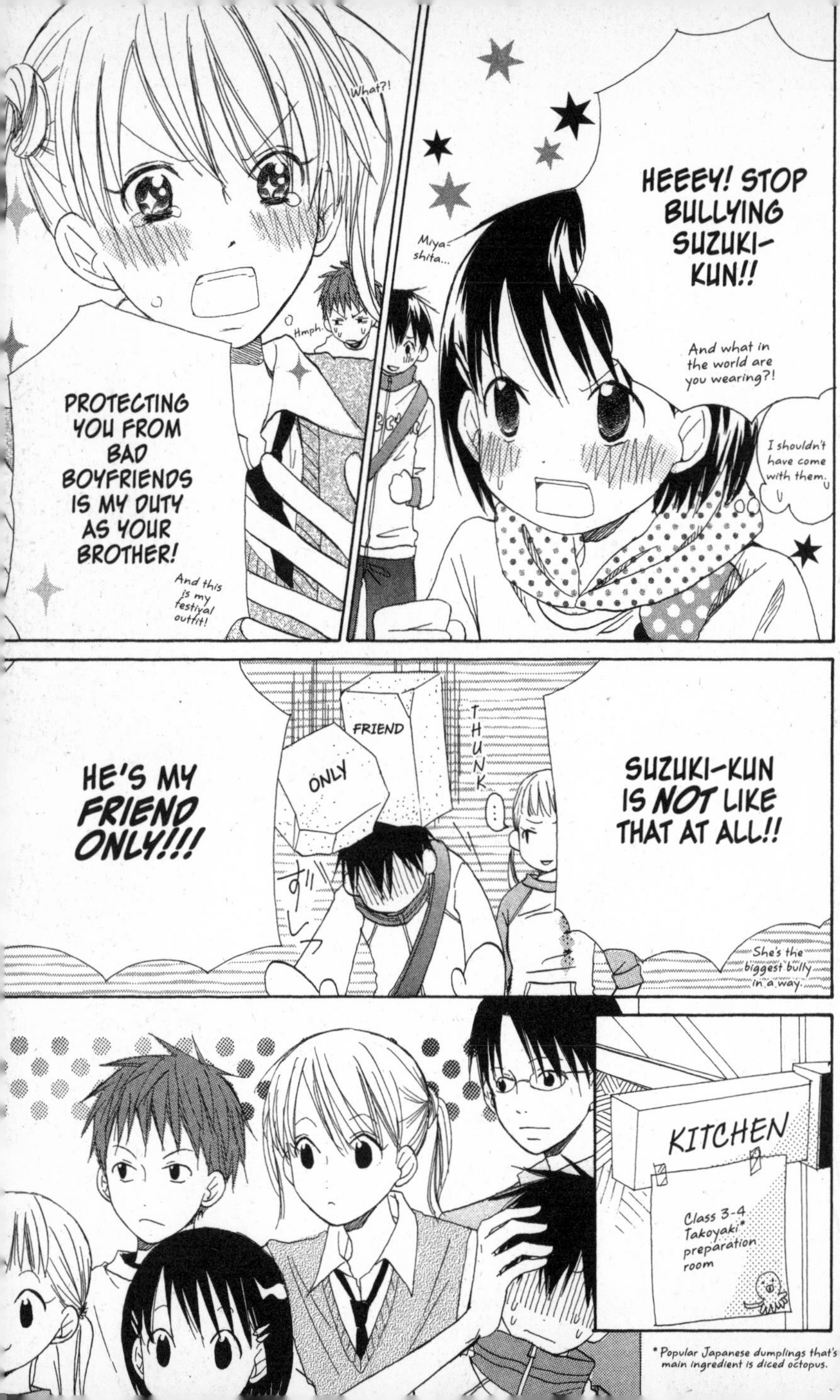
HEEEY! STOP BULLYING SUZUKI-KUN!!
Miya-shita...
And what in the world are you wearing?!
I shouldn't have come with them.
What?!
PROTECTING YOU FROM BAD BOYFRIENDS IS MY DUTY AS YOUR BROTHER!
And this is my festival outfit!
Hmph.
SUZUKI-KUN IS NOT LIKE THAT AT ALL!!
THUNK
...
FRIEND
ONLY
HE'S MY FRIEND ONLY!!!
She's the biggest bully in a way.
KITCHEN
Class 3-4 Takoyaki* preparation room

* Popular Japanese dumplings that's main ingredient is diced octopus.

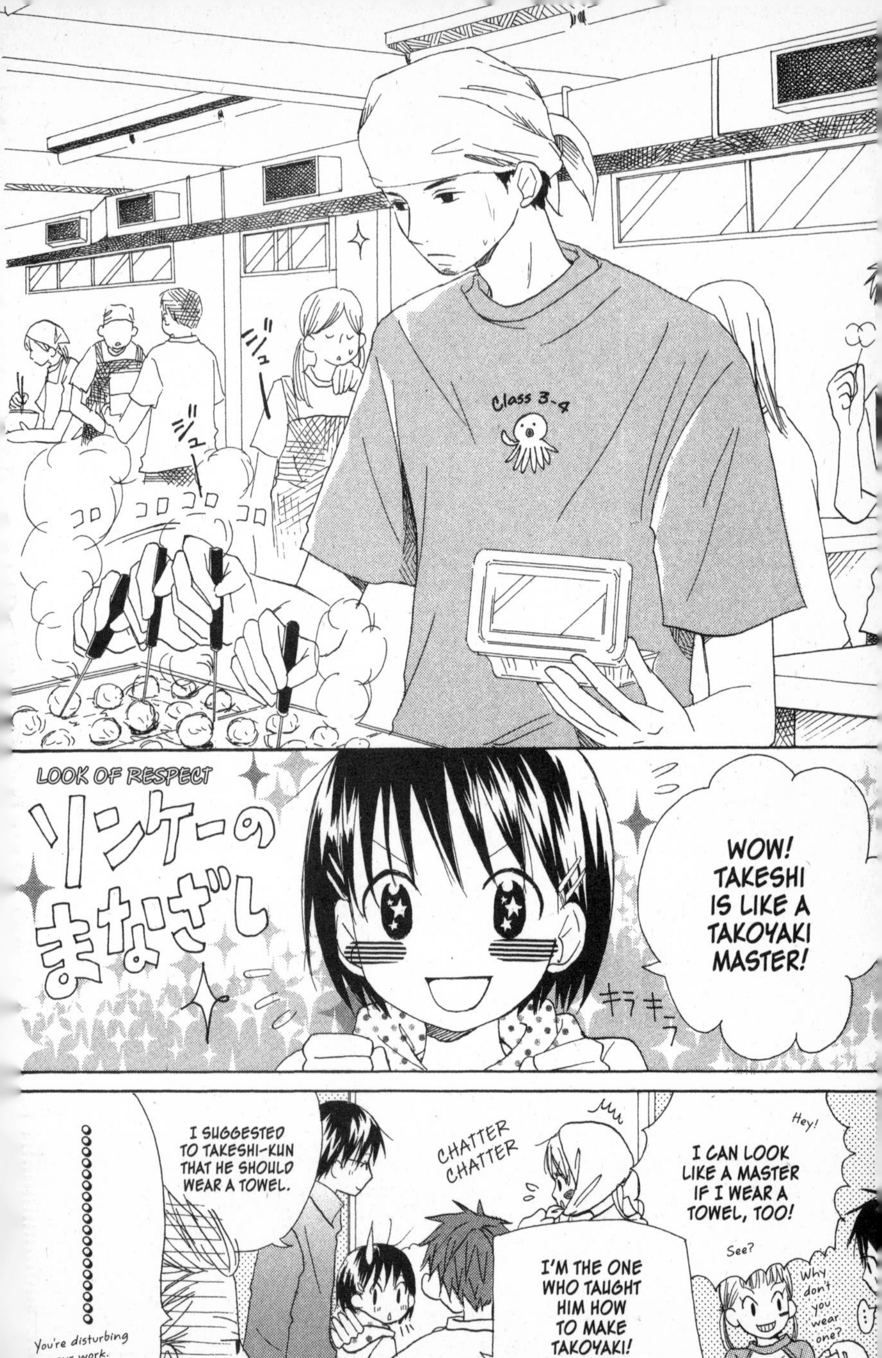
ジュー
ジュー
コロ コロ コロ コロ
Class 3-4
LOOK OF RESPECT
ソンケーのまなざし
WOW! TAKESHI IS LIKE A TAKOYAKI MASTER!
キラキラ
Hey!
I CAN LOOK LIKE A MASTER IF I WEAR A TOWEL, TOO!
See?
Why don't you wear one?
CHATTER CHATTER
I'M THE ONE WHO TAUGHT HIM HOW TO MAKE TAKOYAKI!
I SUGGESTED TO TAKESHI-KUN THAT HE SHOULD WEAR A TOWEL.
You're disturbing our work.

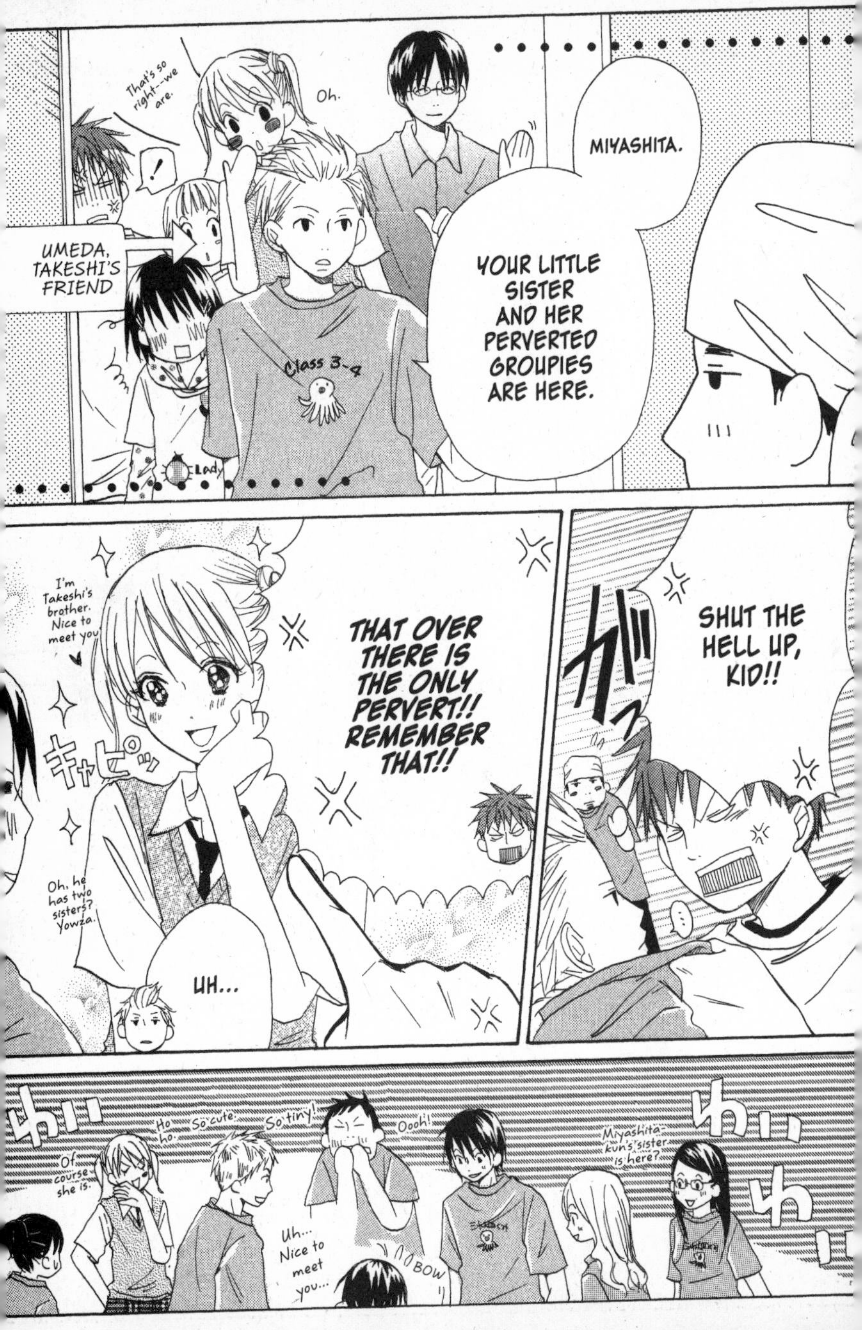
MIYASHITA.
YOUR LITTLE SISTER AND HER PERVERTED GROUPIES ARE HERE.
Oh.
That's so right--we are.
!
UMEDA, TAKESHI'S FRIEND
Class 3-4
Lady
SHUT THE HELL UP, KID!!
...
THAT OVER THERE IS THE ONLY PERVERT!! REMEMBER THAT!!
I'm Takeshi's brother. Nice to meet you
キャピッ
Oh, he has two sisters? Yowza.
UH...
Miyashita-kun's sister is here?
Oooh!
So tiny!
So cute.
Ho ho.
Of course she is.
Uh... Nice to meet you...
BOW

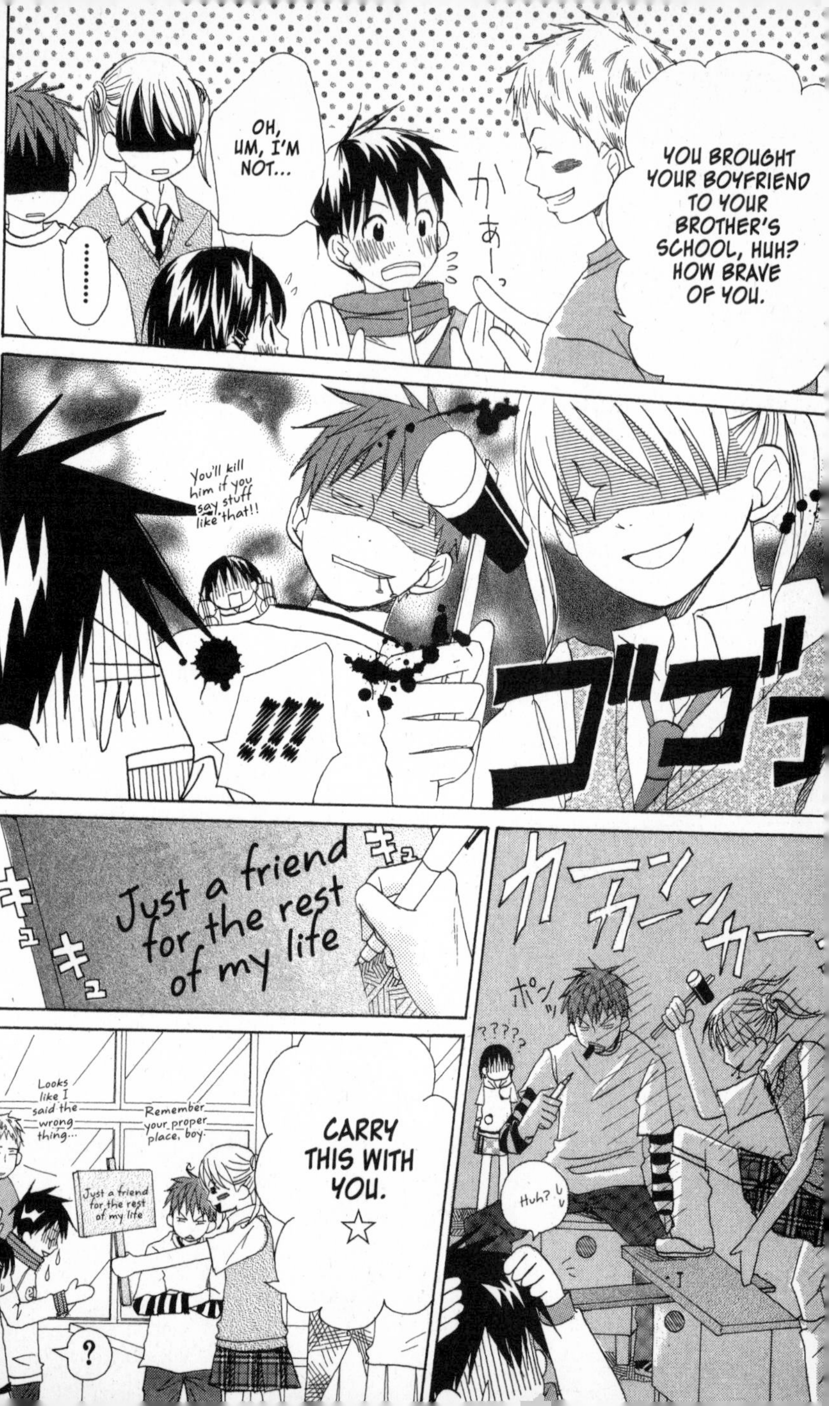

YOU BROUGHT YOUR BOYFRIEND TO YOUR BROTHER'S SCHOOL, HUH? HOW BRAVE OF YOU.
かあーっ
OH, UM, I'M NOT...
....
ゴゴゴ
You'll kill him if you say stuff like that!!
!!!
カーン
カーン
カー
ポンッ
????
Huh?
キュ
キュ
キュ
Just a friend for the rest of my life
CARRY THIS WITH YOU. ☆
Remember your proper place, boy.
Looks like I said the wrong thing...
Just a friend for the rest of my life
?

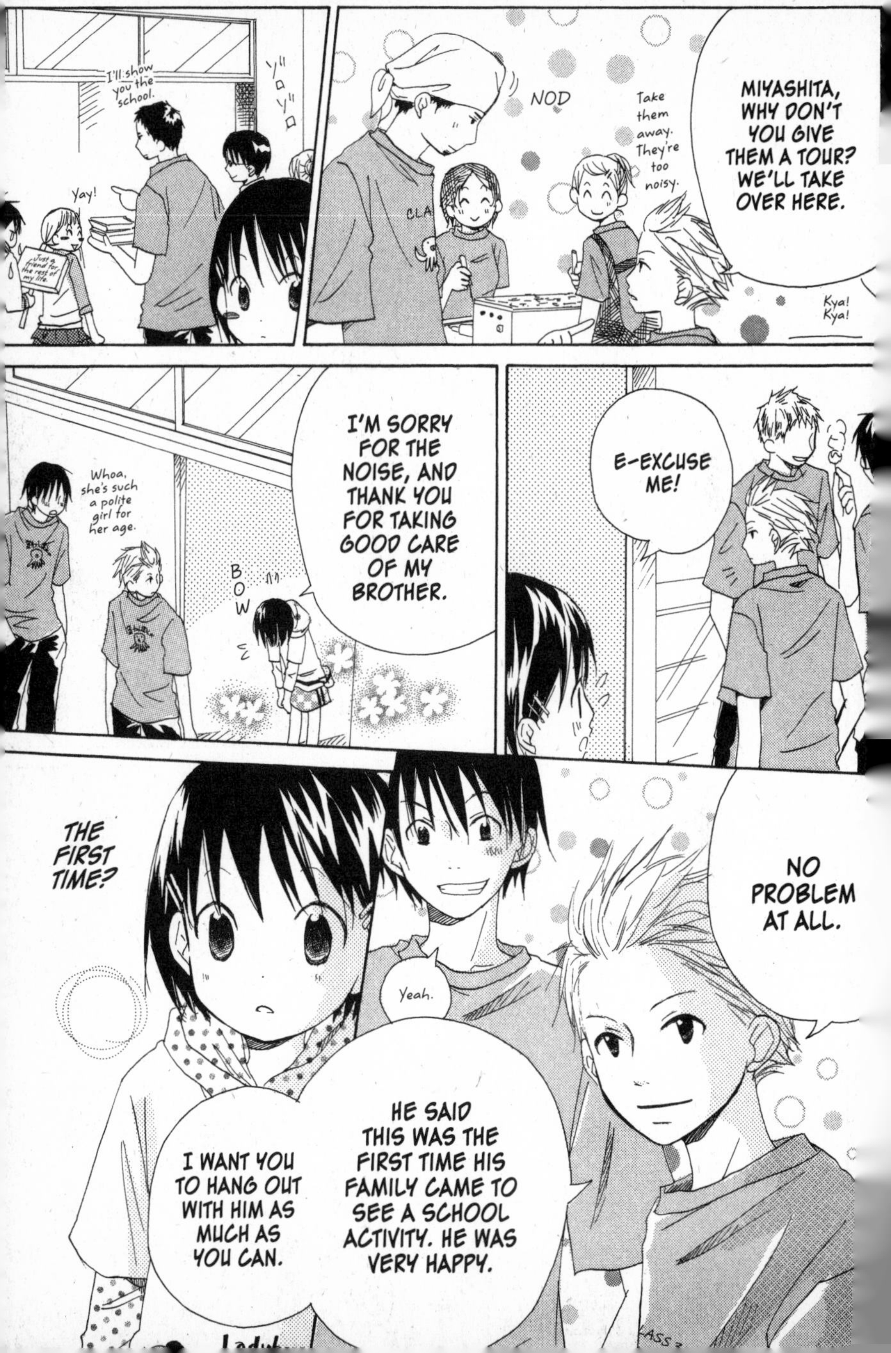
MIYASHITA, WHY DON'T YOU GIVE THEM A TOUR? WE'LL TAKE OVER HERE.
Kya! Kya!
Take them away. They're too noisy.
NOD
I'll show you the school.
ゾロゾロ
Yay!
Just a friend for the rest of my life.
E-EXCUSE ME!
I'M SORRY FOR THE NOISE, AND THANK YOU FOR TAKING GOOD CARE OF MY BROTHER.
BOW
Whoa, she's such a polite girl for her age.
NO PROBLEM AT ALL.
Yeah.
HE SAID THIS WAS THE FIRST TIME HIS FAMILY CAME TO SEE A SCHOOL ACTIVITY. HE WAS VERY HAPPY.
I WANT YOU TO HANG OUT WITH HIM AS MUCH AS YOU CAN.
THE FIRST TIME?

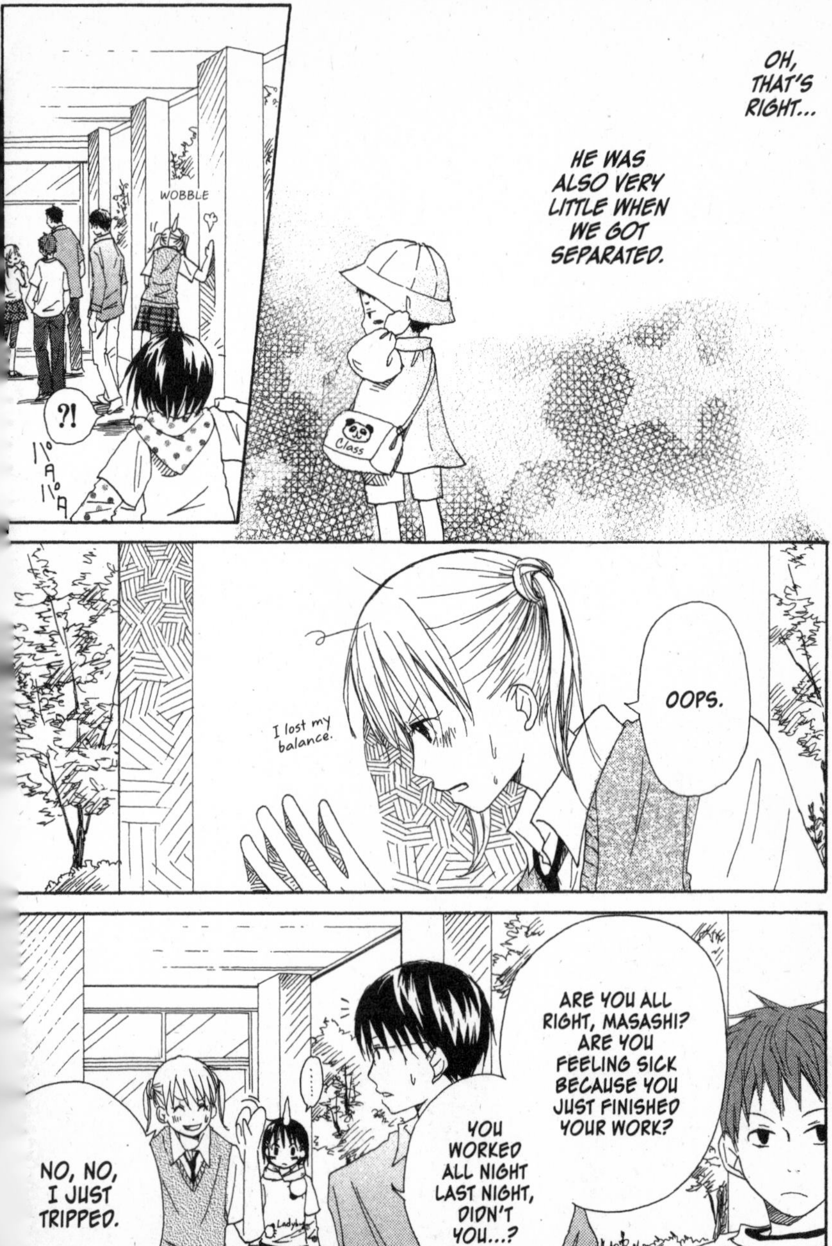
OH, THAT'S RIGHT...
HE WAS ALSO VERY LITTLE WHEN WE GOT SEPARATED.
WOBBLE
?!
パタパタ
OOPS.
I lost my balance.
ARE YOU ALL RIGHT, MASASHI? ARE YOU FEELING SICK BECAUSE YOU JUST FINISHED YOUR WORK?
YOU WORKED ALL NIGHT LAST NIGHT, DIDN'T YOU...?
......
NO, NO, I JUST TRIPPED.
Don't worry.

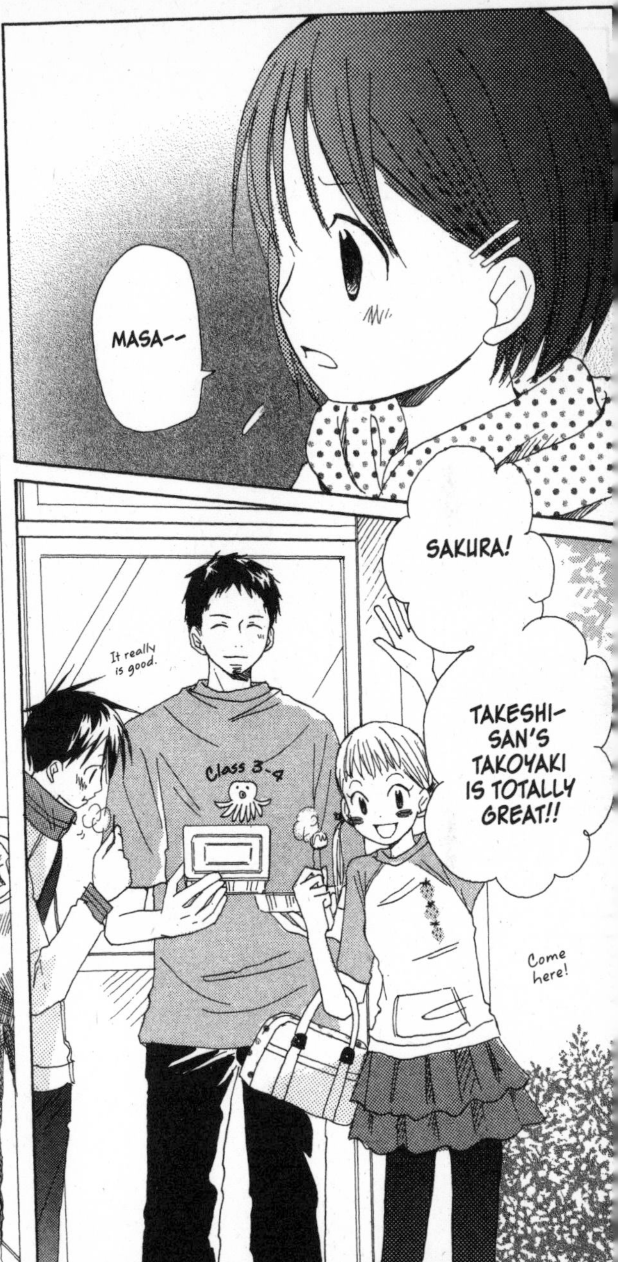
MASA--
SAKURA!
TAKESHI-SAN'S TAKOYAKI IS TOTALLY GREAT!!
Come here!
Class 3-4
It really is good.

☆ 3 ☆

I have two older sisters. I'd like to introduce the younger one to you.

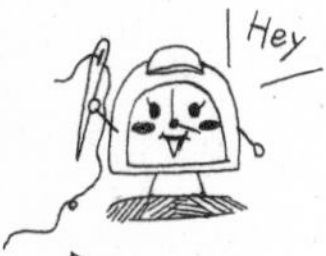
Hey

She has a needle because her job is to make clothes.

At first she hated my penname because she thought the look of the kanji for "Hari" was creepy. She didn't know it was hiragana.

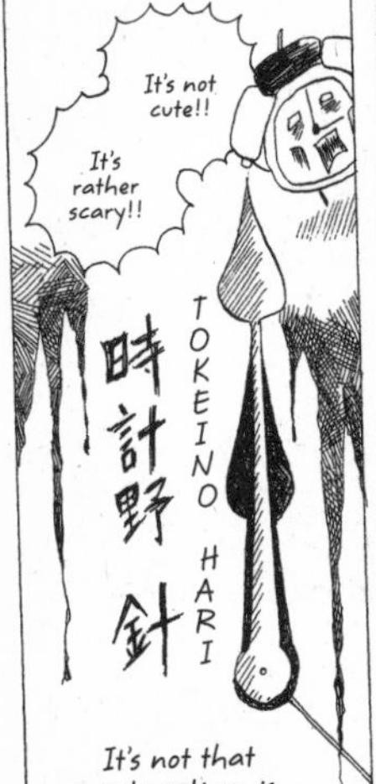
It's not cute!!
It's rather scary!!
時計野針
TOKEINO HARI

It's not that interesting, is it? Sorry.

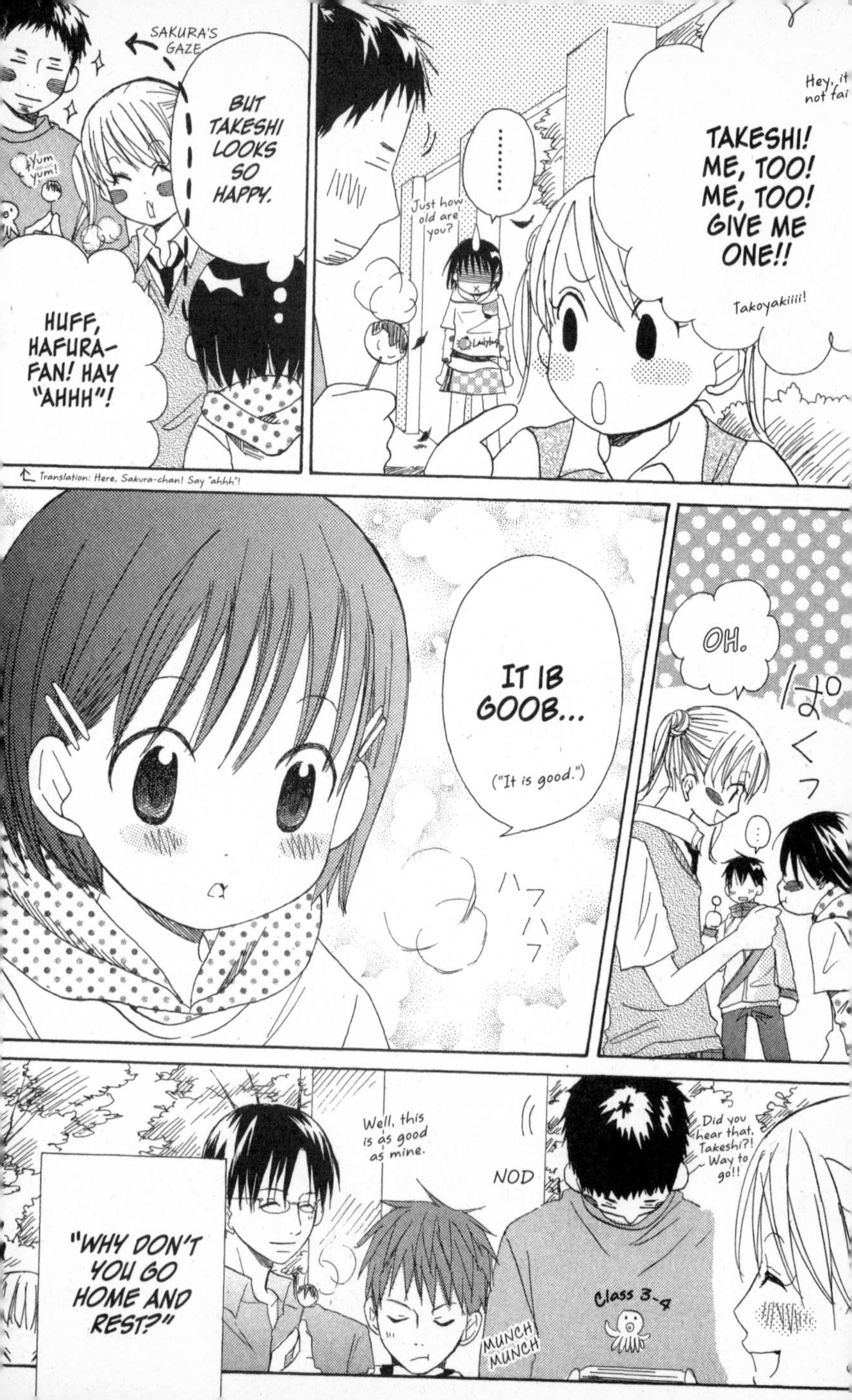
Hey, it not fai
TAKESHI! ME, TOO! ME, TOO! GIVE ME ONE!!
Takoyakiiii!
......
Just how old are you?
SAKURA'S GAZE
BUT TAKESHI LOOKS SO HAPPY.
Yum yum!
HUFF, HAFURA-FAN! HAY "AHHH"!
Translation: Here, Sakura-chan! Say "ahhh"!
OH.
ぱくっ
...
IT IB GOOB...
("It is good.")
ハフハフ
Did you hear that, Takeshi?! Way to go!!
NOD
Class 3-4
MUNCH MUNCH
Well, this is as good as mine.
"WHY DON'T YOU GO HOME AND REST?"

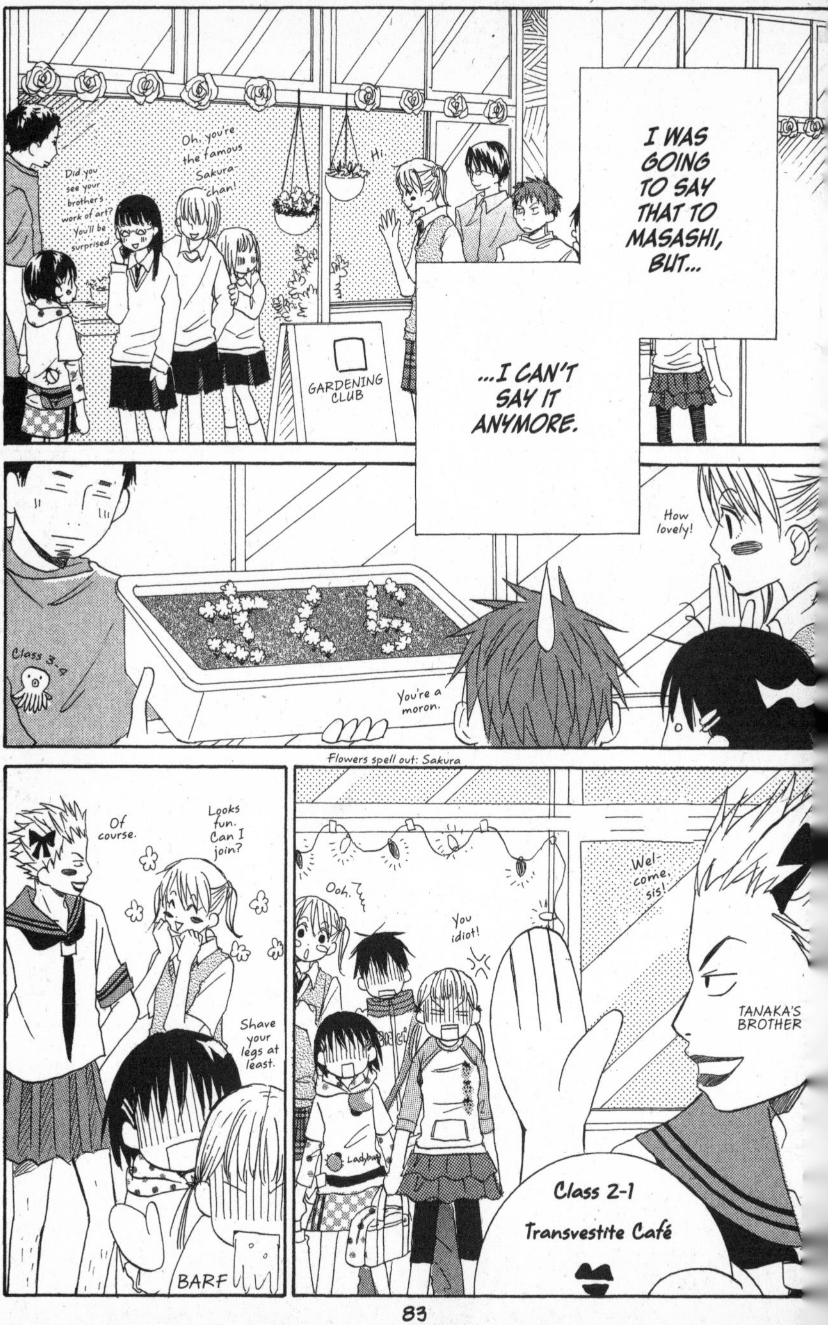
I WAS GOING TO SAY THAT TO MASASHI, BUT...
...I CAN'T SAY IT ANYMORE.
Hi
Oh, you're the famous Sakura-chan!
Did you see your brother's work of art? You'll be surprised.
GARDENING CLUB
How lovely!
You're a moron.
Class 3-4
Flowers spell out: Sakura
Wel-come, sis!
TANAKA'S BROTHER
You idiot!
Ooh.
Ladybug
Class 2-1
Transvestite Café
Looks fun. Can I join?
Of course.
Shave your legs at least.
BARF

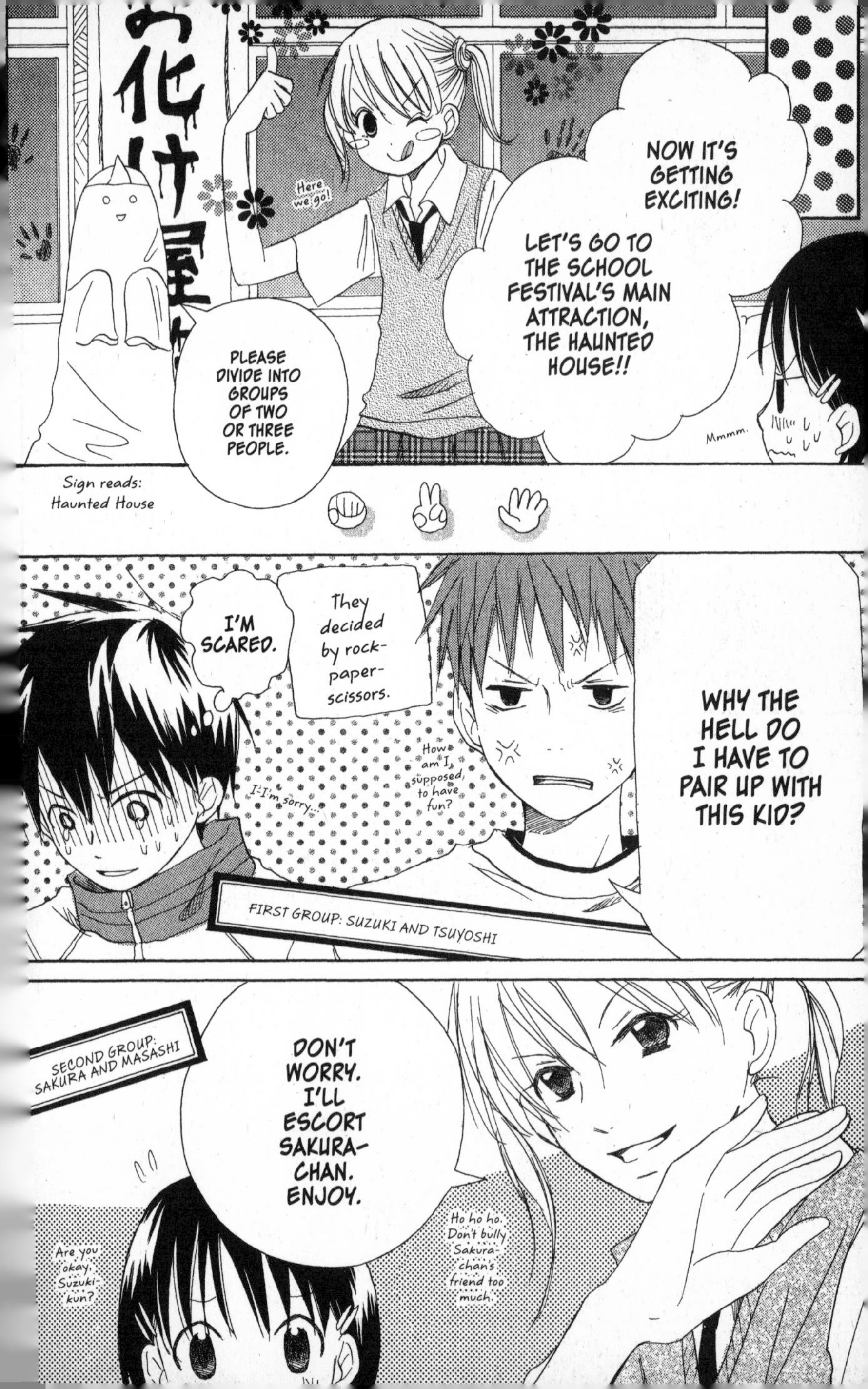
NOW IT'S GETTING EXCITING!
LET'S GO TO THE SCHOOL FESTIVAL'S MAIN ATTRACTION, THE HAUNTED HOUSE!!
Mmmm.
Here we go!
PLEASE DIVIDE INTO GROUPS OF TWO OR THREE PEOPLE.
Sign reads: Haunted House
WHY THE HELL DO I HAVE TO PAIR UP WITH THIS KID?
How am I supposed to have fun?
They decided by rock-paper-scissors.
I'M SCARED.
I-I'm sorry...
FIRST GROUP: SUZUKI AND TSUYOSHI
Ho ho ho. Don't bully Sakura-chan's friend too much.
DON'T WORRY. I'LL ESCORT SAKURA-CHAN. ENJOY.
SECOND GROUP: SAKURA AND MASASHI
Are you okay, Suzuki-kun?

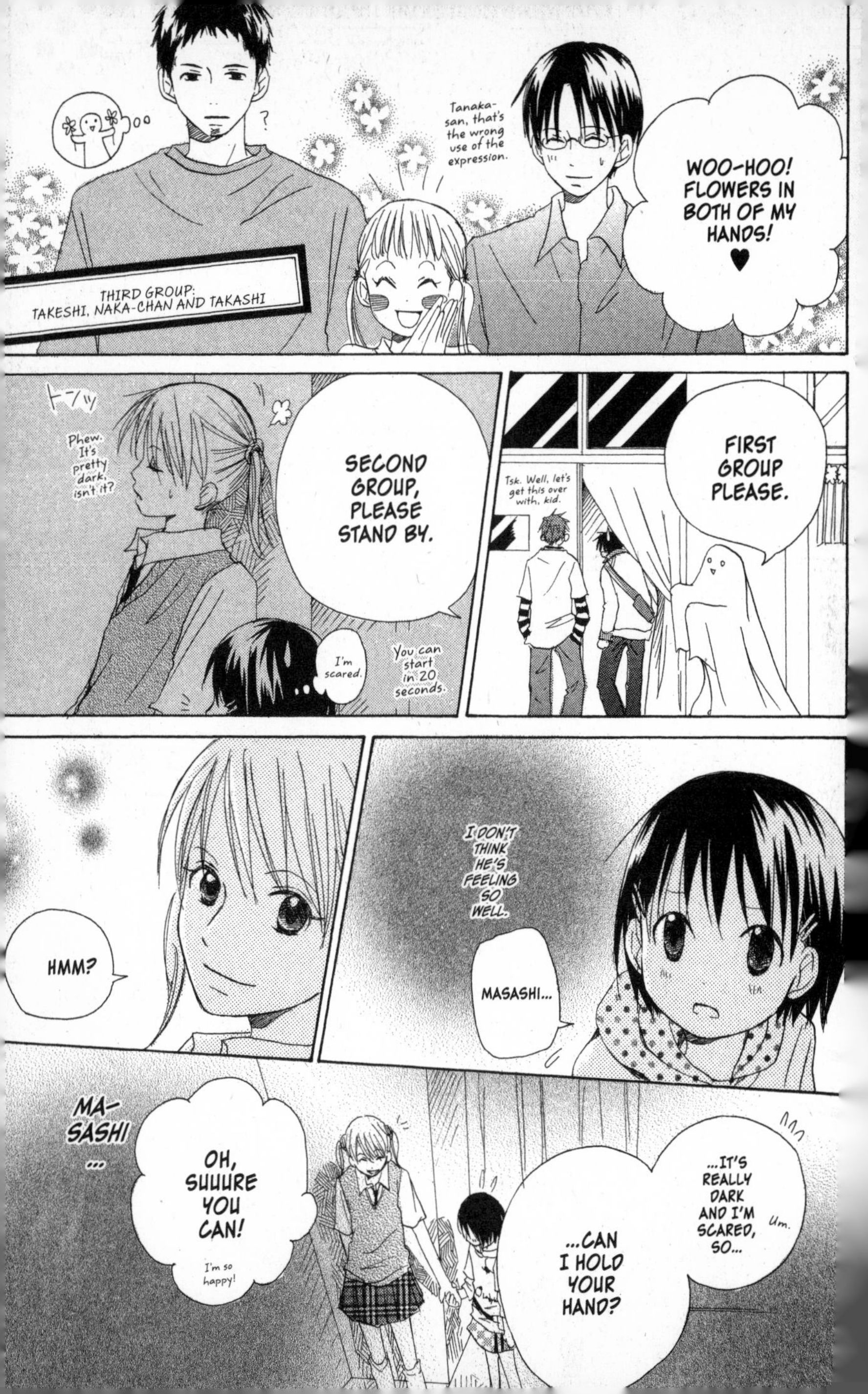
WOO-HOO! FLOWERS IN BOTH OF MY HANDS! ♥
Tanaka-san, that's the wrong use of the expression.
?
THIRD GROUP: TAKESHI, NAKA-CHAN AND TAKASHI
FIRST GROUP PLEASE.
Tsk. Well, let's get this over with, kid.
SECOND GROUP, PLEASE STAND BY.
You can start in 20 seconds.
I'm scared.
Phew. It's pretty dark, isn't it?
I DON'T THINK HE'S FEELING SO WELL.
MASASHI...
HMM?
...IT'S REALLY DARK AND I'M SCARED, SO...
Um.
...CAN I HOLD YOUR HAND?
OH, SUUURE YOU CAN!
I'm so happy!
MA-SASHI...

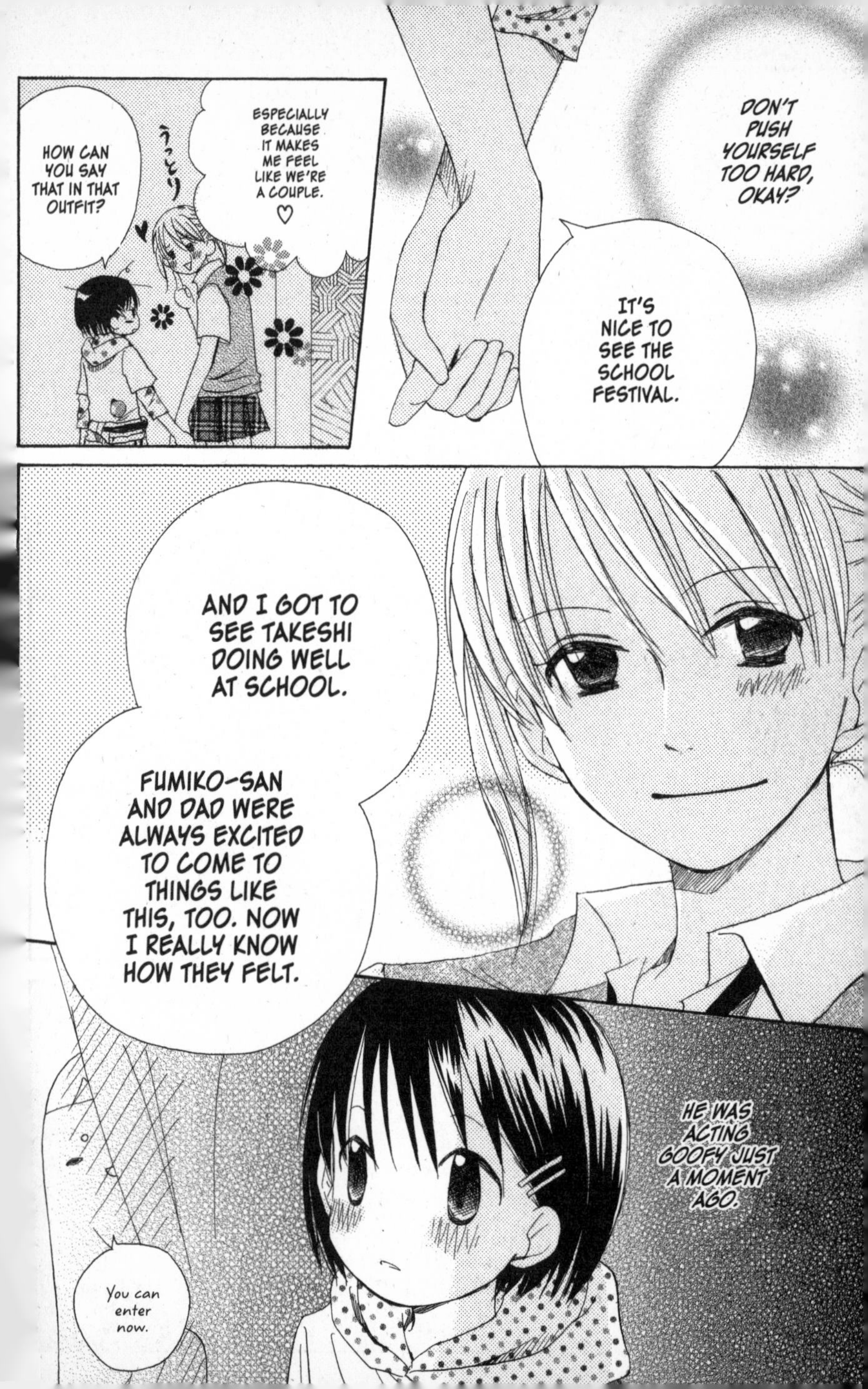

DON'T PUSH YOURSELF TOO HARD, OKAY?
IT'S NICE TO SEE THE SCHOOL FESTIVAL.
ESPECIALLY BECAUSE IT MAKES ME FEEL LIKE WE'RE A COUPLE. ♡
うっとり
HOW CAN YOU SAY THAT IN THAT OUTFIT?
AND I GOT TO SEE TAKESHI DOING WELL AT SCHOOL.
FUMIKO-SAN AND DAD WERE ALWAYS EXCITED TO COME TO THINGS LIKE THIS, TOO. NOW I REALLY KNOW HOW THEY FELT.
HE WAS ACTING GOOFY JUST A MOMENT AGO.
You can enter now.

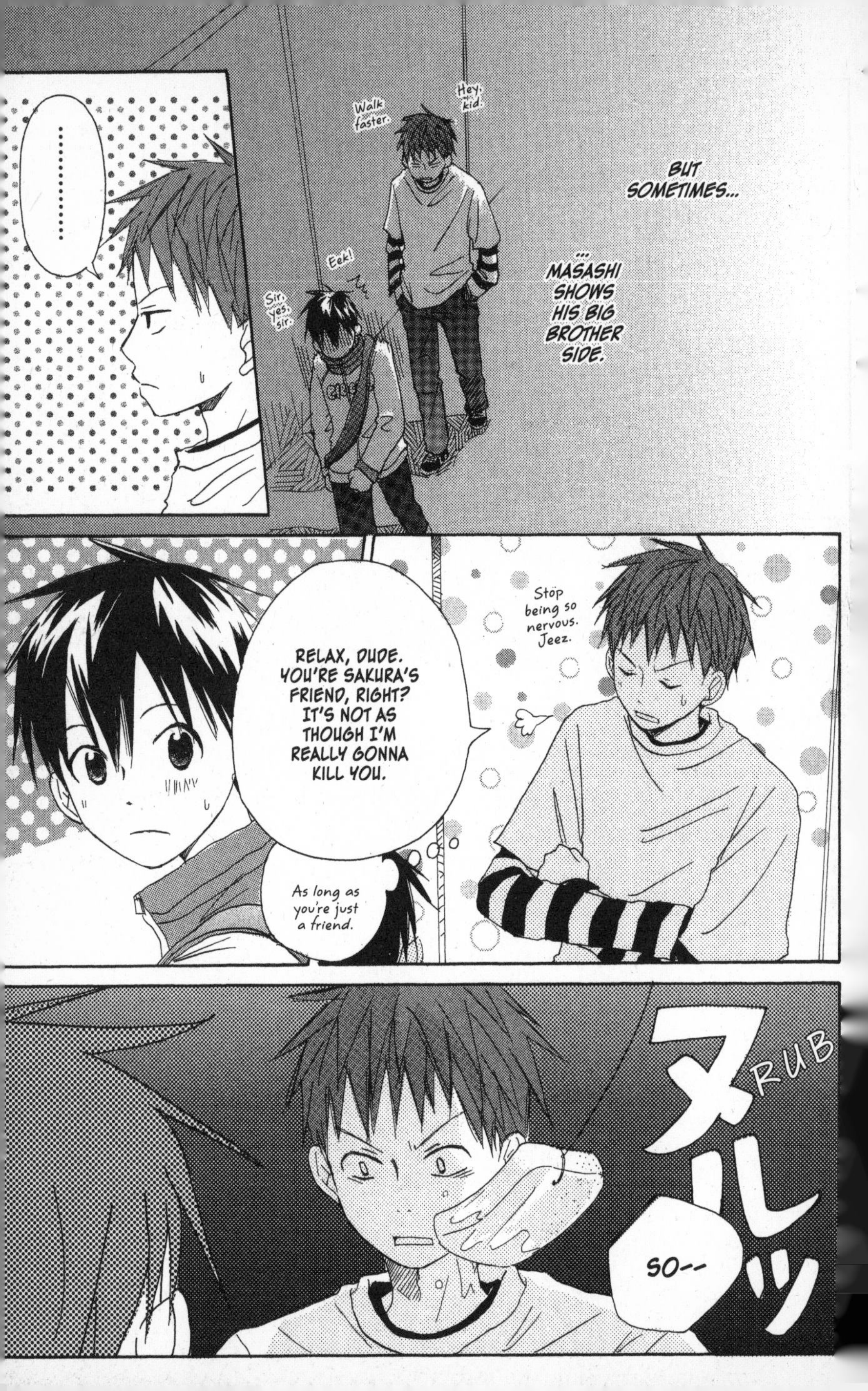
BUT SOMETIMES...
Hey, kid.
Walk faster.
Eek!
Sir. Yes, sir.
...MASASHI SHOWS HIS BIG BROTHER SIDE.
......
Stop being so nervous. Jeez.
RELAX, DUDE. YOU'RE SAKURA'S FRIEND, RIGHT? IT'S NOT AS THOUGH I'M REALLY GONNA KILL YOU.
As long as you're just a friend.
RUB
SO--

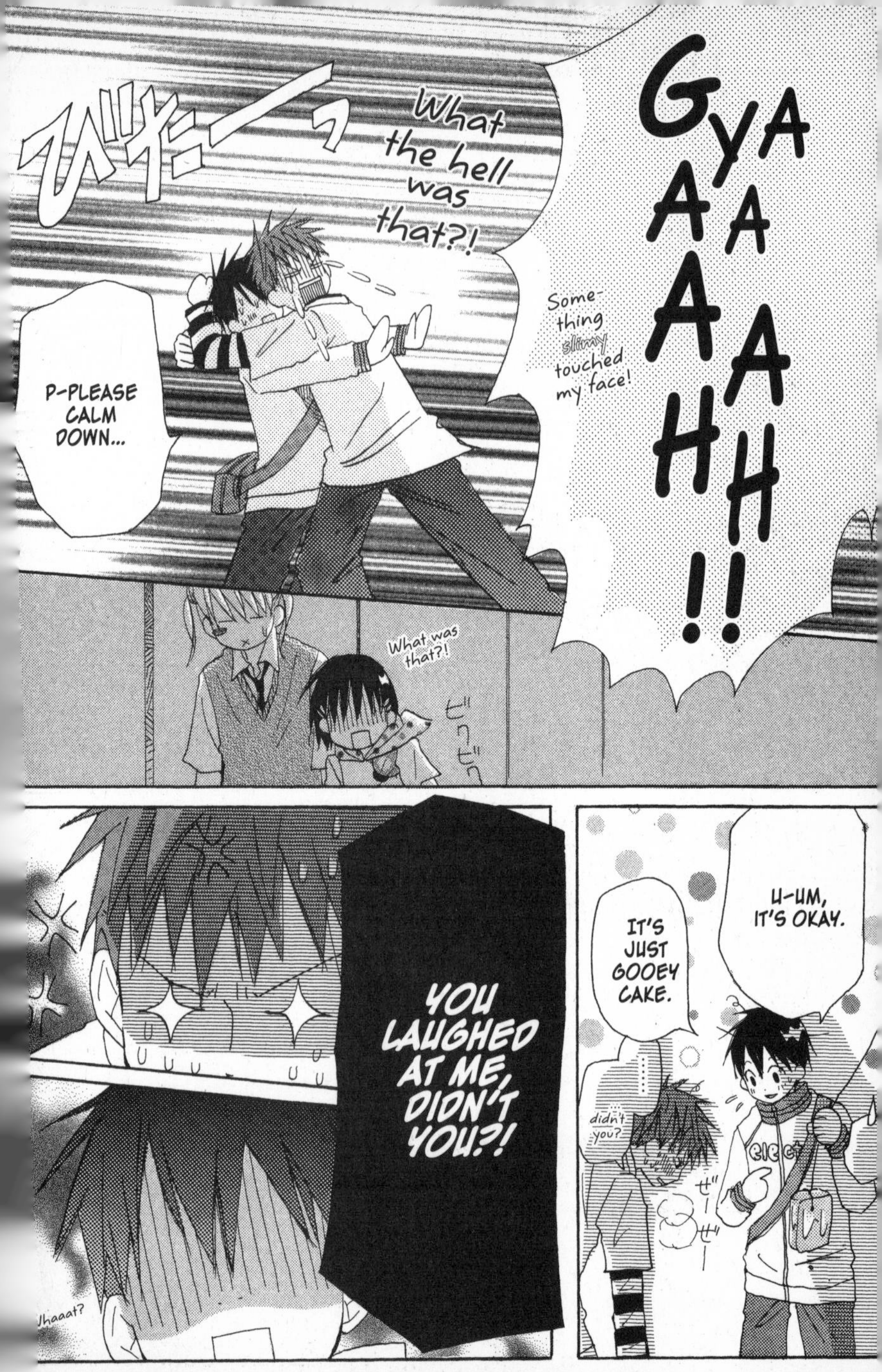
GYAAAAAHH!!
Something slimy touched my face!
What the hell was that?!
P-PLEASE CALM DOWN...
What was that?!
U-UM, IT'S OKAY.
IT'S JUST GOOEY CAKE.
......
didn't you?
YOU LAUGHED AT ME, DIDN'T YOU?!
Whaaat?

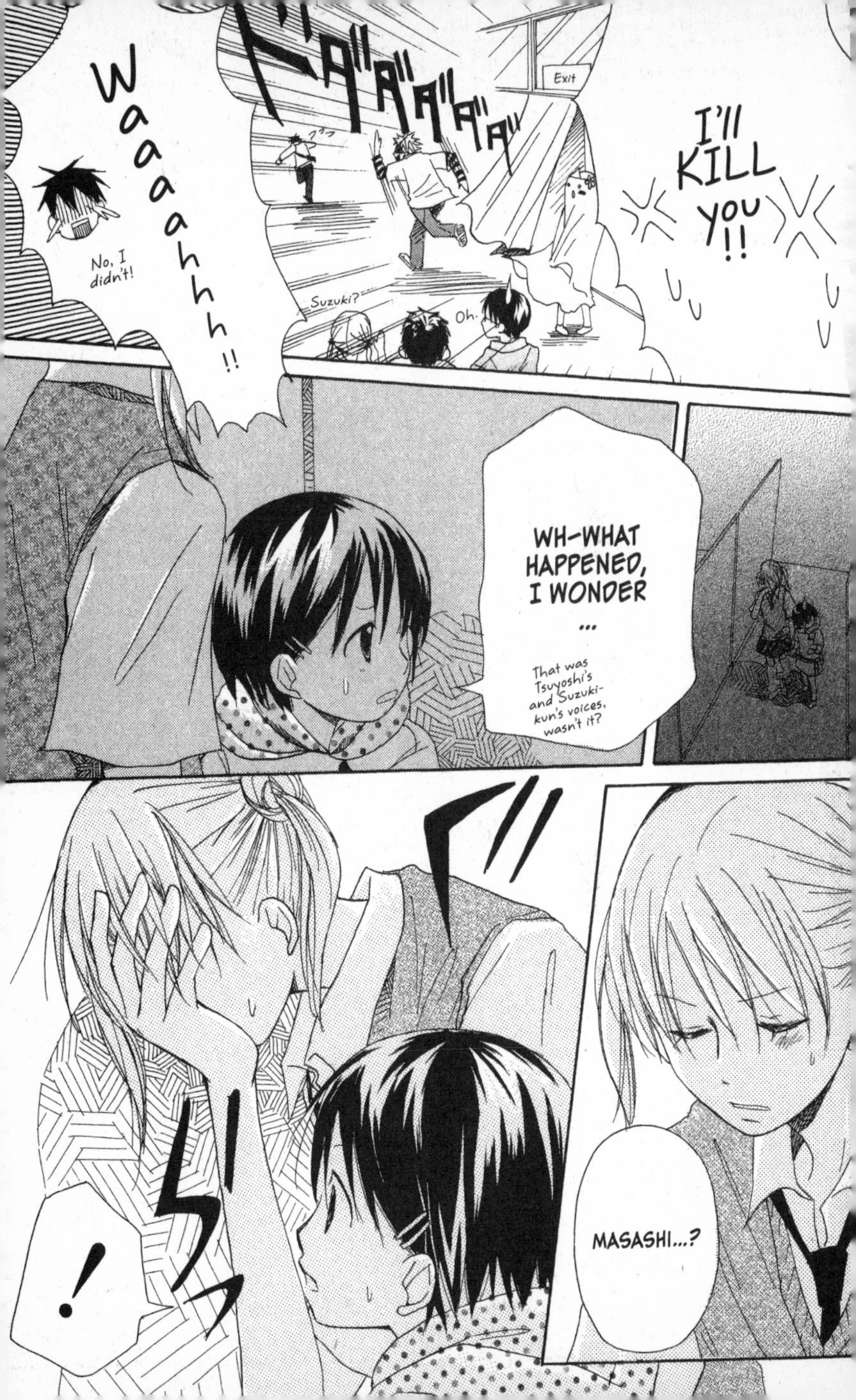

Exit
I'll KILL you!!
Oh.
Suzuki?
Waaaaahhhh!!
No, I didn't!
WH-WHAT HAPPENED, I WONDER ...
That was Tsuyoshi's and Suzuki-kun's voices, wasn't it?
MASASHI...?
!

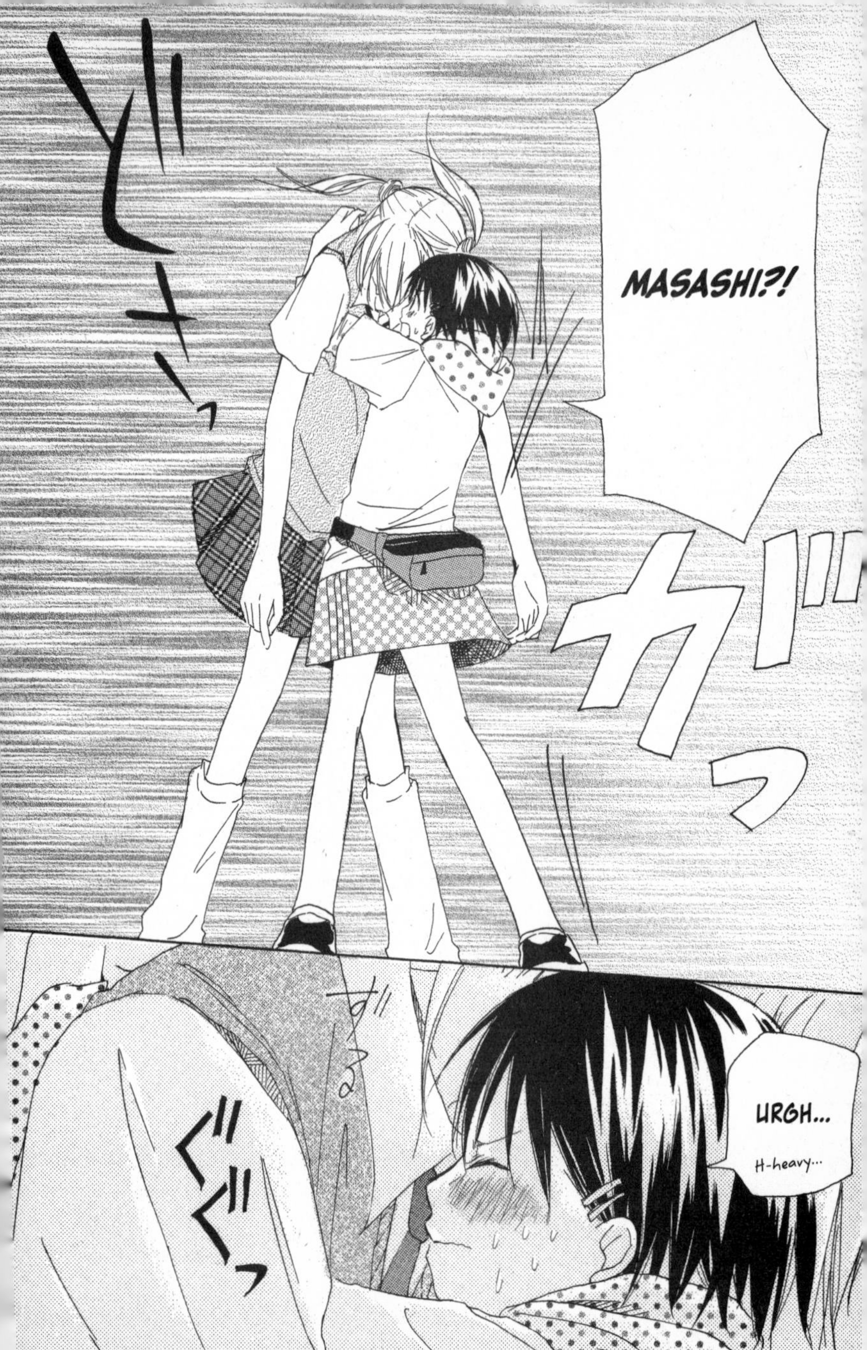
MASASHI?!
URGH...
H-heavy...

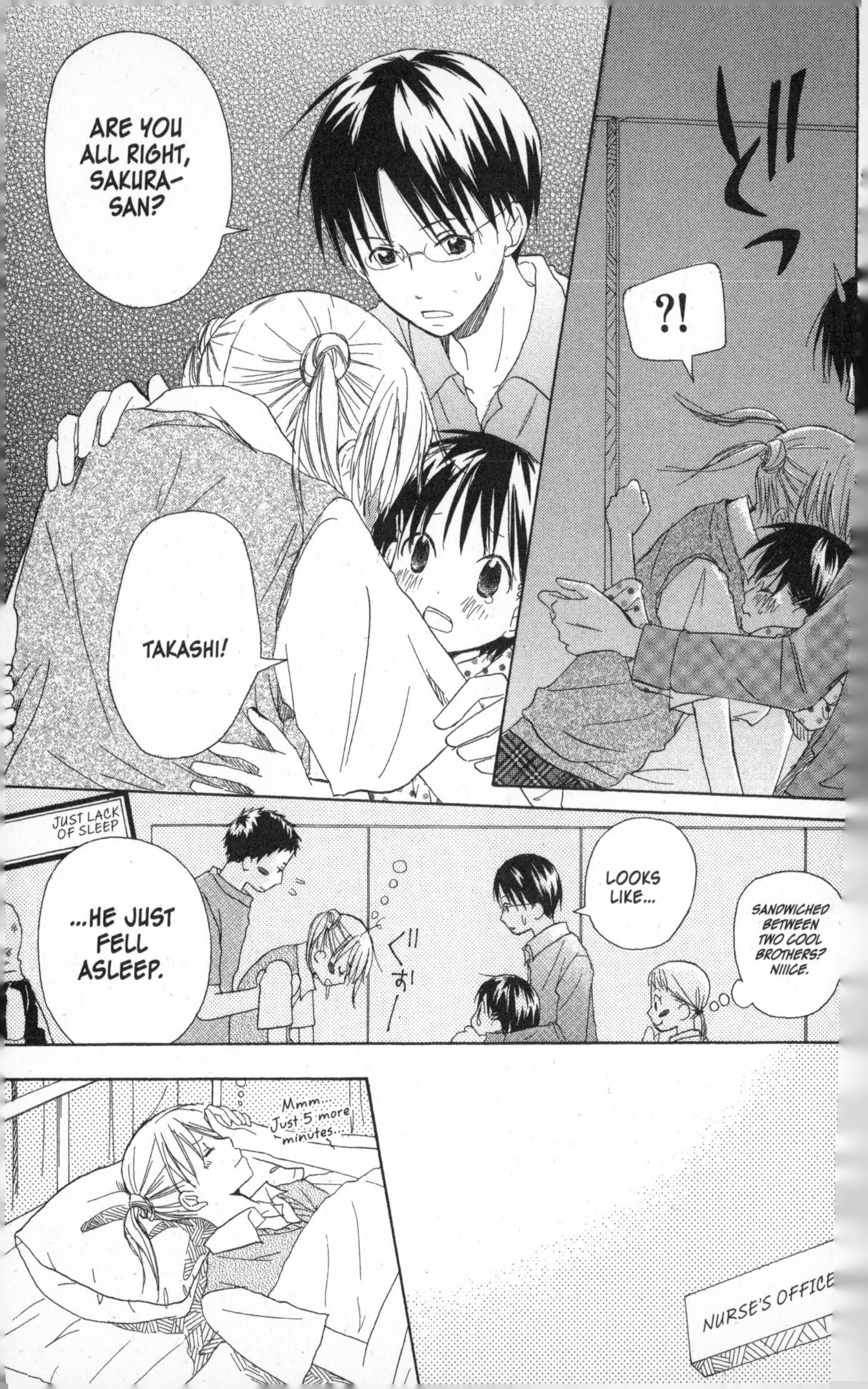
どっ
?!
ARE YOU ALL RIGHT, SAKURA-SAN?
TAKASHI!
SANDWICHED BETWEEN TWO COOL BROTHERS? NIIICE.
LOOKS LIKE...
...HE JUST FELL ASLEEP.
JUST LACK OF SLEEP
Mmm... Just 5 more minutes...
NURSE'S OFFICE

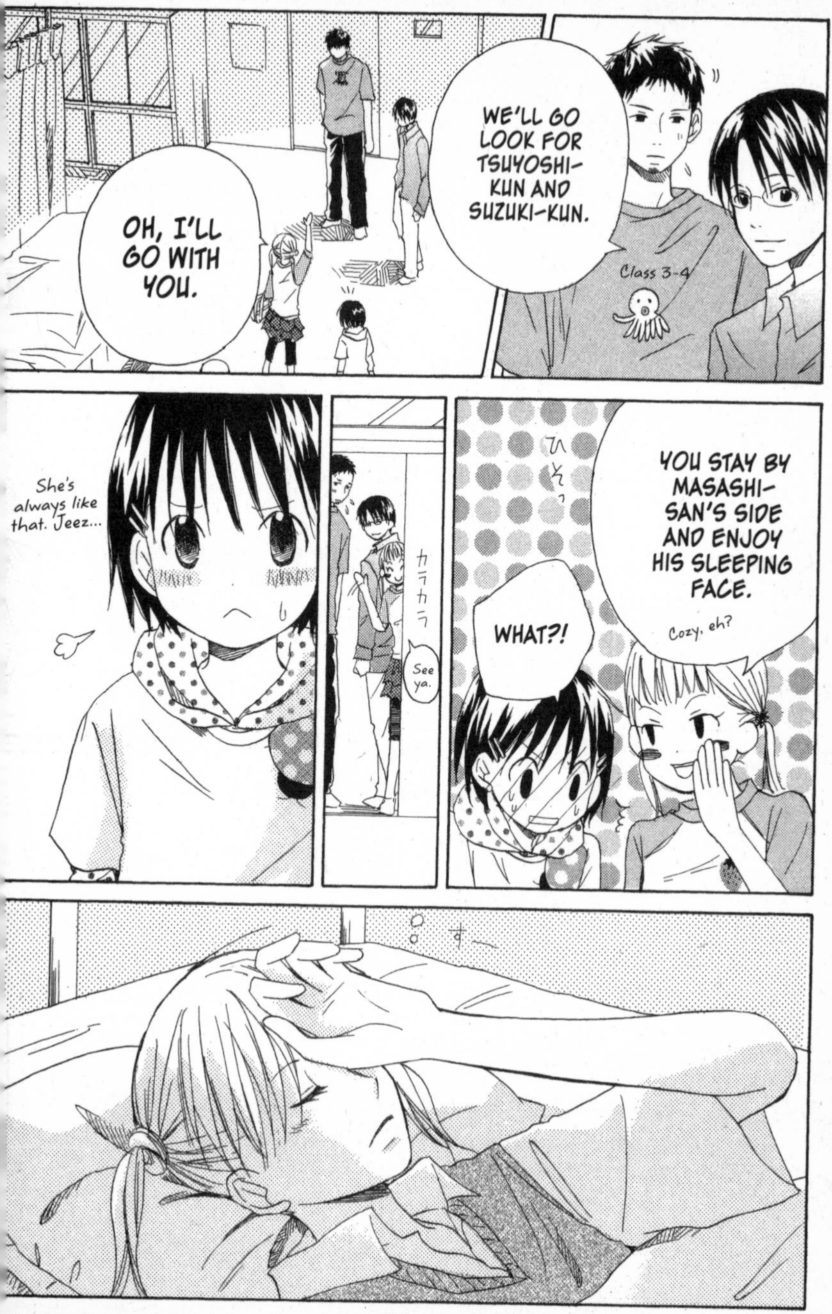
WE'LL GO LOOK FOR TSUYOSHI-KUN AND SUZUKI-KUN.
Class 3-4
OH, I'LL GO WITH YOU.
ひそっ
YOU STAY BY MASASHI-SAN'S SIDE AND ENJOY HIS SLEEPING FACE.
Cozy, eh?
WHAT?!
カラカラ
See ya.
She's always like that. Jeez...
すー

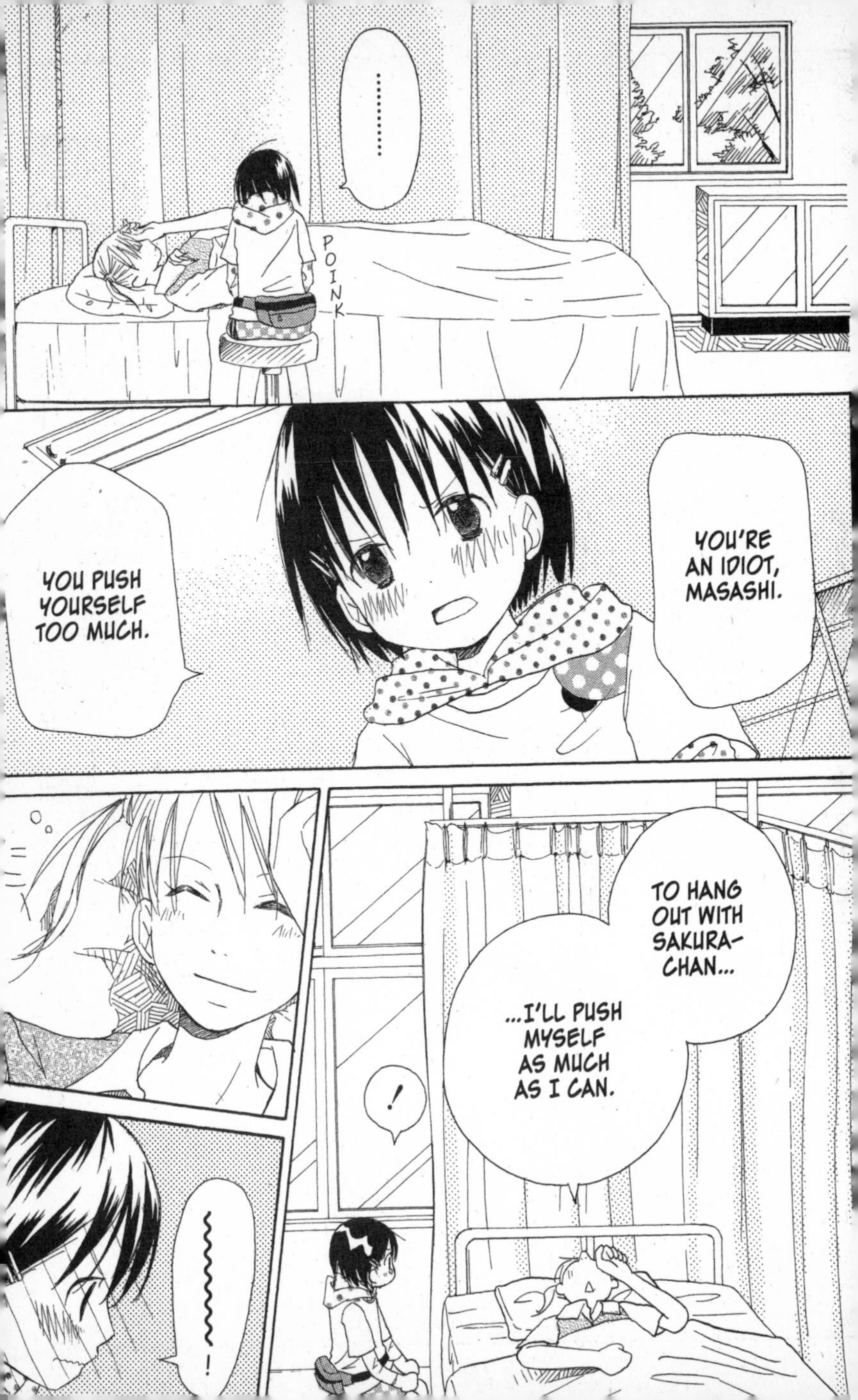
......
POINK
YOU'RE AN IDIOT, MASASHI.
YOU PUSH YOURSELF TOO MUCH.
TO HANG OUT WITH SAKURA-CHAN...
...I'LL PUSH MYSELF AS MUCH AS I CAN.
!
~~~~~~!
~~~~~~

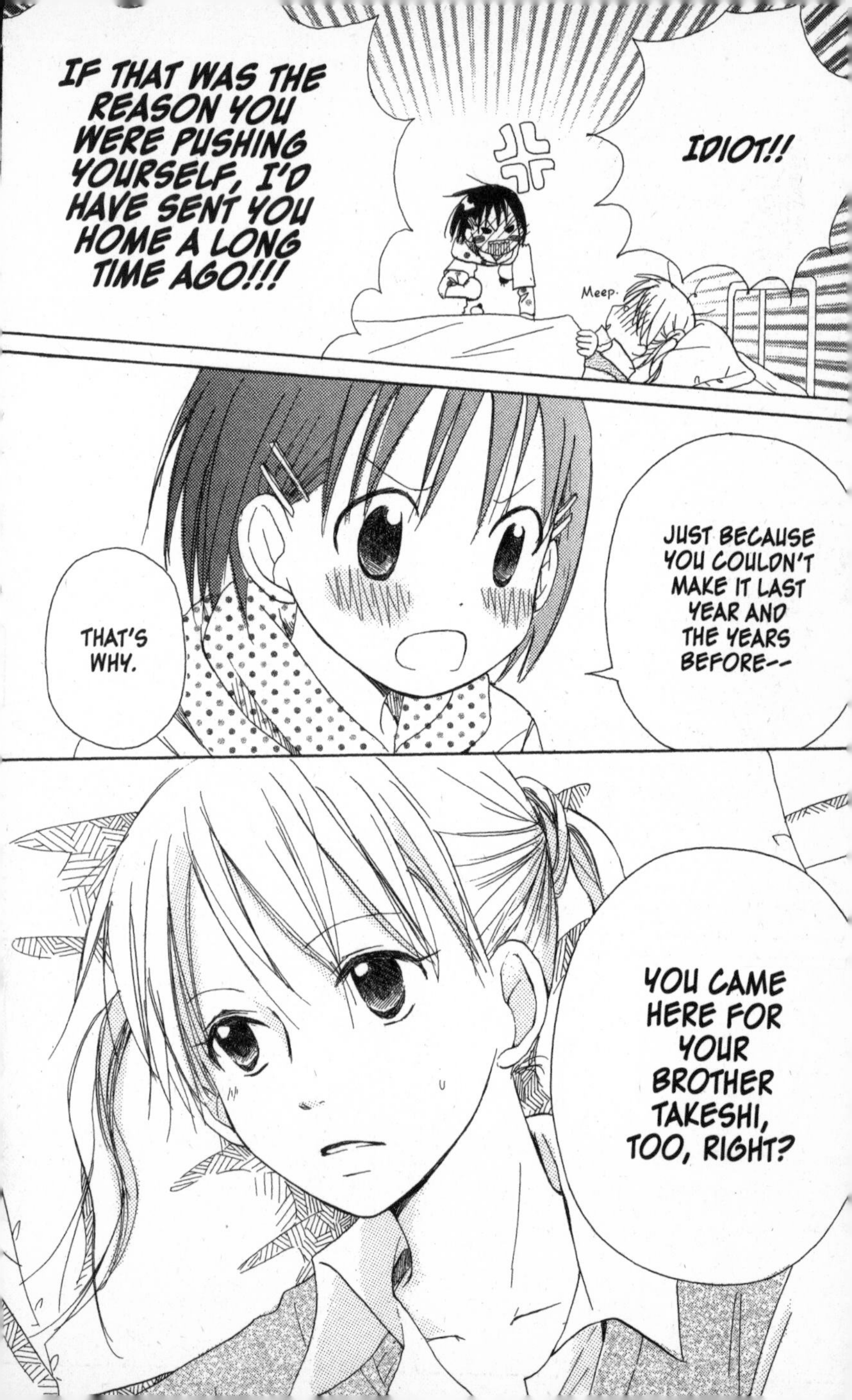
IDIOT!!
IF THAT WAS THE REASON YOU WERE PUSHING YOURSELF, I'D HAVE SENT YOU HOME A LONG TIME AGO!!!
Meep.
JUST BECAUSE YOU COULDN'T MAKE IT LAST YEAR AND THE YEARS BEFORE--
THAT'S WHY.
YOU CAME HERE FOR YOUR BROTHER TAKESHI, TOO, RIGHT?

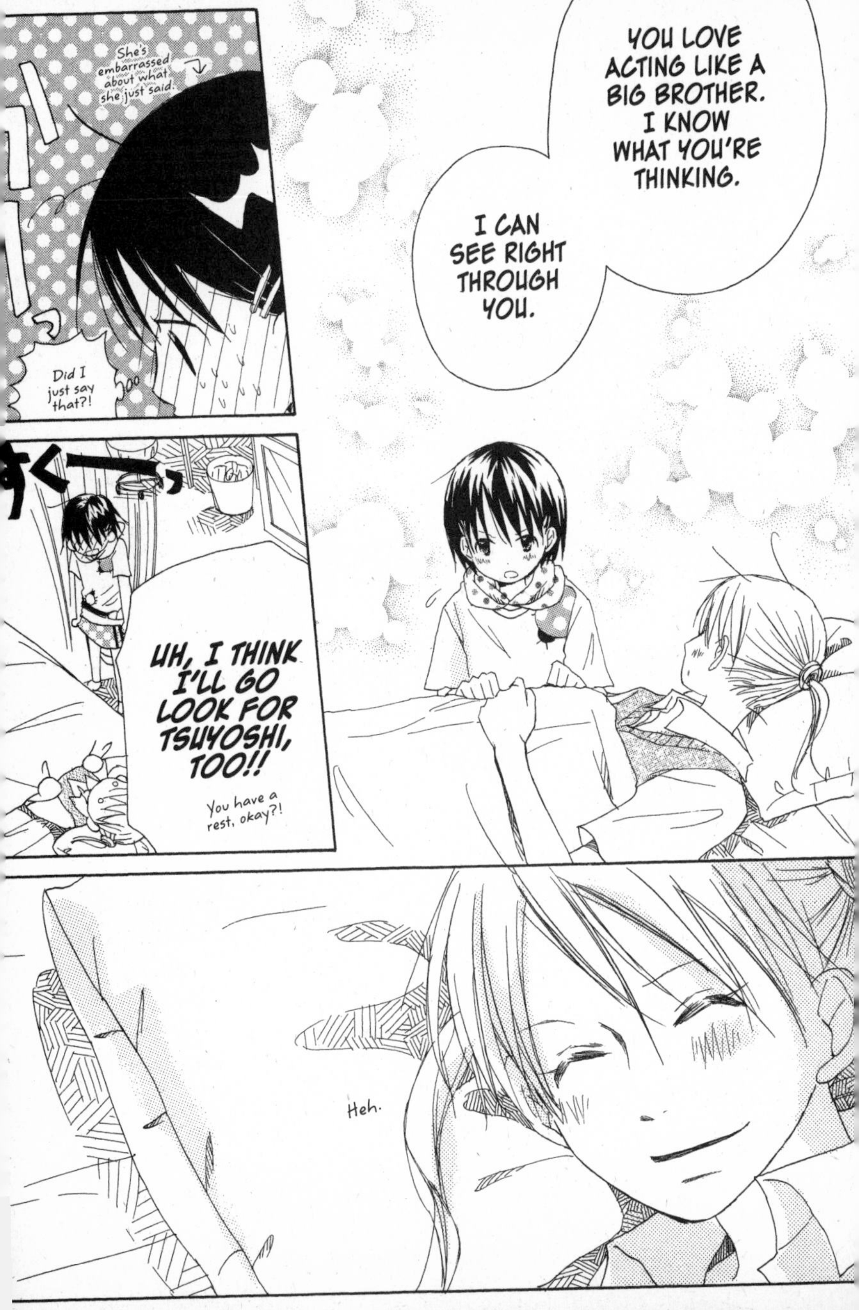
YOU LOVE ACTING LIKE A BIG BROTHER. I KNOW WHAT YOU'RE THINKING.
I CAN SEE RIGHT THROUGH YOU.
She's embarrassed about what she just said.
Did I just say that?!
すくーっ
UH, I THINK I'LL GO LOOK FOR TSUYOSHI, TOO!!
You have a rest, okay?!
Heh.

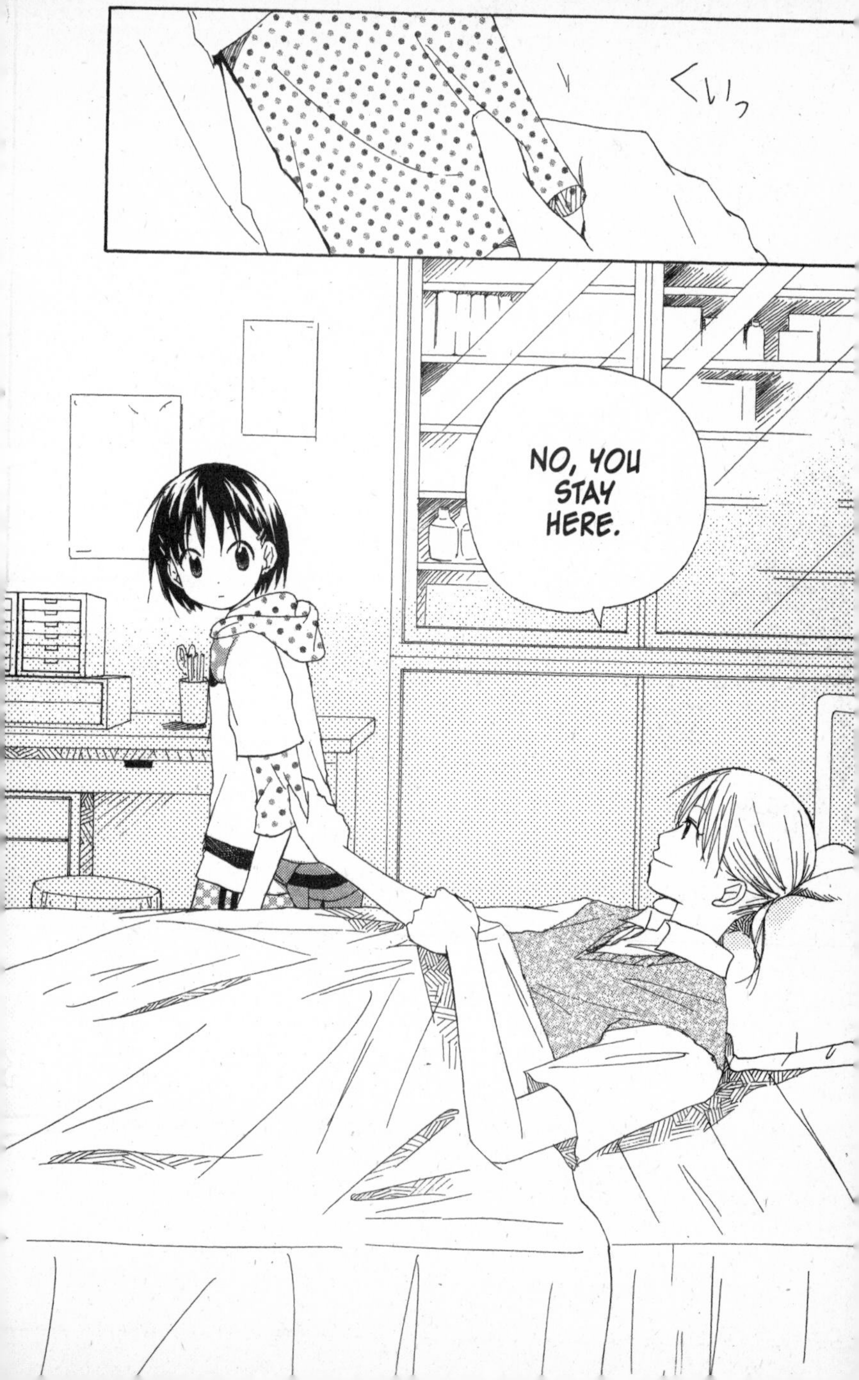
くいっ
NO, YOU STAY HERE.

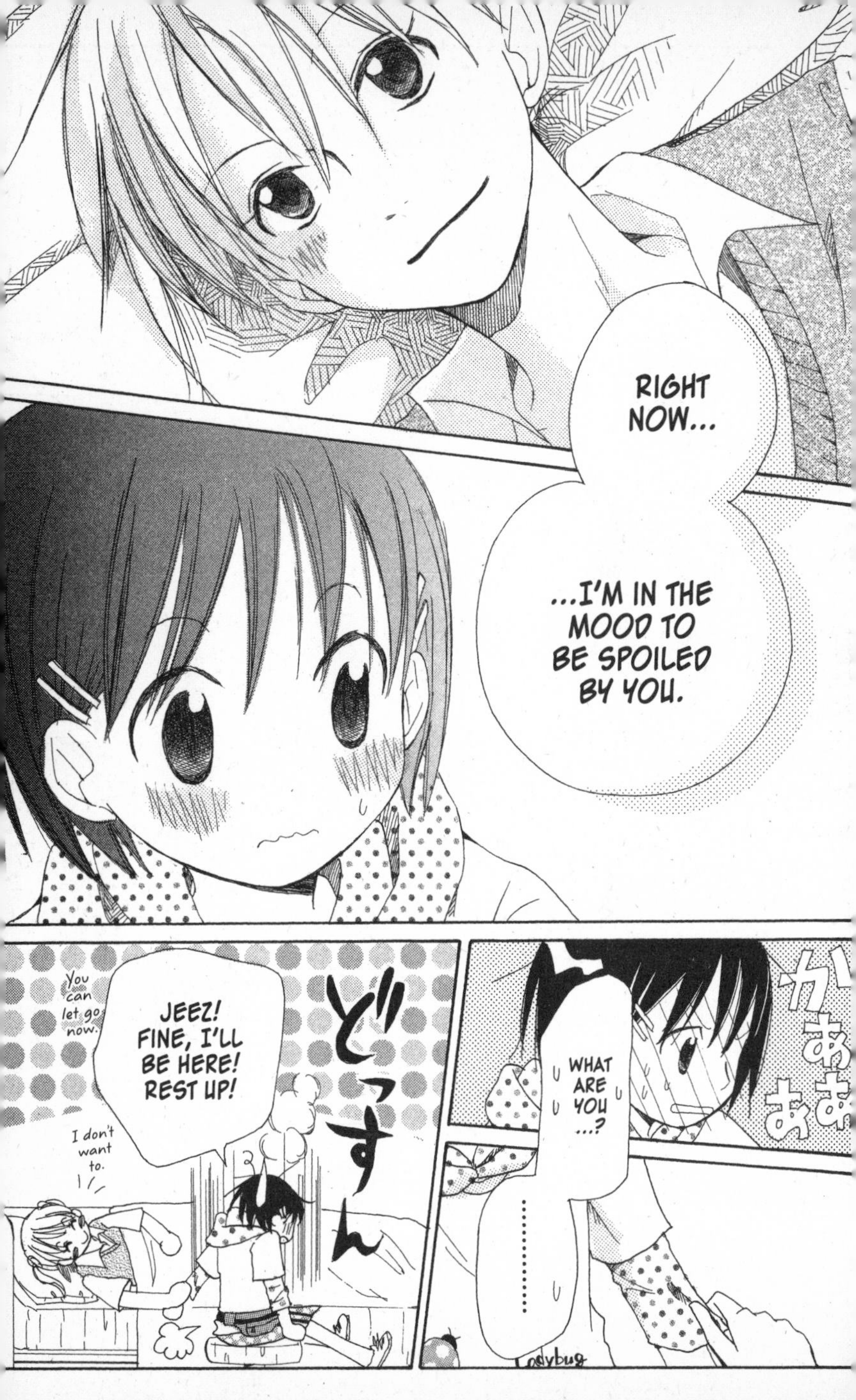
RIGHT NOW...
...I'M IN THE MOOD TO BE SPOILED BY YOU.
かあああ
WHAT ARE YOU ...?
......
Ladybug
どっすん
JEEZ! FINE, I'LL BE HERE! REST UP!
You can let go now.
I don't want to.

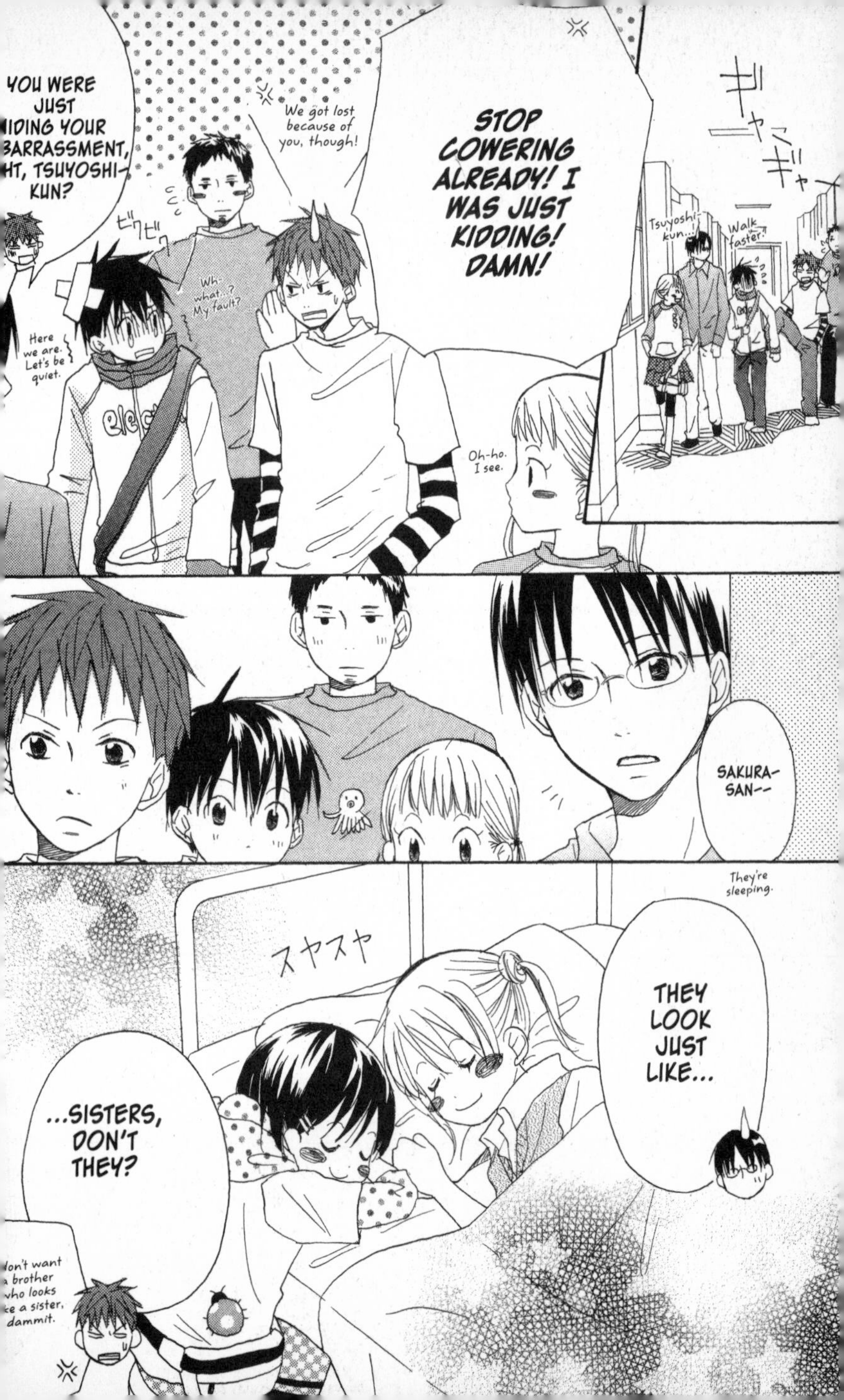
ギャーギャー
Tsuyoshi-kun...!
Walk faster!
STOP COWERING ALREADY! I WAS JUST KIDDING! DAMN!
We got lost because of you, though!
YOU WERE JUST IIDING YOUR BARRASSMENT, HT, TSUYOSHI-KUN?
ビクビク
Wh-what..? My fault?
Here we are. Let's be quiet.
Oh-ho. I see.
SAKURA-SAN--
They're sleeping.
スヤスヤ
THEY LOOK JUST LIKE...
...SISTERS, DON'T THEY?
on't want a brother who looks e a sister, dammit.

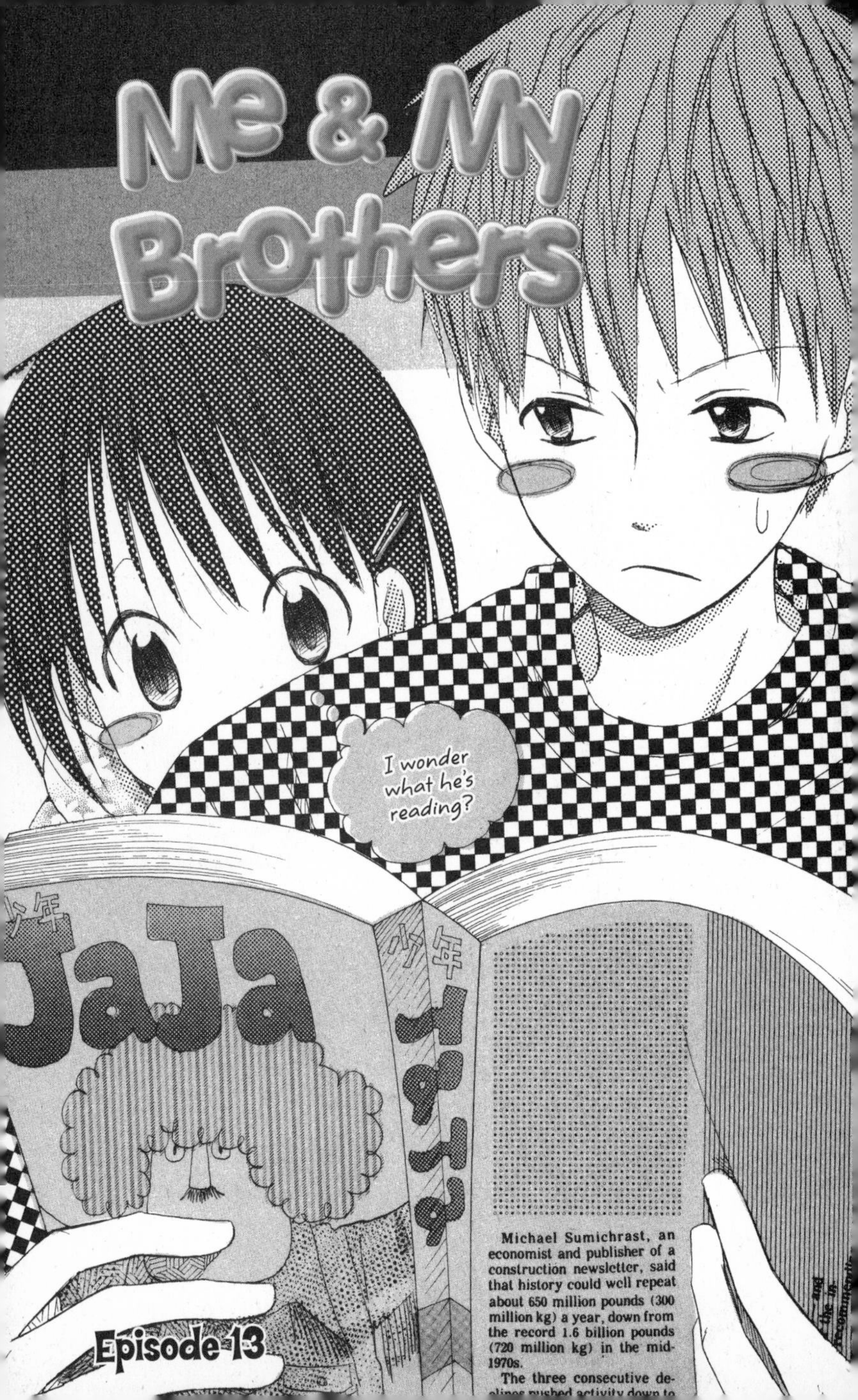
Me & My Brothers
I wonder what he's reading?
少年
JaJa
少年
Michael Sumichrast, an economist and publisher of a construction newsletter, said that history could well repeat about 650 million pounds (300 million kg) a year, down from the record 1.6 billion pounds (720 million kg) in the mid-1970s.
The three consecutive de-
Episode 13

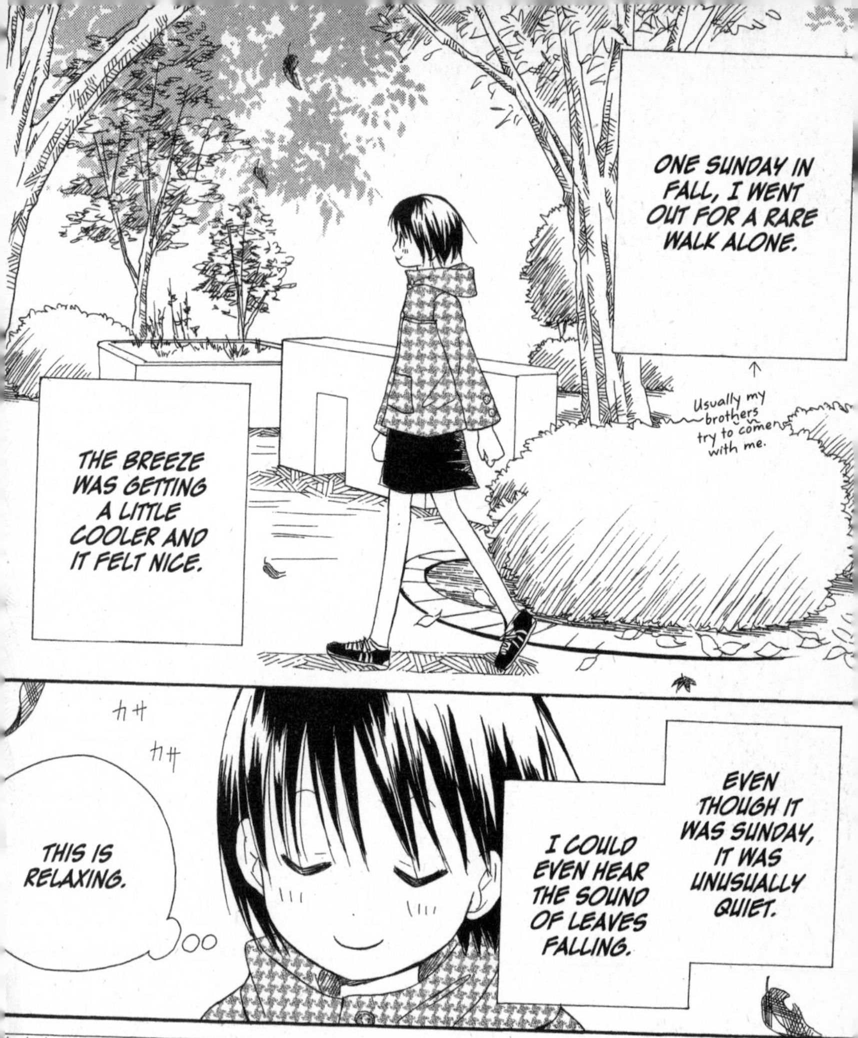
ONE SUNDAY IN FALL, I WENT OUT FOR A RARE WALK ALONE.
Usually my brothers try to come with me.
THE BREEZE WAS GETTING A LITTLE COOLER AND IT FELT NICE.
EVEN THOUGH IT WAS SUNDAY, IT WAS UNUSUALLY QUIET.
I COULD EVEN HEAR THE SOUND OF LEAVES FALLING.
カサ
カサ
THIS IS RELAXING.

The self-introductions I wrote before were actually written for the first magazine installment of Me and My Brothers.

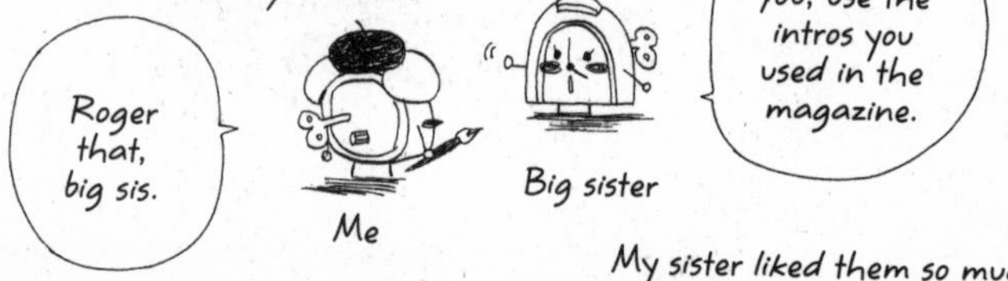
You, use the intros you used in the magazine.
Big sister
Me
Roger that, big sis.

My sister liked them so much, I ended up using them again.

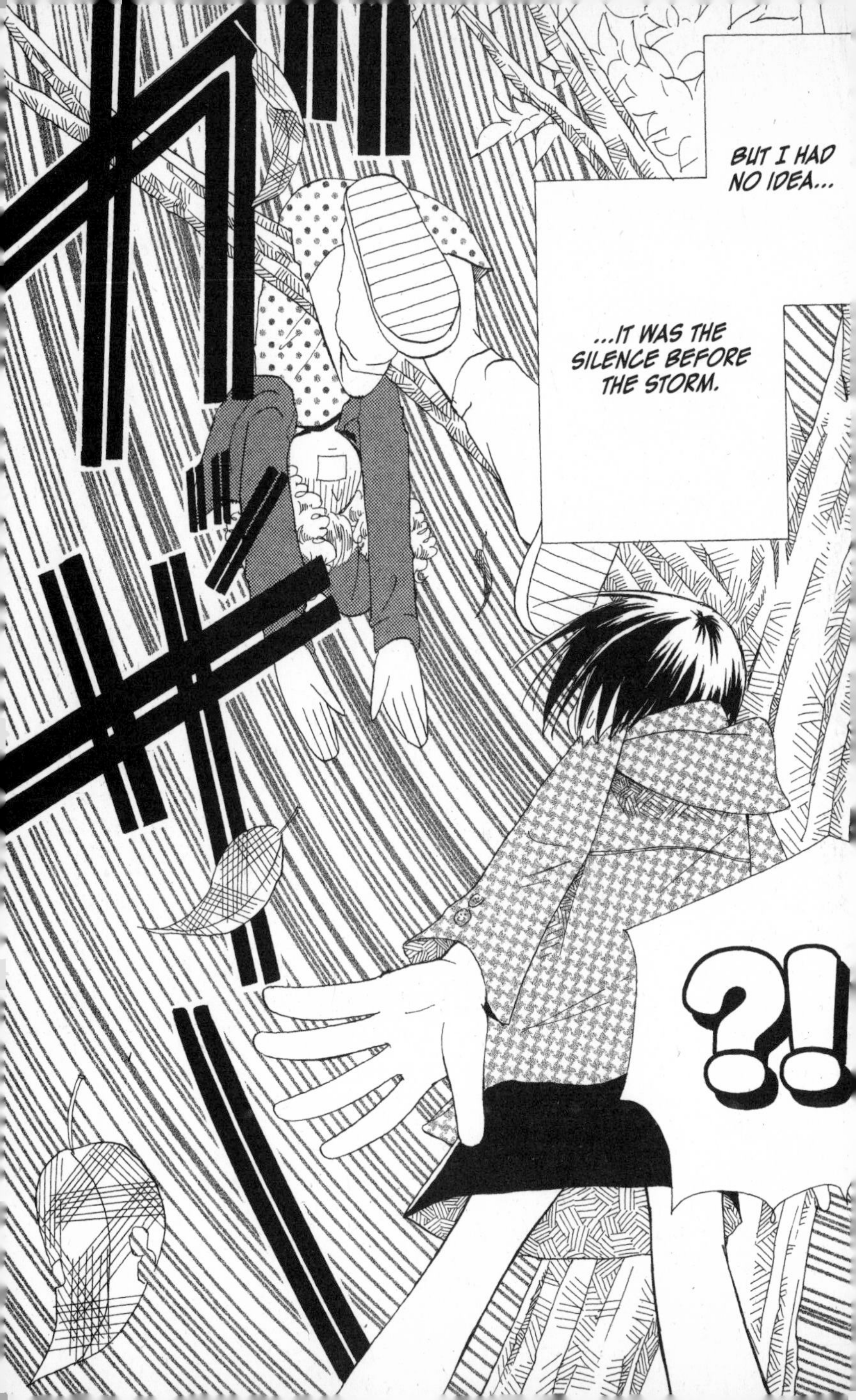
BUT I HAD NO IDEA...
...IT WAS THE SILENCE BEFORE THE STORM.
?!

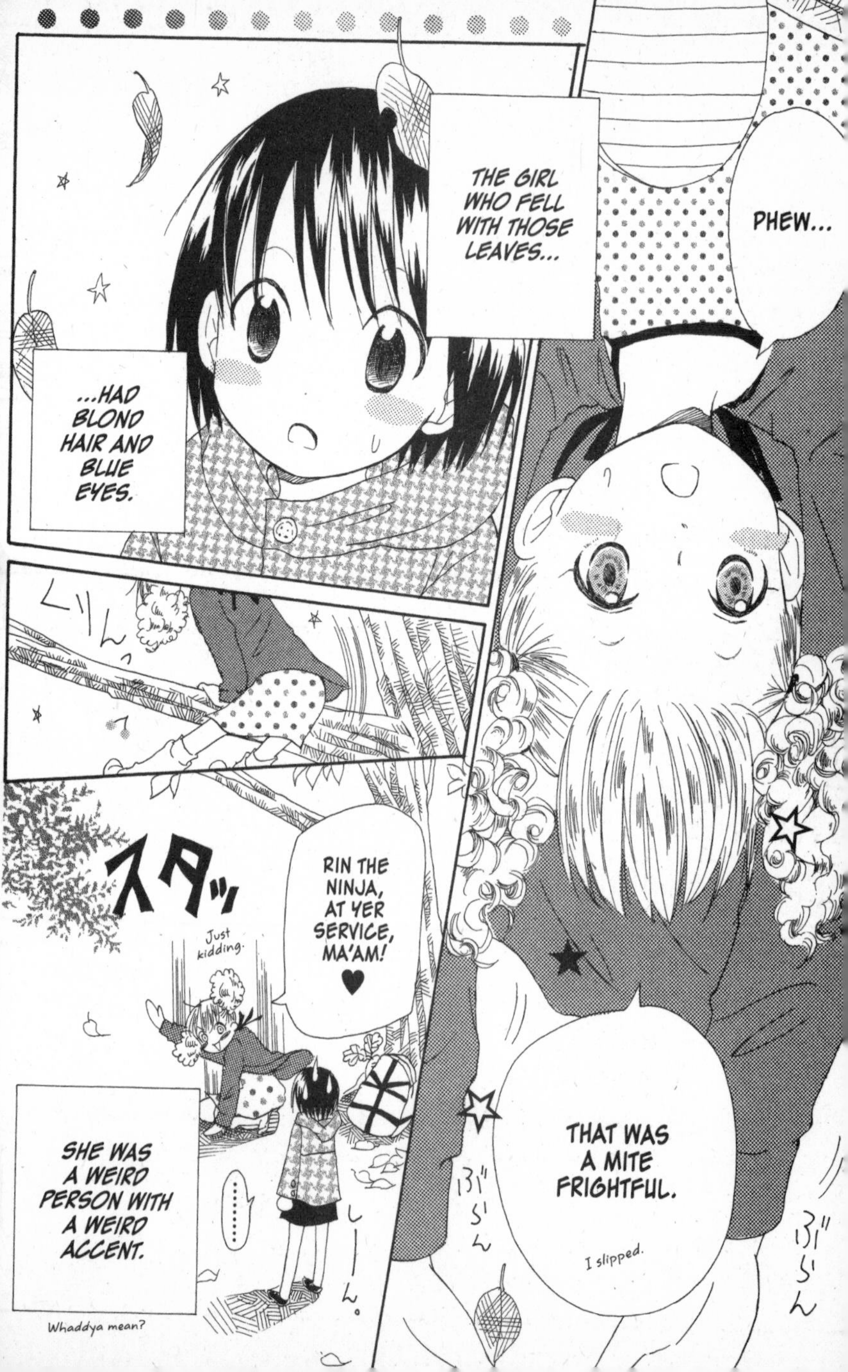
PHEW...
THAT WAS A MITE FRIGHTFUL.
I slipped.
ぶらん
ぶらん
THE GIRL WHO FELL WITH THOSE LEAVES...
...HAD BLOND HAIR AND BLUE EYES.
ムりんっ
スタッ
RIN THE NINJA, AT YER SERVICE, MA'AM! ♥
Just kidding.
SHE WAS A WEIRD PERSON WITH A WEIRD ACCENT.
......
しーん。
Whaddya mean?

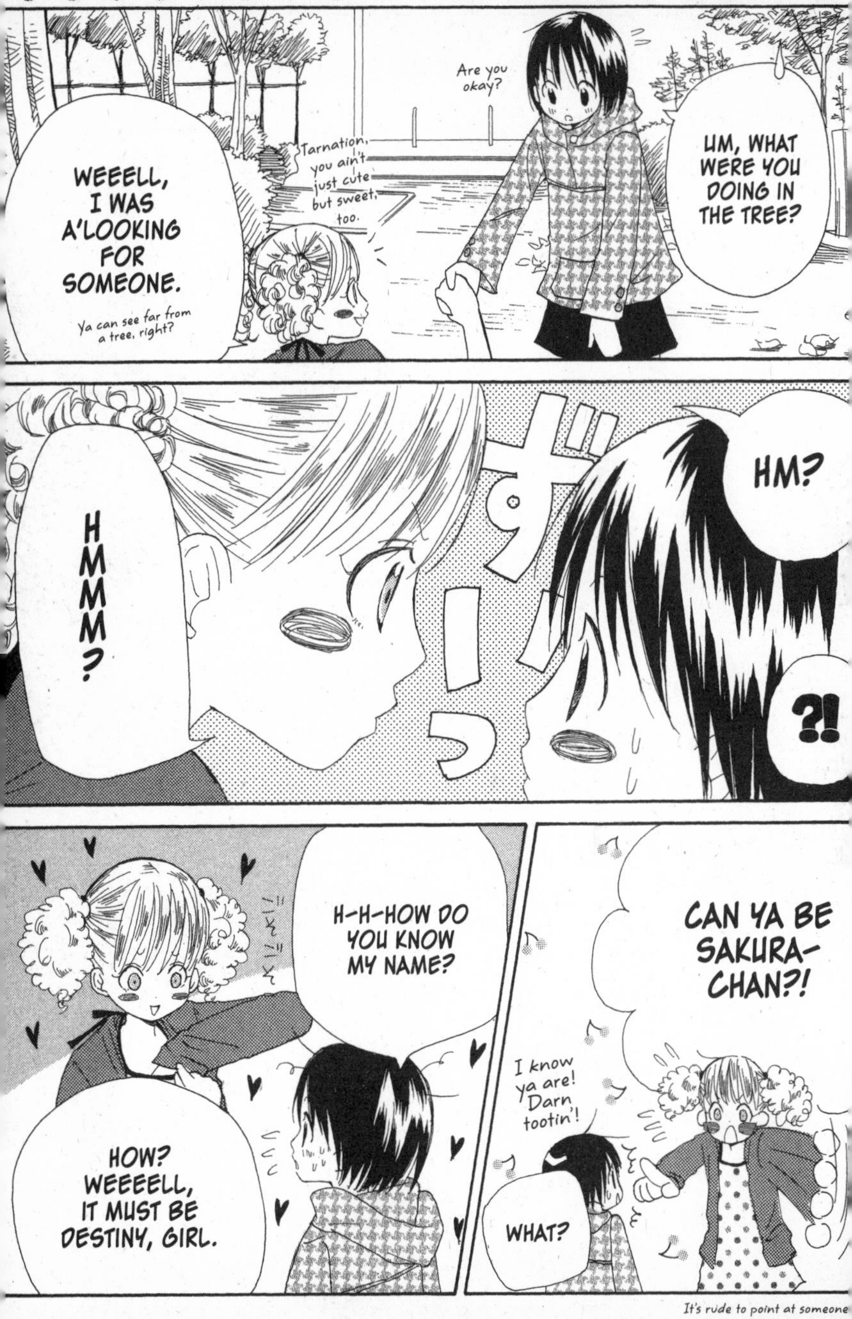
Are you okay?
UM, WHAT WERE YOU DOING IN THE TREE?
Tarnation, you ain't just cute but sweet, too.
WEEELL, I WAS A'LOOKING FOR SOMEONE.
Ya can see far from a tree, right?
HM?
ずいっ
?!
HMMM?
CAN YA BE SAKURA-CHAN?!
I know ya are! Darn tootin'!
WHAT?
H-H-HOW DO YOU KNOW MY NAME?
HOW? WEEEELL, IT MUST BE DESTINY, GIRL.

It's rude to point at someone

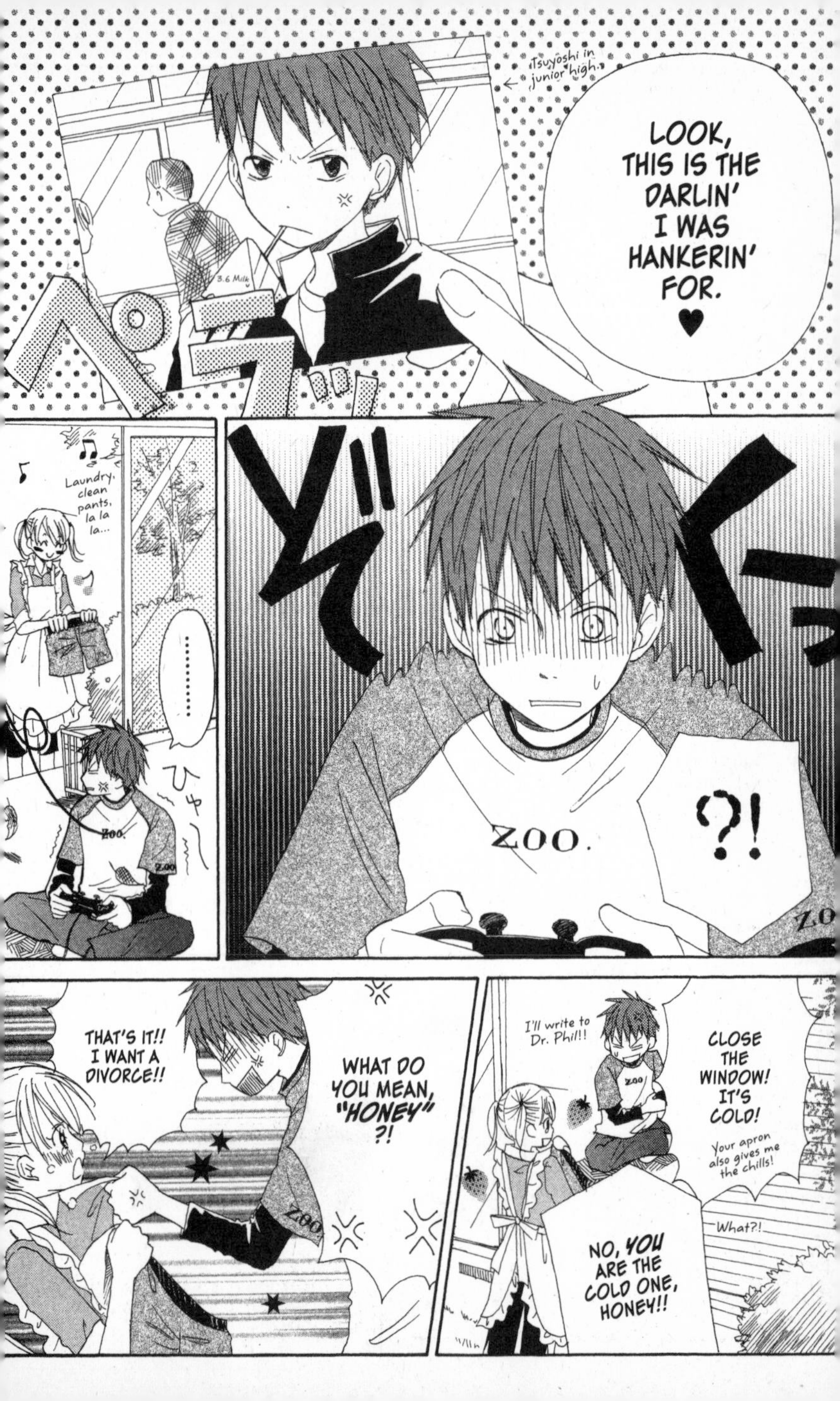

LOOK, THIS IS THE DARLIN' I WAS HANKERIN' FOR. ♥
Tsuyoshi in junior high.
3.6 Milk
?!
ZOO.
Laundry, clean pants, la la la...
......
ZOO.
CLOSE THE WINDOW! IT'S COLD!
Your apron also gives me the chills!
I'll write to Dr. Phil!!
What?!
NO, YOU ARE THE COLD ONE, HONEY!!
WHAT DO YOU MEAN, "HONEY"?!
THAT'S IT!! I WANT A DIVORCE!!

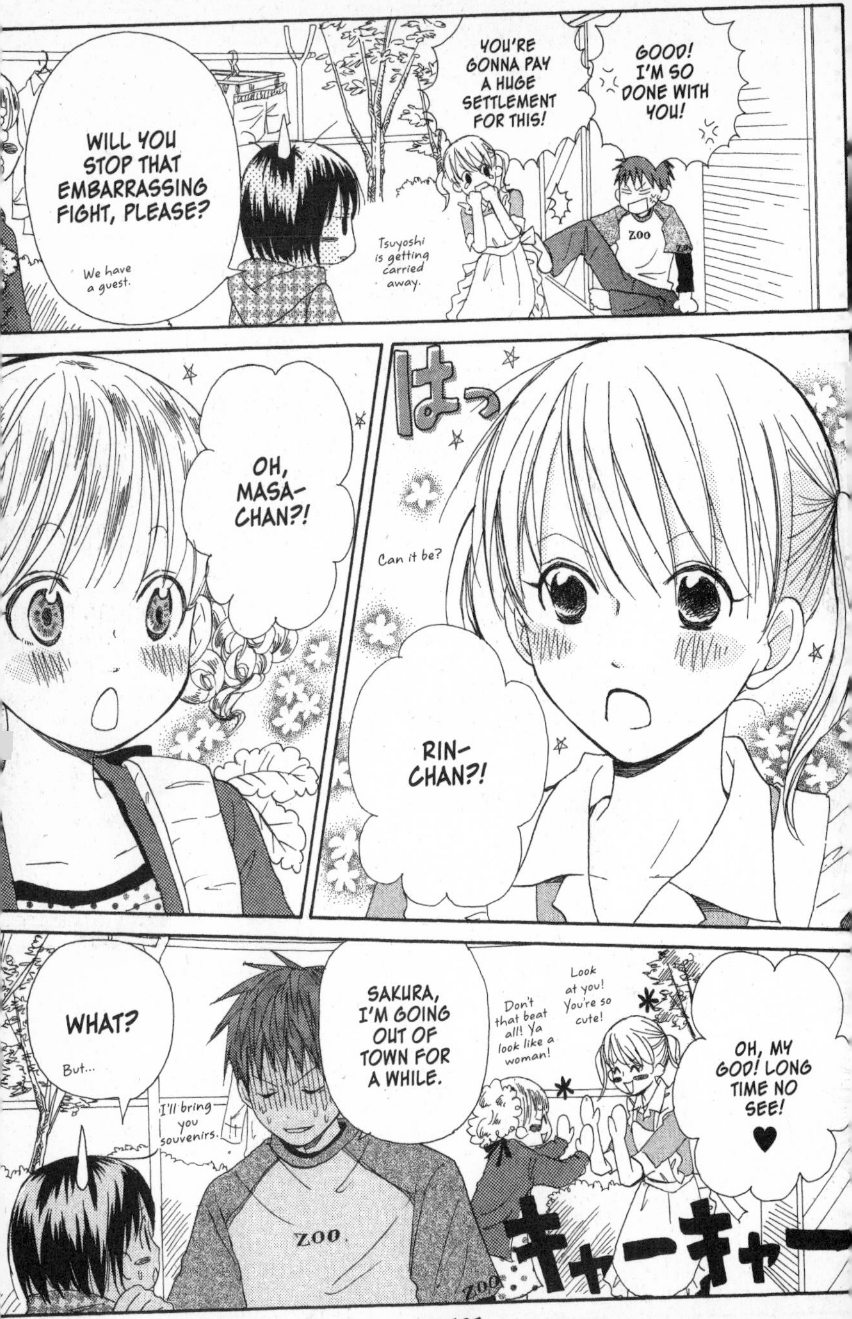
GOOD! I'M SO DONE WITH YOU!
YOU'RE GONNA PAY A HUGE SETTLEMENT FOR THIS!
ZOO
Tsuyoshi is getting carried away.
WILL YOU STOP THAT EMBARRASSING FIGHT, PLEASE?
We have a guest.
はっ
Can it be?
RIN-CHAN?!
OH, MASA-CHAN?!
OH, MY GOD! LONG TIME NO SEE! ♥
Look at you! You're so cute!
Don't that beat all! Ya look like a woman!
キャーキャー
SAKURA, I'M GOING OUT OF TOWN FOR A WHILE.
I'll bring you souvenirs.
ZOO
WHAT?
But...

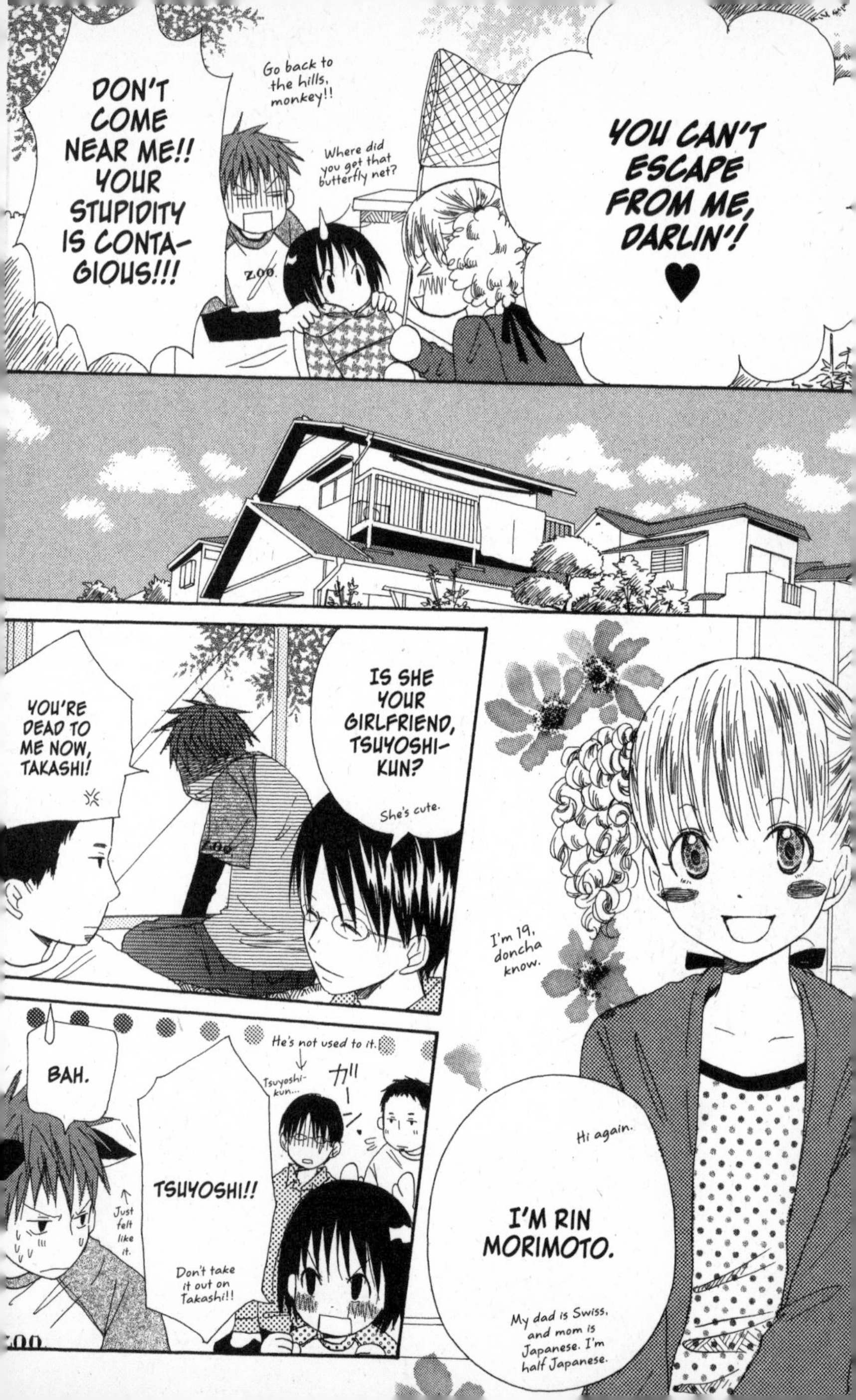
YOU CAN'T ESCAPE FROM ME, DARLIN'! ♥
Go back to the hills, monkey!!
Where did you get that butterfly net?
DON'T COME NEAR ME!! YOUR STUPIDITY IS CONTA-GIOUS!!!
I'm 19, doncha know.
Hi again.
I'M RIN MORIMOTO.
My dad is Swiss, and mom is Japanese. I'm half Japanese.
IS SHE YOUR GIRLFRIEND, TSUYOSHI-KUN?
She's cute.
YOU'RE DEAD TO ME NOW, TAKASHI!
He's not used to it.
Tsuyoshi-kun...
TSUYOSHI!!
Don't take it out on Takashi!!
BAH.
Just felt like it.

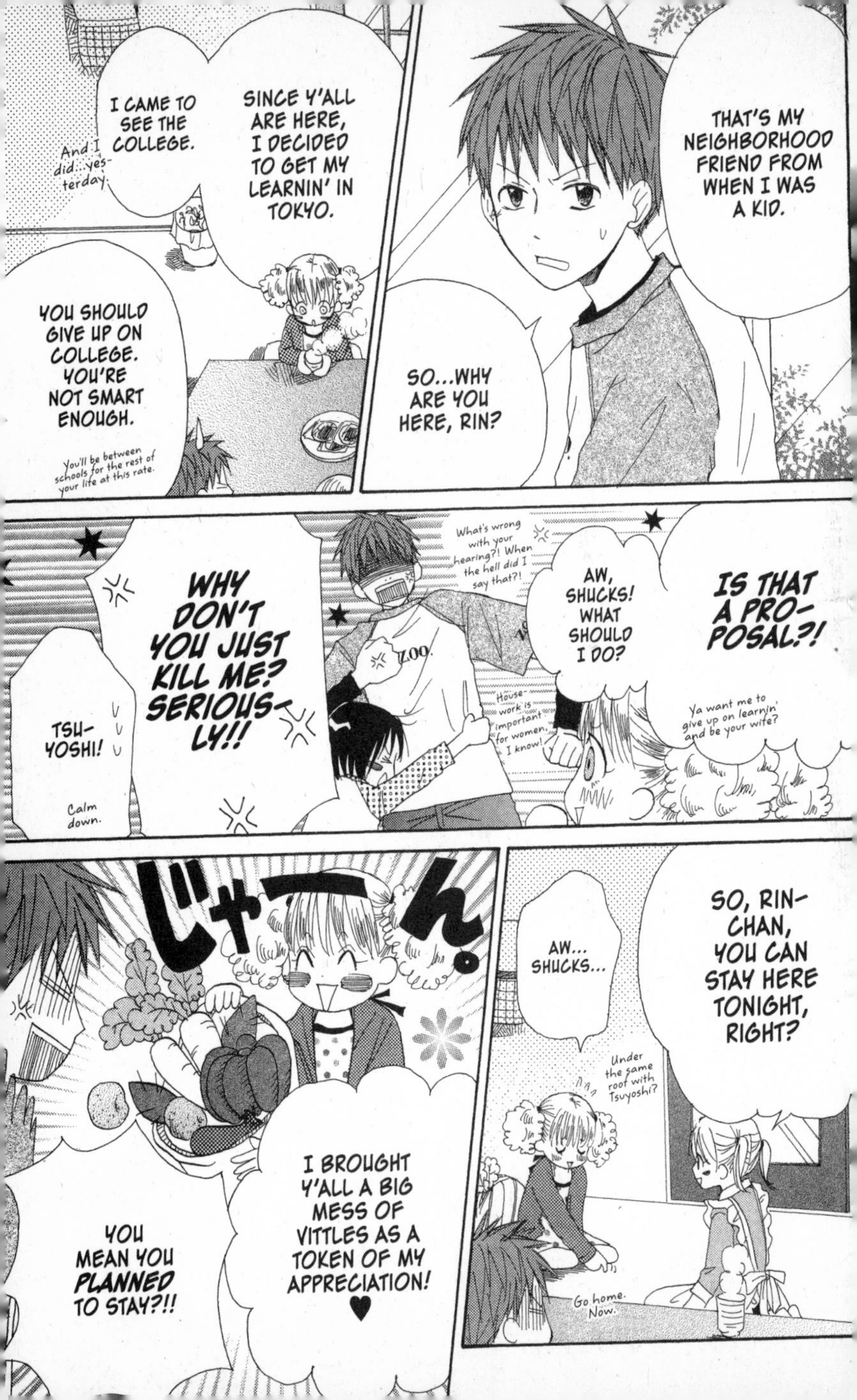
THAT'S MY NEIGHBORHOOD FRIEND FROM WHEN I WAS A KID.
SO...WHY ARE YOU HERE, RIN?
SINCE Y'ALL ARE HERE, I DECIDED TO GET MY LEARNIN' IN TOKYO.
I CAME TO SEE THE COLLEGE.
And I did...yesterday.
YOU SHOULD GIVE UP ON COLLEGE. YOU'RE NOT SMART ENOUGH.
You'll be between schools for the rest of your life at this rate.
IS THAT A PROPOSAL?!
Ya want me to give up on learnin' and be your wife?
AW, SHUCKS! WHAT SHOULD I DO?
Housework is important for women, I know!
What's wrong with your hearing?! When the hell did I say that?!
WHY DON'T YOU JUST KILL ME? SERIOUSLY!!
TSUYOSHI!
Calm down.
SO, RIN-CHAN, YOU CAN STAY HERE TONIGHT, RIGHT?
AW... SHUCKS...
Under the same roof with Tsuyoshi?
Go home. Now.
じゃーん。
I BROUGHT Y'ALL A BIG MESS OF VITTLES AS A TOKEN OF MY APPRECIATION! ♥
YOU MEAN YOU PLANNED TO STAY?!!

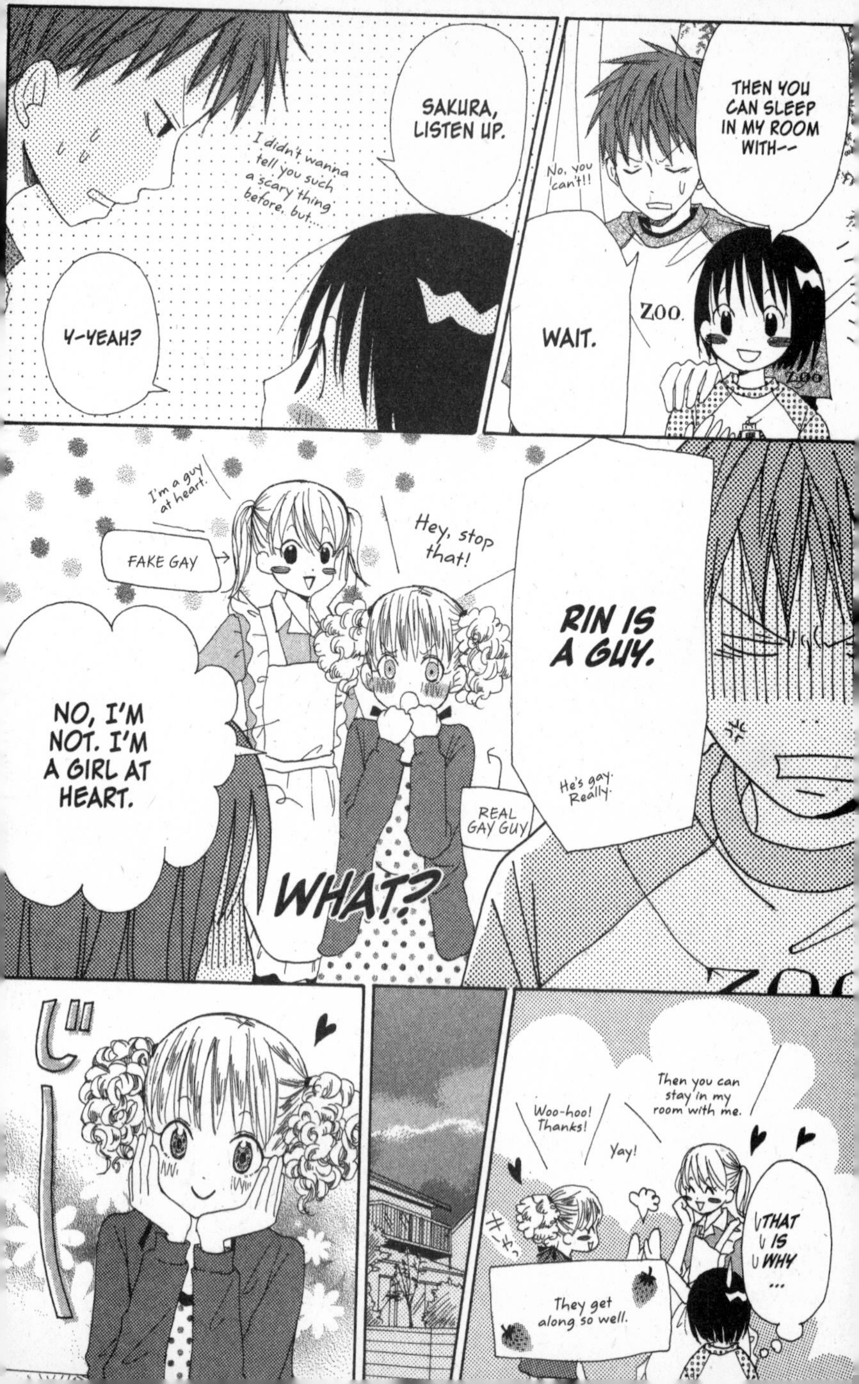
THEN YOU CAN SLEEP IN MY ROOM WITH--
No, you can't!!
ZOO.
WAIT.
SAKURA, LISTEN UP.
I didn't wanna tell you such a scary thing before, but...
Y-YEAH?
RIN IS A GUY.
He's gay. Really.
Hey, stop that!
I'm a guy at heart.
FAKE GAY
NO, I'M NOT. I'M A GIRL AT HEART.
REAL GAY GUY
WHAT?
Then you can stay in my room with me.
Woo-hoo! Thanks!
Yay!
THAT IS WHY ...
They get along so well.
じー

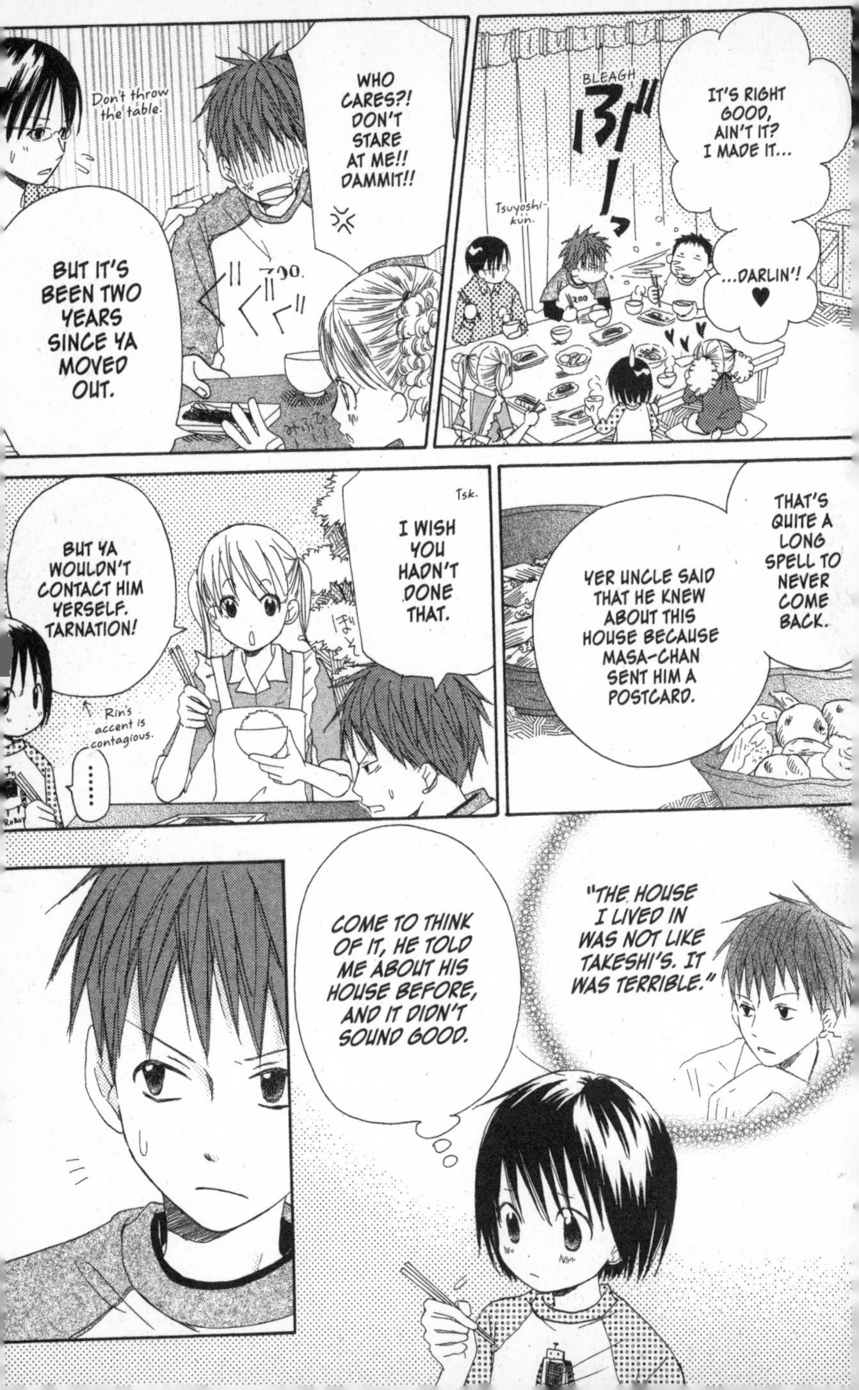
IT'S RIGHT GOOD, AIN'T IT? I MADE IT...
BLEAGH
...DARLIN'! ♥
Tsuyoshi-kun.
WHO CARES?! DON'T STARE AT ME!! DAMMIT!!
Don't throw the table.
BUT IT'S BEEN TWO YEARS SINCE YA MOVED OUT.
THAT'S QUITE A LONG SPELL TO NEVER COME BACK.
YER UNCLE SAID THAT HE KNEW ABOUT THIS HOUSE BECAUSE MASA-CHAN SENT HIM A POSTCARD.
Tsk.
I WISH YOU HADN'T DONE THAT.
BUT YA WOULDN'T CONTACT HIM YERSELF. TARNATION!
Rin's accent is contagious.
......
"THE HOUSE I LIVED IN WAS NOT LIKE TAKESHI'S. IT WAS TERRIBLE."
COME TO THINK OF IT, HE TOLD ME ABOUT HIS HOUSE BEFORE, AND IT DIDN'T SOUND GOOD.

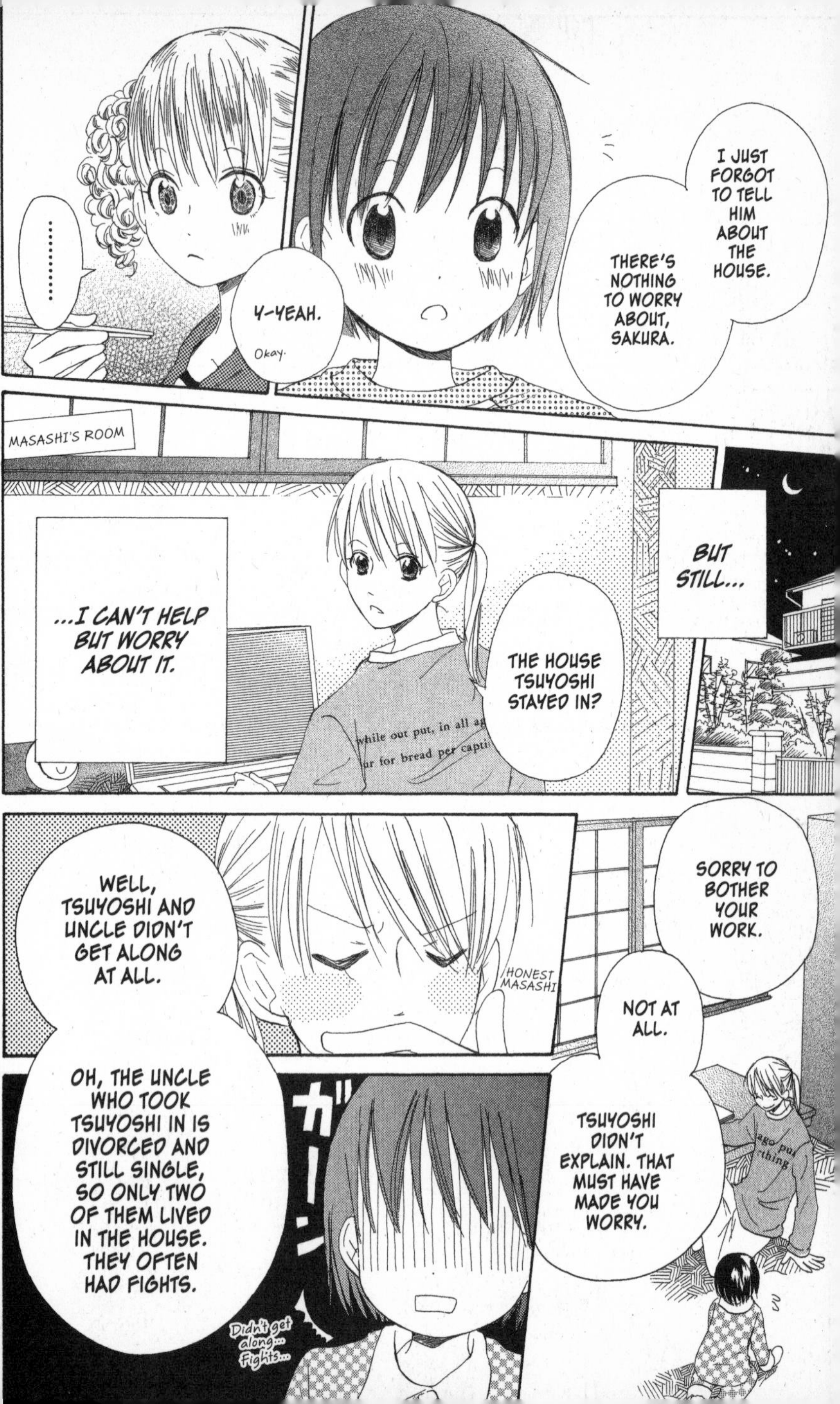
I JUST FORGOT TO TELL HIM ABOUT THE HOUSE.
THERE'S NOTHING TO WORRY ABOUT, SAKURA.
Y-YEAH.
Okay.
......
BUT STILL...
...I CAN'T HELP BUT WORRY ABOUT IT.
MASASHI'S ROOM
THE HOUSE TSUYOSHI STAYED IN?
while out put, in all ag
ur for bread per capit
SORRY TO BOTHER YOUR WORK.
NOT AT ALL.
WELL, TSUYOSHI AND UNCLE DIDN'T GET ALONG AT ALL.
HONEST MASASHI
TSUYOSHI DIDN'T EXPLAIN. THAT MUST HAVE MADE YOU WORRY.
OH, THE UNCLE WHO TOOK TSUYOSHI IN IS DIVORCED AND STILL SINGLE, SO ONLY TWO OF THEM LIVED IN THE HOUSE. THEY OFTEN HAD FIGHTS.
ガーン
Didn't get along... Fights...

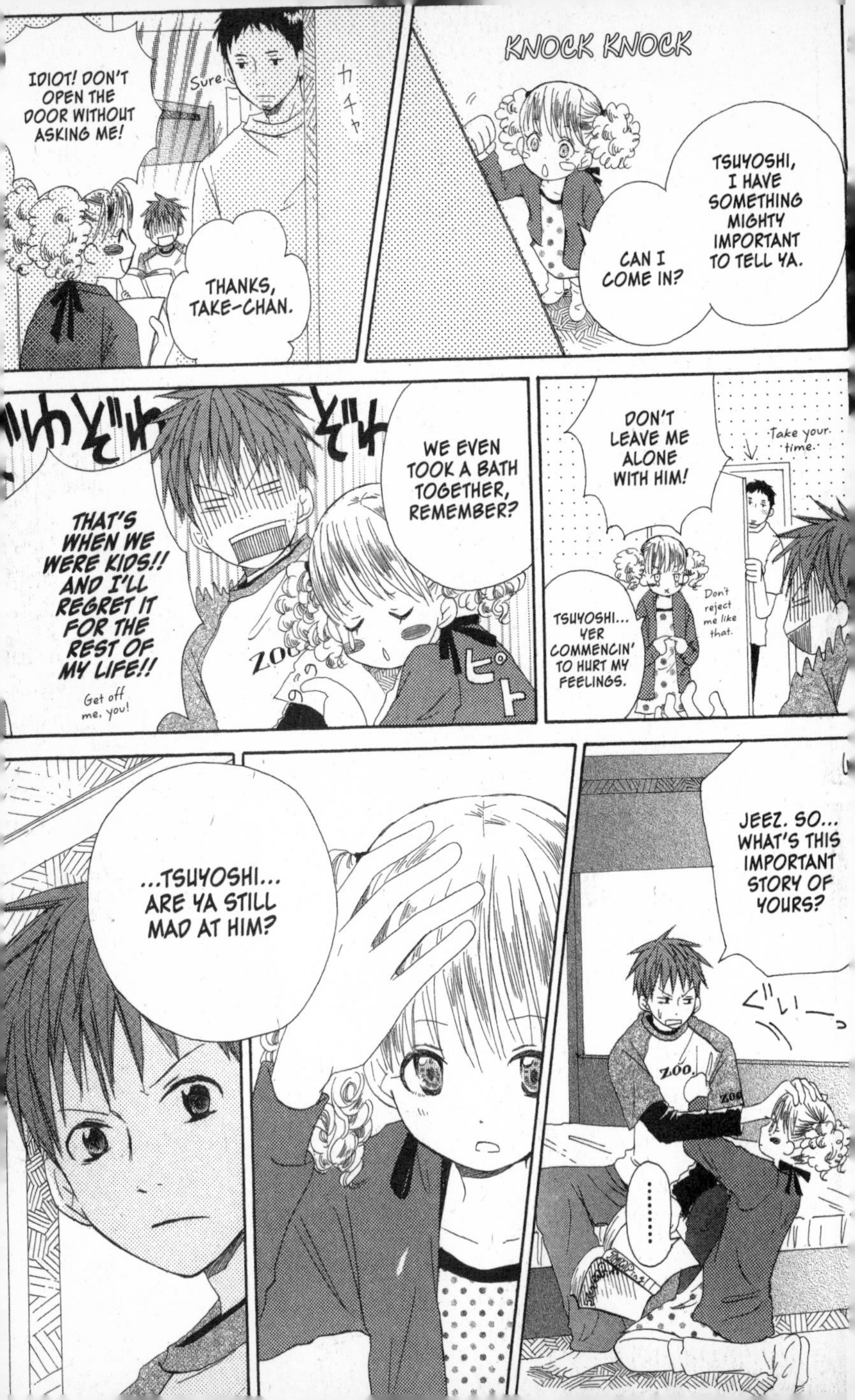
KNOCK KNOCK
TSUYOSHI, I HAVE SOMETHING MIGHTY IMPORTANT TO TELL YA.
CAN I COME IN?
カチャ
Sure.
IDIOT! DON'T OPEN THE DOOR WITHOUT ASKING ME!
THANKS, TAKE-CHAN.
DON'T LEAVE ME ALONE WITH HIM!
Take your time.
Don't reject me like that.
TSUYOSHI... YER COMMENCIN' TO HURT MY FEELINGS.
WE EVEN TOOK A BATH TOGETHER, REMEMBER?
ピト
THAT'S WHEN WE WERE KIDS!! AND I'LL REGRET IT FOR THE REST OF MY LIFE!!
Get off me, you!
JEEZ. SO... WHAT'S THIS IMPORTANT STORY OF YOURS?
......
...TSUYOSHI... ARE YA STILL MAD AT HIM?

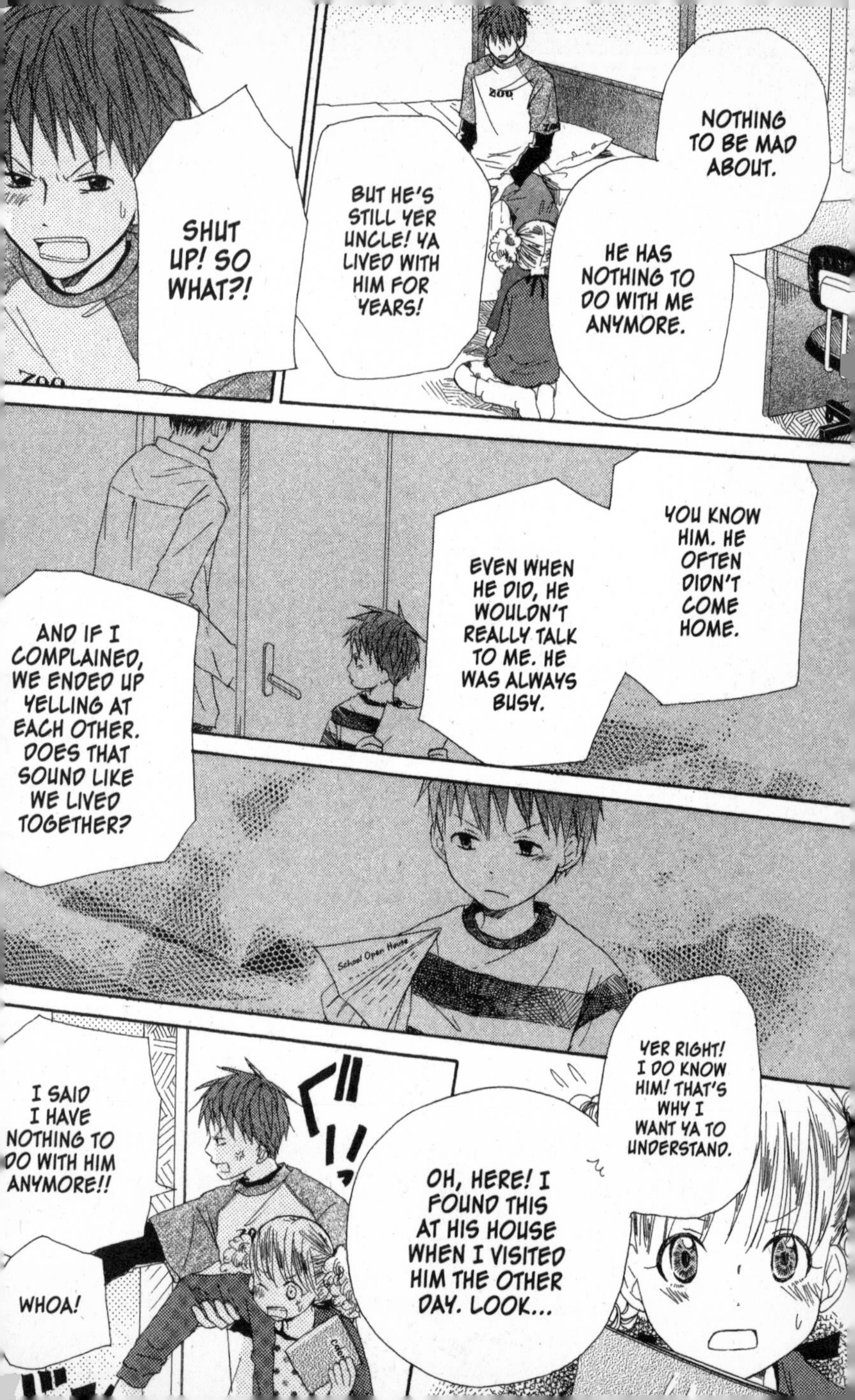
NOTHING TO BE MAD ABOUT.
HE HAS NOTHING TO DO WITH ME ANYMORE.
BUT HE'S STILL YER UNCLE! YA LIVED WITH HIM FOR YEARS!
SHUT UP! SO WHAT?!
YOU KNOW HIM. HE OFTEN DIDN'T COME HOME.
EVEN WHEN HE DID, HE WOULDN'T REALLY TALK TO ME. HE WAS ALWAYS BUSY.
AND IF I COMPLAINED, WE ENDED UP YELLING AT EACH OTHER. DOES THAT SOUND LIKE WE LIVED TOGETHER?
School Open House
YER RIGHT! I DO KNOW HIM! THAT'S WHY I WANT YA TO UNDERSTAND.
OH, HERE! I FOUND THIS AT HIS HOUSE WHEN I VISITED HIM THE OTHER DAY. LOOK...
I SAID I HAVE NOTHING TO DO WITH HIM ANYMORE!!
WHOA!

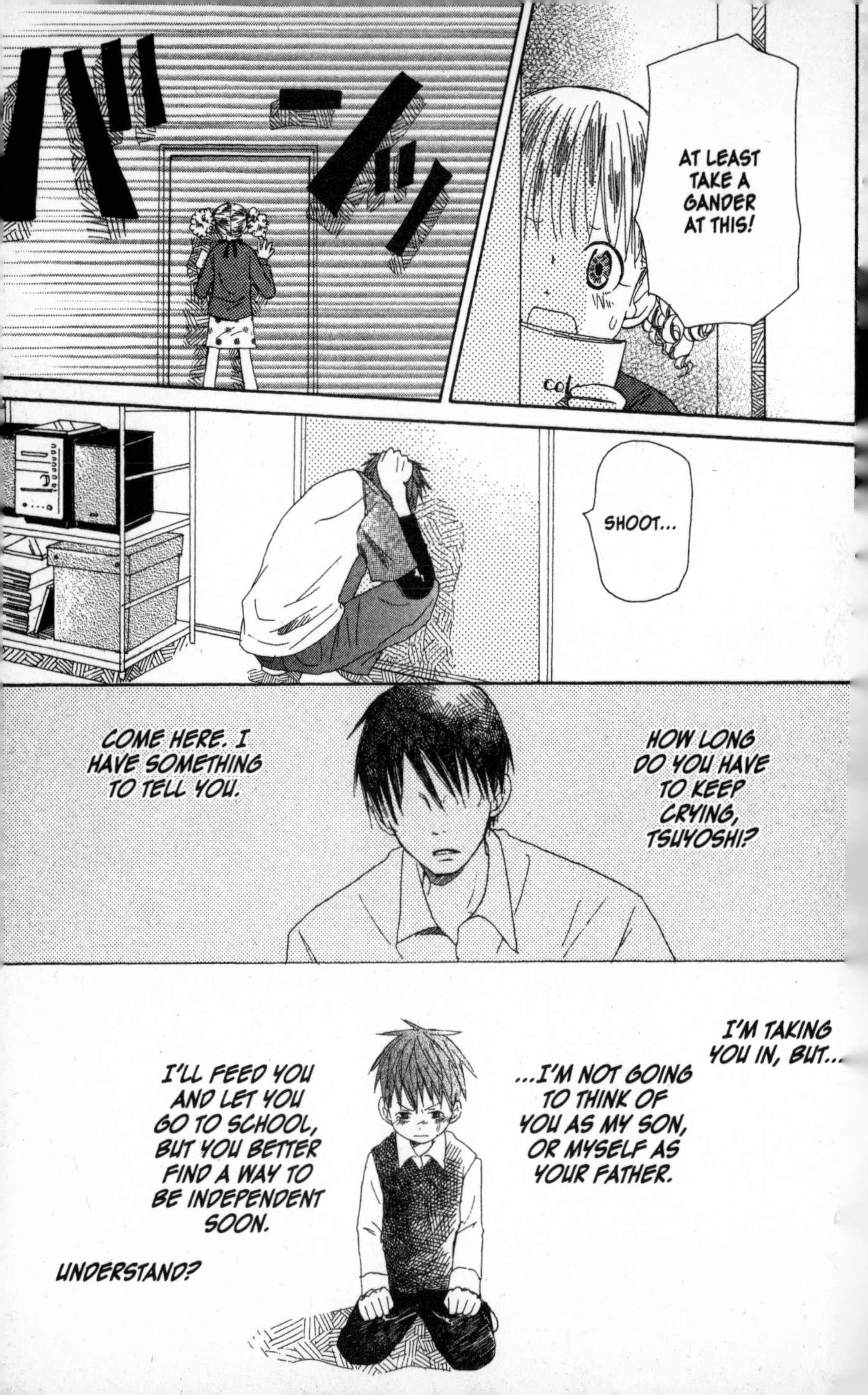
AT LEAST TAKE A GANDER AT THIS!
SHOOT...
HOW LONG DO YOU HAVE TO KEEP CRYING, TSUYOSHI?
COME HERE. I HAVE SOMETHING TO TELL YOU.
I'M TAKING YOU IN, BUT...
...I'M NOT GOING TO THINK OF YOU AS MY SON, OR MYSELF AS YOUR FATHER.
I'LL FEED YOU AND LET YOU GO TO SCHOOL, BUT YOU BETTER FIND A WAY TO BE INDEPENDENT SOON.
UNDERSTAND?

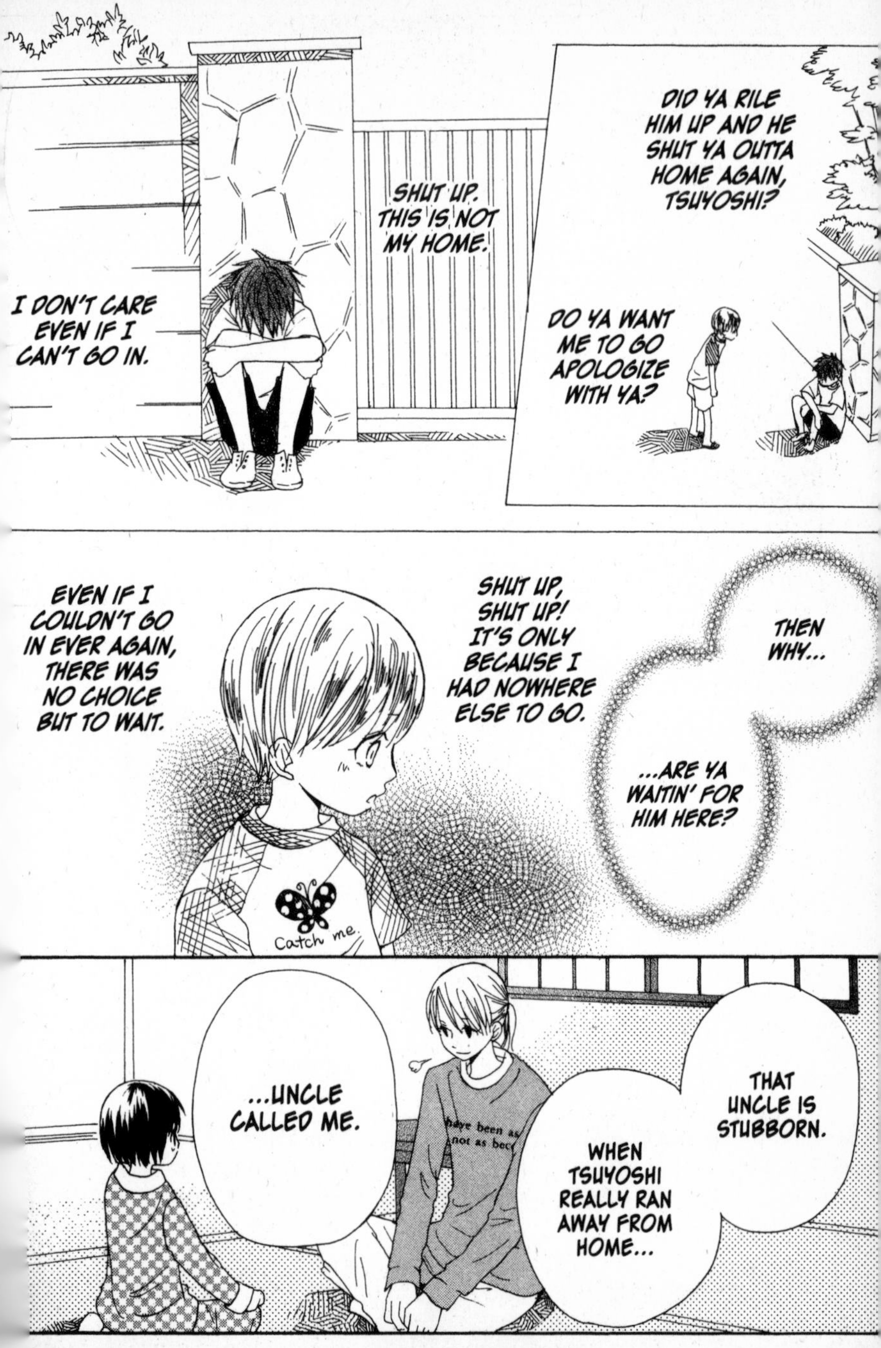
DID YA RILE HIM UP AND HE SHUT YA OUTTA HOME AGAIN, TSUYOSHI?
DO YA WANT ME TO GO APOLOGIZE WITH YA?
SHUT UP. THIS IS NOT MY HOME.
I DON'T CARE EVEN IF I CAN'T GO IN.
THEN WHY...
...ARE YA WAITIN' FOR HIM HERE?
SHUT UP, SHUT UP! IT'S ONLY BECAUSE I HAD NOWHERE ELSE TO GO.
EVEN IF I COULDN'T GO IN EVER AGAIN, THERE WAS NO CHOICE BUT TO WAIT.
Catch me.
THAT UNCLE IS STUBBORN.
WHEN TSUYOSHI REALLY RAN AWAY FROM HOME...
...UNCLE CALLED ME.

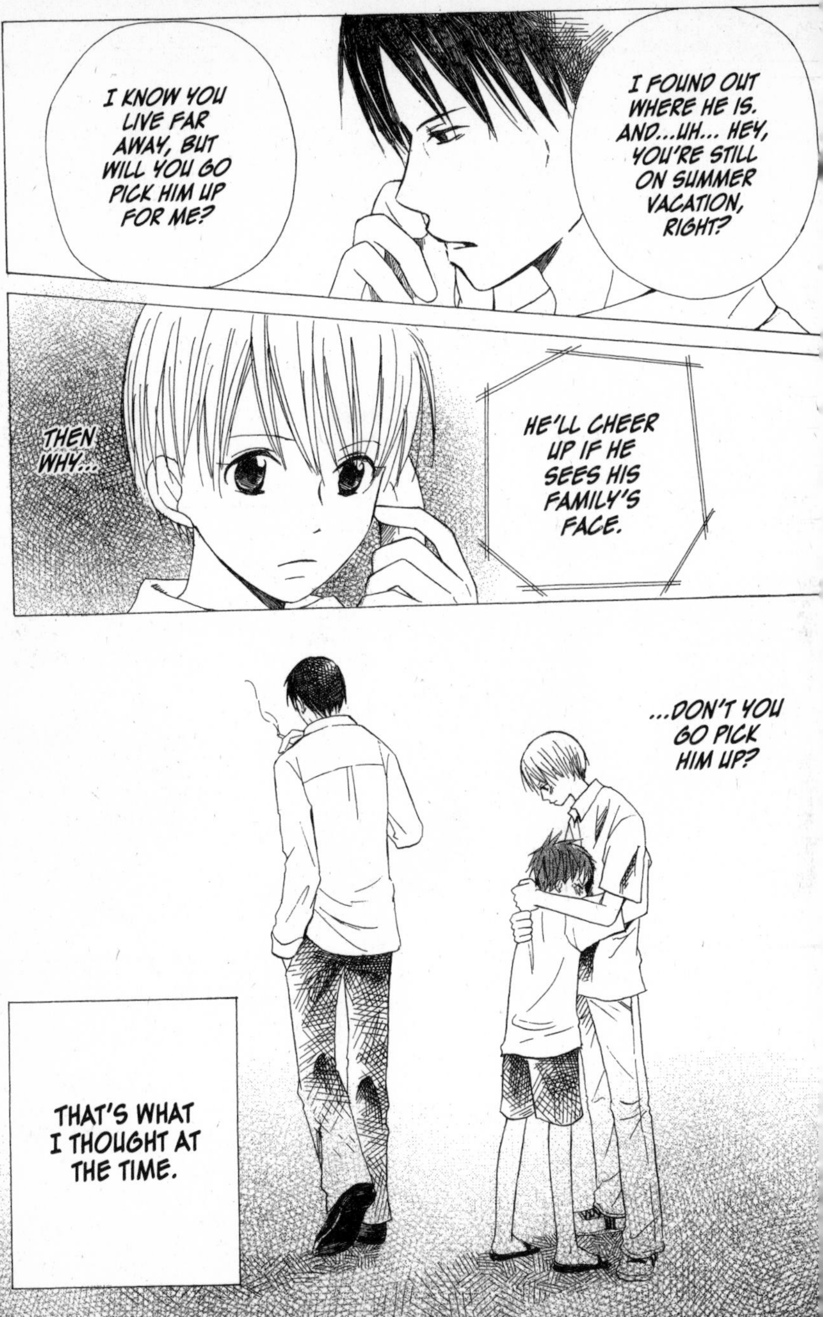
I FOUND OUT WHERE HE IS. AND...UH... HEY, YOU'RE STILL ON SUMMER VACATION, RIGHT?
I KNOW YOU LIVE FAR AWAY, BUT WILL YOU GO PICK HIM UP FOR ME?
HE'LL CHEER UP IF HE SEES HIS FAMILY'S FACE.
THEN WHY...
...DON'T YOU GO PICK HIM UP?
THAT'S WHAT I THOUGHT AT THE TIME.

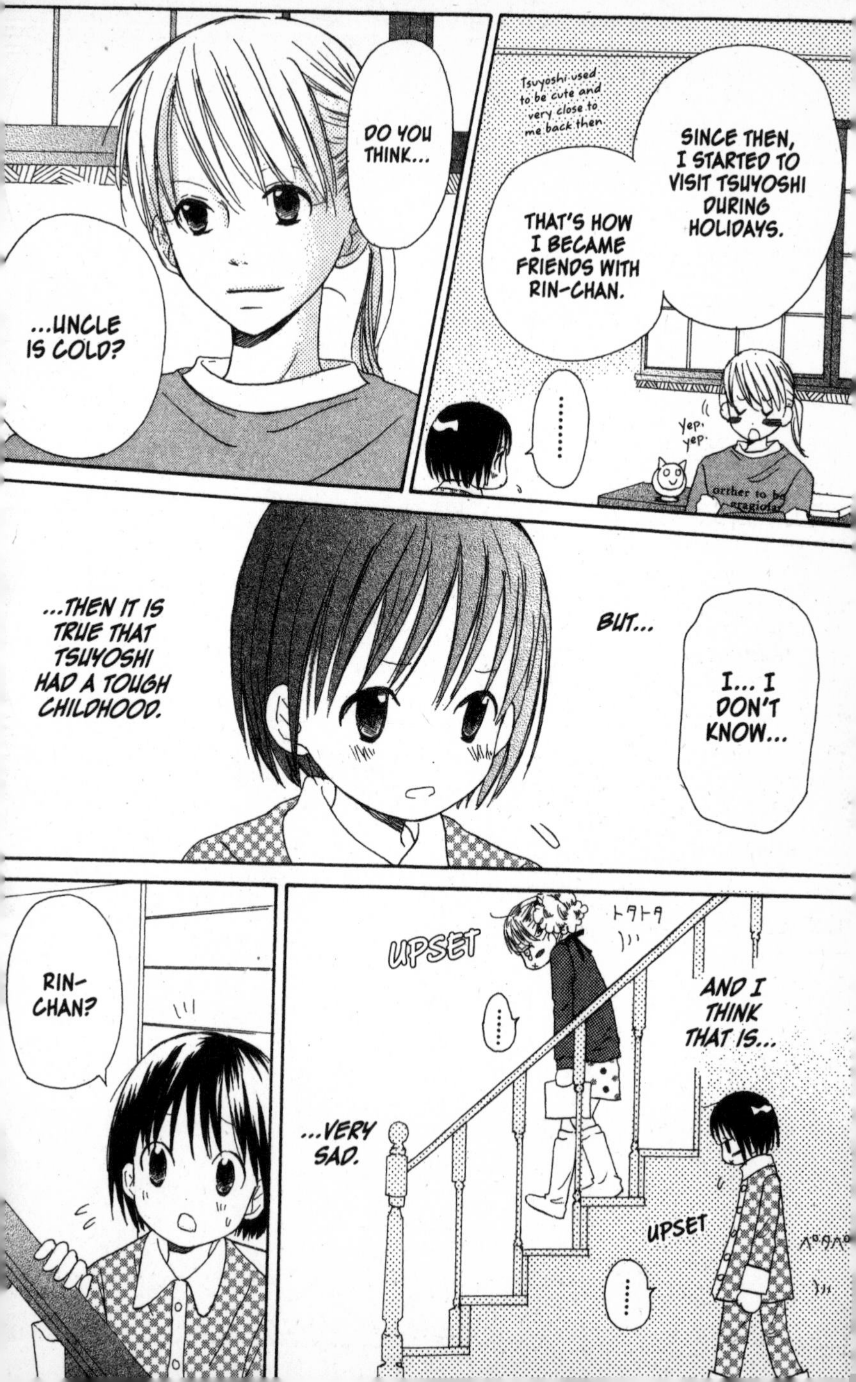
Tsuyoshi used to be cute and very close to me back then.
SINCE THEN, I STARTED TO VISIT TSUYOSHI DURING HOLIDAYS.
THAT'S HOW I BECAME FRIENDS WITH RIN-CHAN.
....
Yep. yep.
DO YOU THINK...
...UNCLE IS COLD?
I... I DON'T KNOW...
BUT...
...THEN IT IS TRUE THAT TSUYOSHI HAD A TOUGH CHILDHOOD.
トタトタ
UPSET
AND I THINK THAT IS...
......
...VERY SAD.
UPSET
......
RIN-CHAN?

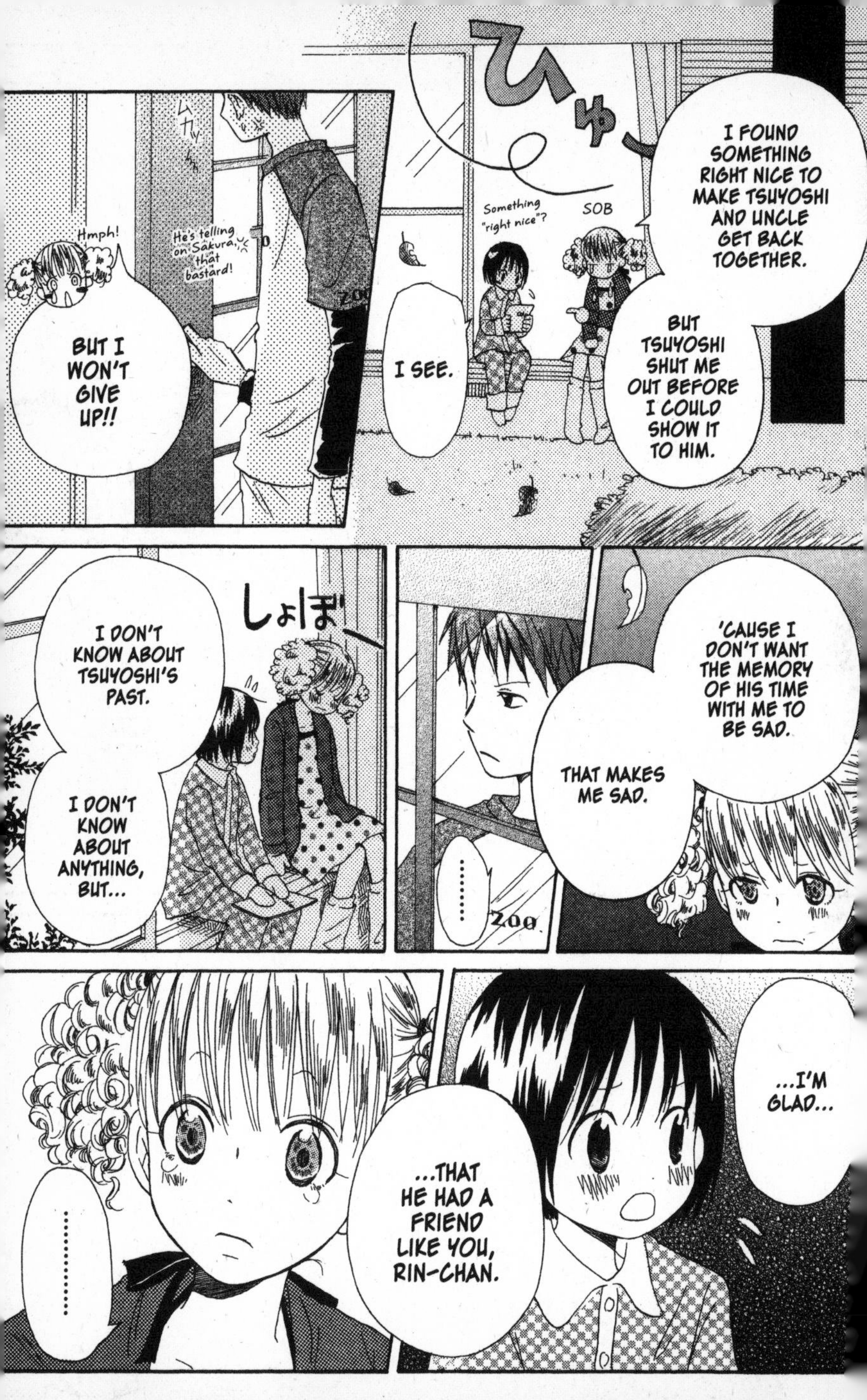

ひゅ～
I FOUND SOMETHING RIGHT NICE TO MAKE TSUYOSHI AND UNCLE GET BACK TOGETHER.
SOB
BUT TSUYOSHI SHUT ME OUT BEFORE I COULD SHOW IT TO HIM.
Something "right nice"?
I SEE.
ムカッ
He's telling on Sakura, that bastard!
Hmph!
BUT I WON'T GIVE UP!!
'CAUSE I DON'T WANT THE MEMORY OF HIS TIME WITH ME TO BE SAD.
THAT MAKES ME SAD.
......
しょぼ
I DON'T KNOW ABOUT TSUYOSHI'S PAST.
I DON'T KNOW ABOUT ANYTHING, BUT...
...I'M GLAD...
...THAT HE HAD A FRIEND LIKE YOU, RIN-CHAN.
....

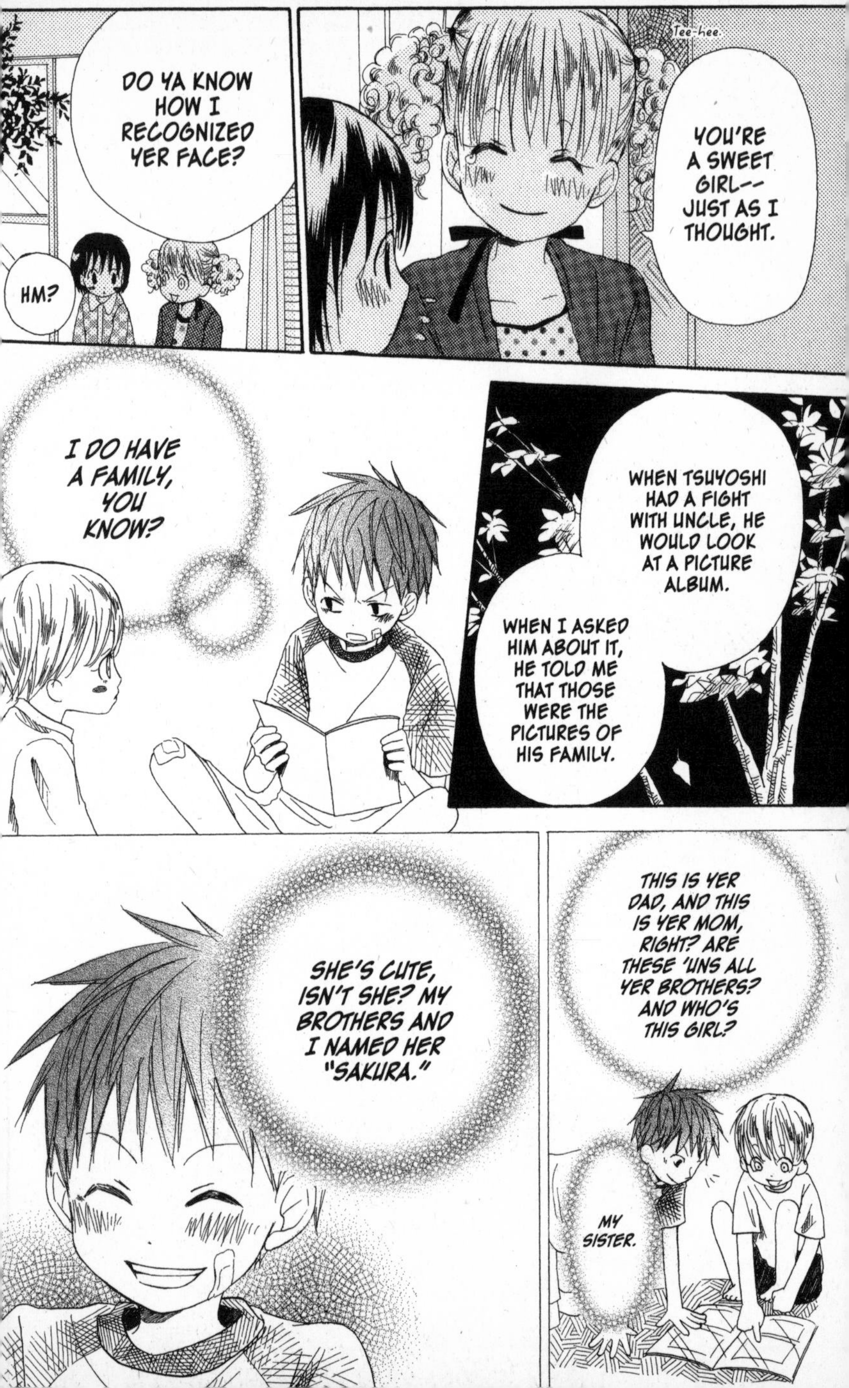
Tee-hee.
YOU'RE A SWEET GIRL-- JUST AS I THOUGHT.
DO YA KNOW HOW I RECOGNIZED YER FACE?
HM?
WHEN TSUYOSHI HAD A FIGHT WITH UNCLE, HE WOULD LOOK AT A PICTURE ALBUM.
WHEN I ASKED HIM ABOUT IT, HE TOLD ME THAT THOSE WERE THE PICTURES OF HIS FAMILY.
I DO HAVE A FAMILY, YOU KNOW?
THIS IS YER DAD, AND THIS IS YER MOM, RIGHT? ARE THESE 'UNS ALL YER BROTHERS? AND WHO'S THIS GIRL?
MY SISTER.
SHE'S CUTE, ISN'T SHE? MY BROTHERS AND I NAMED HER "SAKURA."

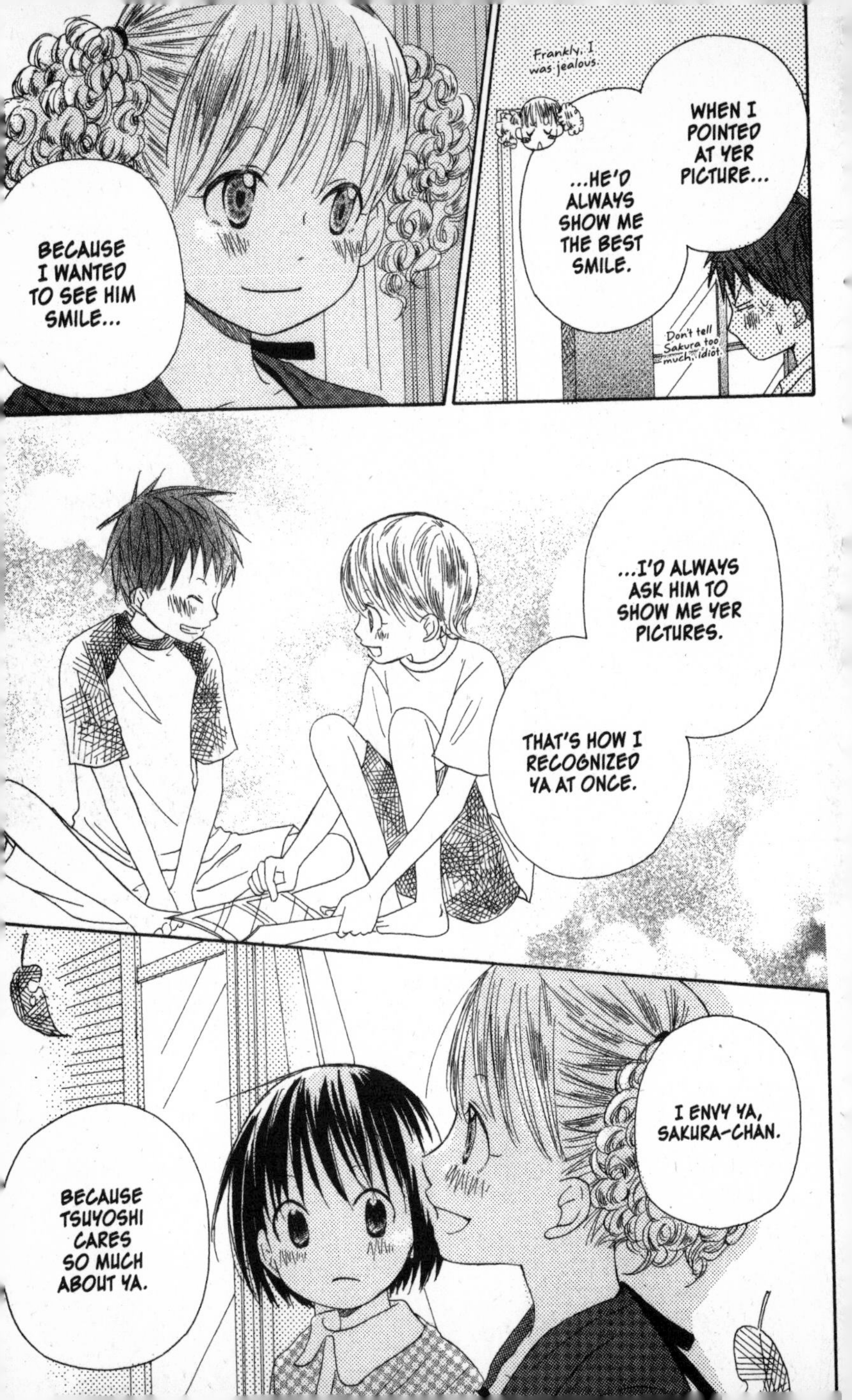
Frankly, I was jealous.
WHEN I POINTED AT YER PICTURE...
...HE'D ALWAYS SHOW ME THE BEST SMILE.
Don't tell Sakura too much, idiot.
BECAUSE I WANTED TO SEE HIM SMILE...
...I'D ALWAYS ASK HIM TO SHOW ME YER PICTURES.
THAT'S HOW I RECOGNIZED YA AT ONCE.
I ENVY YA, SAKURA-CHAN.
BECAUSE TSUYOSHI CARES SO MUCH ABOUT YA.

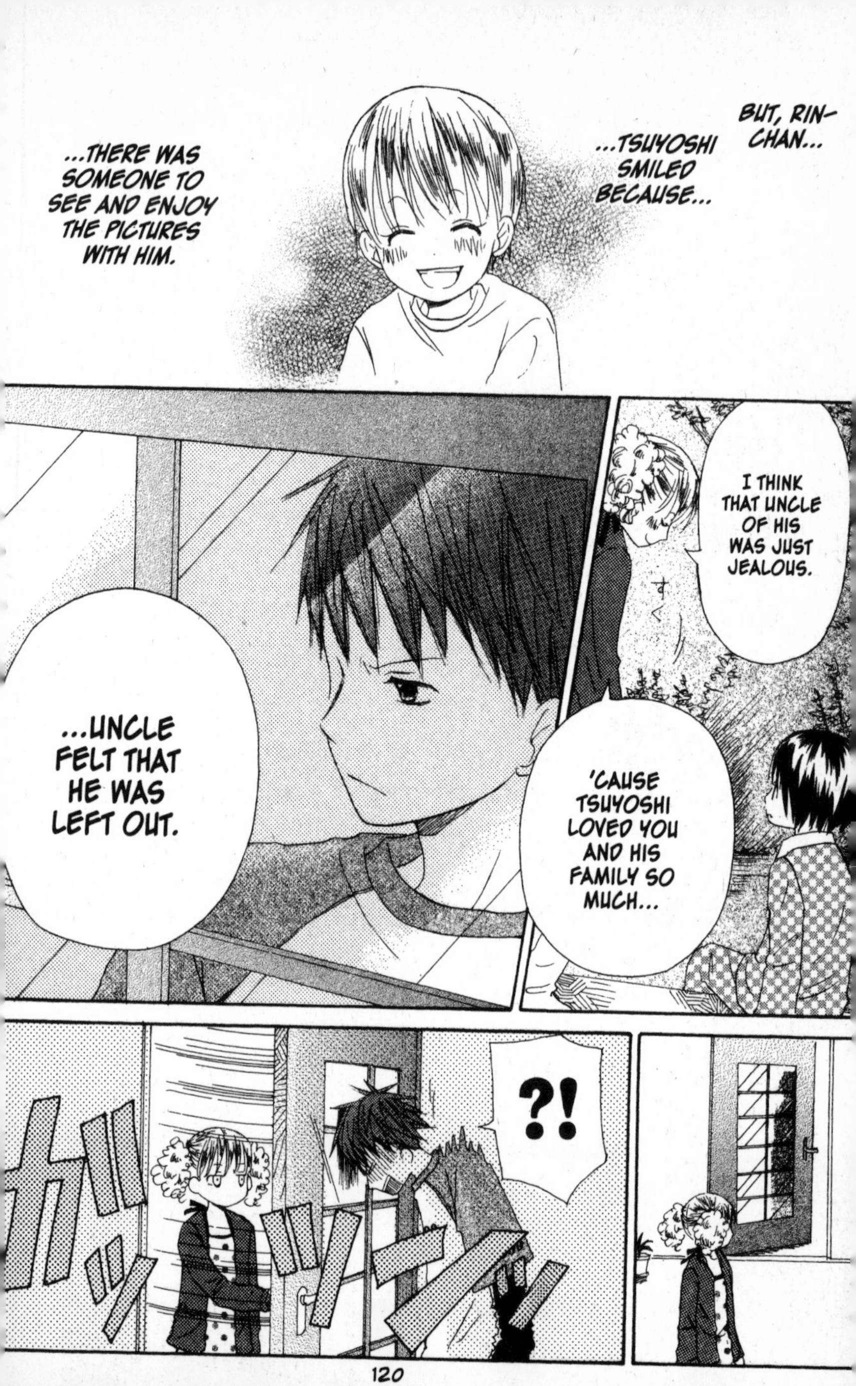
BUT, RIN-CHAN...
...TSUYOSHI SMILED BECAUSE...
...THERE WAS SOMEONE TO SEE AND ENJOY THE PICTURES WITH HIM.
I THINK THAT UNCLE OF HIS WAS JUST JEALOUS.
すく
'CAUSE TSUYOSHI LOVED YOU AND HIS FAMILY SO MUCH...
...UNCLE FELT THAT HE WAS LEFT OUT.
?!

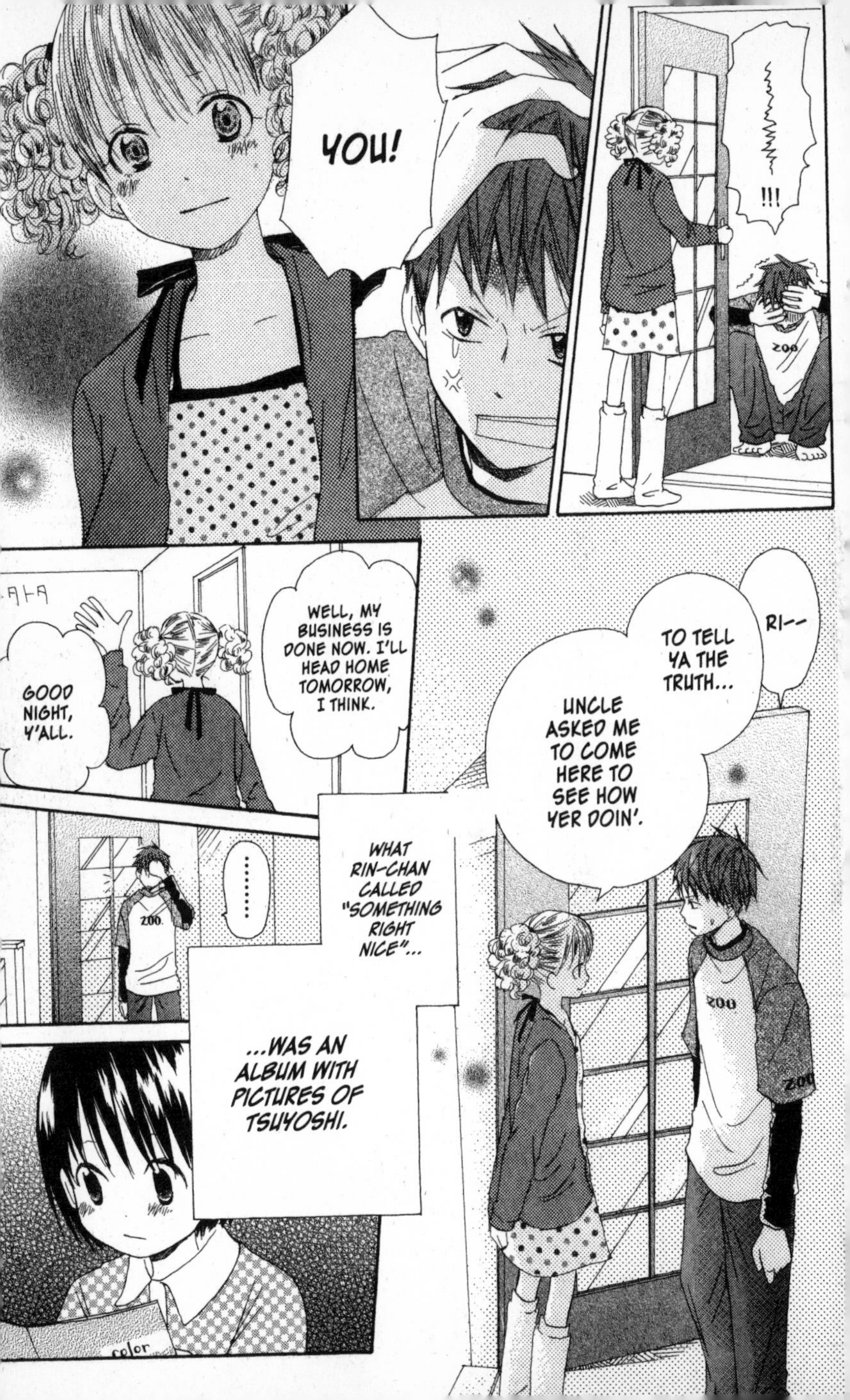

!!!
YOU!
RI--
TO TELL YA THE TRUTH...
UNCLE ASKED ME TO COME HERE TO SEE HOW YER DOIN'.
WELL, MY BUSINESS IS DONE NOW. I'LL HEAD HOME TOMORROW, I THINK.
GOOD NIGHT, Y'ALL.
......
WHAT RIN-CHAN CALLED "SOMETHING RIGHT NICE"...
...WAS AN ALBUM WITH PICTURES OF TSUYOSHI.
color

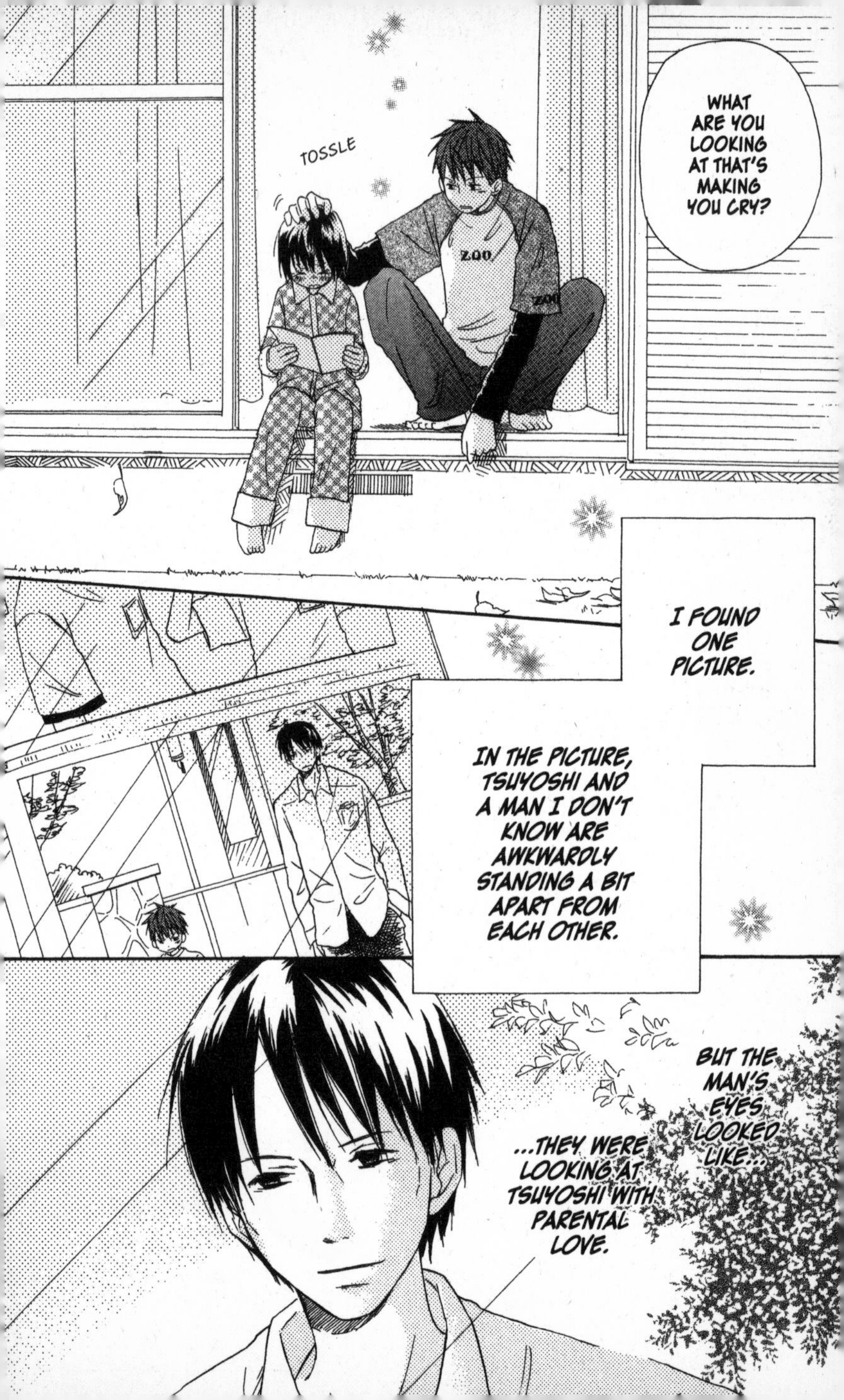

WHAT ARE YOU LOOKING AT THAT'S MAKING YOU CRY?
TOSSLE
I FOUND ONE PICTURE.
IN THE PICTURE, TSUYOSHI AND A MAN I DON'T KNOW ARE AWKWARDLY STANDING A BIT APART FROM EACH OTHER.
BUT THE MAN'S EYES LOOKED LIKE...
...THEY WERE LOOKING AT TSUYOSHI WITH PARENTAL LOVE.

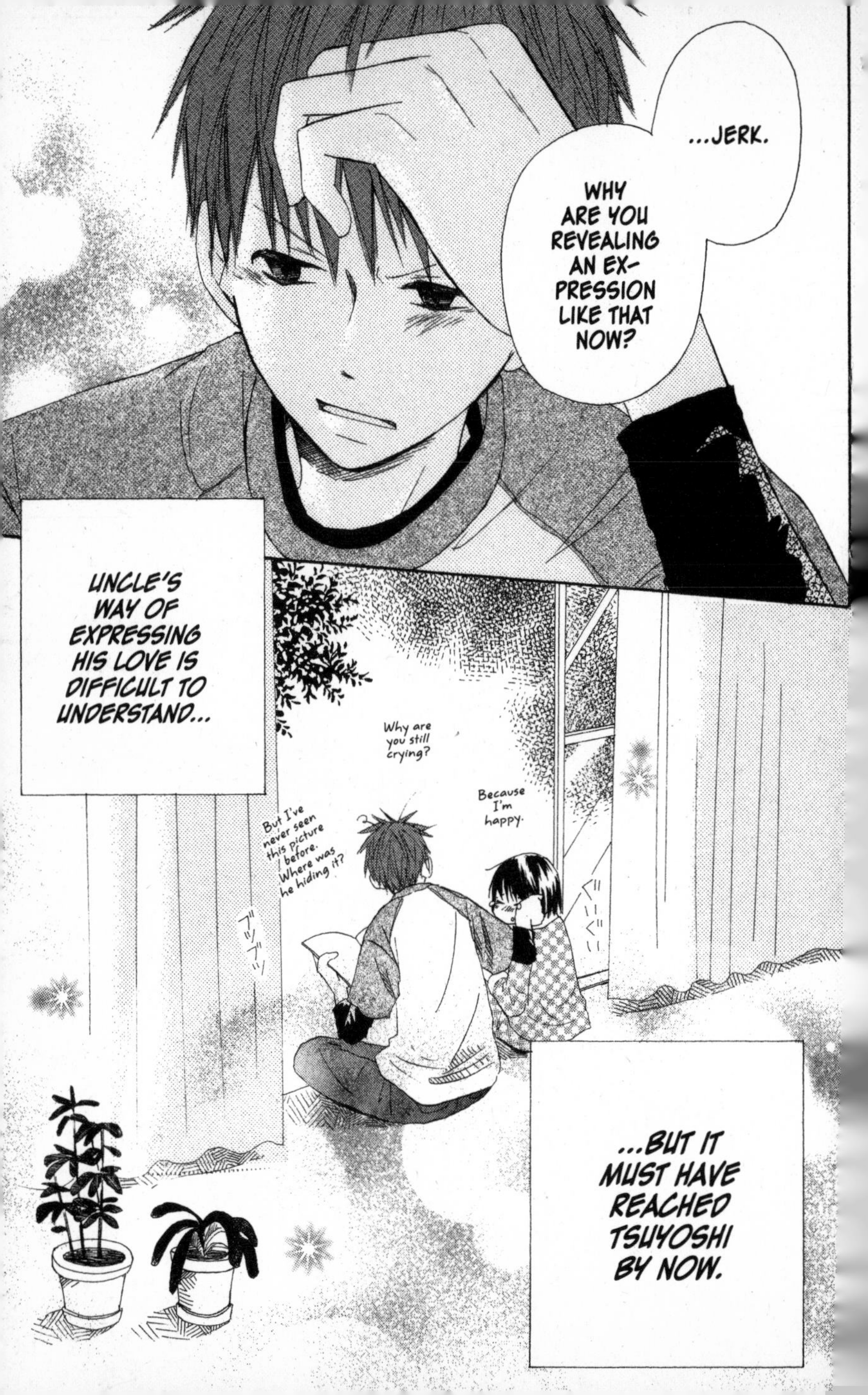
...JERK.
WHY ARE YOU REVEALING AN EXPRESSION LIKE THAT NOW?
UNCLE'S WAY OF EXPRESSING HIS LOVE IS DIFFICULT TO UNDERSTAND...
Why are you still crying?
Because I'm happy.
But I've never seen this picture before. Where was he hiding it?
ブツブツ
...BUT IT MUST HAVE REACHED TSUYOSHI BY NOW.

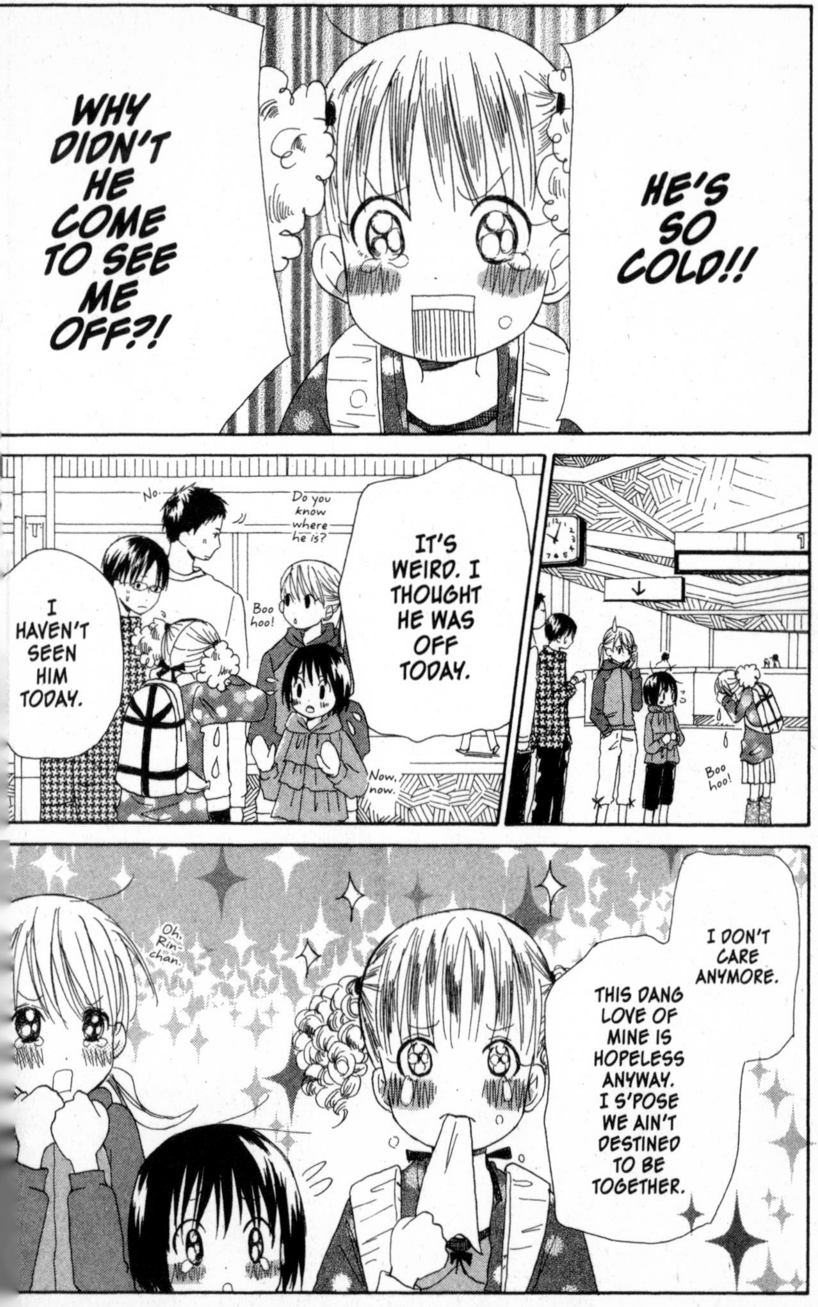
HE'S SO COLD!!
WHY DIDN'T HE COME TO SEE ME OFF?!
Boo hoo!
IT'S WEIRD. I THOUGHT HE WAS OFF TODAY.
Do you know where he is?
No.
Boo hoo!
I HAVEN'T SEEN HIM TODAY.
Now, now.
I DON'T CARE ANYMORE.
THIS DANG LOVE OF MINE IS HOPELESS ANYWAY. I S'POSE WE AIN'T DESTINED TO BE TOGETHER.
Oh, Rin-chan.

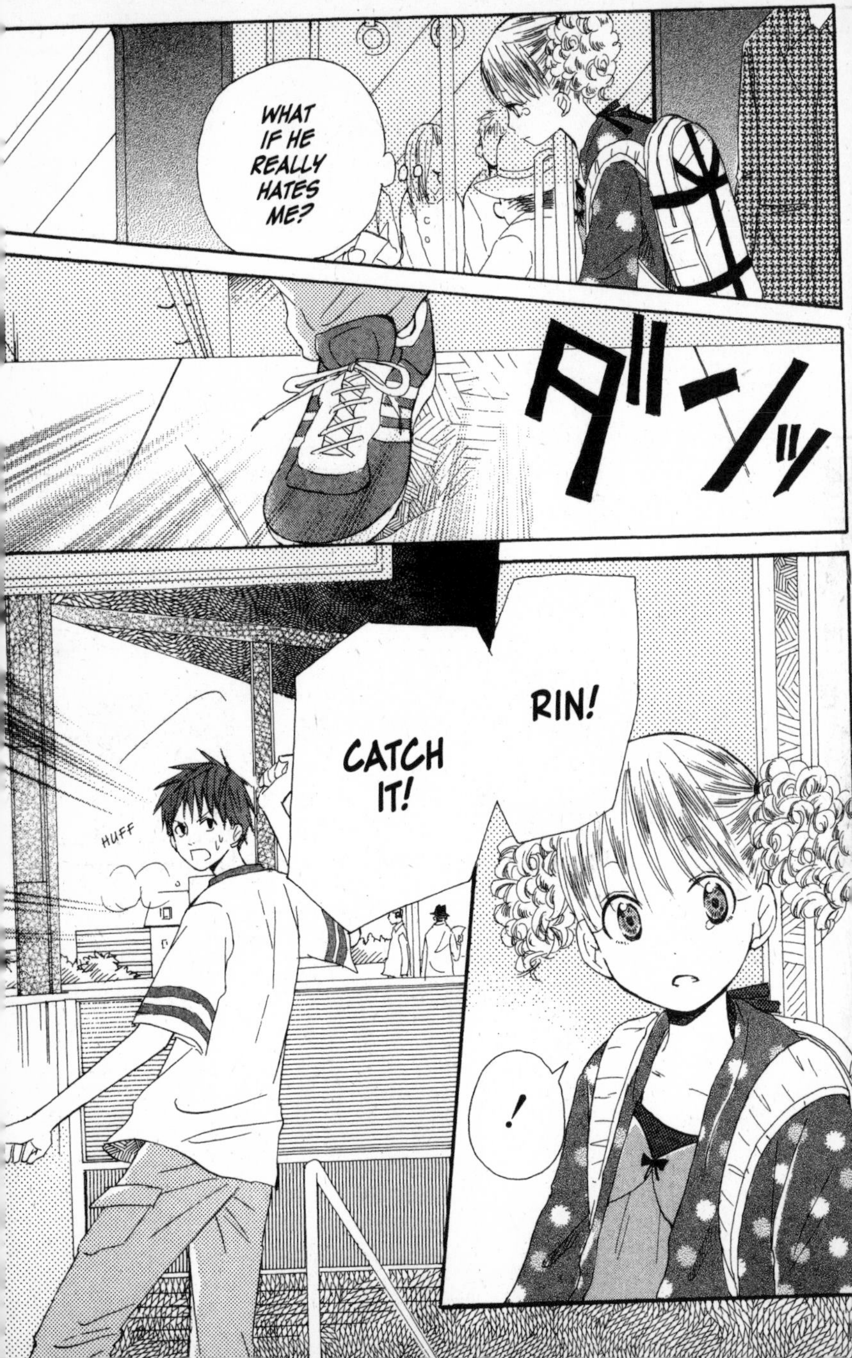
WHAT IF HE REALLY HATES ME?
ダーンッ
RIN!
CATCH IT!
HUFF
!

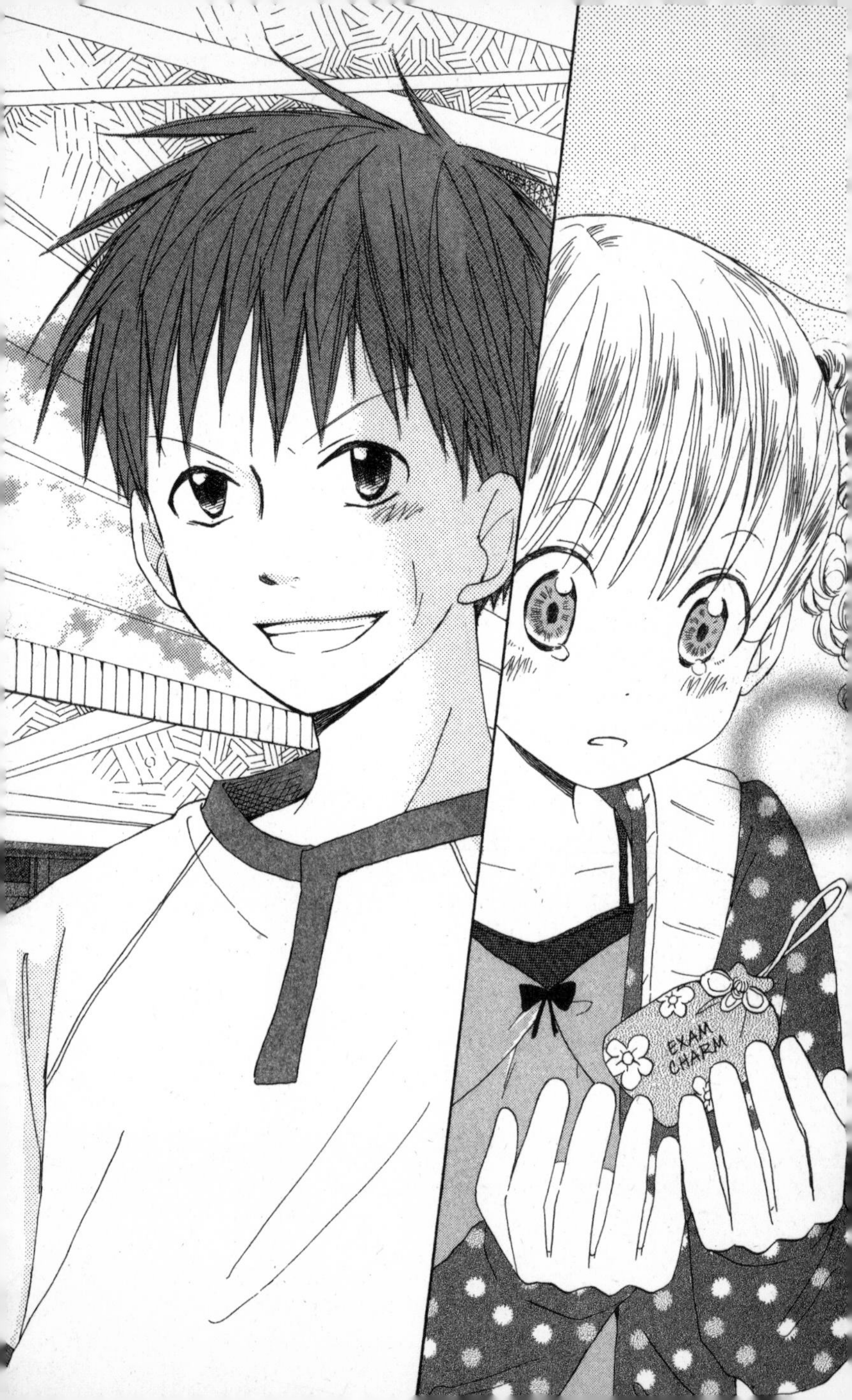
EXAM CHARM

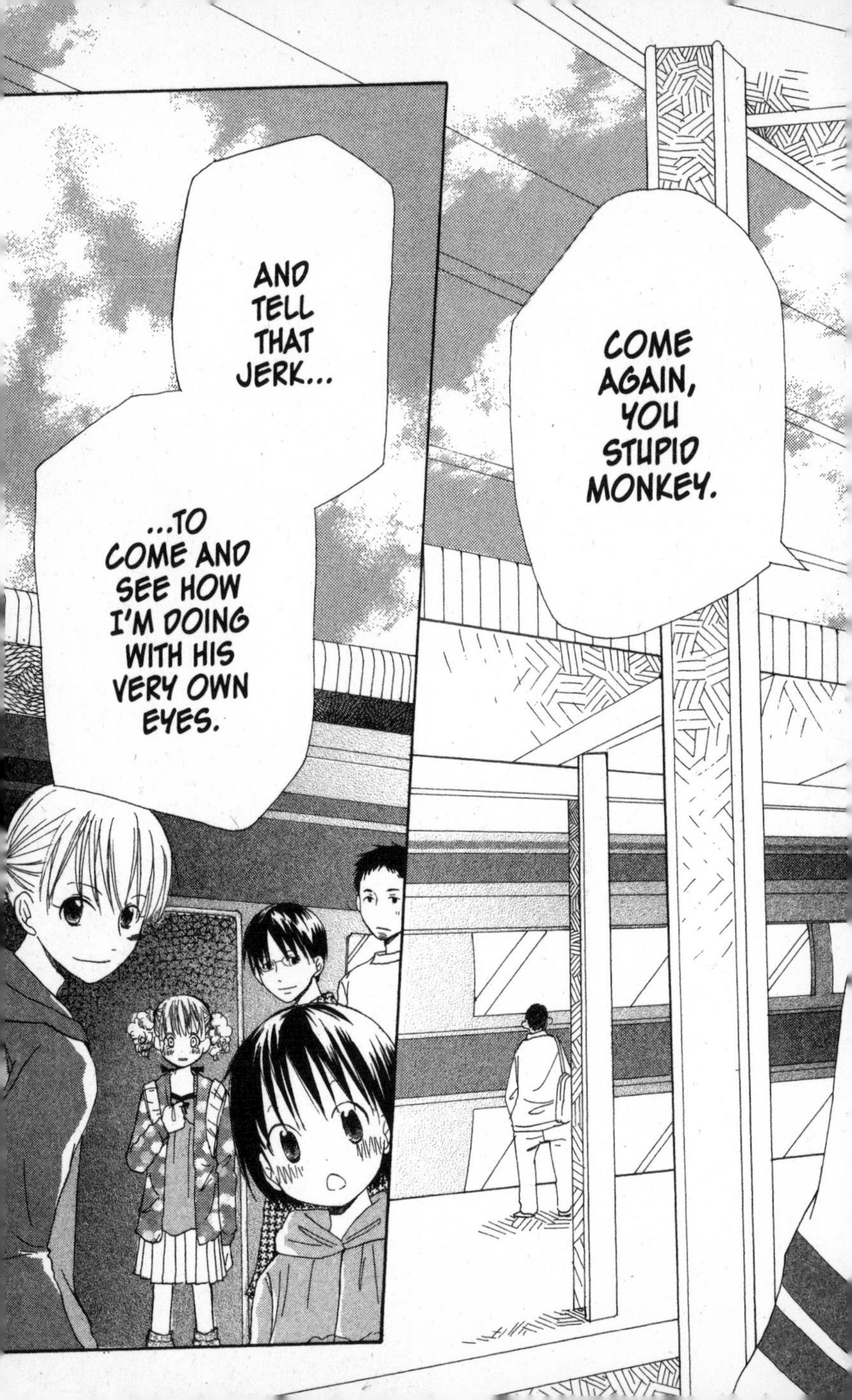
COME AGAIN, YOU STUPID MONKEY.
AND TELL THAT JERK...
...TO COME AND SEE HOW I'M DOING WITH HIS VERY OWN EYES.

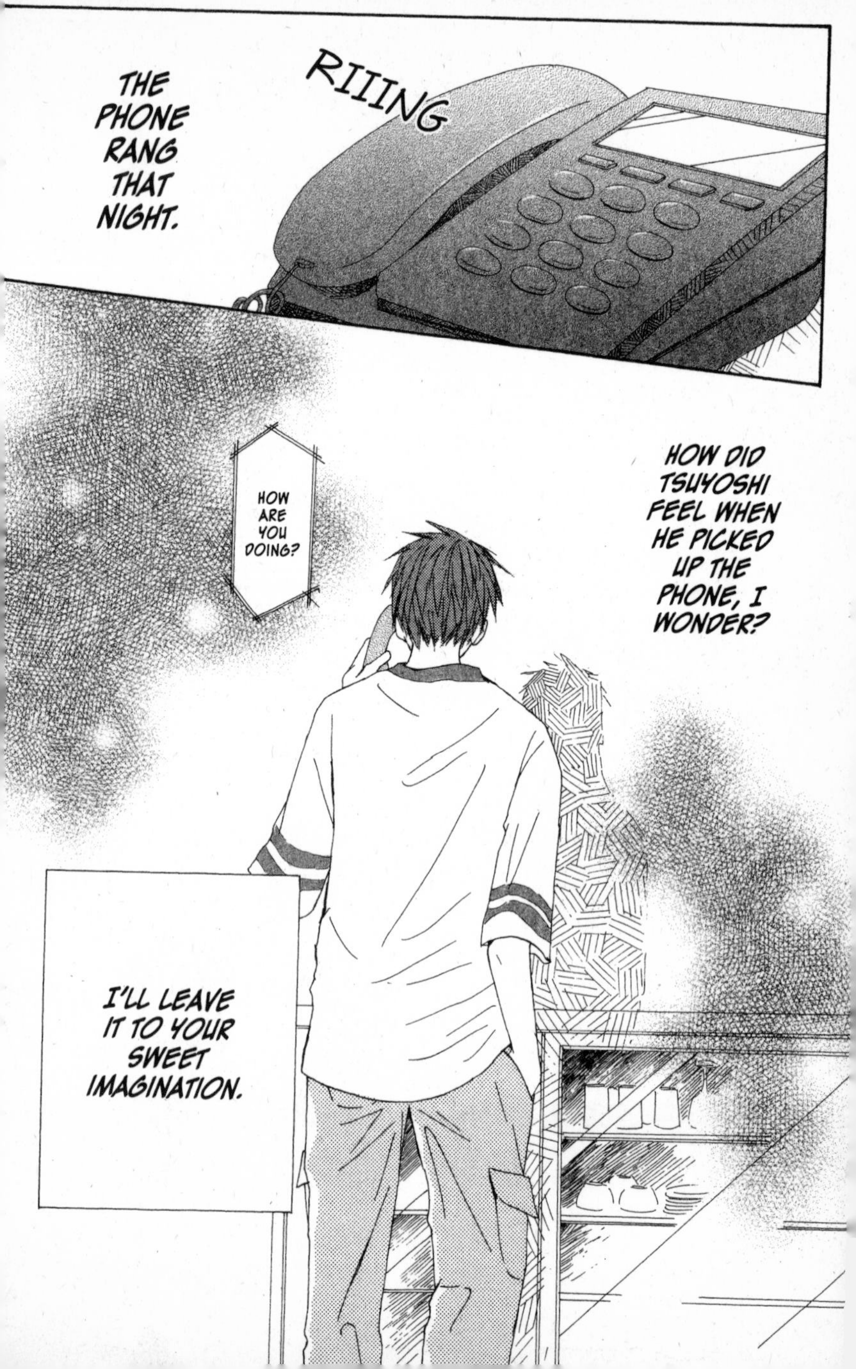
RIIING
THE PHONE RANG THAT NIGHT.
HOW DID TSUYOSHI FEEL WHEN HE PICKED UP THE PHONE, I WONDER?
HOW ARE YOU DOING?
I'LL LEAVE IT TO YOUR SWEET IMAGINATION.

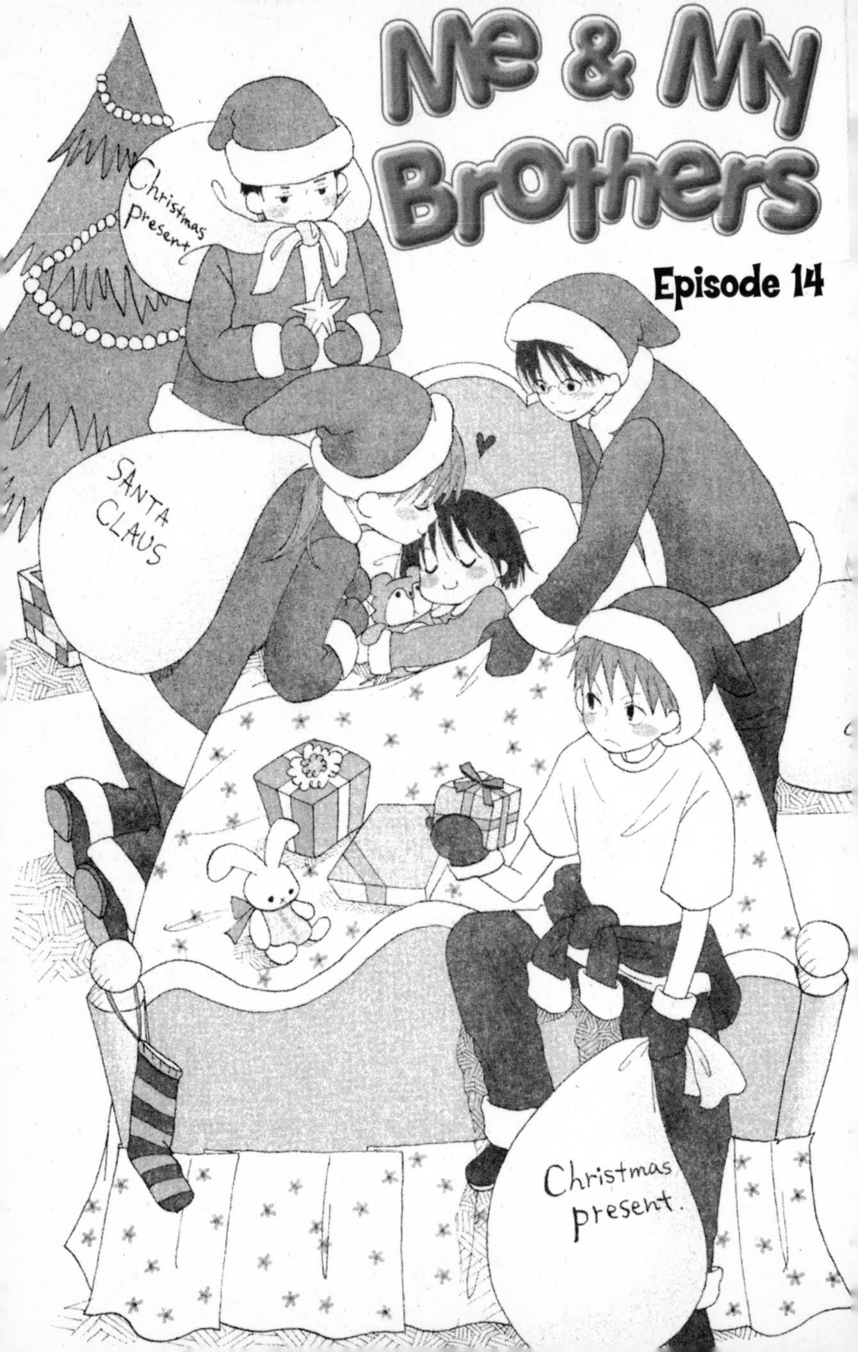
Me & My Brothers
Episode 14
Christmas present
SANTA CLAUS
Christmas present.

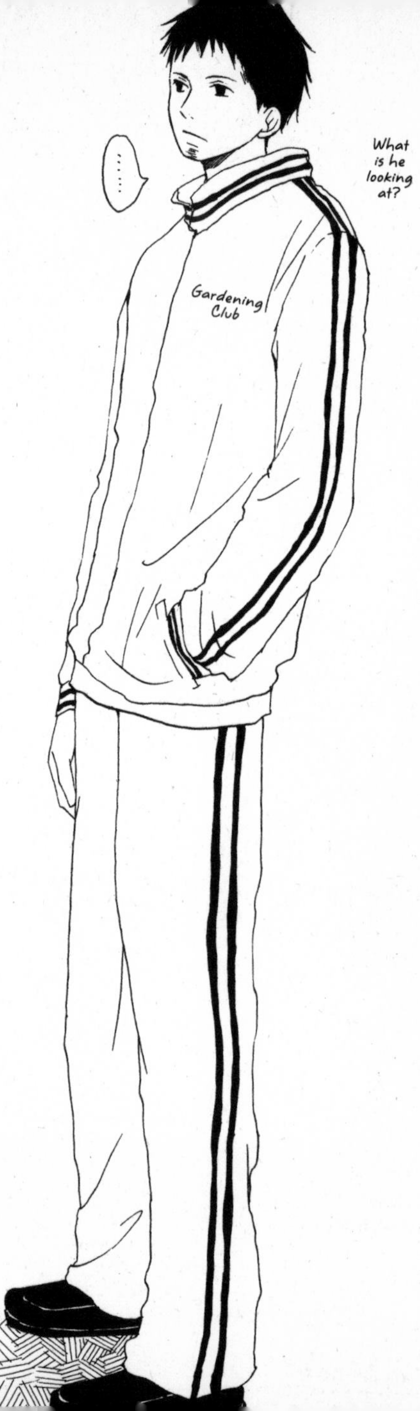
……
Gardening Club
What is he looking at?

Takeshi Miyashita

Date of Birth:
April 2nd, 1986
Aries
Blood type: O

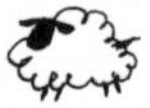

Hobby: Gardening

Height: 187cm

Likes: Trees, flowers and small things

Hates: Low doorways (...how lame)

Charm point: Soul patch

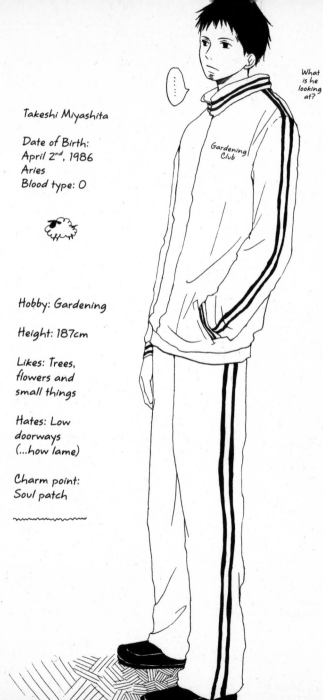

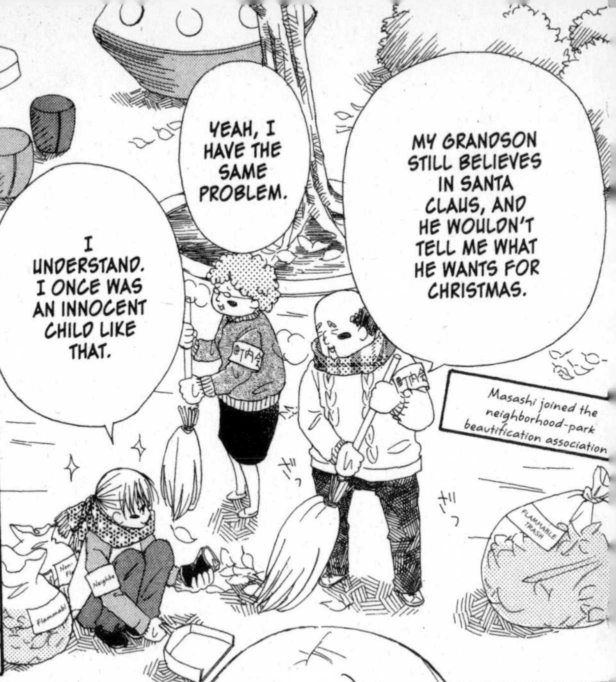
MY GRANDSON STILL BELIEVES IN SANTA CLAUS, AND HE WOULDN'T TELL ME WHAT HE WANTS FOR CHRISTMAS.
Masashi joined the neighborhood-park beautification association
FLAMMABLE TRASH
YEAH, I HAVE THE SAME PROBLEM.
I UNDERSTAND. I ONCE WAS AN INNOCENT CHILD LIKE THAT.

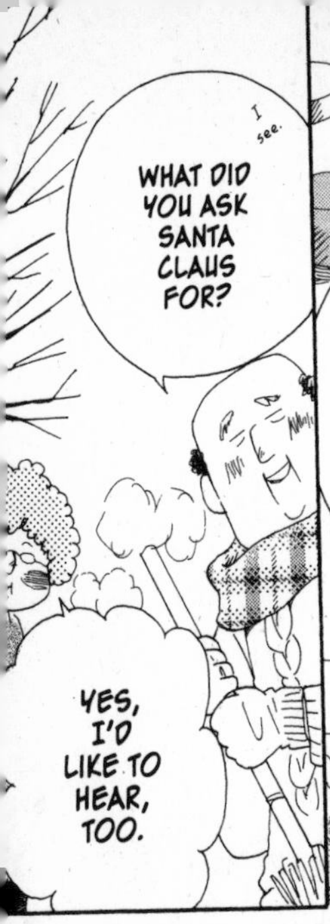
I see.
WHAT DID YOU ASK SANTA CLAUS FOR?
YES, I'D LIKE TO HEAR, TOO.

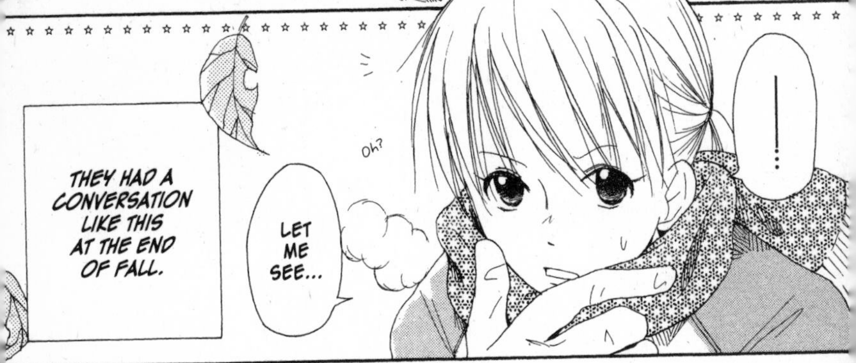
......!
Oh?
LET ME SEE...
THEY HAD A CONVERSATION LIKE THIS AT THE END OF FALL.

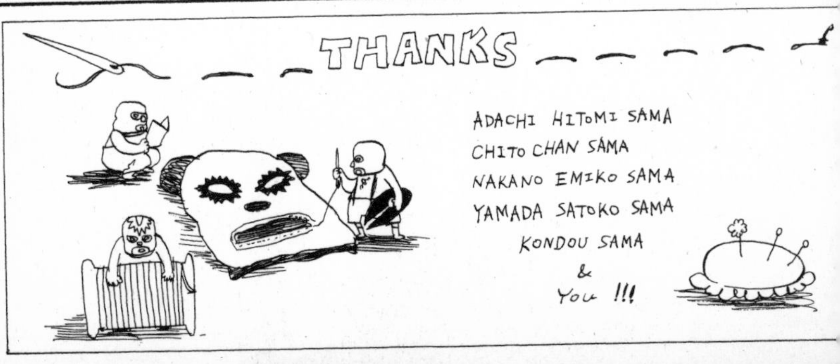
THANKS
ADACHI HITOMI SAMA
CHITO CHAN SAMA
NAKANO EMIKO SAMA
YAMADA SATOKO SAMA
KONDOU SAMA
&
YOU !!!

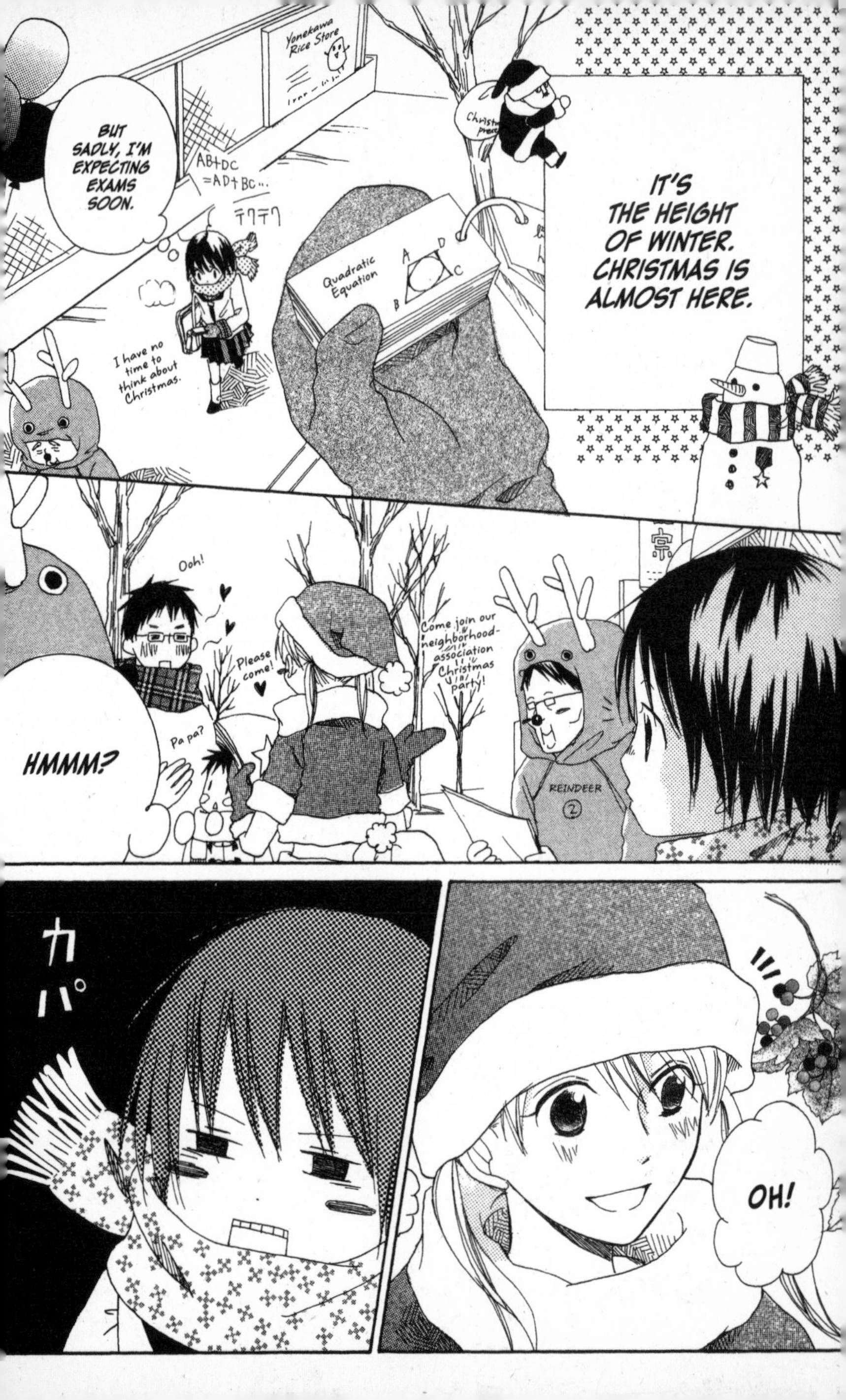
IT'S THE HEIGHT OF WINTER. CHRISTMAS IS ALMOST HERE.
Yonekawa Rice Store
Quadratic Equation
BUT SADLY, I'M EXPECTING EXAMS SOON.
AB+DC =AD+BC...
テクテク
I have no time to think about Christmas.
Come join our neighborhood-association Christmas party!
REINDEER
Please come!
Ooh!
Pa pa?
HMMM?
OH!
カパ

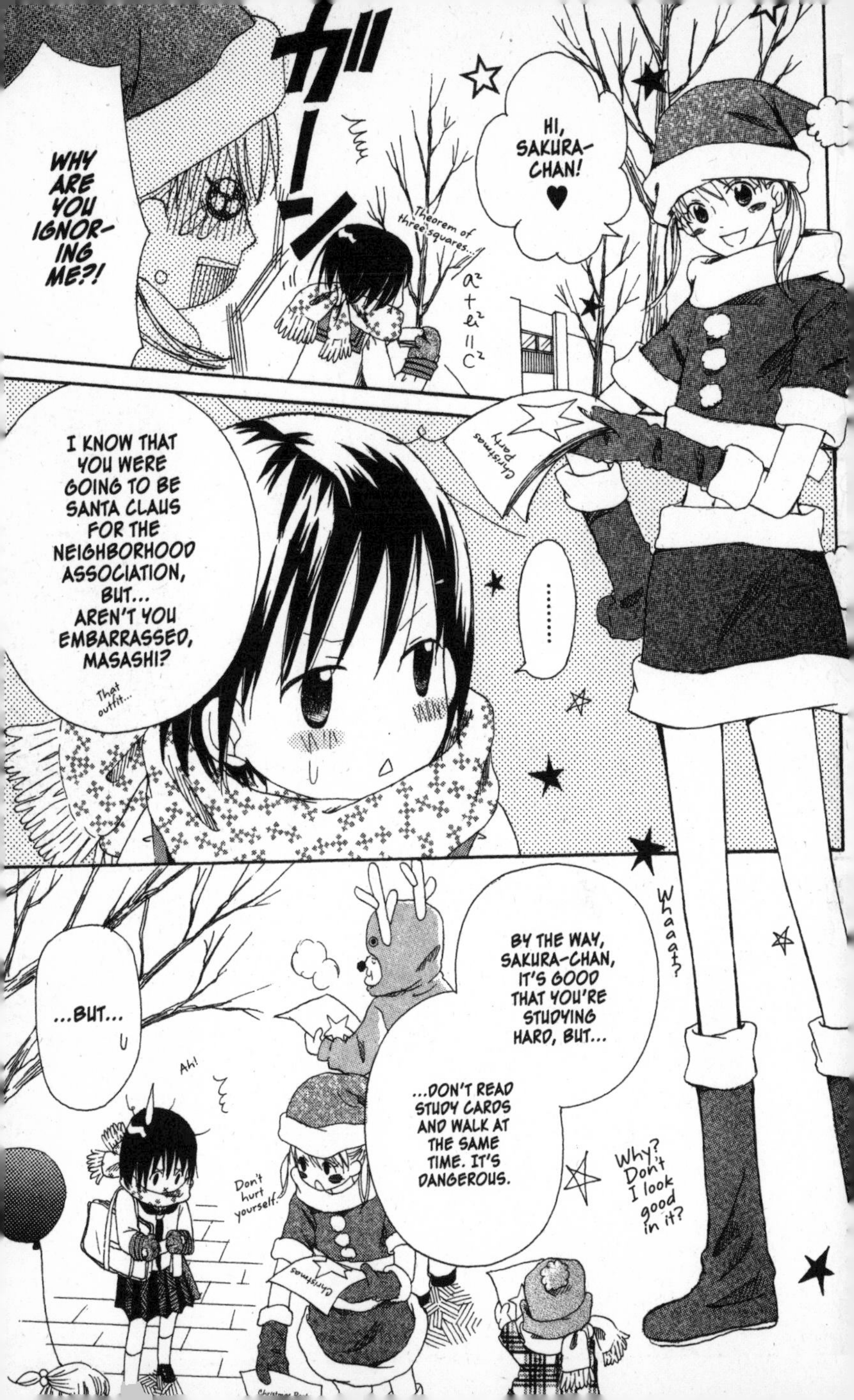

HI, SAKURA-CHAN! ♥
ガーン
Theorem of three squares...
a² + b² = c²
WHY ARE YOU IGNORING ME?!
......
I KNOW THAT YOU WERE GOING TO BE SANTA CLAUS FOR THE NEIGHBORHOOD ASSOCIATION, BUT... AREN'T YOU EMBARRASSED, MASASHI?
That outfit...
Whaaaat?
Why? Don't I look good in it?
BY THE WAY, SAKURA-CHAN, IT'S GOOD THAT YOU'RE STUDYING HARD, BUT...
...DON'T READ STUDY CARDS AND WALK AT THE SAME TIME. IT'S DANGEROUS.
Don't hurt yourself.
Ah!
...BUT...

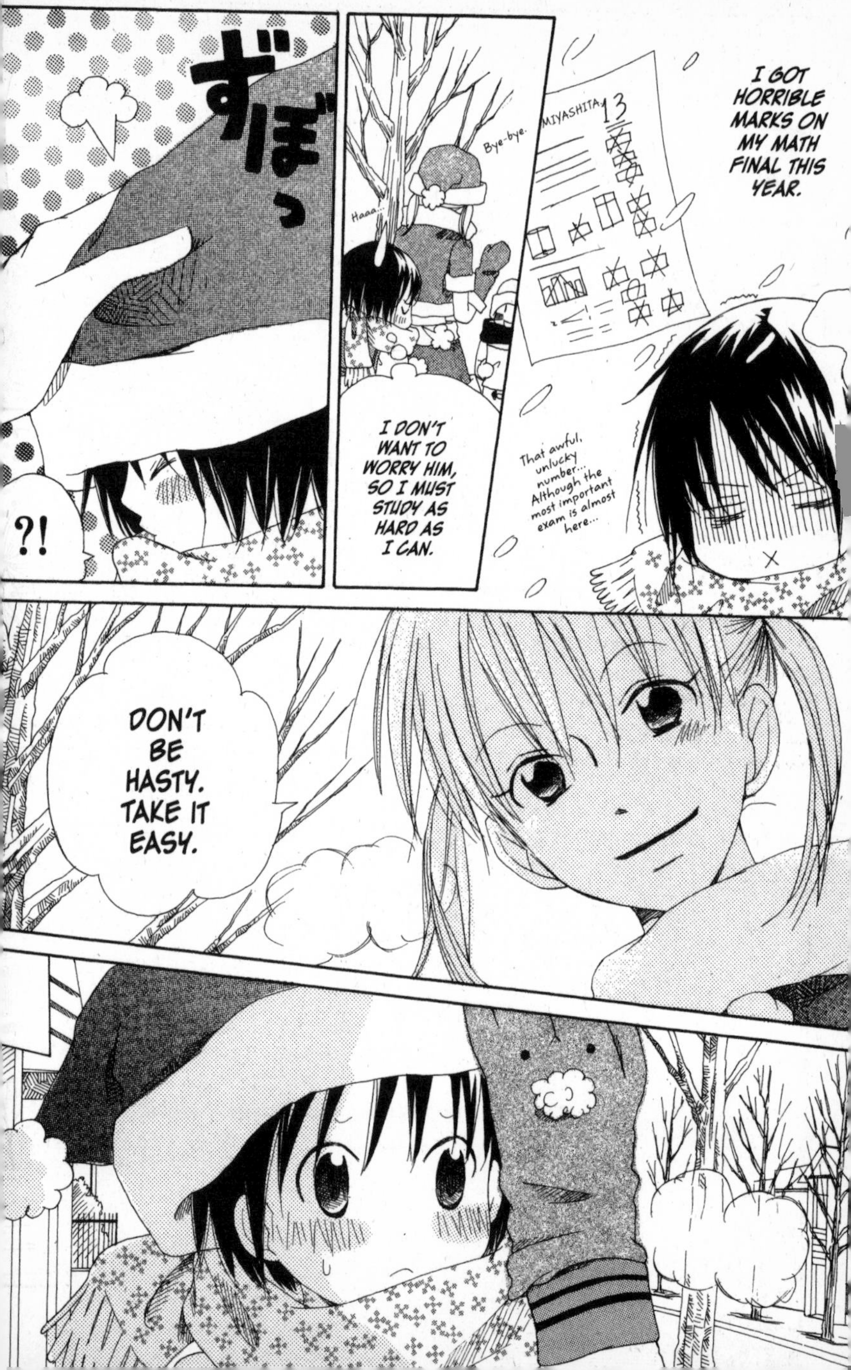

I GOT HORRIBLE MARKS ON MY MATH FINAL THIS YEAR.
MIYASHITA 13
That awful, unlucky number... Although the most important exam is almost here...
Bye-bye.
Haaa...
I DON'T WANT TO WORRY HIM, SO I MUST STUDY AS HARD AS I CAN.
ずぼっ
?!
DON'T BE HASTY. TAKE IT EASY.

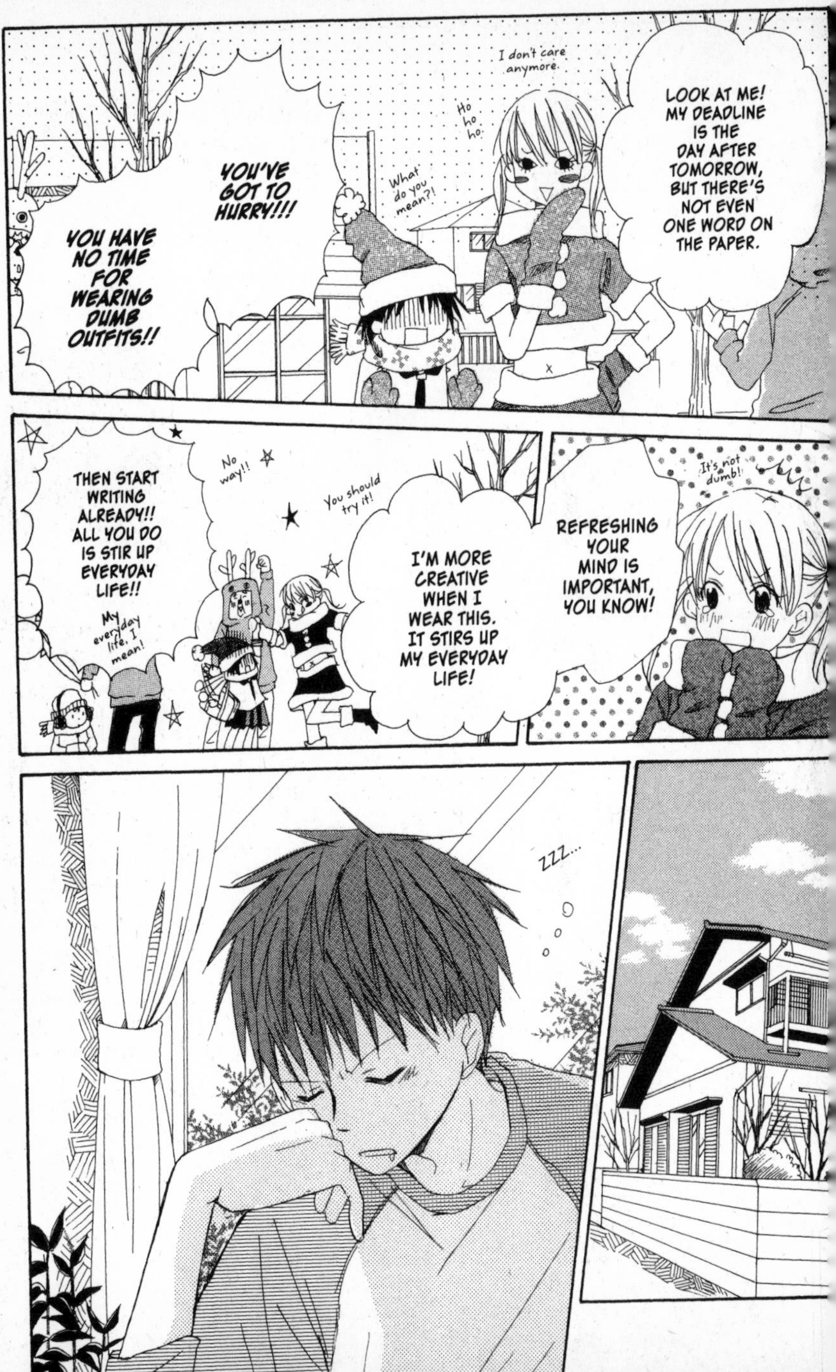
LOOK AT ME! MY DEADLINE IS THE DAY AFTER TOMORROW, BUT THERE'S NOT EVEN ONE WORD ON THE PAPER.
I don't care anymore.
Ho ho ho.
What do you mean?!
YOU'VE GOT TO HURRY!!!
YOU HAVE NO TIME FOR WEARING DUMB OUTFITS!!
It's not dumb!
REFRESHING YOUR MIND IS IMPORTANT, YOU KNOW!
You should try it!
I'M MORE CREATIVE WHEN I WEAR THIS. IT STIRS UP MY EVERYDAY LIFE!
No way!!
THEN START WRITING ALREADY!! ALL YOU DO IS STIR UP EVERYDAY LIFE!!
My everyday life, I mean!
ZZZ...

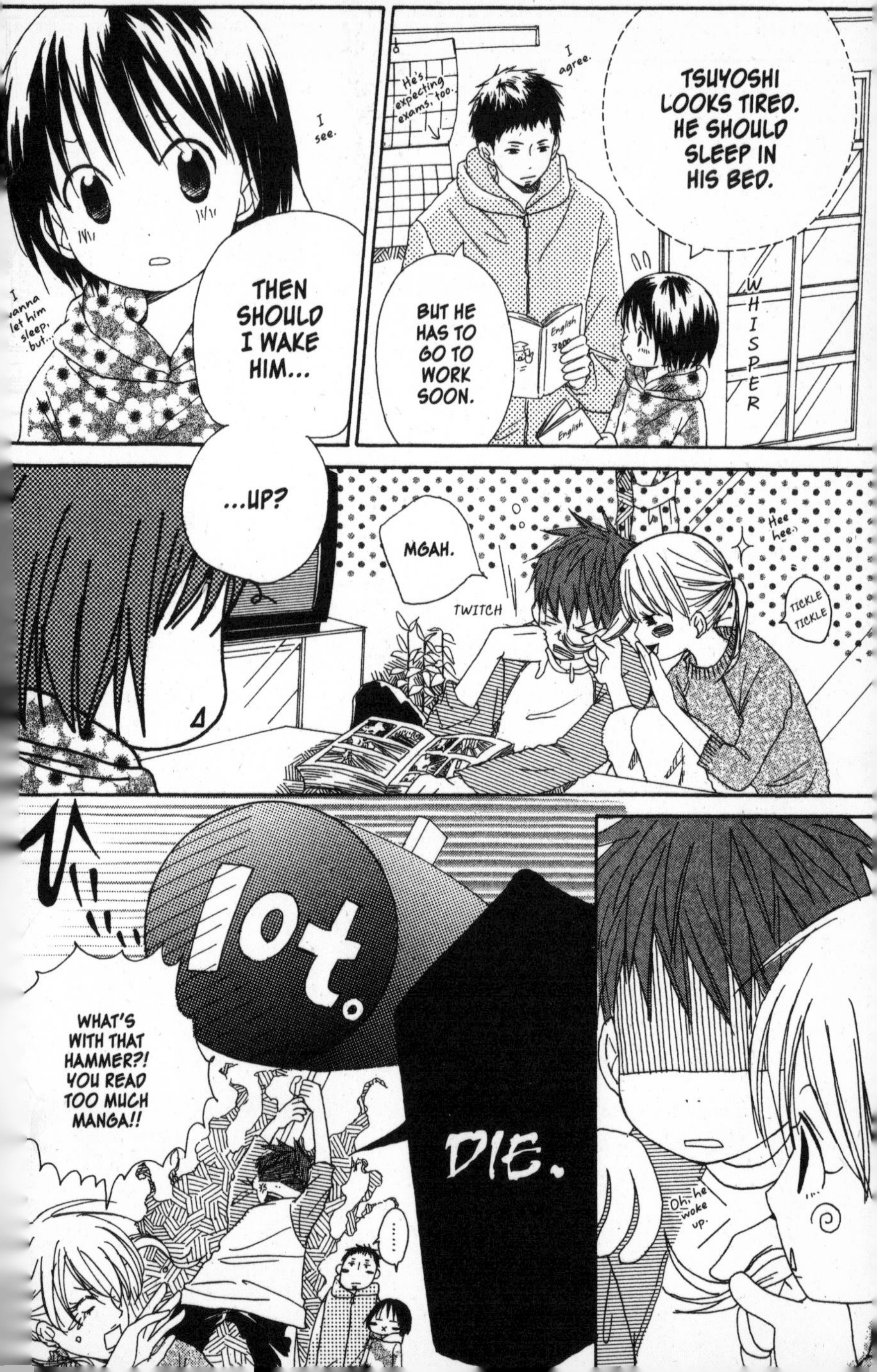
TSUYOSHI LOOKS TIRED. HE SHOULD SLEEP IN HIS BED.
WHISPER
I agree.
He's expecting exams, too.
BUT HE HAS TO GO TO WORK SOON.
English 3000
English
I see.
THEN SHOULD I WAKE HIM...
I wanna let him sleep, but...
...UP?
Hee hee.
TICKLE TICKLE
MGAH.
TWITCH
DIE.
Oh, he woke up.
...
10t.
WHAT'S WITH THAT HAMMER?! YOU READ TOO MUCH MANGA!!
......

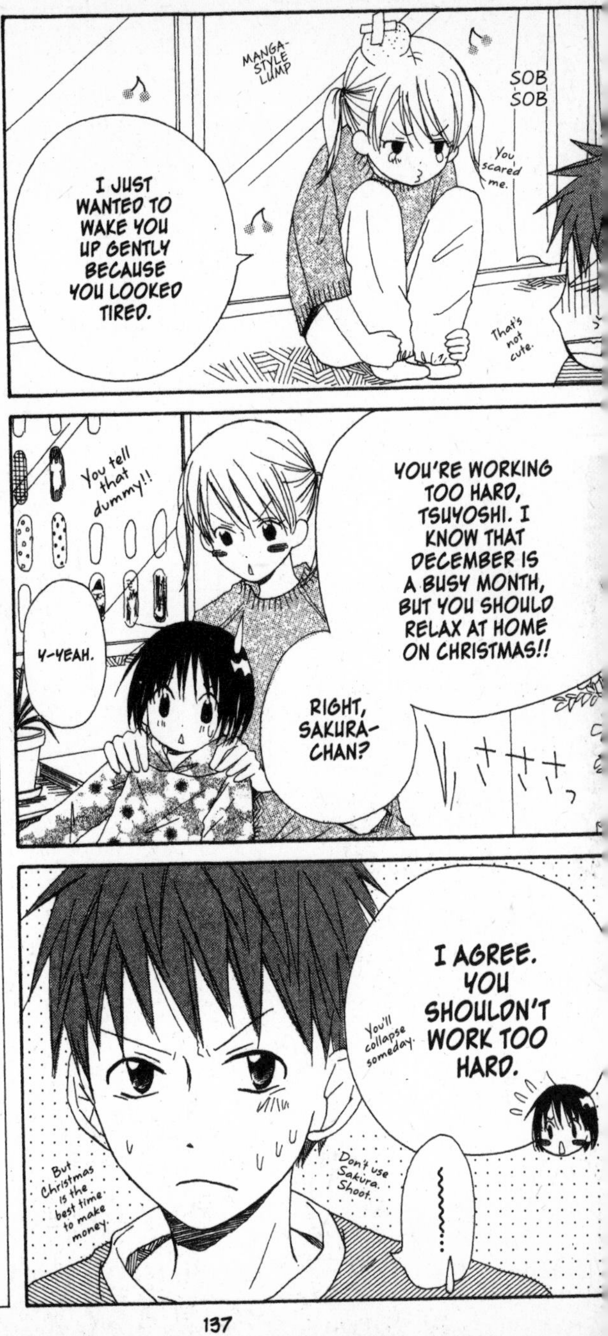
SOB SOB
You scared me.
That's not cute.
MANGA-STYLE LUMP
I JUST WANTED TO WAKE YOU UP GENTLY BECAUSE YOU LOOKED TIRED.
YOU'RE WORKING TOO HARD, TSUYOSHI. I KNOW THAT DECEMBER IS A BUSY MONTH, BUT YOU SHOULD RELAX AT HOME ON CHRISTMAS!!
RIGHT, SAKURA-CHAN?
You tell that dummy!!
Y-YEAH.
I AGREE. YOU SHOULDN'T WORK TOO HARD.
You'll collapse someday.
......
Don't use Sakura. Shoot.
But Christmas is the best time to make money.

☆4☆

About fireflies.

When I was on a firefly hunt, I really slapped them to the ground.
A lot of people around me have never even seen fireflies. I thought that everyone slapped them with a fan to catch them, but now I'm not so sure. Let me know if you think I'm correct.
Let's make the "Firefly Slapping Association."

...Firefly fans will kill me.

I'm sorry.
I won't do it again.

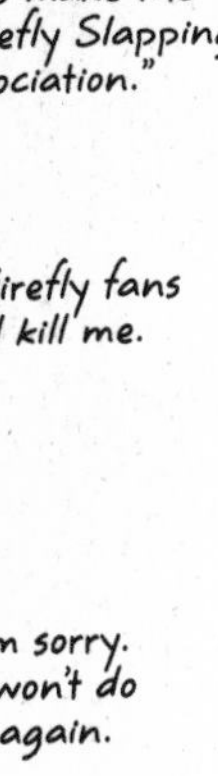

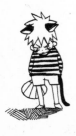

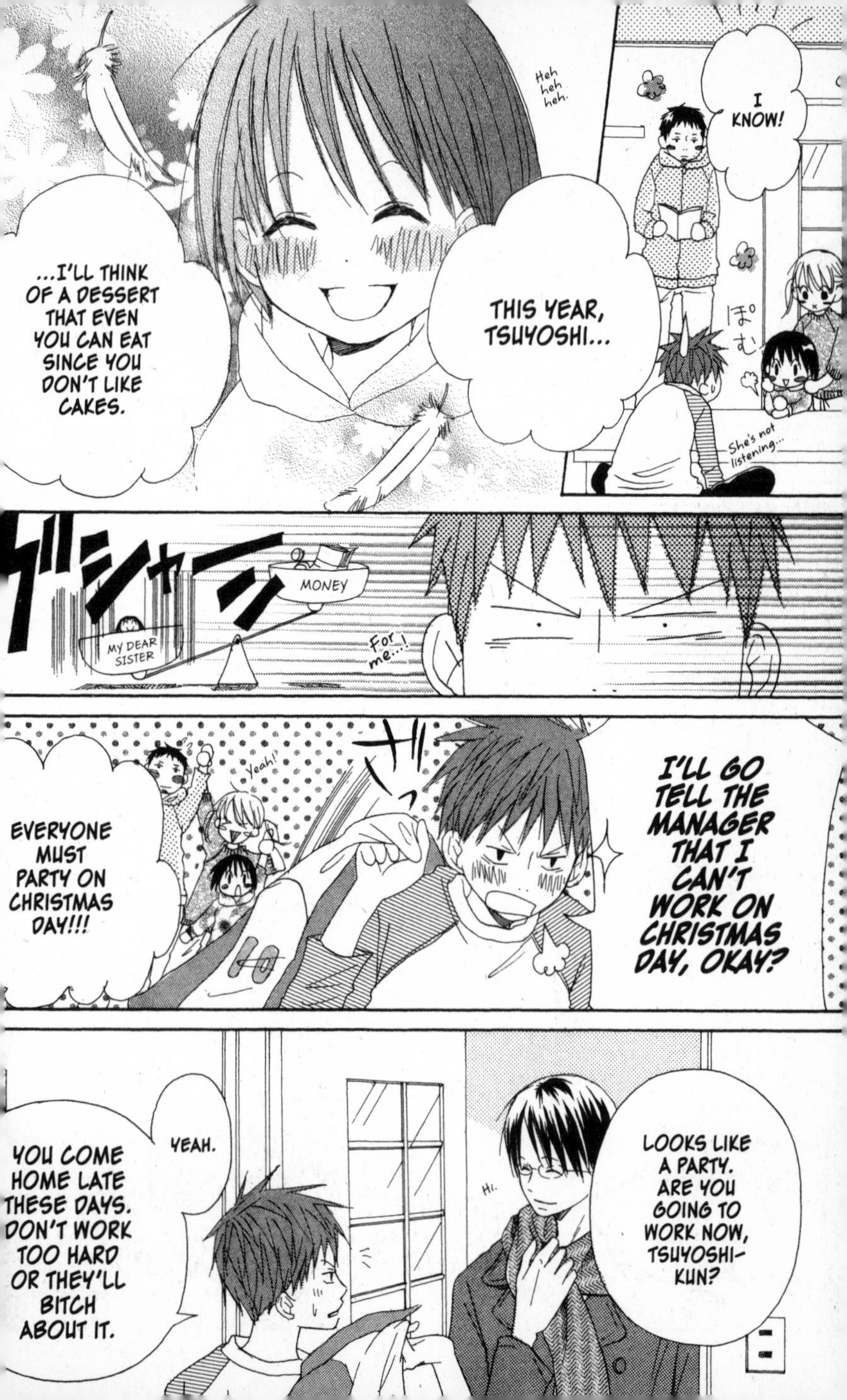
I KNOW!
ぽむ
She's not listening...
Heh heh heh.
THIS YEAR, TSUYOSHI...
...I'LL THINK OF A DESSERT THAT EVEN YOU CAN EAT SINCE YOU DON'T LIKE CAKES.
ザシャーン
MONEY
MY DEAR SISTER
For me...!
I'LL GO TELL THE MANAGER THAT I CAN'T WORK ON CHRISTMAS DAY, OKAY?
EVERYONE MUST PARTY ON CHRISTMAS DAY!!!
Yeah!
LOOKS LIKE A PARTY. ARE YOU GOING TO WORK NOW, TSUYOSHI-KUN?
Hi.
YEAH.
YOU COME HOME LATE THESE DAYS. DON'T WORK TOO HARD OR THEY'LL BITCH ABOUT IT.

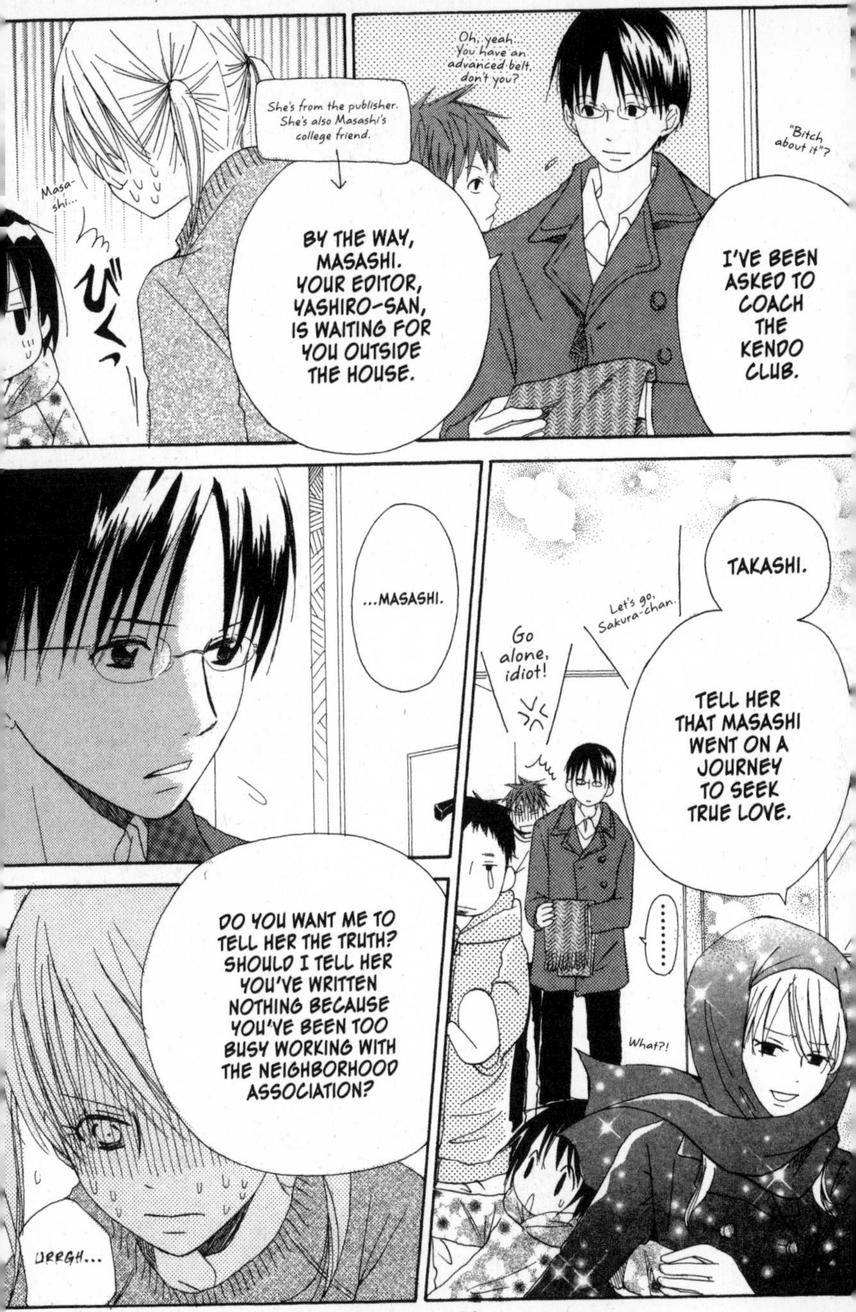
"Bitch about it"?
I'VE BEEN ASKED TO COACH THE KENDO CLUB.
Oh, yeah. You have an advanced belt, don't you?
She's from the publisher. She's also Masashi's college friend.
BY THE WAY, MASASHI. YOUR EDITOR, YASHIRO-SAN, IS WAITING FOR YOU OUTSIDE THE HOUSE.
Masa-shi...
びくっ
TAKASHI.
TELL HER THAT MASASHI WENT ON A JOURNEY TO SEEK TRUE LOVE.
Let's go, Sakura-chan.
Go alone, idiot!
......
What?!
...MASASHI.
DO YOU WANT ME TO TELL HER THE TRUTH? SHOULD I TELL HER YOU'VE WRITTEN NOTHING BECAUSE YOU'VE BEEN TOO BUSY WORKING WITH THE NEIGHBORHOOD ASSOCIATION?
URRGH...

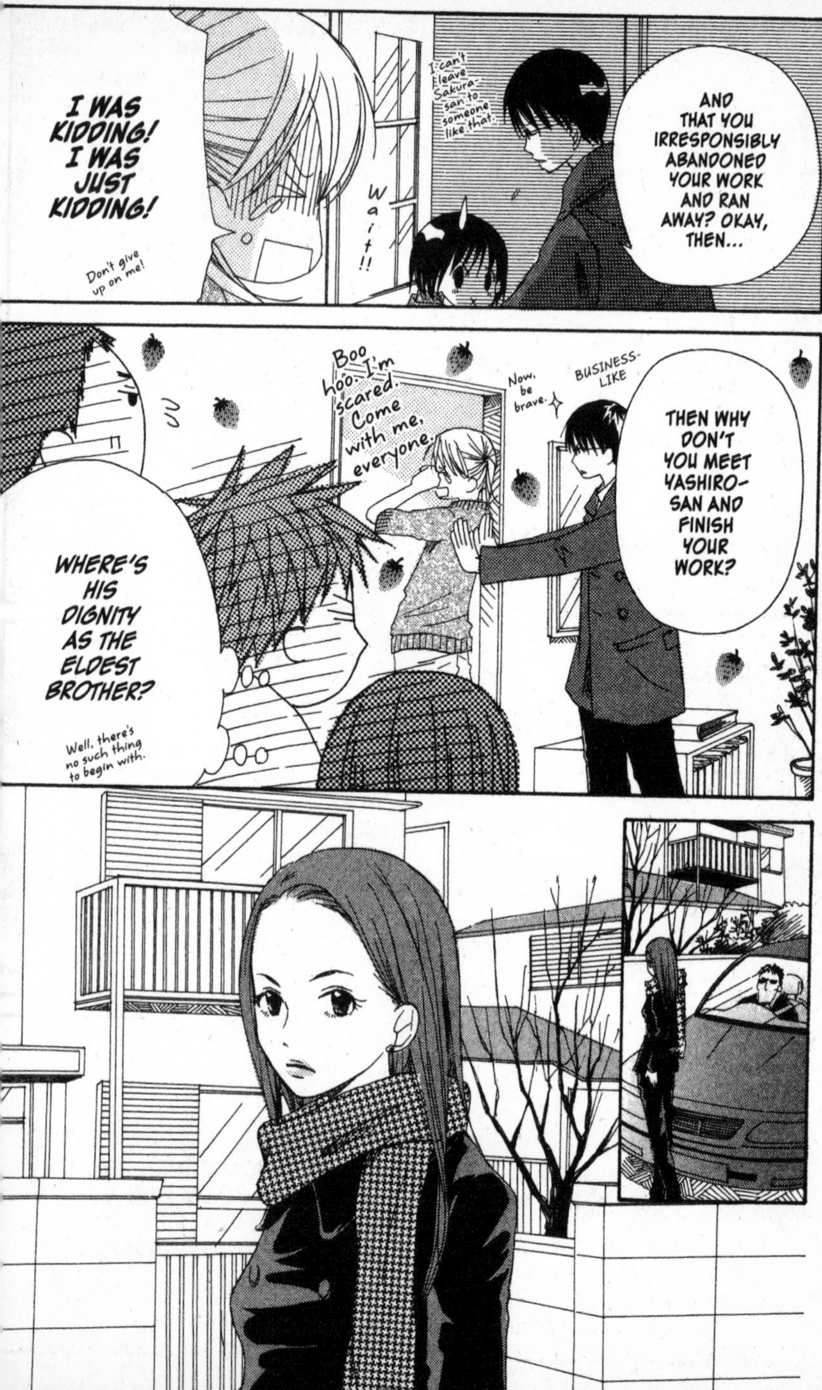
AND THAT YOU IRRESPONSIBLY ABANDONED YOUR WORK AND RAN AWAY? OKAY, THEN...
I can't leave Sakura-san to someone like that.
Wait!!
I WAS KIDDING! I WAS JUST KIDDING!
Don't give up on me!
THEN WHY DON'T YOU MEET YASHIRO-SAN AND FINISH YOUR WORK?
BUSINESS-LIKE
Now, be brave.
Boo hoo. I'm scared. Come with me, everyone.
WHERE'S HIS DIGNITY AS THE ELDEST BROTHER?
Well, there's no such thing to begin with.

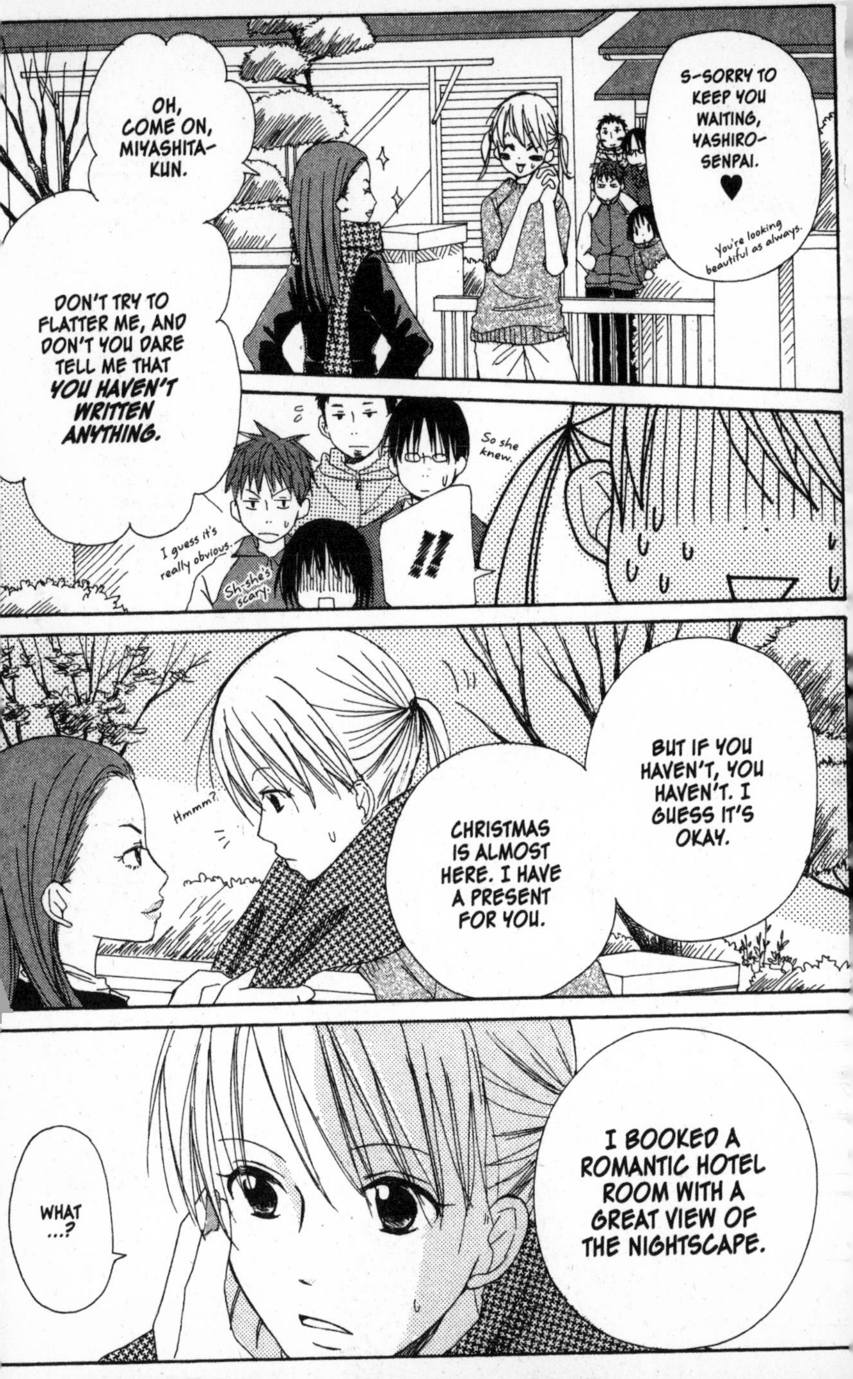
S-SORRY TO KEEP YOU WAITING, YASHIRO-SENPAI. ♥
You're looking beautiful as always.
OH, COME ON, MIYASHITA-KUN.
DON'T TRY TO FLATTER ME, AND DON'T YOU DARE TELL ME THAT ***YOU HAVEN'T WRITTEN ANYTHING.***
!!
So she knew.
Sh-she's scary.
I guess it's really obvious.
BUT IF YOU HAVEN'T, YOU HAVEN'T. I GUESS IT'S OKAY.
CHRISTMAS IS ALMOST HERE. I HAVE A PRESENT FOR YOU.
Hmmm?
I BOOKED A ROMANTIC HOTEL ROOM WITH A GREAT VIEW OF THE NIGHTSCAPE.
WHAT ...?

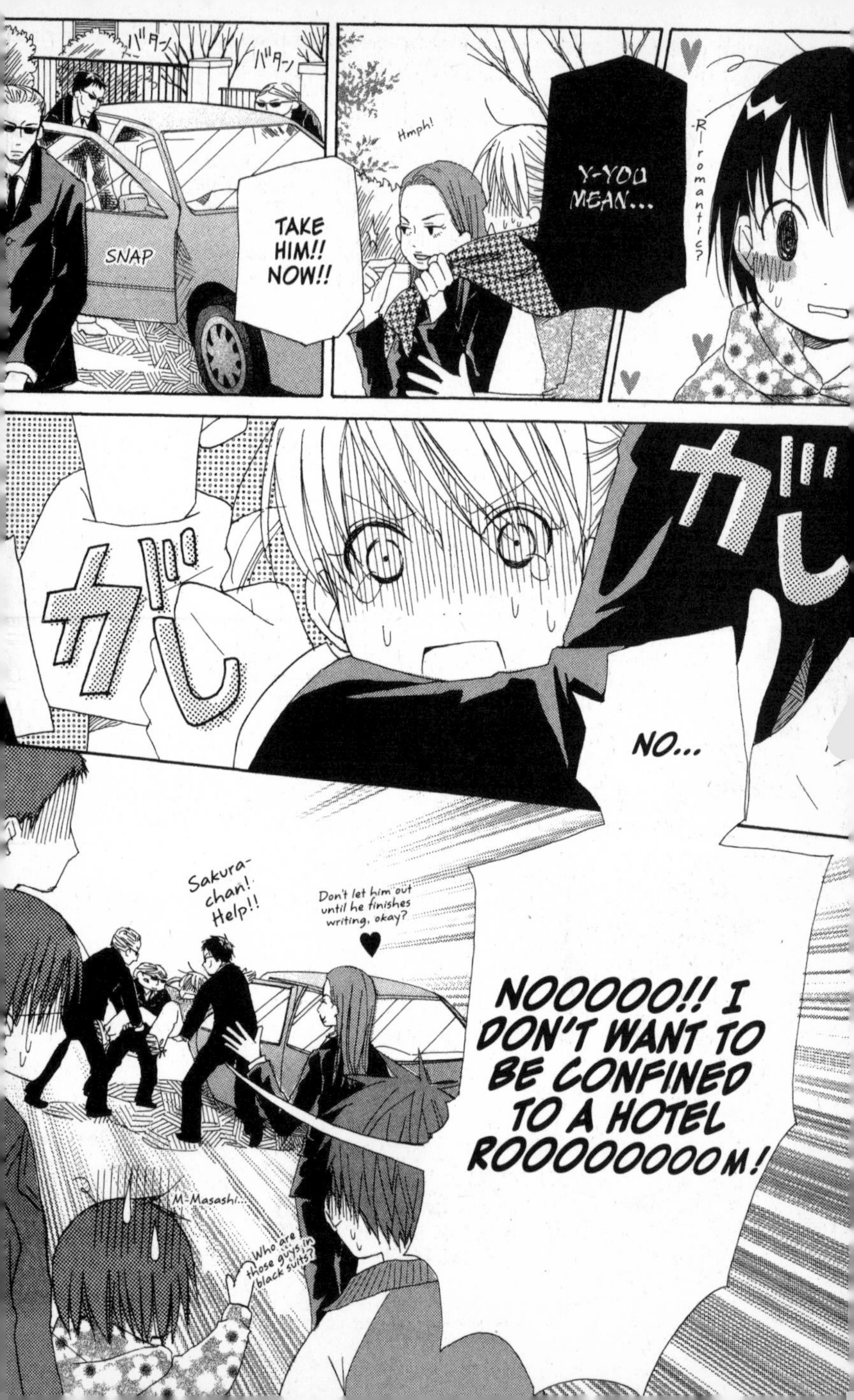
R-romantic?
Y-YOU MEAN...
Hmph!
TAKE HIM!! NOW!!
バターン
バターン
SNAP
ガし
NO...
ガし
NOOOOO!! I DON'T WANT TO BE CONFINED TO A HOTEL ROOOOOOOOM!
Don't let him out until he finishes writing, okay?
Sakura-chan! Help!!
M-Masashi...
Who are those guys in black suits?

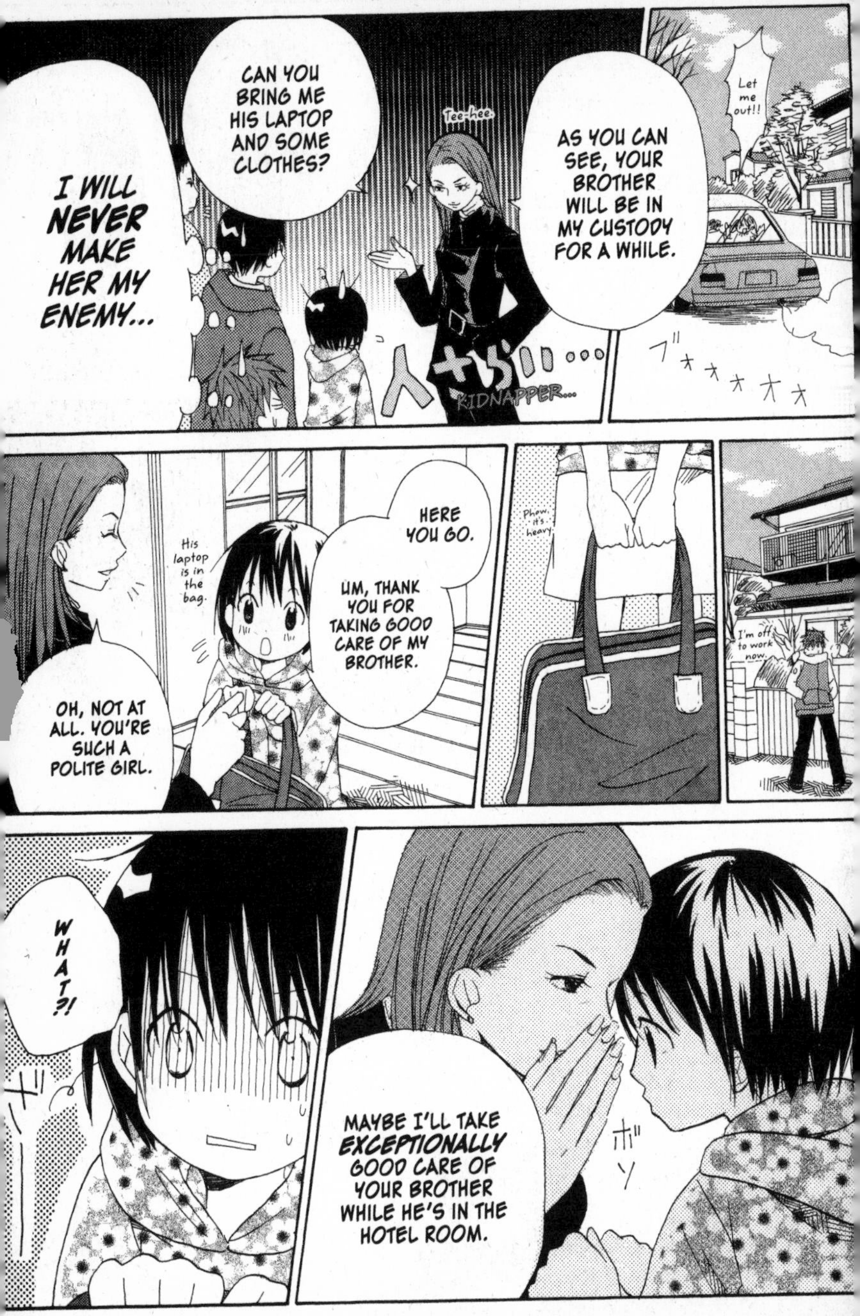

Let me out!!
As you can see, your brother will be in my custody for a while.
Tee-hee.
Can you bring me his laptop and some clothes?
KIDNAPPER...
I WILL NEVER MAKE HER MY ENEMY...
I'm off to work now.
Phew, it's heavy.
Here you go.
Um, thank you for taking good care of my brother.
His laptop is in the bag.
Oh, not at all. You're such a polite girl.
Maybe I'll take exceptionally good care of your brother while he's in the hotel room.
WHAT?!

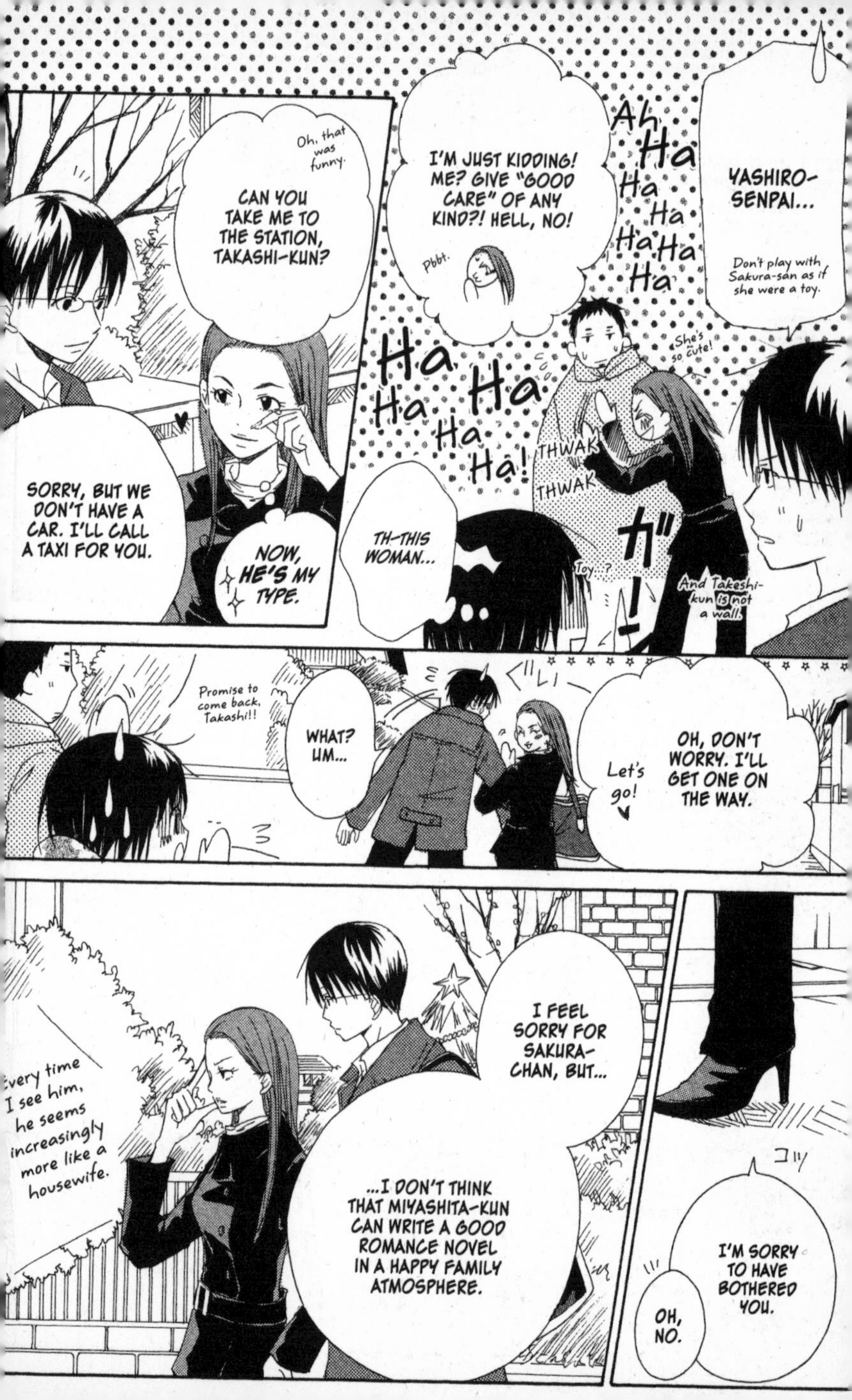
YASHIRO-SENPAI...
Don't play with Sakura-san as if she were a toy.
Ah Ha Ha Ha Ha Ha Ha
I'M JUST KIDDING! ME? GIVE "GOOD CARE" OF ANY KIND?! HELL, NO!
Pbbt.
She's so cute!
Ha Ha Ha Ha Ha!
THWAK
THWAK
TH-THIS WOMAN...
Toy...?
And Takeshi-kun is not a wall.
Oh, that was funny.
CAN YOU TAKE ME TO THE STATION, TAKASHI-KUN?
SORRY, BUT WE DON'T HAVE A CAR. I'LL CALL A TAXI FOR YOU.
NOW, HE'S MY TYPE.
OH, DON'T WORRY. I'LL GET ONE ON THE WAY.
Let's go!
WHAT? UM...
Promise to come back, Takashi!!
I'M SORRY TO HAVE BOTHERED YOU.
OH, NO.
I FEEL SORRY FOR SAKURA-CHAN, BUT...
...I DON'T THINK THAT MIYASHITA-KUN CAN WRITE A GOOD ROMANCE NOVEL IN A HAPPY FAMILY ATMOSPHERE.
Every time I see him, he seems increasingly more like a housewife.

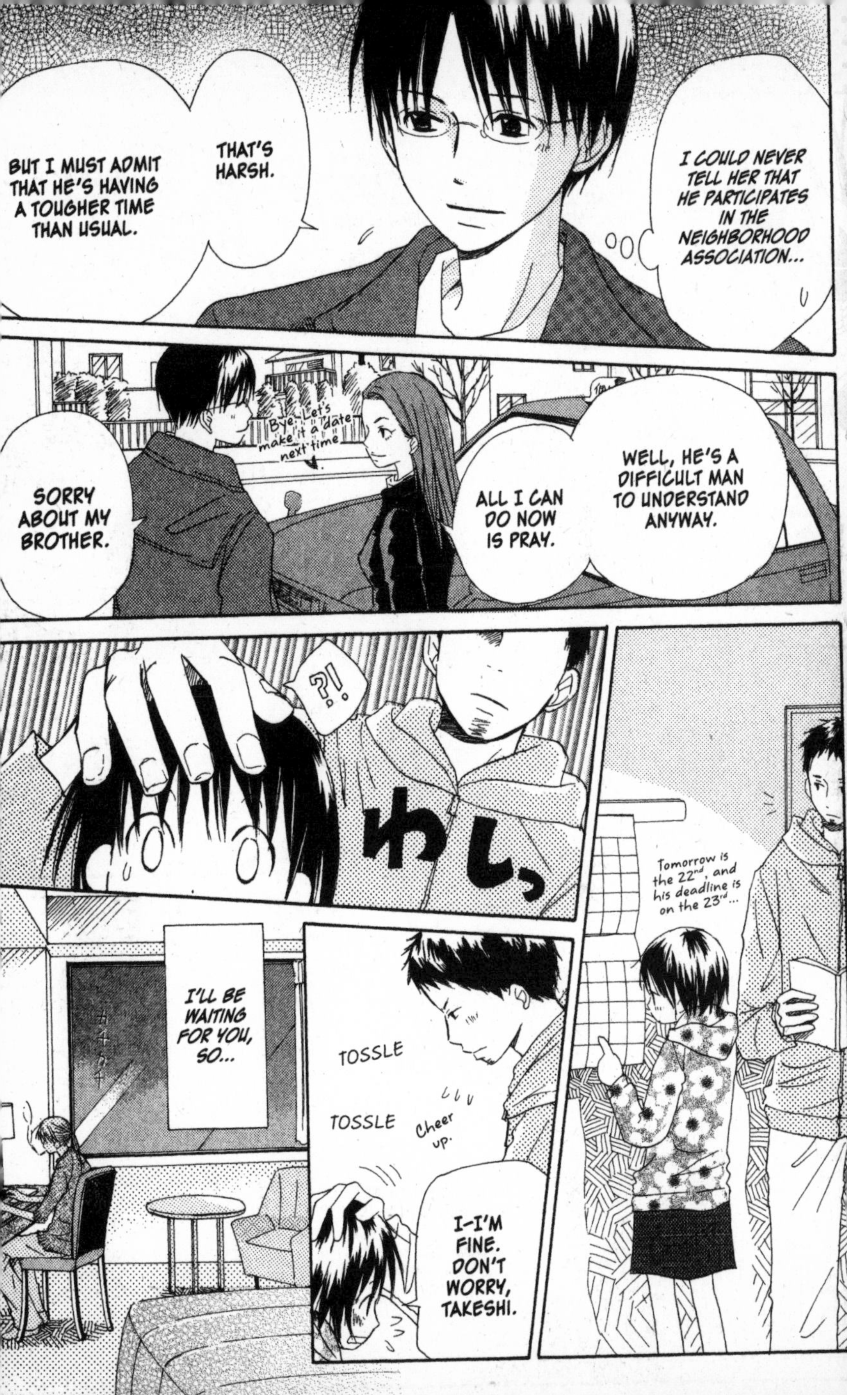
I COULD NEVER TELL HER THAT HE PARTICIPATES IN THE NEIGHBORHOOD ASSOCIATION...
THAT'S HARSH.
BUT I MUST ADMIT THAT HE'S HAVING A TOUGHER TIME THAN USUAL.
WELL, HE'S A DIFFICULT MAN TO UNDERSTAND ANYWAY.
ALL I CAN DO NOW IS PRAY.
Bye. Let's make it a date next time.
SORRY ABOUT MY BROTHER.
Tomorrow is the 22nd, and his deadline is on the 23rd...
?!
TOSSLE
TOSSLE
Cheer up.
I-I'M FINE. DON'T WORRY, TAKESHI.
I'LL BE WAITING FOR YOU, SO...

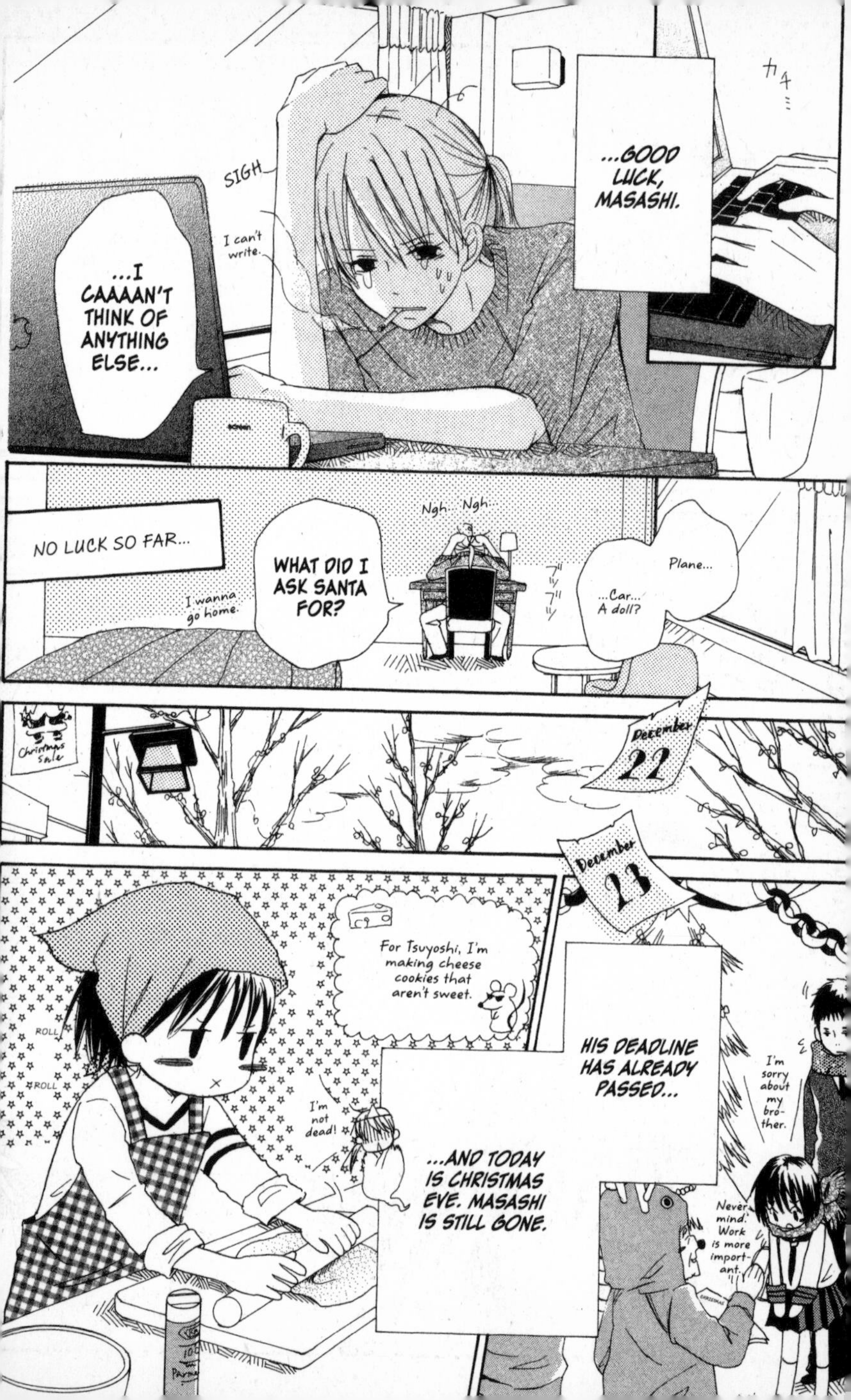
カタ
...GOOD LUCK, MASASHI.
SIGH
I can't write.
...I CAAAAN'T THINK OF ANYTHING ELSE...
Plane...
...Car... A doll?
ブツブツ
Ngh. Ngh..
WHAT DID I ASK SANTA FOR?
I wanna go home.
NO LUCK SO FAR...
December 22
Christmas Sale
December 23
I'm sorry about my bro-ther.
Never mind. Work is more import-ant.
HIS DEADLINE HAS ALREADY PASSED...
...AND TODAY IS CHRISTMAS EVE. MASASHI IS STILL GONE.
For Tsuyoshi, I'm making cheese cookies that aren't sweet.
I'm not dead!
ROLL
ROLL

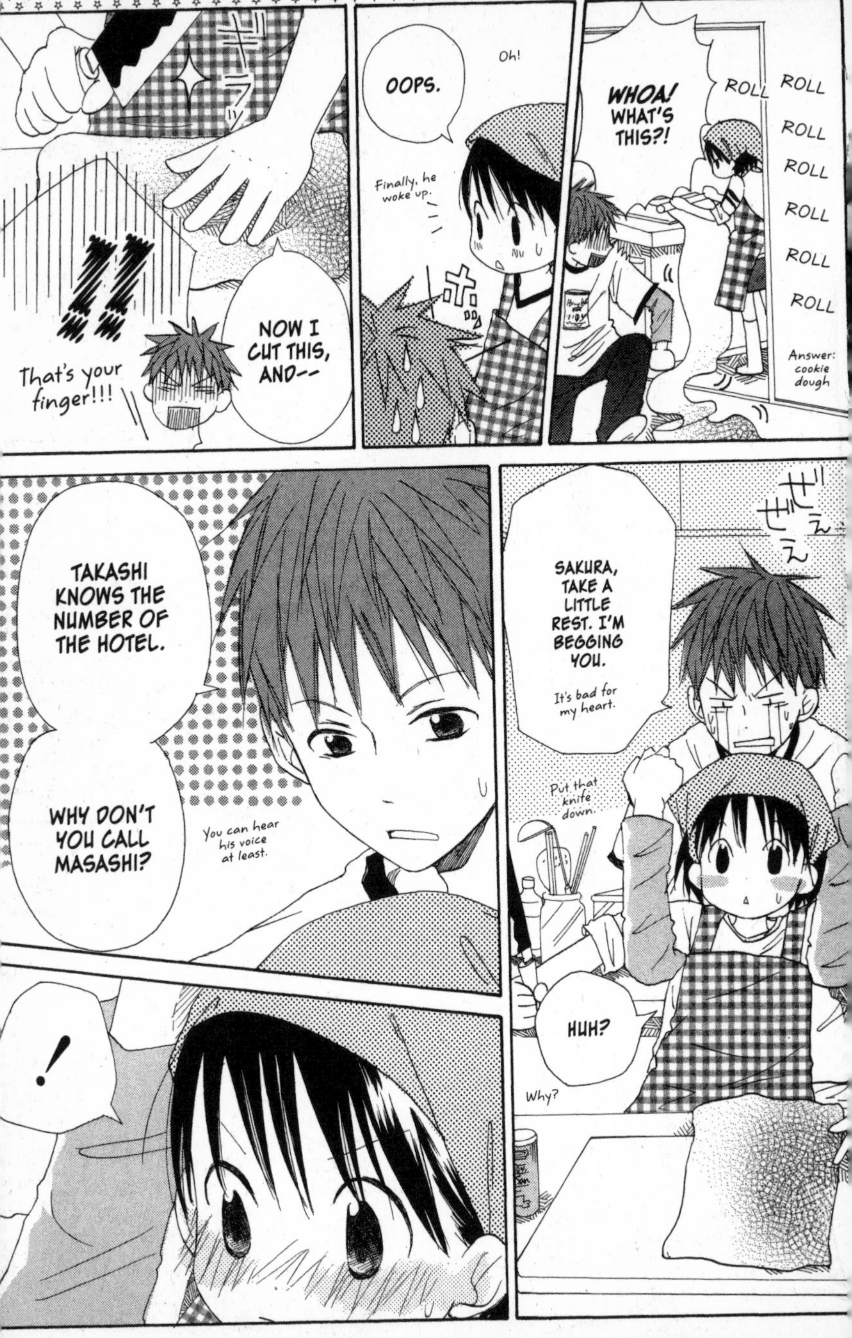
WHOA! WHAT'S THIS?!
ROLL ROLL ROLL ROLL ROLL ROLL
Answer: cookie dough
Oh!
OOPS.
Finally, he woke up.
NOW I CUT THIS, AND--
That's your finger!!!
ぜぇ ぜぇ
SAKURA, TAKE A LITTLE REST. I'M BEGGING YOU.
It's bad for my heart.
Put that knife down.
HUH?
Why?
TAKASHI KNOWS THE NUMBER OF THE HOTEL.
WHY DON'T YOU CALL MASASHI?
You can hear his voice at least.
!

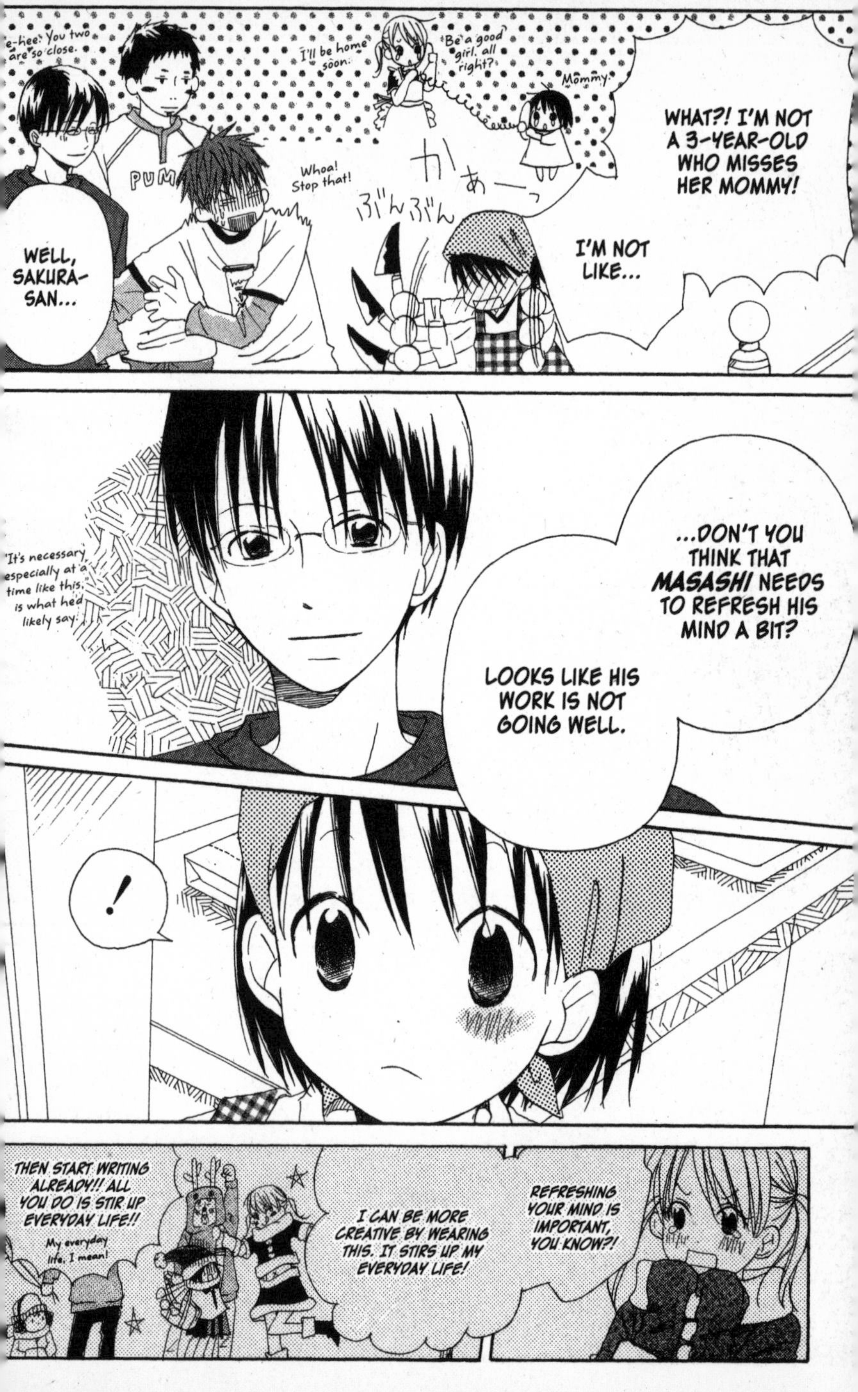
WHAT?! I'M NOT A 3-YEAR-OLD WHO MISSES HER MOMMY!
Mommy.
Be a good girl, all right?
I'll be home soon.
e-hee! You two are so close.
I'M NOT LIKE...
かあーっ
ぶんぶん
Whoa! Stop that!
WELL, SAKURA-SAN...
...DON'T YOU THINK THAT *MASASHI* NEEDS TO REFRESH HIS MIND A BIT?
LOOKS LIKE HIS WORK IS NOT GOING WELL.
"It's necessary especially at a time like this," is what he'd likely say.
!
REFRESHING YOUR MIND IS IMPORTANT, YOU KNOW?!
I CAN BE MORE CREATIVE BY WEARING THIS. IT STIRS UP MY EVERYDAY LIFE!
THEN START WRITING ALREADY!! ALL YOU DO IS STIR UP EVERYDAY LIFE!!
My everyday life, I mean!

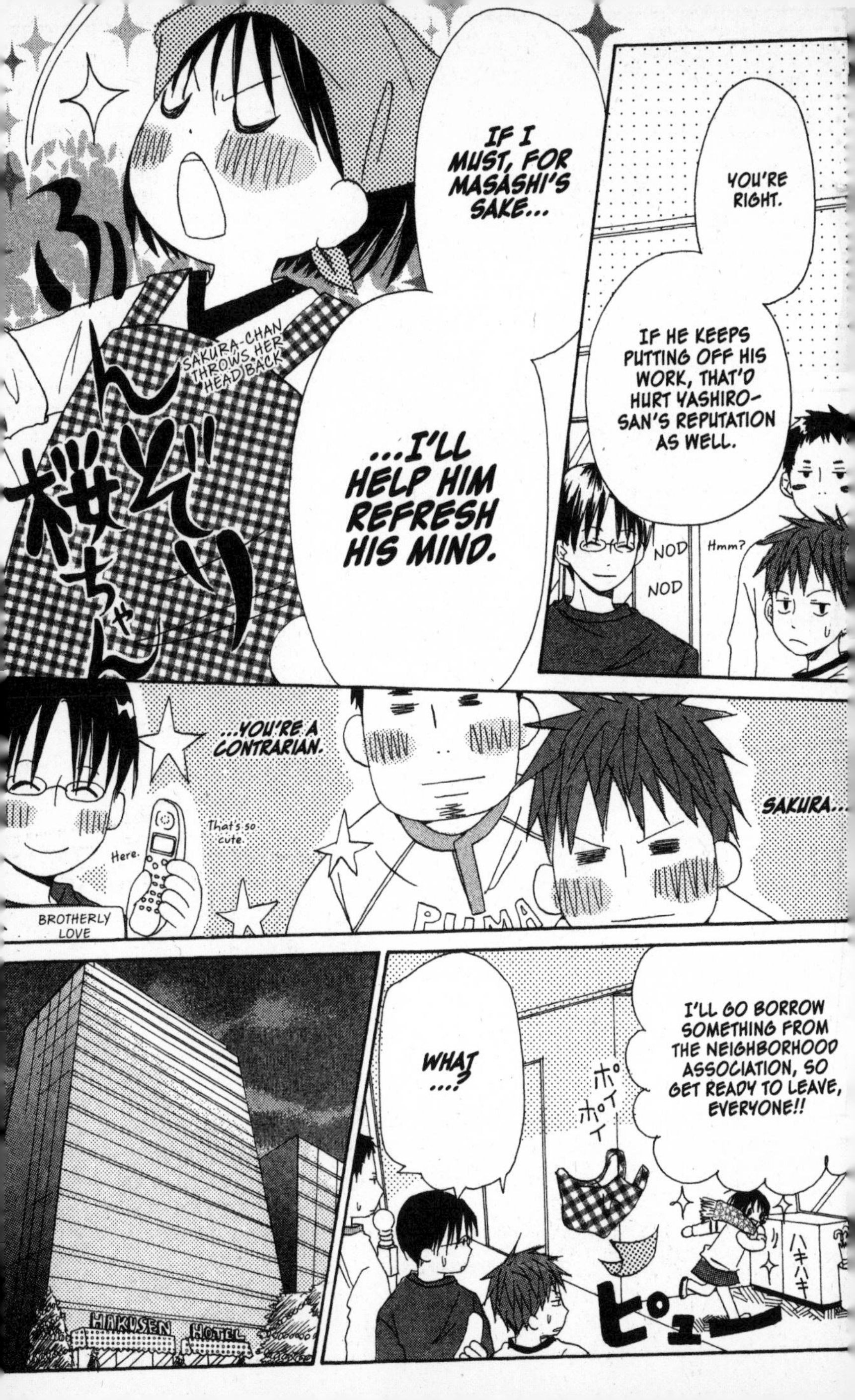
YOU'RE RIGHT.
IF HE KEEPS PUTTING OFF HIS WORK, THAT'D HURT YASHIRO-SAN'S REPUTATION AS WELL.
NOD
NOD
Hmm?
IF I MUST, FOR MASASHI'S SAKE...
...I'LL HELP HIM REFRESH HIS MIND.
SAKURA-CHAN THROWS HER HEAD BACK
SAKURA...
...YOU'RE A CONTRARIAN.
That's so cute.
Here.
BROTHERLY LOVE
I'LL GO BORROW SOMETHING FROM THE NEIGHBORHOOD ASSOCIATION, SO GET READY TO LEAVE, EVERYONE!!
ハキハキ
ピュー
ポイ
ポイ
WHAT...?
HAKUSEN HOTEL

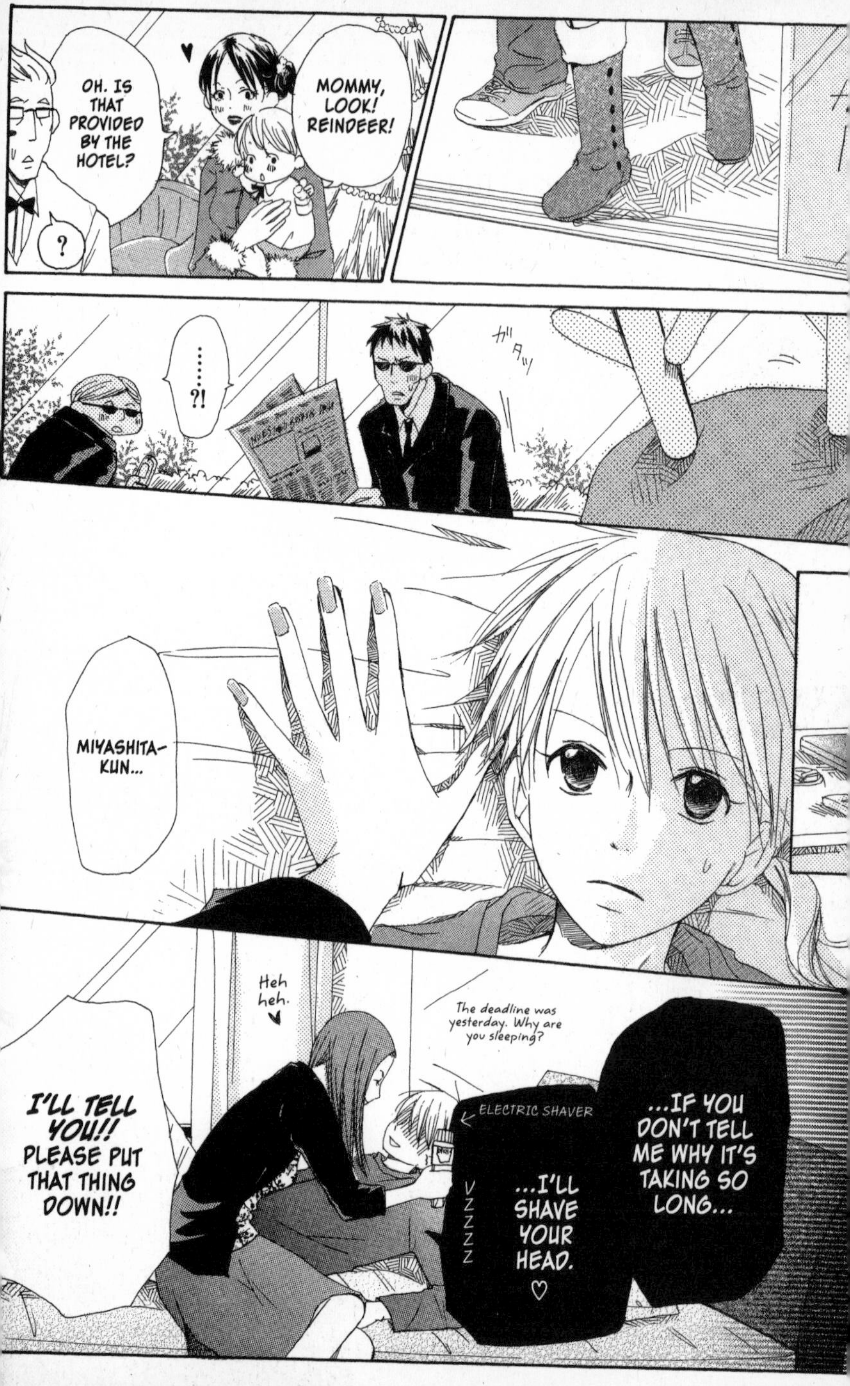
MOMMY, LOOK! REINDEER!
OH. IS THAT PROVIDED BY THE HOTEL?
?
ガタッ
......?!
MIYASHITA-KUN...
...IF YOU DON'T TELL ME WHY IT'S TAKING SO LONG...
...I'LL SHAVE YOUR HEAD. ♡
VZZZZ
ELECTRIC SHAVER
The deadline was yesterday. Why are you sleeping?
Heh heh. ♥
I'LL TELL YOU!! PLEASE PUT THAT THING DOWN!!

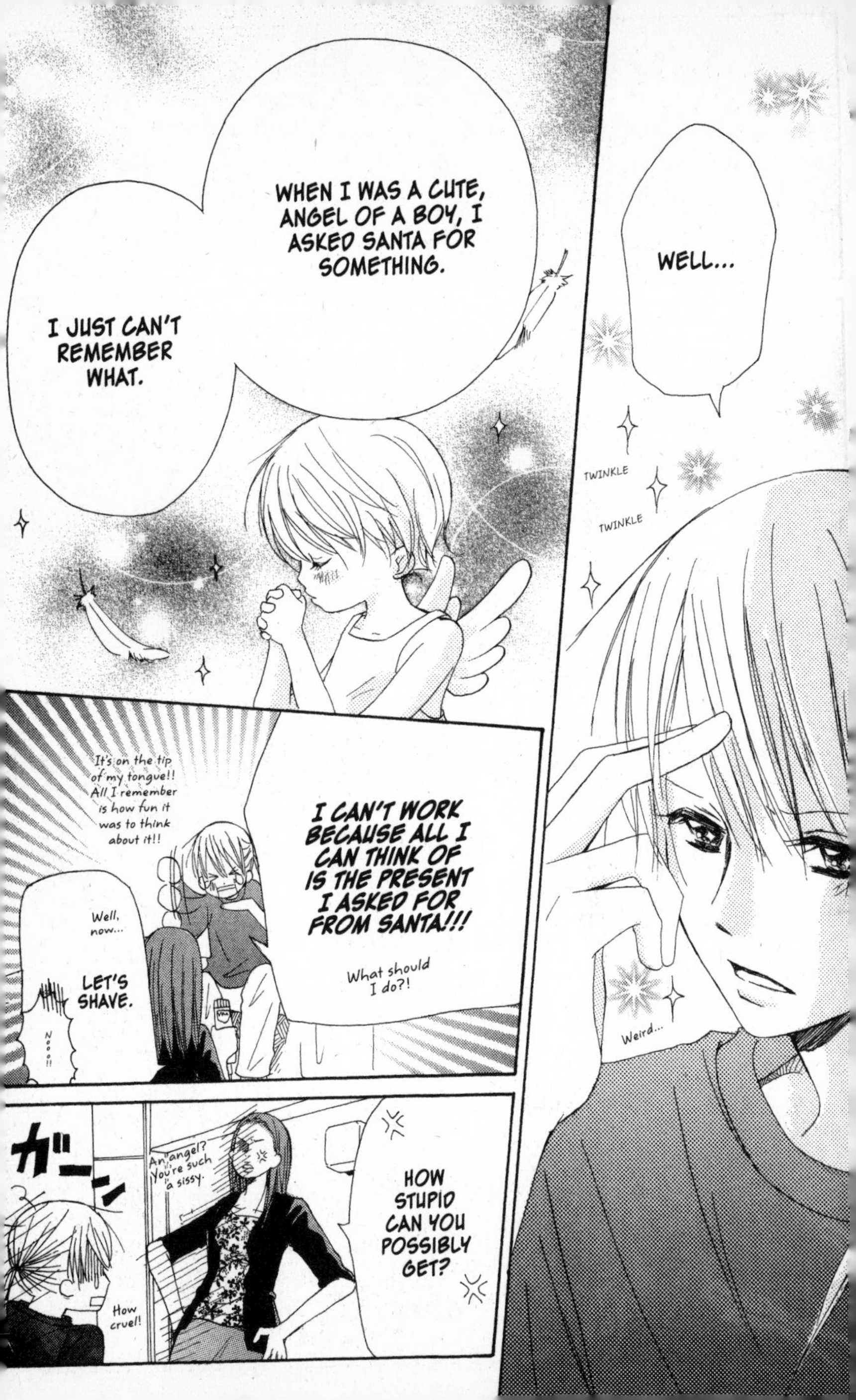
WELL...
TWINKLE
TWINKLE
Weird...
WHEN I WAS A CUTE, ANGEL OF A BOY, I ASKED SANTA FOR SOMETHING.
I JUST CAN'T REMEMBER WHAT.
I CAN'T WORK BECAUSE ALL I CAN THINK OF IS THE PRESENT I ASKED FOR FROM SANTA!!!
What should I do?!
It's on the tip of my tongue!! All I remember is how fun it was to think about it!!
Well, now...
LET'S SHAVE.
Noooo!!
HOW STUPID CAN YOU POSSIBLY GET?
An angel? You're such a sissy.
ガーン
How cruel!

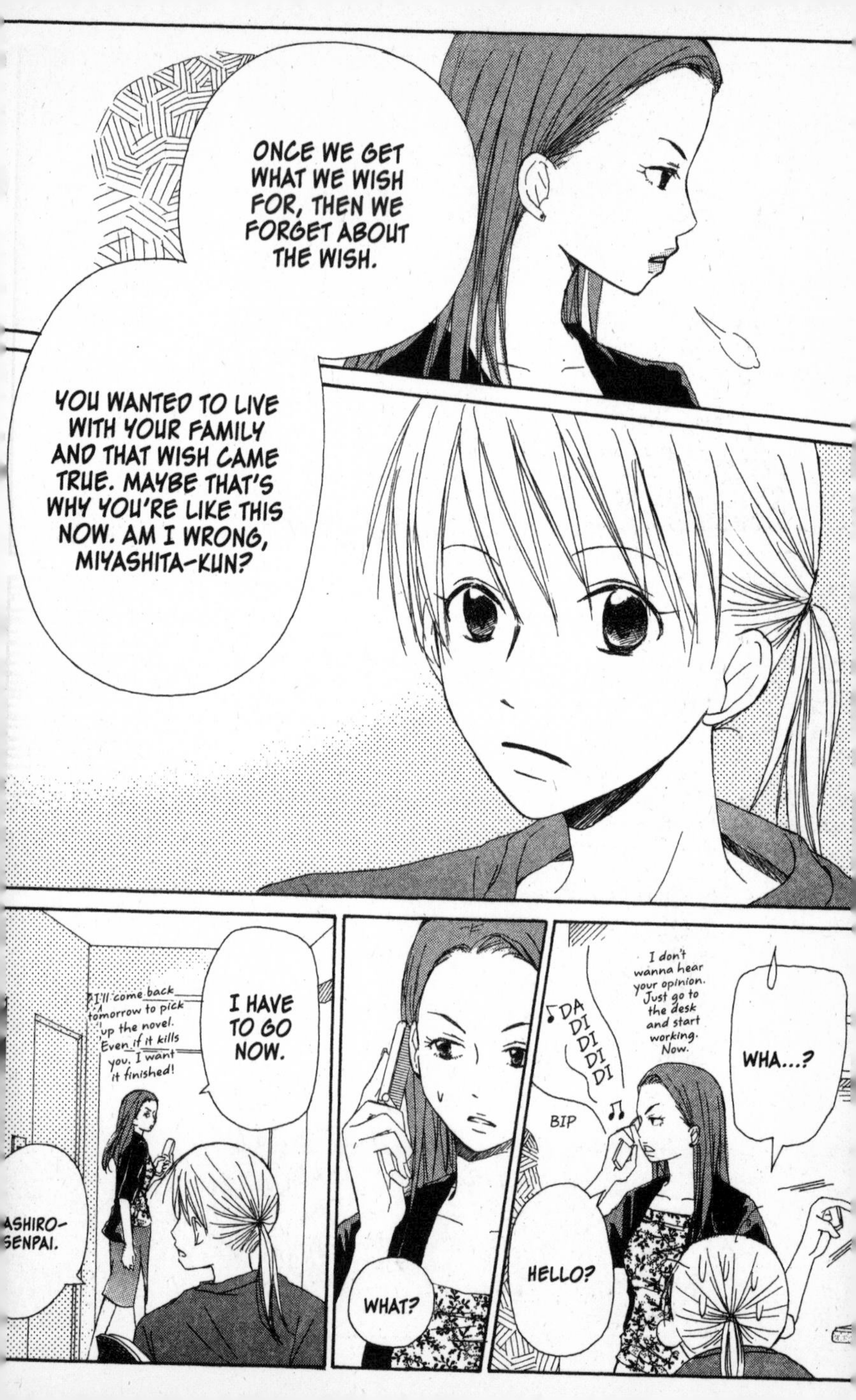
ONCE WE GET WHAT WE WISH FOR, THEN WE FORGET ABOUT THE WISH.
YOU WANTED TO LIVE WITH YOUR FAMILY AND THAT WISH CAME TRUE. MAYBE THAT'S WHY YOU'RE LIKE THIS NOW. AM I WRONG, MIYASHITA-KUN?
WHA...?
I don't wanna hear your opinion. Just go to the desk and start working. Now.
DA DI DI DI DI
BIP
HELLO?
WHAT?
I HAVE TO GO NOW.
I'll come back tomorrow to pick up the novel. Even if it kills you, I want it finished!
ASHIRO-SENPAI.

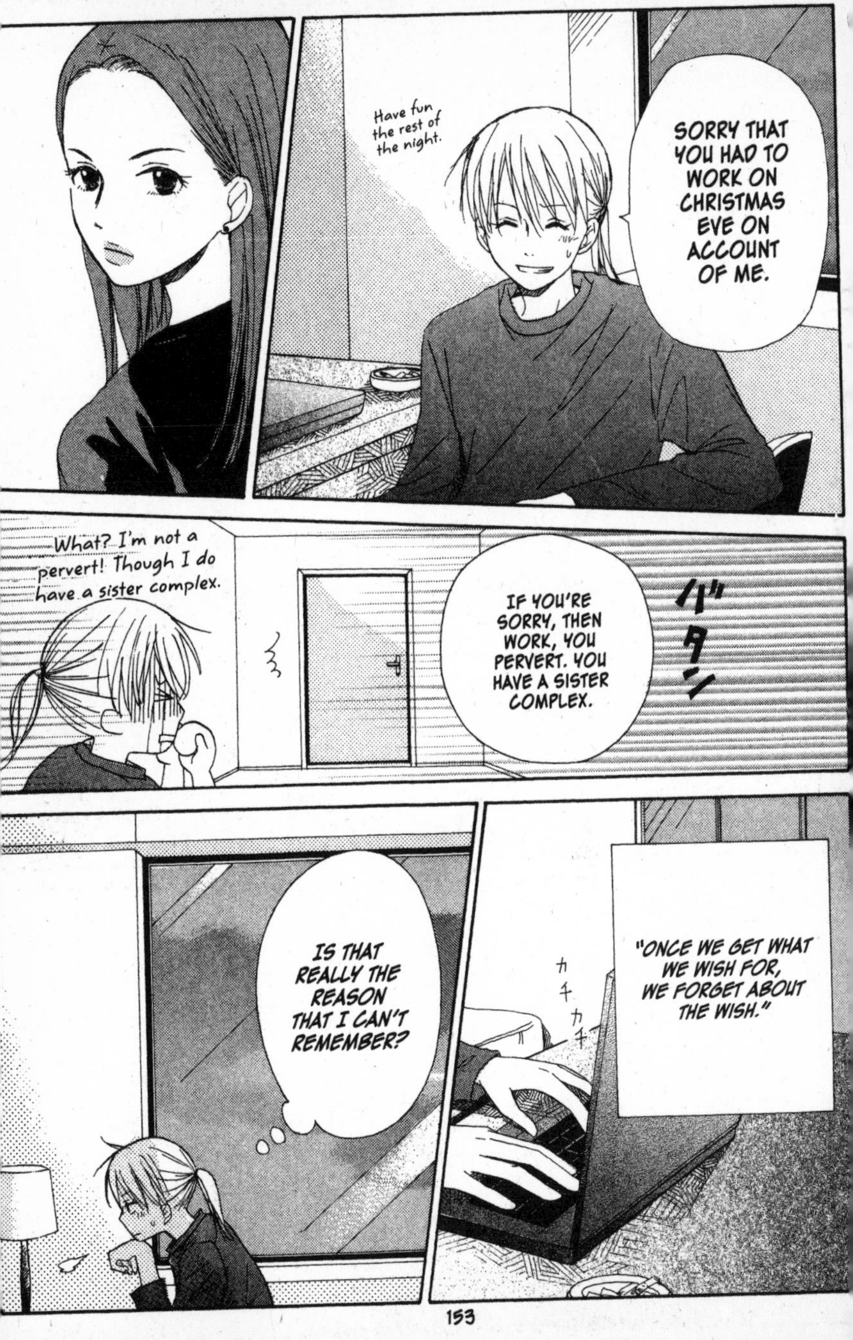
SORRY THAT YOU HAD TO WORK ON CHRISTMAS EVE ON ACCOUNT OF ME.
Have fun the rest of the night.
バタン
IF YOU'RE SORRY, THEN WORK, YOU PERVERT. YOU HAVE A SISTER COMPLEX.
What? I'm not a pervert! Though I do have a sister complex.
"ONCE WE GET WHAT WE WISH FOR, WE FORGET ABOUT THE WISH."
カチカチ
IS THAT REALLY THE REASON THAT I CAN'T REMEMBER?

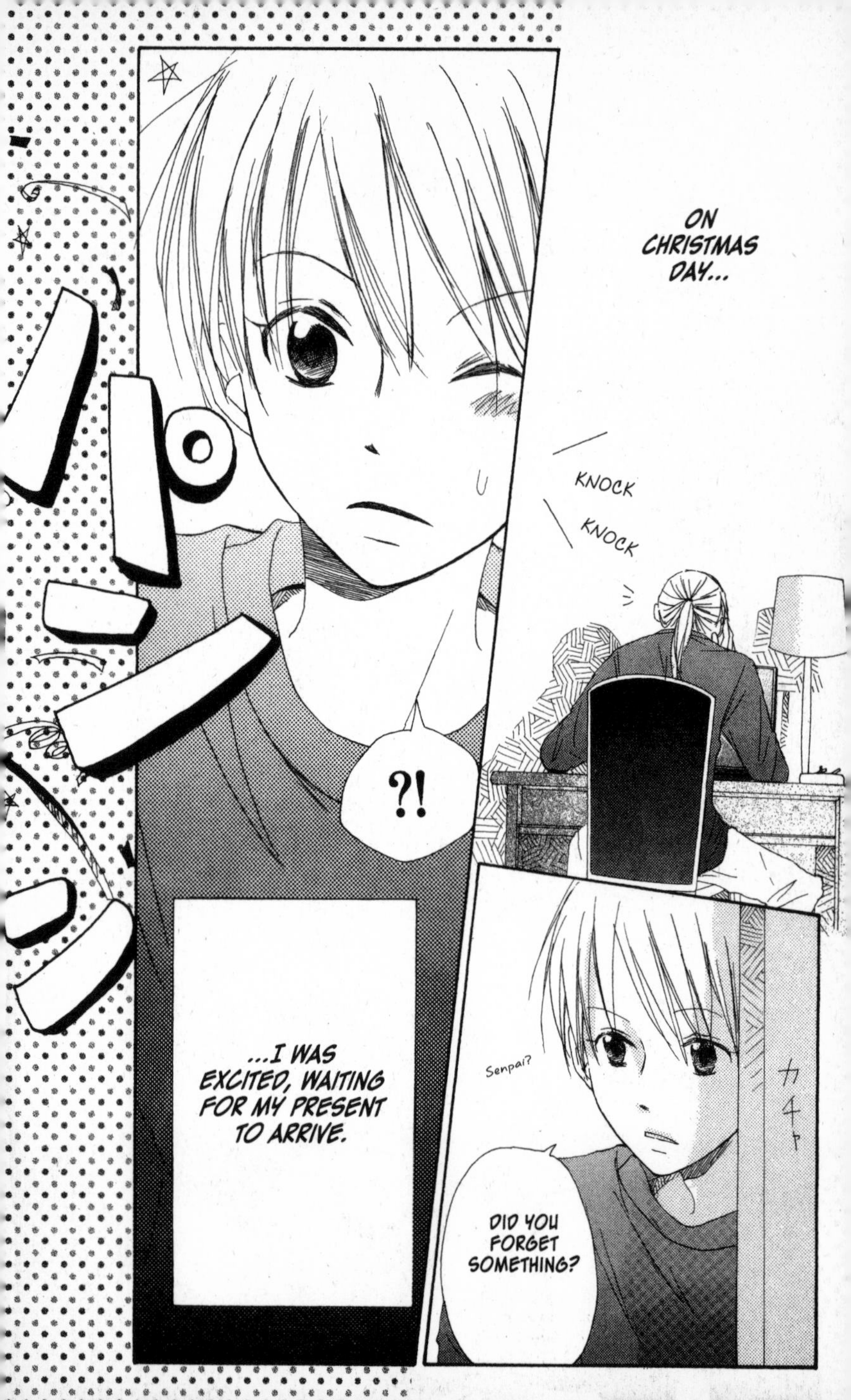
ON CHRISTMAS DAY...
KNOCK
KNOCK
カチャ
Senpai?
DID YOU FORGET SOMETHING?
?!
...I WAS EXCITED, WAITING FOR MY PRESENT TO ARRIVE.

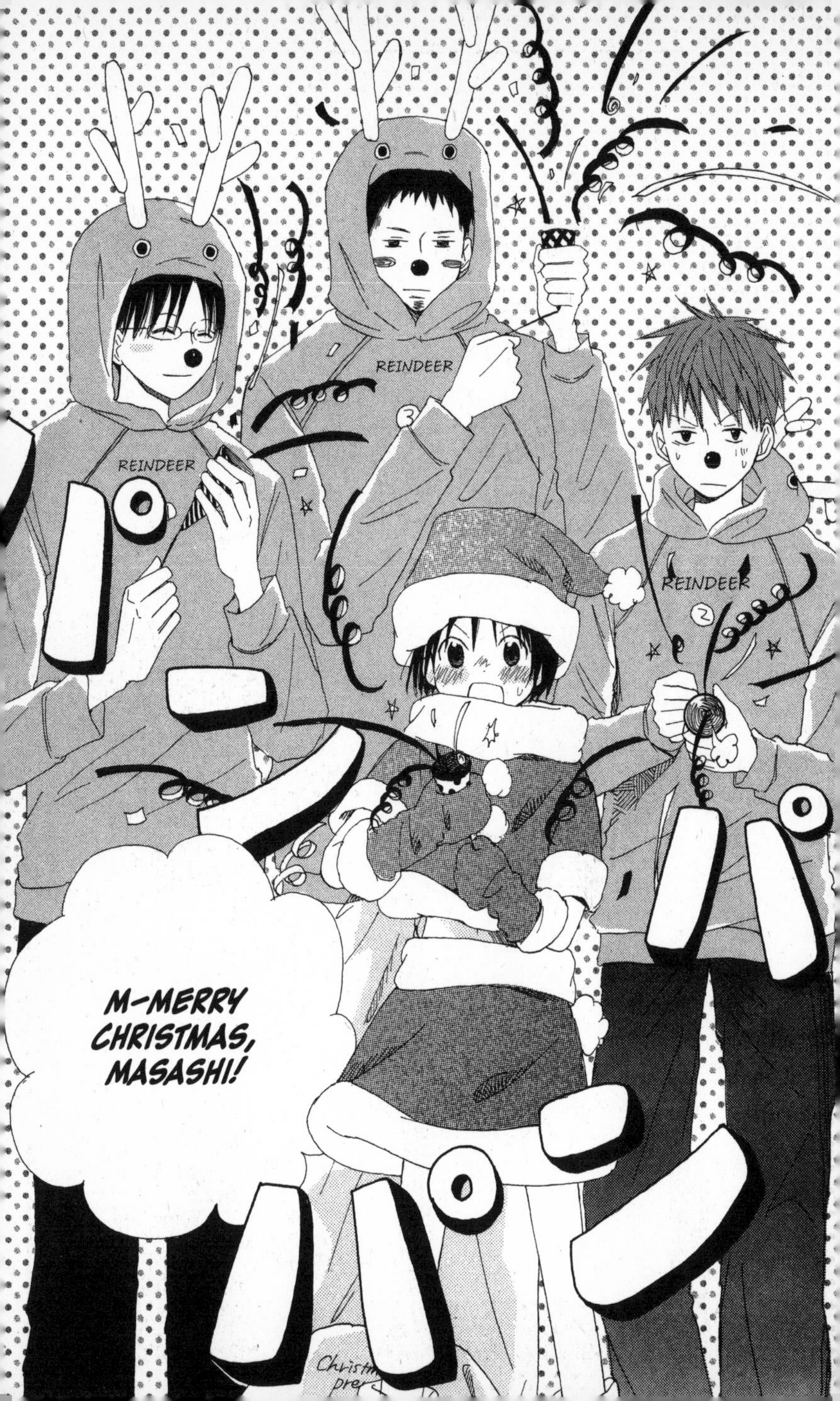
REINDEER
REINDEER
REINDEER
M-MERRY CHRISTMAS, MASASHI!

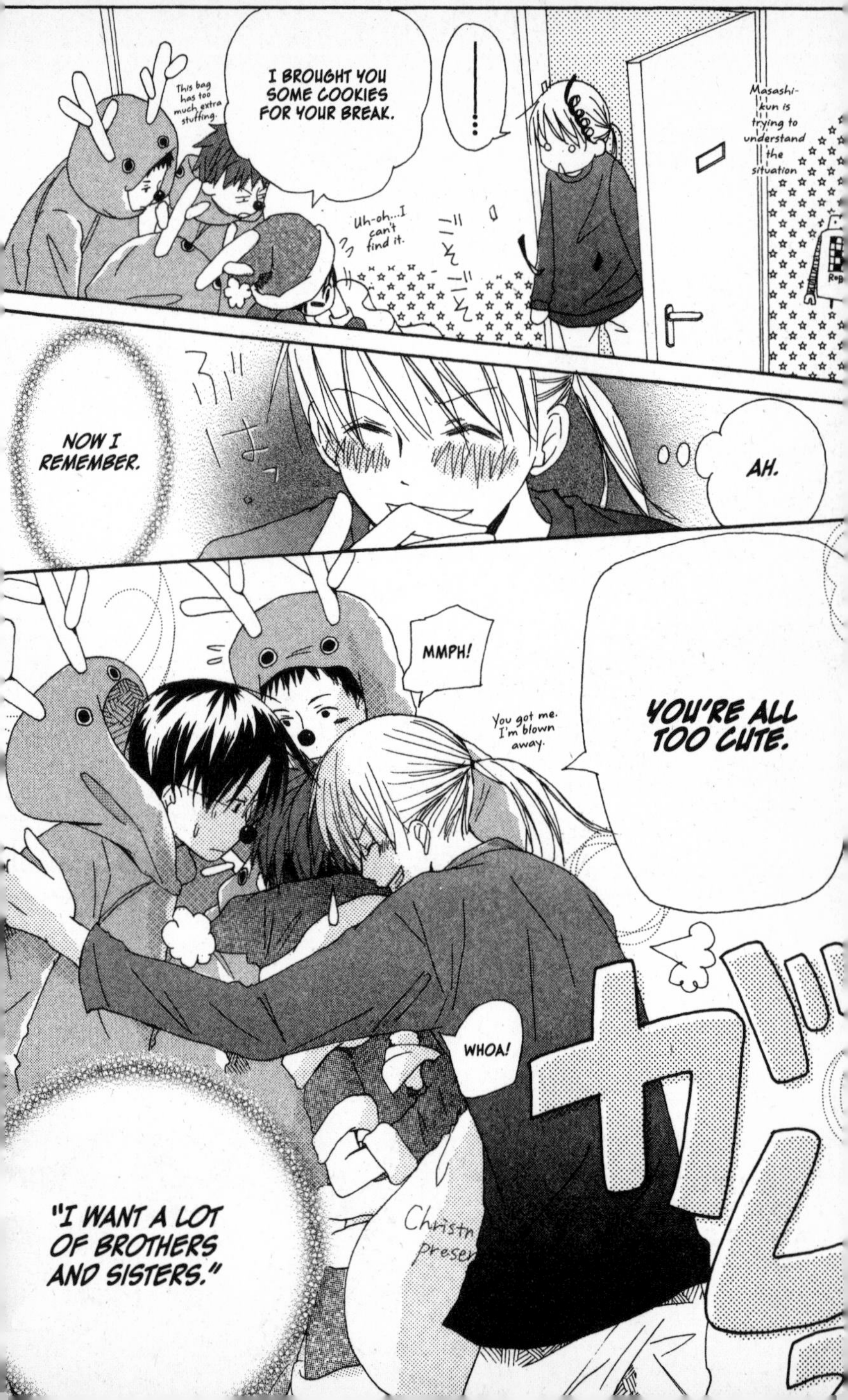
Masashi-kun is trying to understand the situation
!...
I BROUGHT YOU SOME COOKIES FOR YOUR BREAK.
Uh-oh...I can't find it.
This bag has too much extra stuffing.
AH.
NOW I REMEMBER.
YOU'RE ALL TOO CUTE.
You got me. I'm blown away.
MMPH!
WHOA!
"I WANT A LOT OF BROTHERS AND SISTERS."

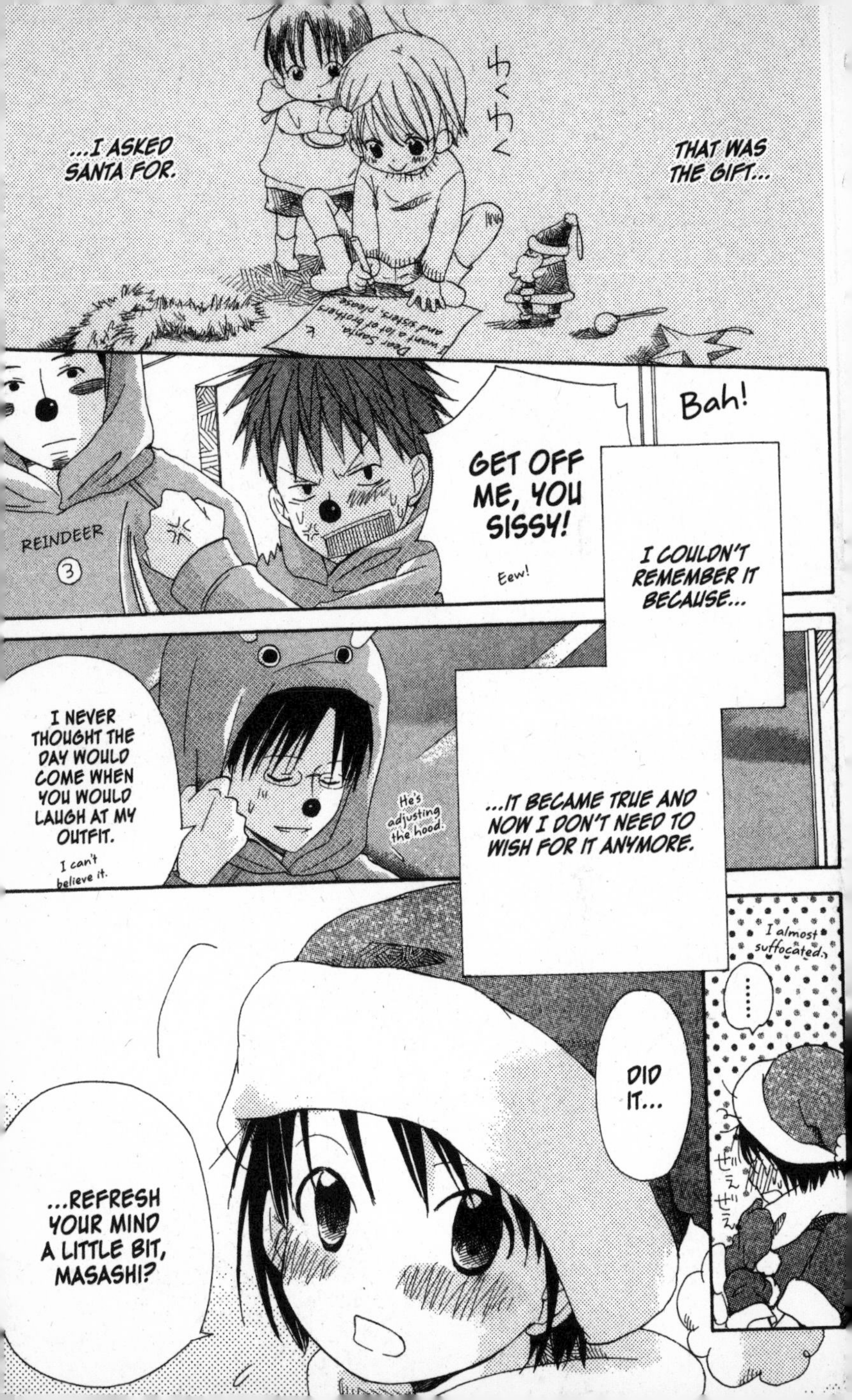
THAT WAS THE GIFT...
わくわく
...I ASKED SANTA FOR.
Dear Santa, I want a lot of brothers and sisters, please
Bah!
I COULDN'T REMEMBER IT BECAUSE...
GET OFF ME, YOU SISSY!
Eew!
REINDEER
3
...IT BECAME TRUE AND NOW I DON'T NEED TO WISH FOR IT ANYMORE.
He's adjusting the hood.
I NEVER THOUGHT THE DAY WOULD COME WHEN YOU WOULD LAUGH AT MY OUTFIT.
I can't believe it.
I almost suffocated.
......
ぜえぜえ
DID IT...
...REFRESH YOUR MIND A LITTLE BIT, MASASHI?

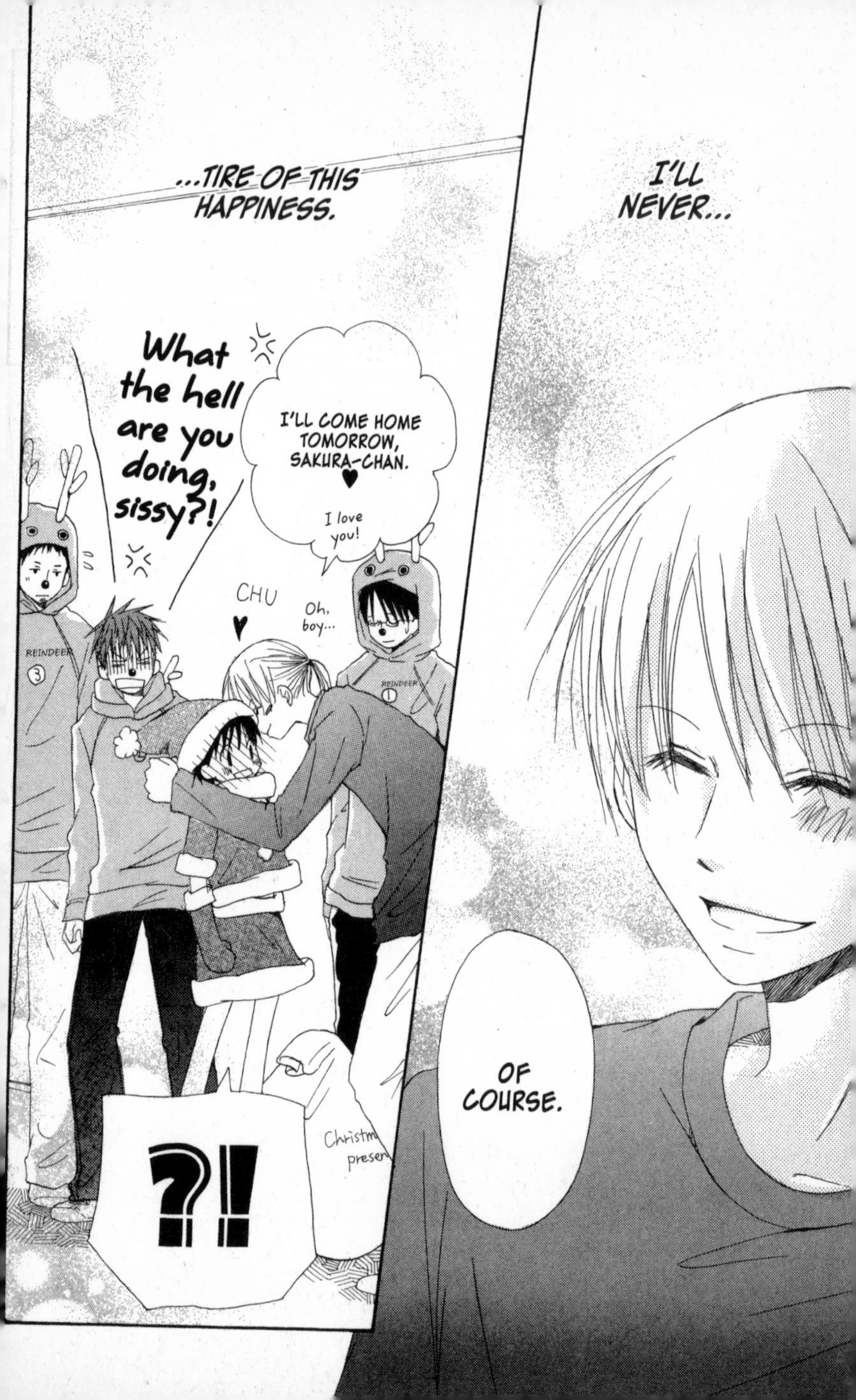
I'LL NEVER...
OF COURSE.
...TIRE OF THIS HAPPINESS.
I'LL COME HOME TOMORROW, SAKURA-CHAN. ♥
I love you!
What the hell are you doing, sissy?!
CHU ♥
Oh, boy...
REINDEER 1
REINDEER 3
?!

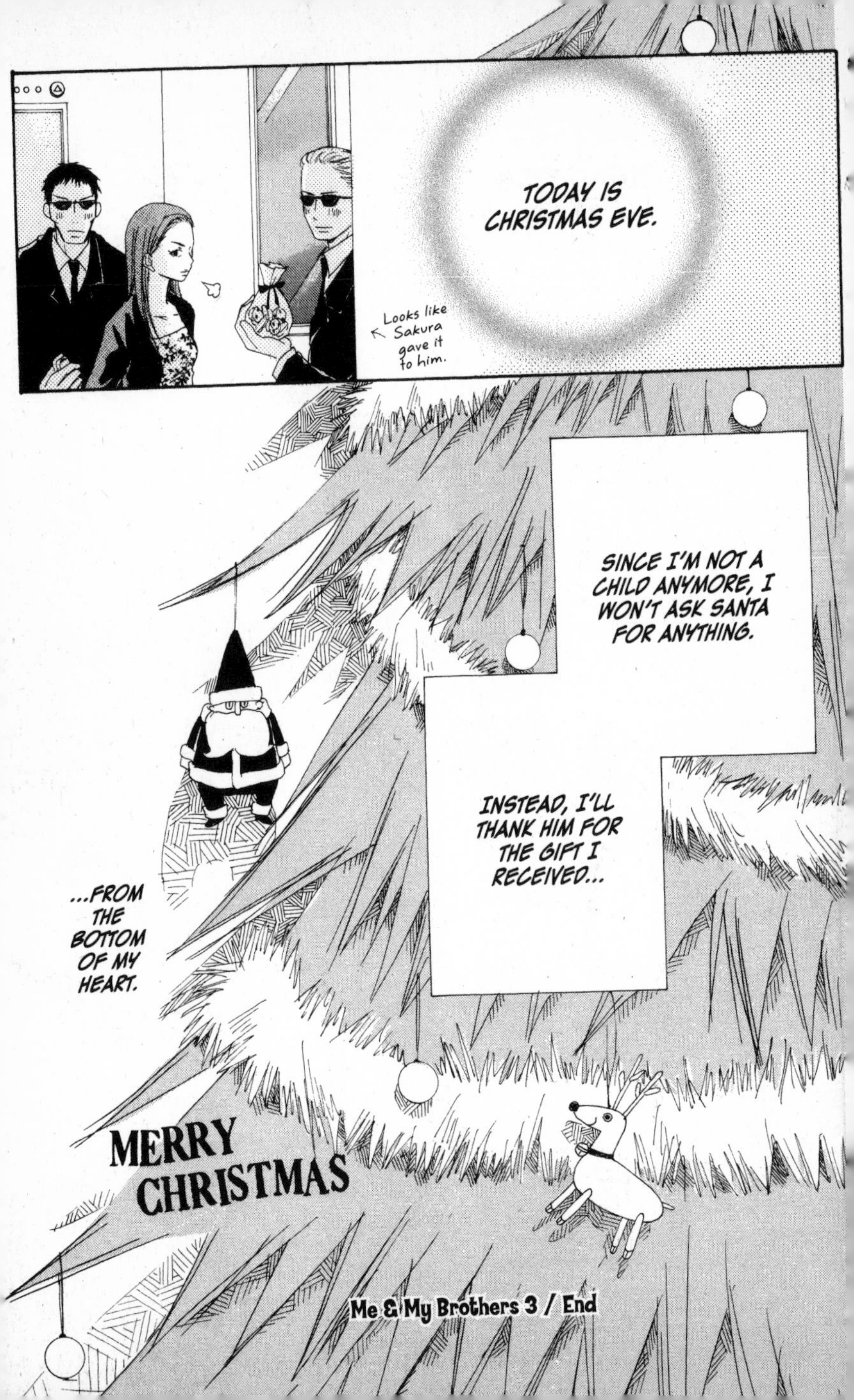
TODAY IS CHRISTMAS EVE.
Looks like Sakura gave it to him.
SINCE I'M NOT A CHILD ANYMORE, I WON'T ASK SANTA FOR ANYTHING.
INSTEAD, I'LL THANK HIM FOR THE GIFT I RECEIVED...
...FROM THE BOTTOM OF MY HEART.
MERRY CHRISTMAS
Me & My Brothers 3 / End

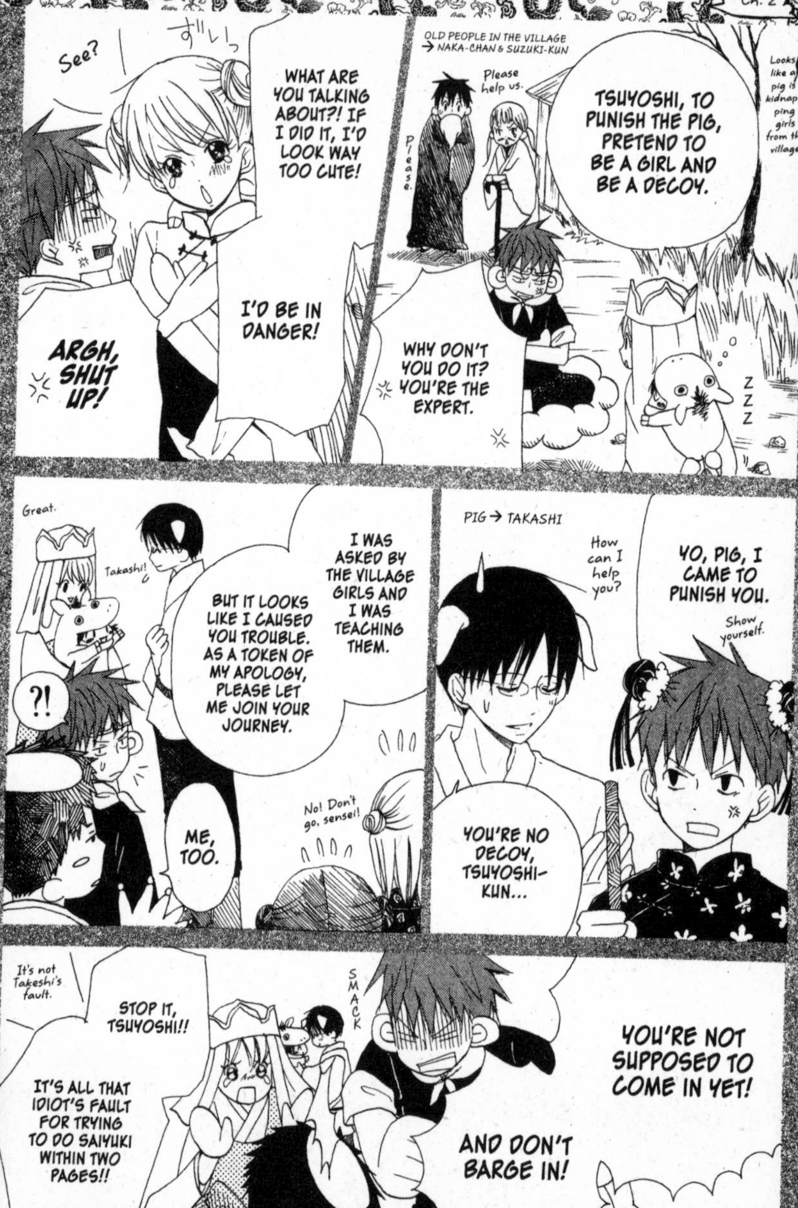
OLD PEOPLE IN THE VILLAGE → NAKA-CHAN & SUZUKI-KUN
Looks like a pig is kidnapping girls from the village.
TSUYOSHI, TO PUNISH THE PIG, PRETEND TO BE A GIRL AND BE A DECOY.
Please help us.
Please.
WHY DON'T YOU DO IT? YOU'RE THE EXPERT.
ZZZ
WHAT ARE YOU TALKING ABOUT?! IF I DID IT, I'D LOOK WAY TOO CUTE!
ずいっ
See?
I'D BE IN DANGER!
ARGH, SHUT UP!
PIG → TAKASHI
YO, PIG, I CAME TO PUNISH YOU.
Show yourself.
How can I help you?
YOU'RE NO DECOY, TSUYOSHI-KUN...
I WAS ASKED BY THE VILLAGE GIRLS AND I WAS TEACHING THEM.
BUT IT LOOKS LIKE I CAUSED YOU TROUBLE. AS A TOKEN OF MY APOLOGY, PLEASE LET ME JOIN YOUR JOURNEY.
Great.
Takashi!
No! Don't go, sensei!
?!
ME, TOO.
YOU'RE NOT SUPPOSED TO COME IN YET!
AND DON'T BARGE IN!
SMACK
STOP IT, TSUYOSHI!!
It's not Takeshi's fault.
IT'S ALL THAT IDIOT'S FAULT FOR TRYING TO DO SAIYUKI WITHIN TWO PAGES!!
I'm sorry.
END

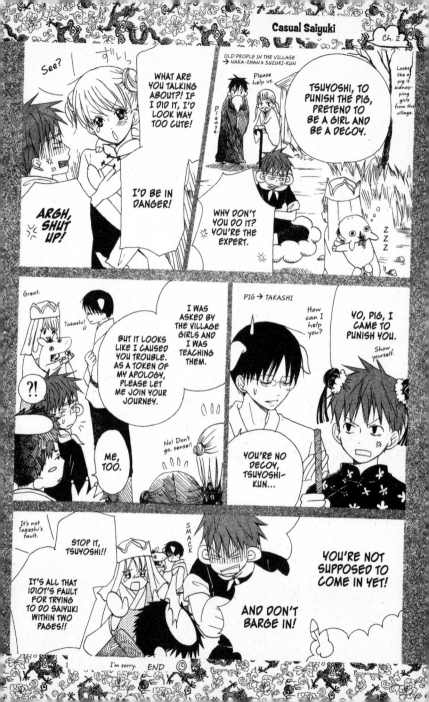

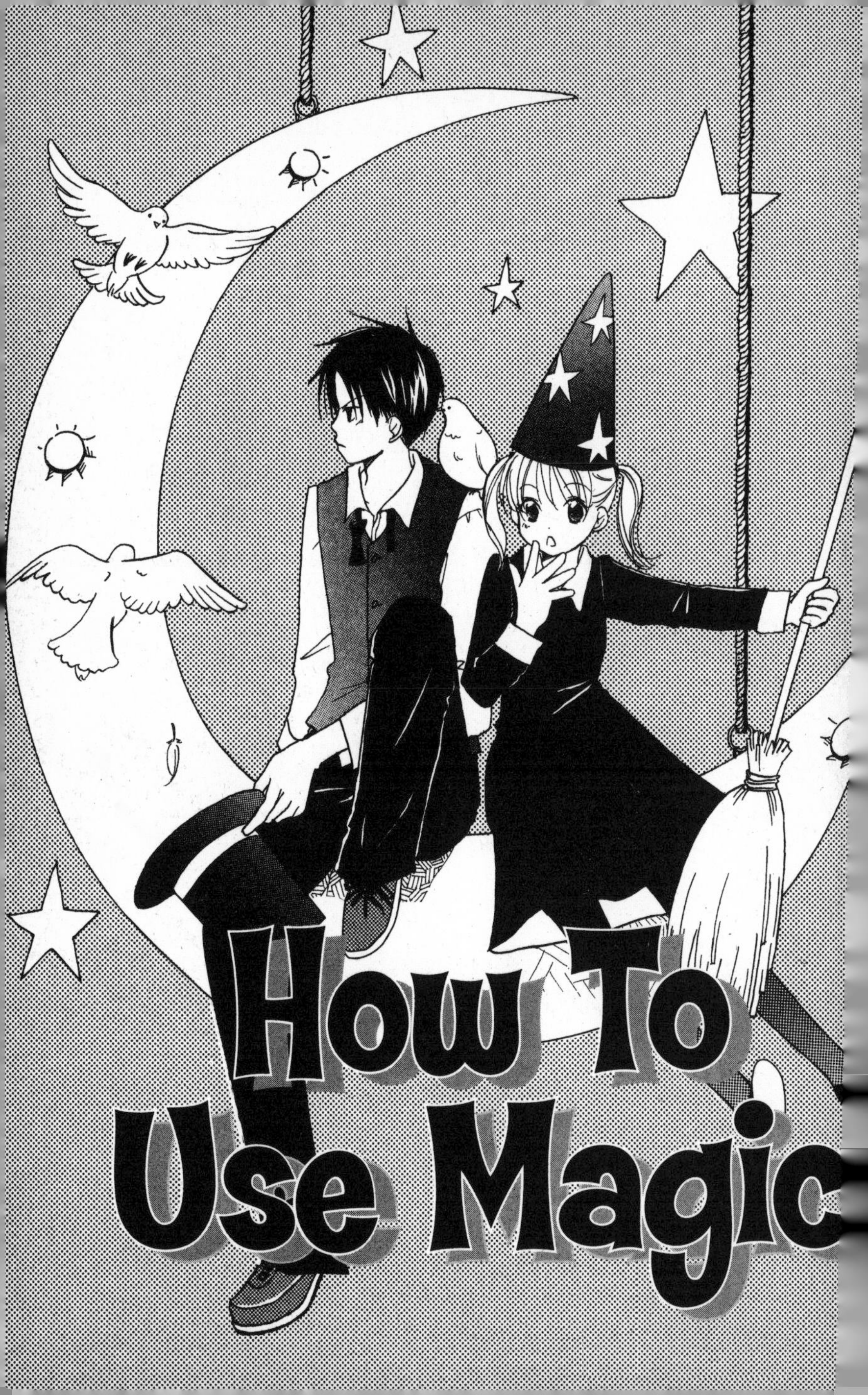
How To
Use Magic

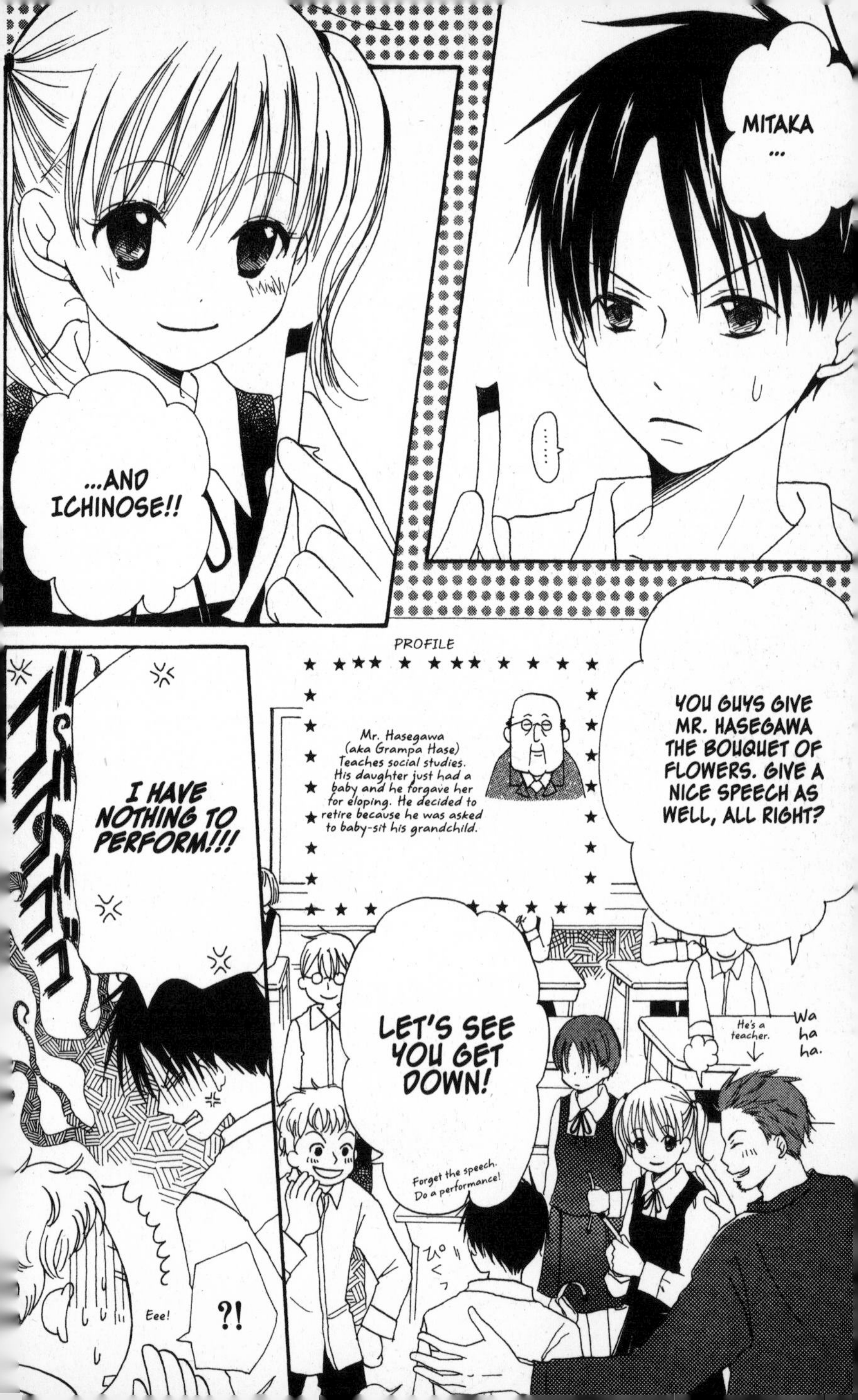
MITAKA ...
......
...AND ICHINOSE!!
YOU GUYS GIVE MR. HASEGAWA THE BOUQUET OF FLOWERS. GIVE A NICE SPEECH AS WELL, ALL RIGHT?
PROFILE
Mr. Hasegawa (aka Grampa Hase) Teaches social studies. His daughter just had a baby and he forgave her for eloping. He decided to retire because he was asked to baby-sit his grandchild.
Wa ha ha.
He's a teacher.
LET'S SEE YOU GET DOWN!
Forget the speech. Do a performance!
I HAVE NOTHING TO PERFORM!!!
?!
Eee!

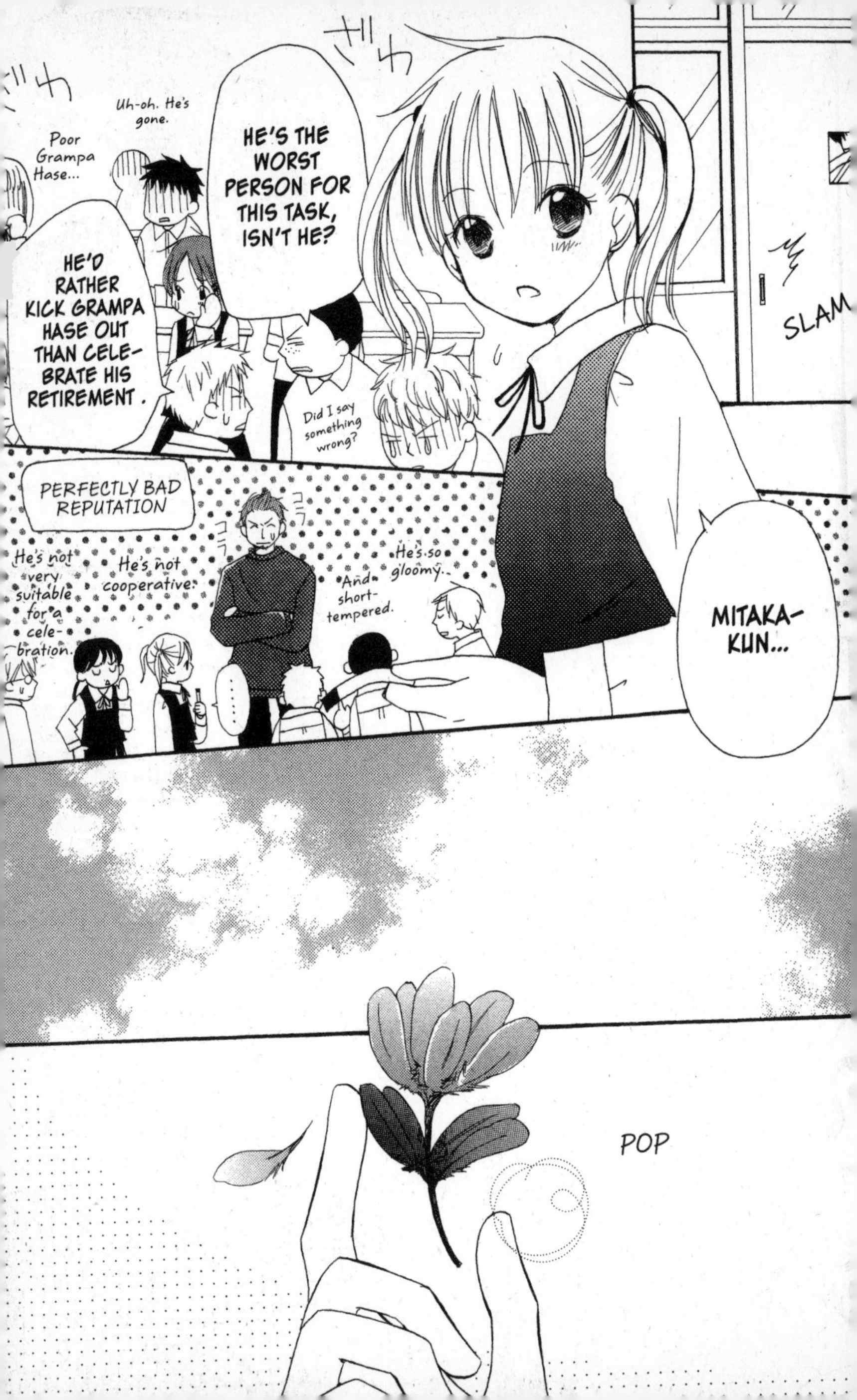
SLAM
ざわ
HE'S THE WORST PERSON FOR THIS TASK, ISN'T HE?
Uh-oh. He's gone.
ざわ
Poor Grampa Hase...
HE'D RATHER KICK GRAMPA HASE OUT THAN CELE-BRATE HIS RETIREMENT.
Did I say something wrong?
MITAKA-KUN...
PERFECTLY BAD REPUTATION
He's so gloomy..
And short-tempered.
コラ
コラ
He's not cooperative.
He's not very suitable for a cele-bration.
......
POP

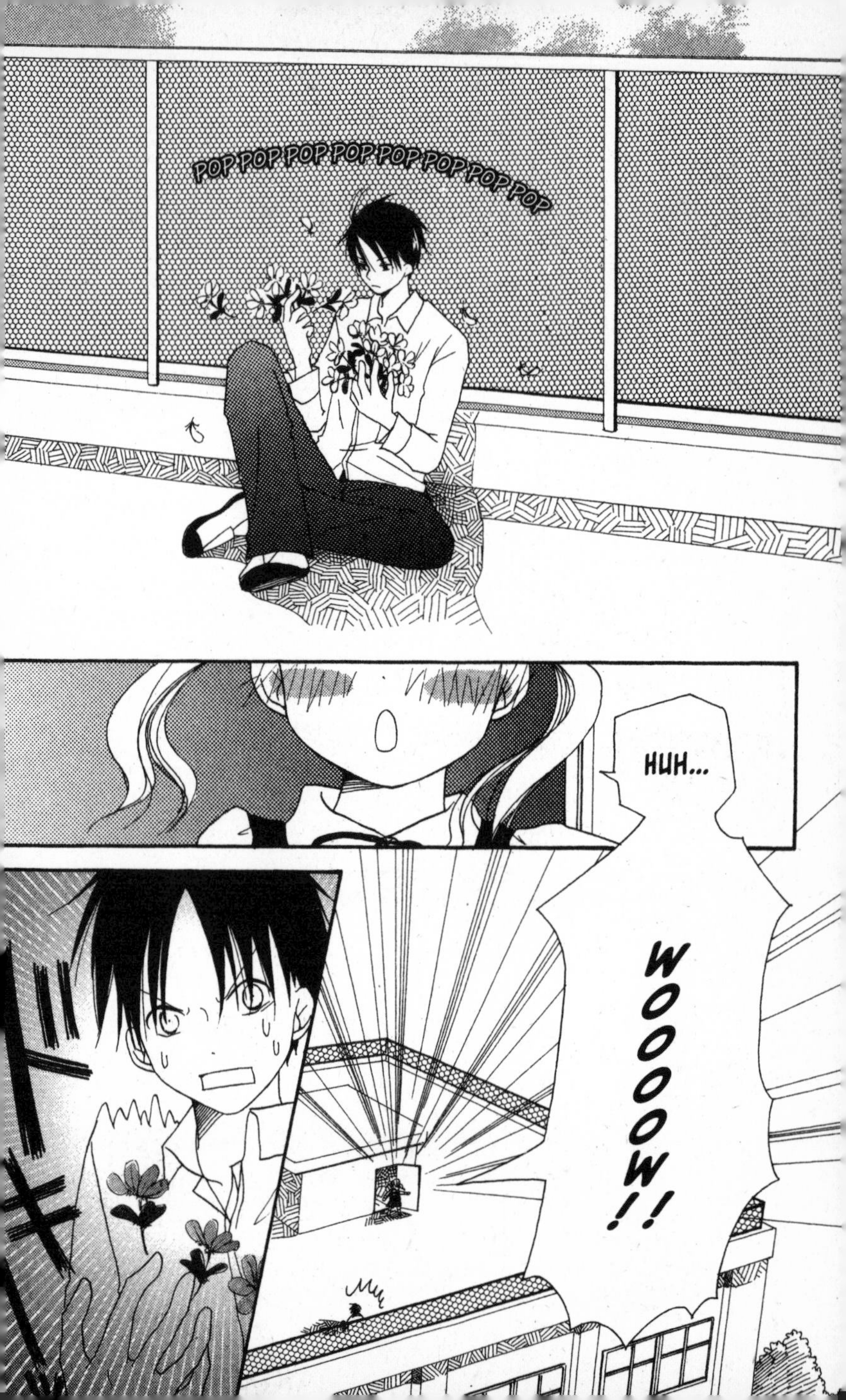
POP POP POP POP POP POP POP POP
HUH...
WOOOOOW!!

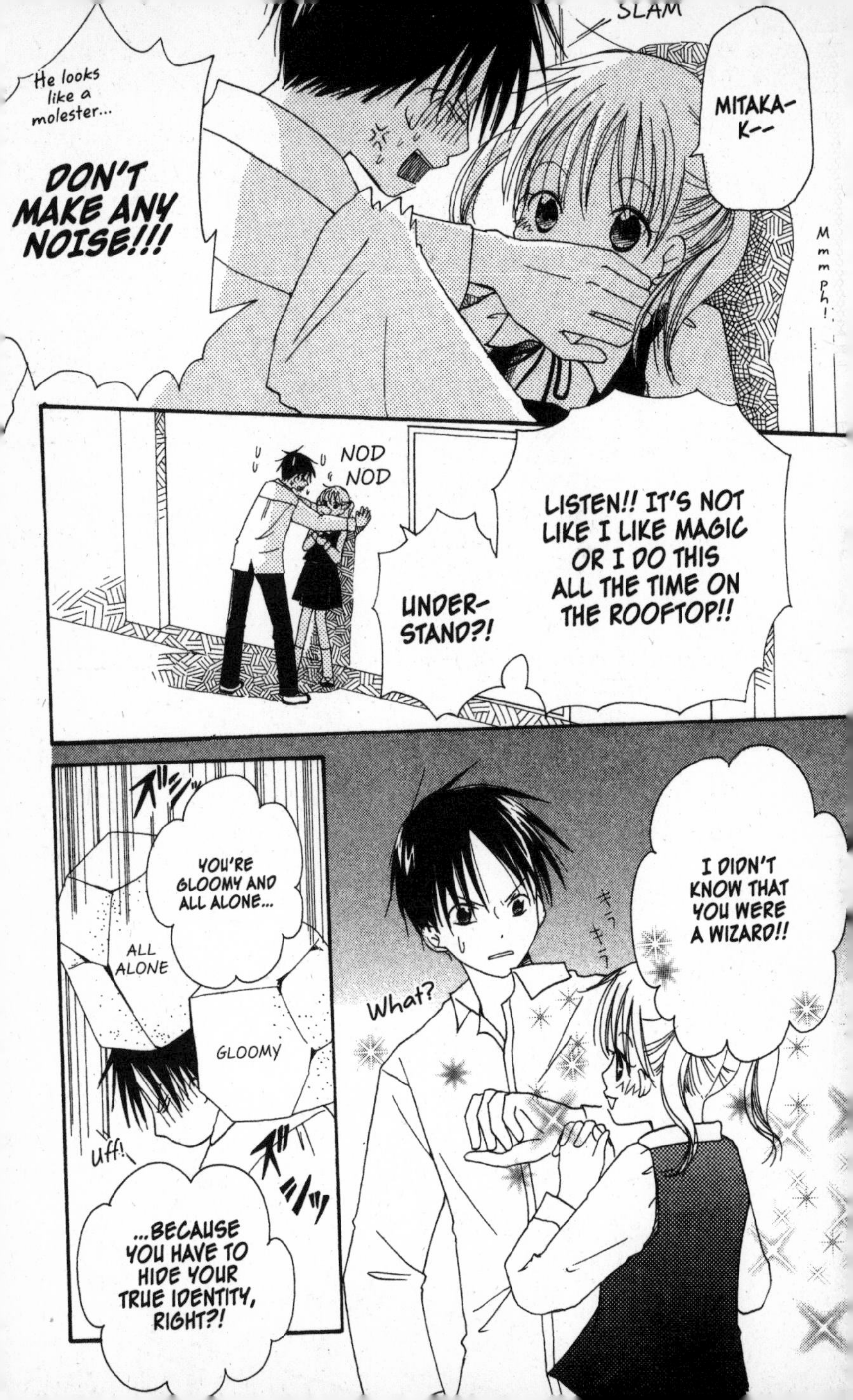
SLAM
MITAKA-K--
Mmmph!
He looks like a molester...
DON'T MAKE ANY NOISE!!!
LISTEN!! IT'S NOT LIKE I LIKE MAGIC OR I DO THIS ALL THE TIME ON THE ROOFTOP!!
UNDER-STAND?!
NOD NOD
I DIDN'T KNOW THAT YOU WERE A WIZARD!!
キラ キラ
What?
YOU'RE GLOOMY AND ALL ALONE...
ALL ALONE
GLOOMY
Uff!
...BECAUSE YOU HAVE TO HIDE YOUR TRUE IDENTITY, RIGHT?!

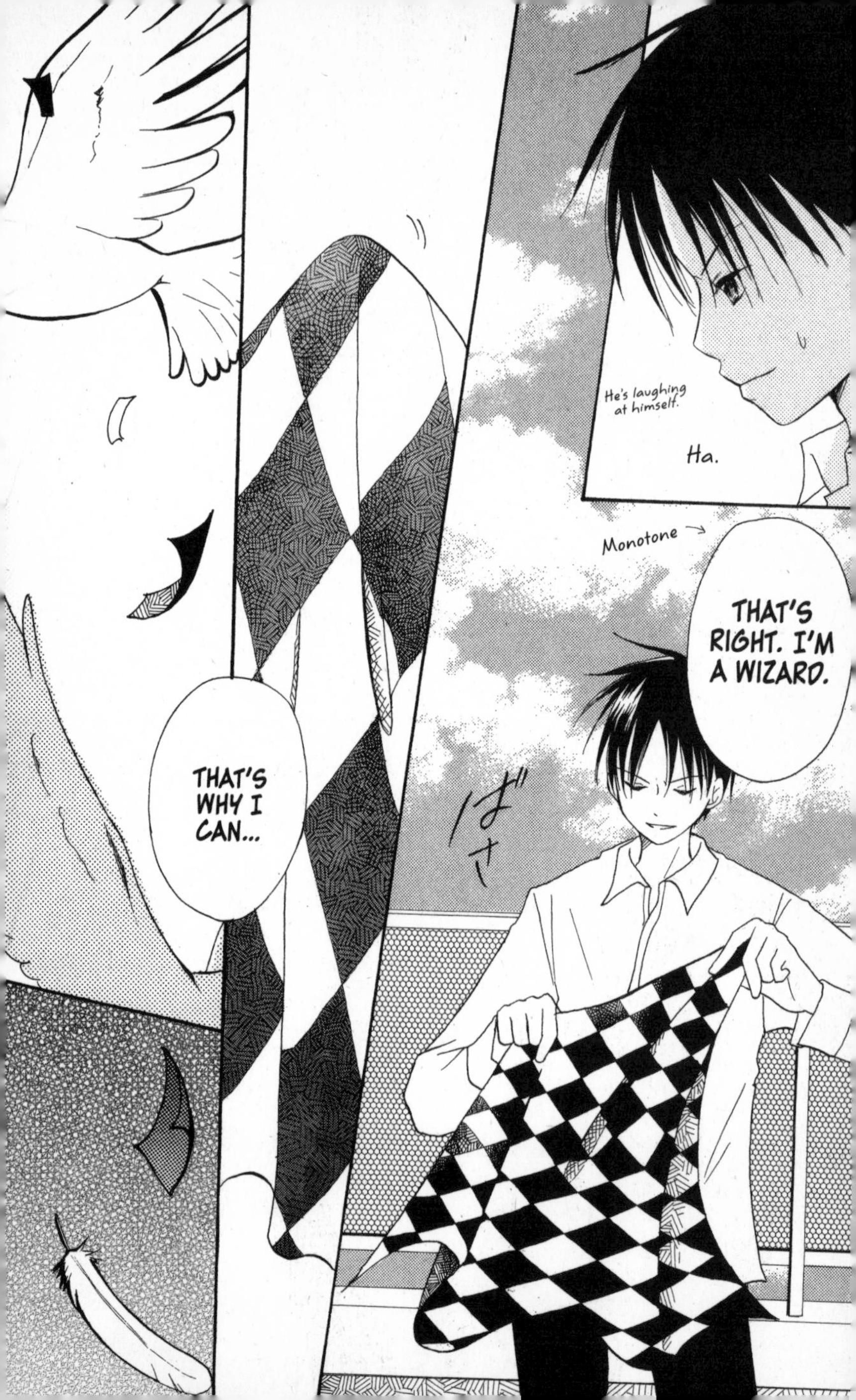
He's laughing at himself.
Ha.
Monotone →
THAT'S RIGHT. I'M A WIZARD.
ばさ
THAT'S WHY I CAN...

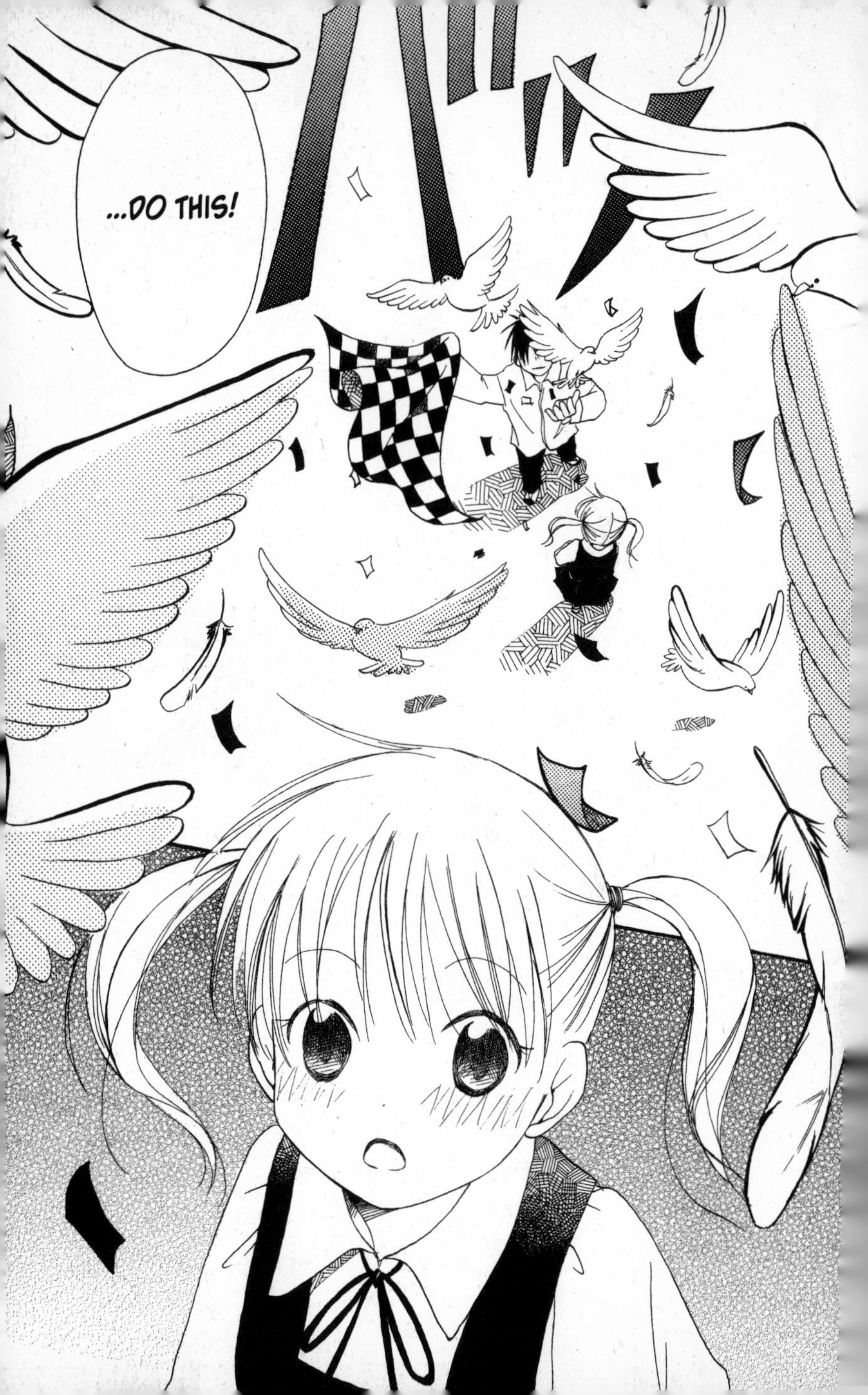
...DO THIS!

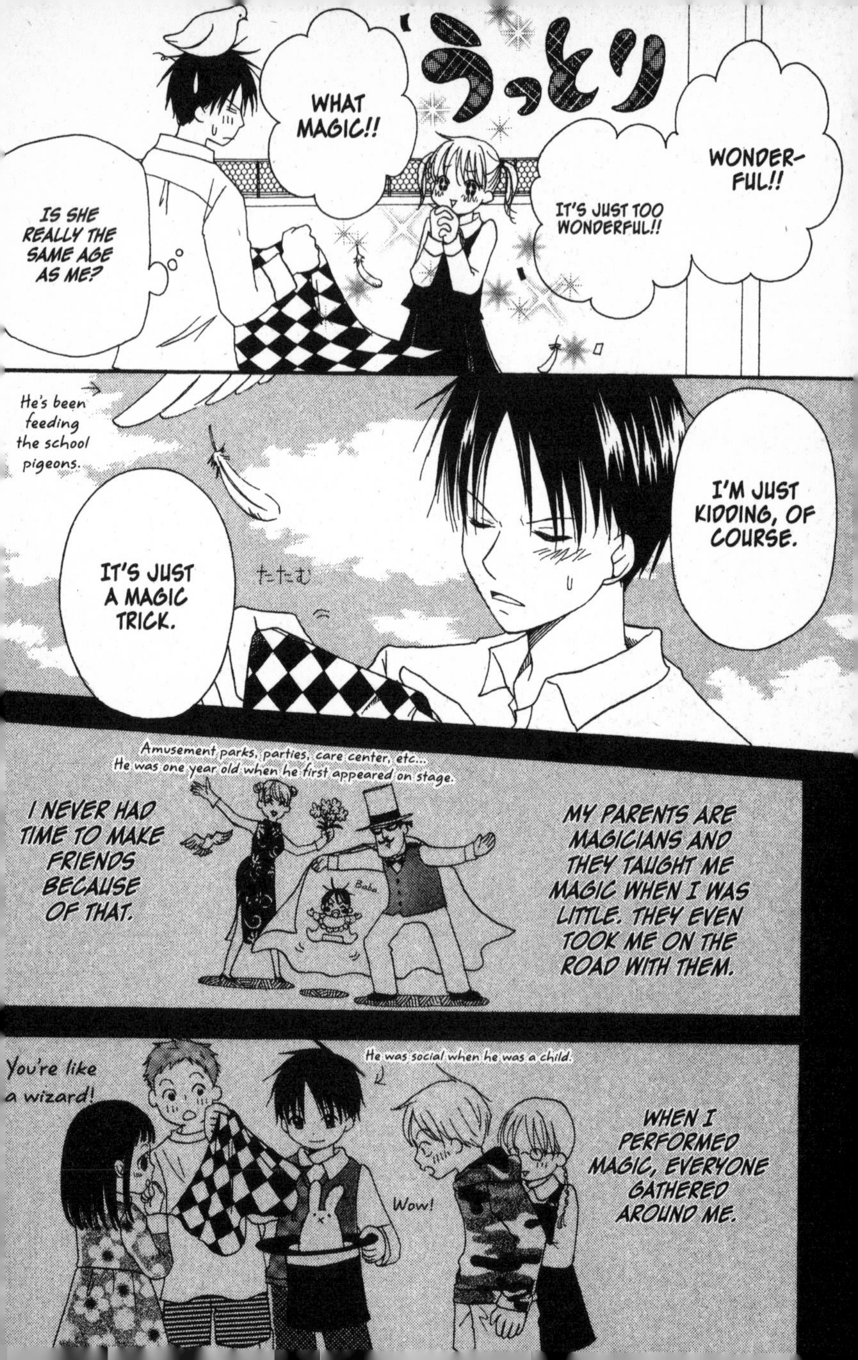
WONDER-FUL!!
IT'S JUST TOO WONDERFUL!!
うっとり
WHAT MAGIC!!
IS SHE REALLY THE SAME AGE AS ME?
I'M JUST KIDDING, OF COURSE.
たたむ
IT'S JUST A MAGIC TRICK.
He's been feeding the school pigeons.
MY PARENTS ARE MAGICIANS AND THEY TAUGHT ME MAGIC WHEN I WAS LITTLE. THEY EVEN TOOK ME ON THE ROAD WITH THEM.
Amusement parks, parties, care center, etc... He was one year old when he first appeared on stage.
I NEVER HAD TIME TO MAKE FRIENDS BECAUSE OF THAT.
WHEN I PERFORMED MAGIC, EVERYONE GATHERED AROUND ME.
He was social when he was a child.
Wow!
You're like a wizard!

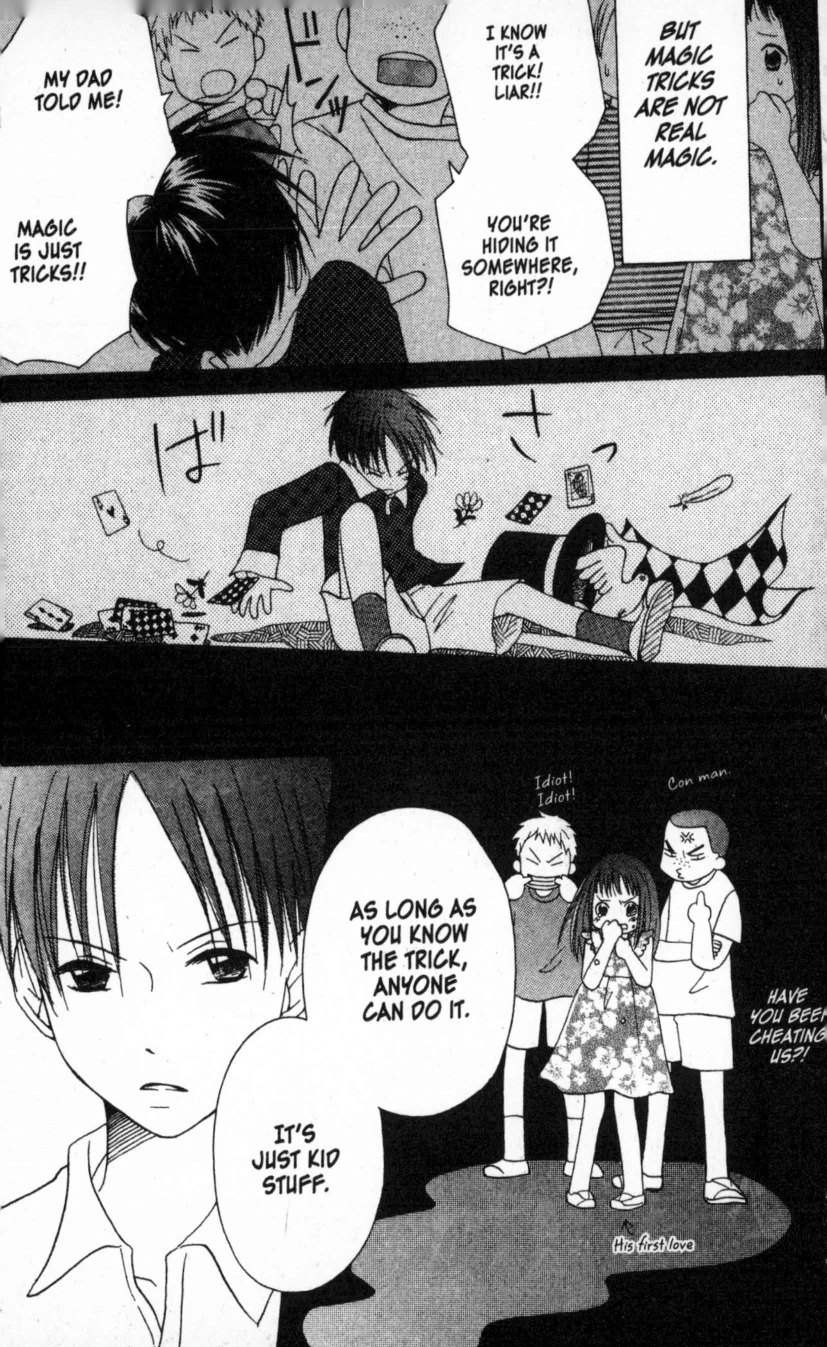
BUT MAGIC TRICKS ARE NOT REAL MAGIC.
I KNOW IT'S A TRICK! LIAR!!
YOU'RE HIDING IT SOMEWHERE, RIGHT?!
MY DAD TOLD ME!
MAGIC IS JUST TRICKS!!
さっ
ばっ
HAVE YOU BEE CHEATING US?!
Con man.
Idiot! Idiot!
AS LONG AS YOU KNOW THE TRICK, ANYONE CAN DO IT.
IT'S JUST KID STUFF.
His first love

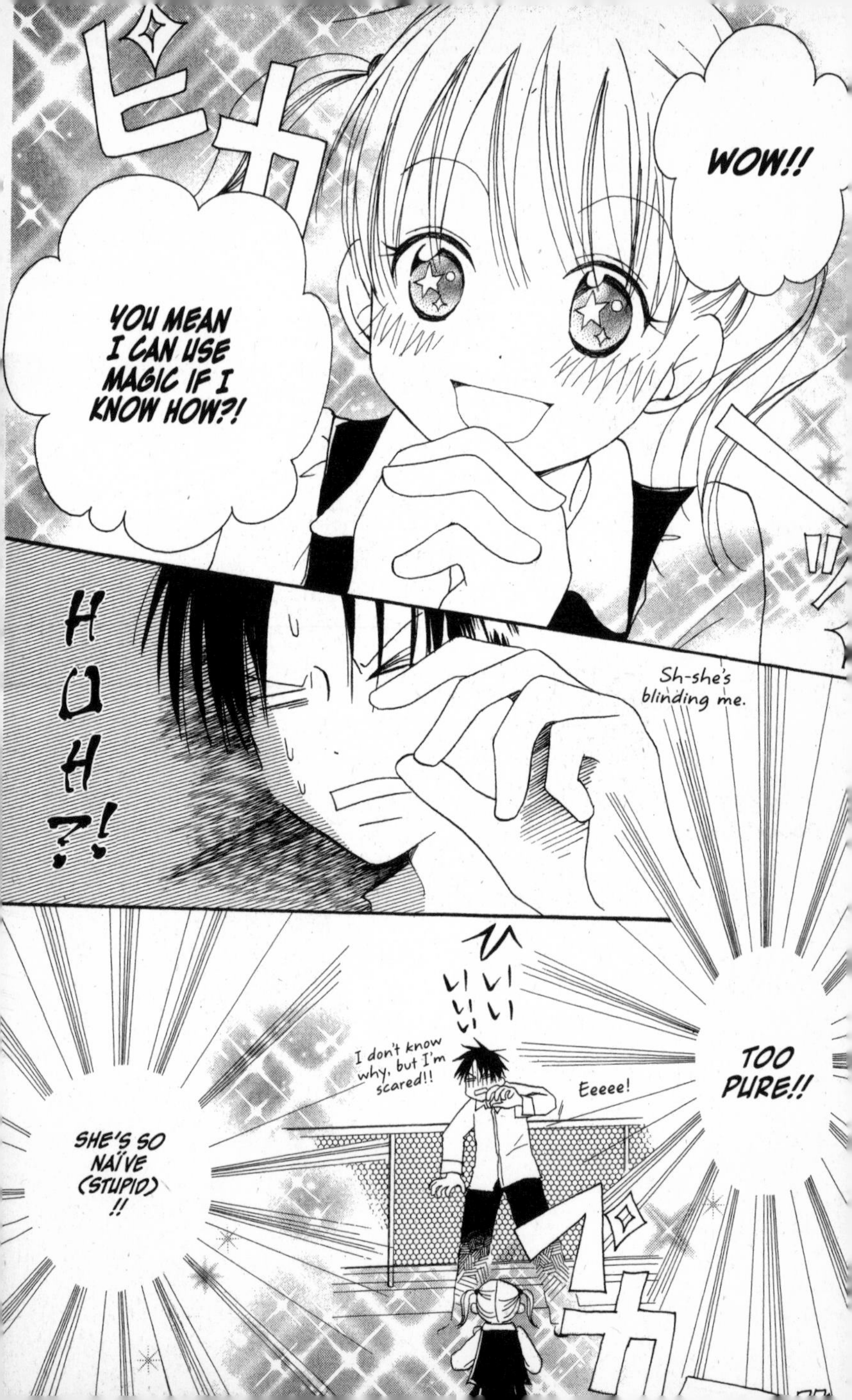
WOW!!
YOU MEAN I CAN USE MAGIC IF I KNOW HOW?!
Sh-she's blinding me.
HUH?!
TOO PURE!!
Eeeee!
I don't know why, but I'm scared!!
SHE'S SO NAÏVE (STUPID) !!

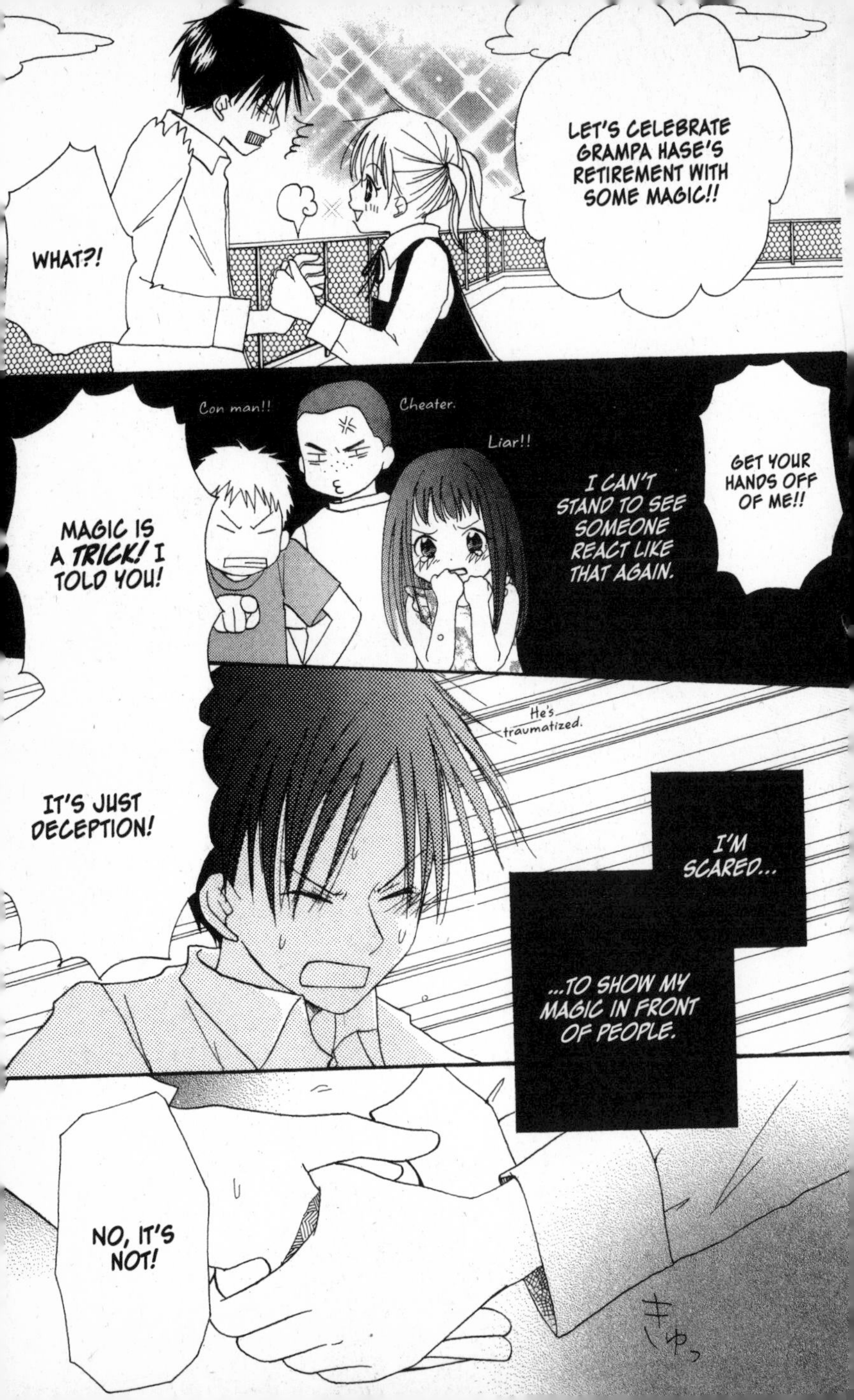
LET'S CELEBRATE GRAMPA HASE'S RETIREMENT WITH SOME MAGIC!!
WHAT?!
GET YOUR HANDS OFF OF ME!!
I CAN'T STAND TO SEE SOMEONE REACT LIKE THAT AGAIN.
Cheater.
Liar!!
Con man!!
MAGIC IS A TRICK! I TOLD YOU!
He's traumatized.
I'M SCARED...
...TO SHOW MY MAGIC IN FRONT OF PEOPLE.
IT'S JUST DECEPTION!
NO, IT'S NOT!
きゅっ

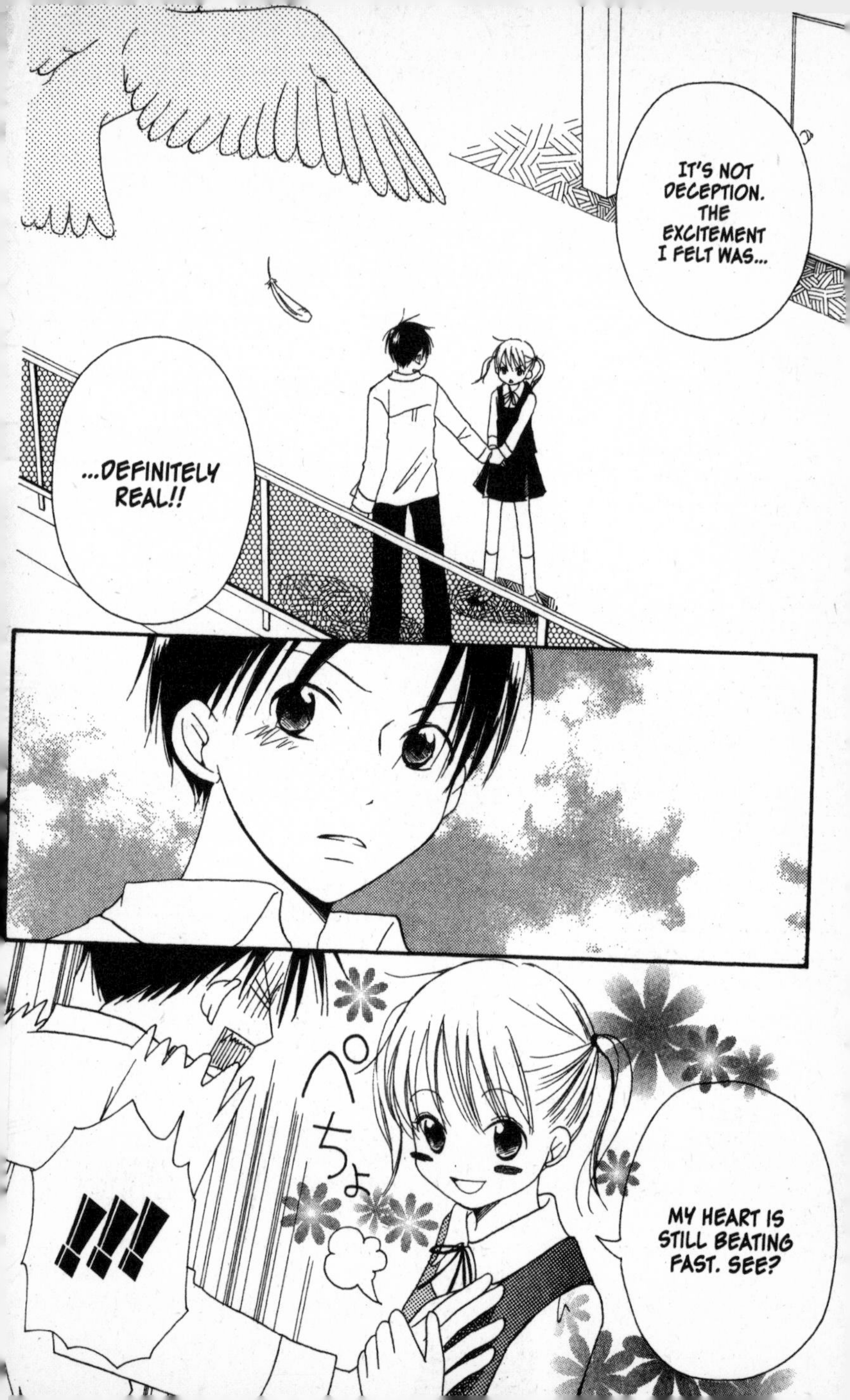
IT'S NOT DECEPTION. THE EXCITEMENT I FELT WAS...
...DEFINITELY REAL!!
MY HEART IS STILL BEATING FAST. SEE?
ぺちょ
!!!

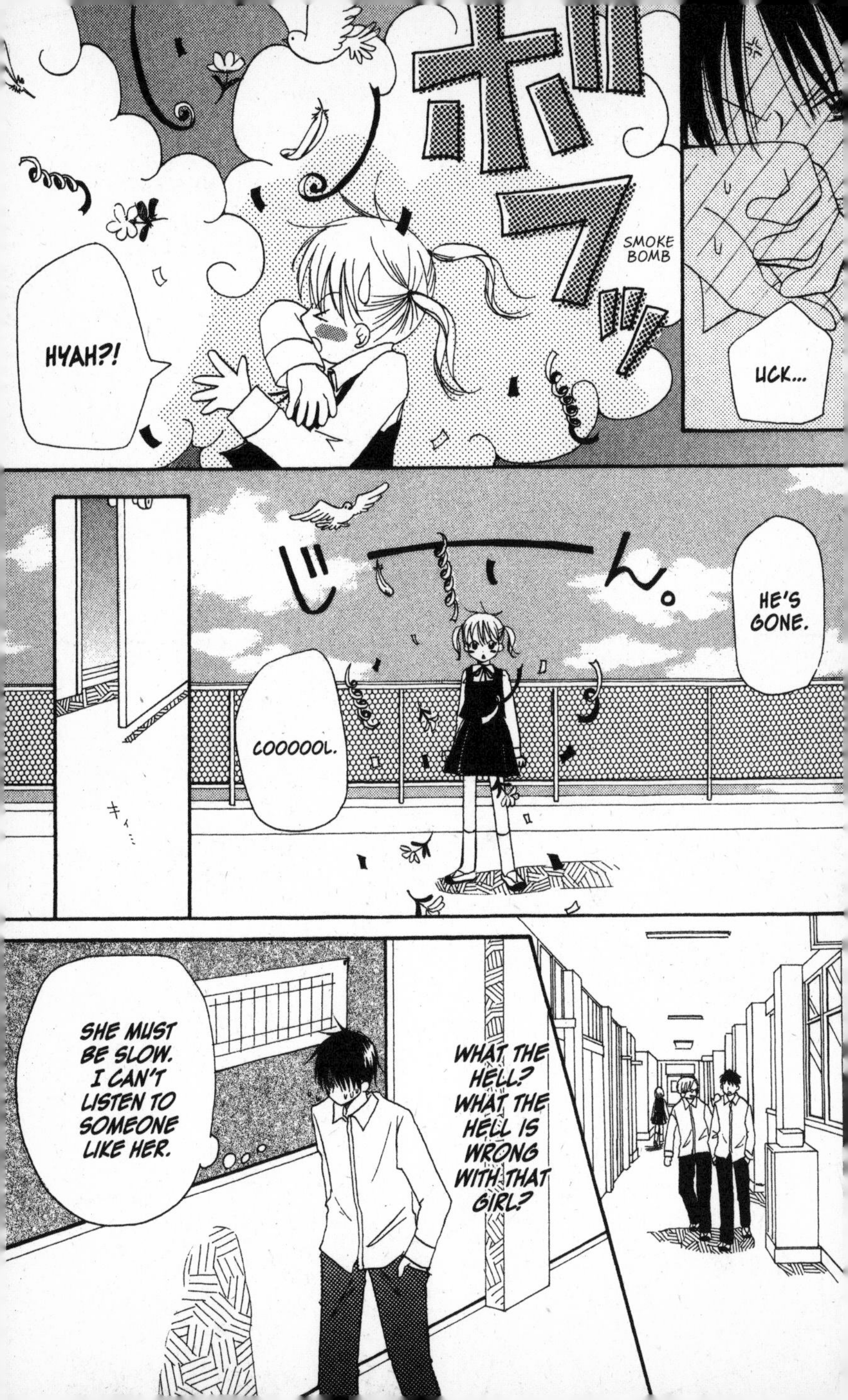
UCK...
ボフッ
SMOKE BOMB
HYAH?!
HE'S GONE.
じーーん。
COOOOOL.
キィ…
WHAT THE HELL? WHAT THE HELL IS WRONG WITH THAT GIRL?
SHE MUST BE SLOW. I CAN'T LISTEN TO SOMEONE LIKE HER.

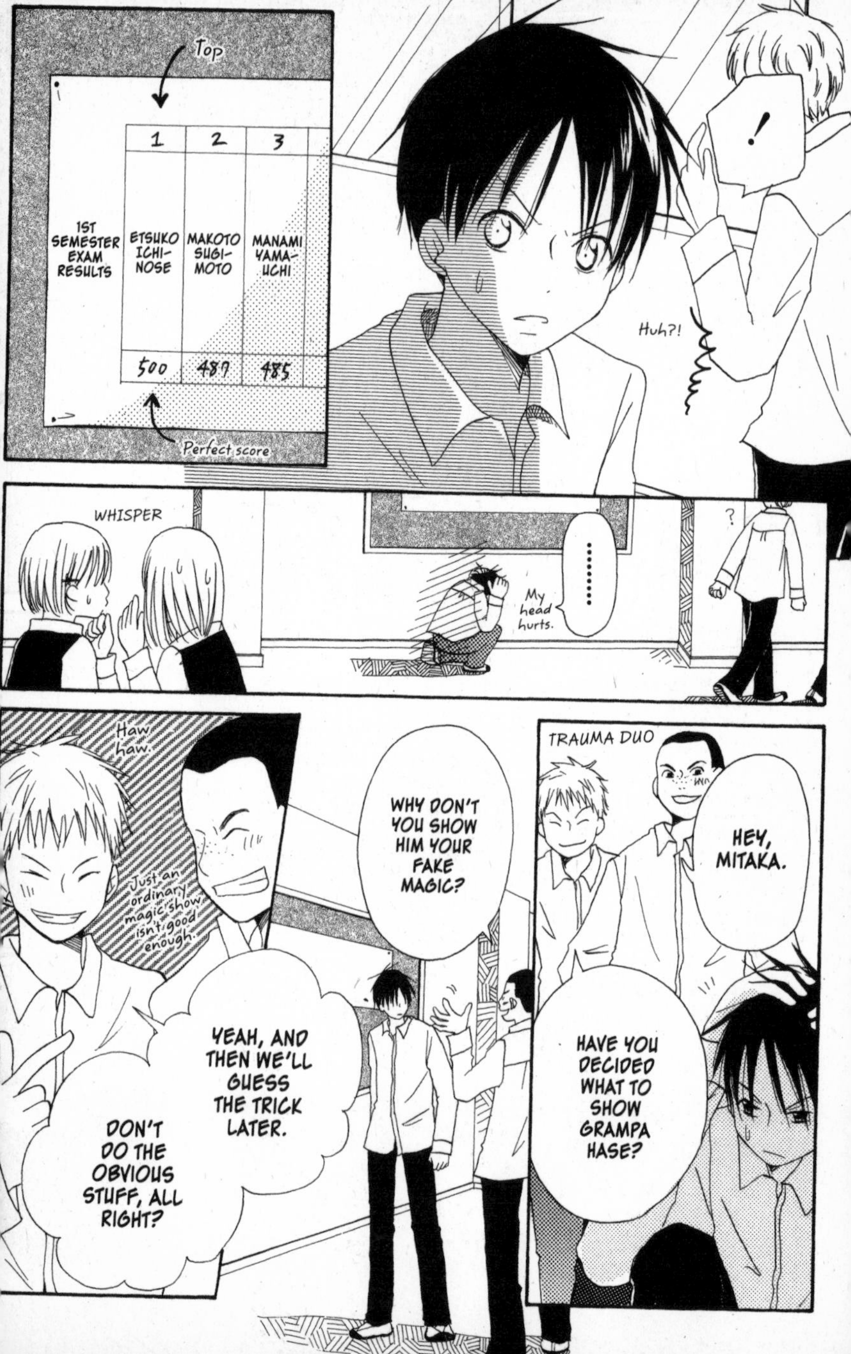
!
Huh?!
Top
1ST SEMESTER EXAM RESULTS
1 ETSUKO ICHINOSE 500
2 MAKOTO SUGIMOTO 487
3 MANAMI YAMAUCHI 485
Perfect score
?
My head hurts.
....
WHISPER
TRAUMA DUO
HEY, MITAKA.
HAVE YOU DECIDED WHAT TO SHOW GRAMPA HASE?
WHY DON'T YOU SHOW HIM YOUR FAKE MAGIC?
Haw haw.
Just an ordinary magic show isn't good enough.
YEAH, AND THEN WE'LL GUESS THE TRICK LATER.
DON'T DO THE OBVIOUS STUFF, ALL RIGHT?

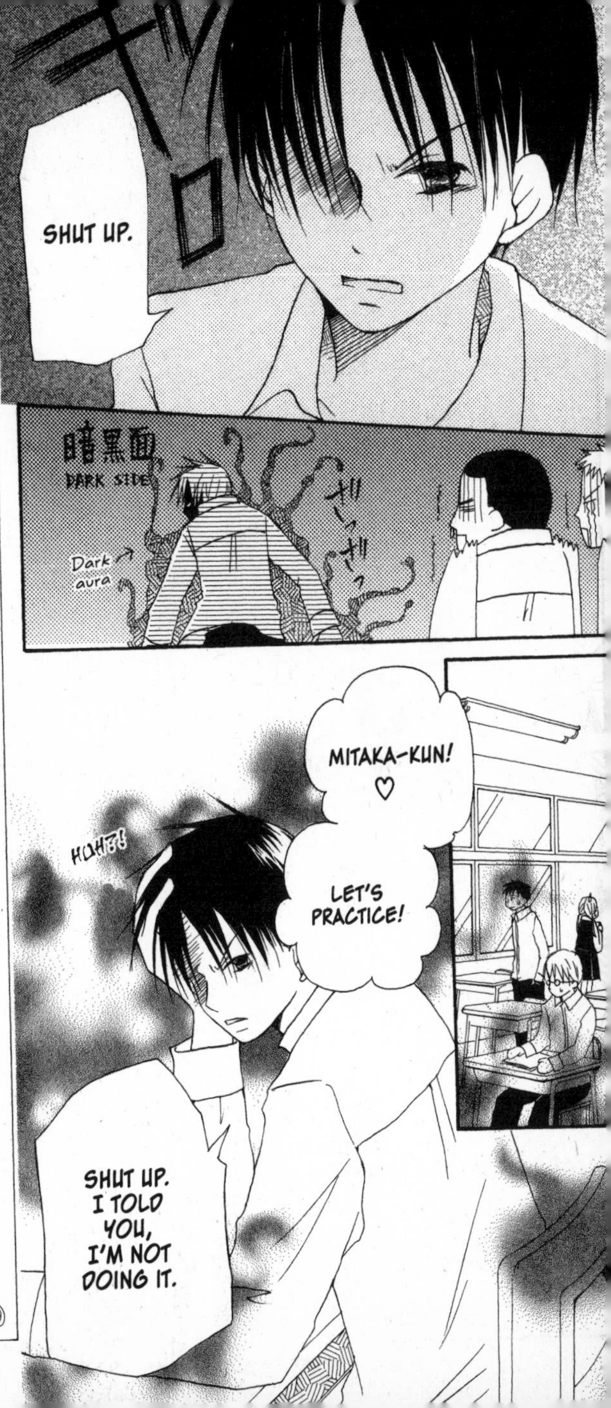
SHUT UP.
暗黒面
DARK SIDE
Dark aura
MITAKA-KUN! ♡
LET'S PRACTICE!
HUH?!
SHUT UP. I TOLD YOU, I'M NOT DOING IT.

☆5☆

I like the characters in this short story. I planned to make Rin a girl like Etsuko, but... Ha ha ha ha ha ha.

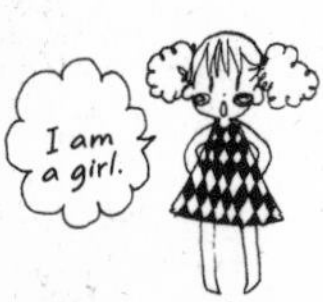
I am a girl.

Sorry about her weird accent, but she's not Japanese, you see?

This is the last column in this volume. Thank you for reading this far.

If you'd like to send me comments about my book, here's the address:
TOKYOPOP
c/o Hyun Joo Kim
5900 Wilshire
Blvd. Ste. 2000
Los Angeles,
CA, 90036

Thank you.

Hari Tokeino

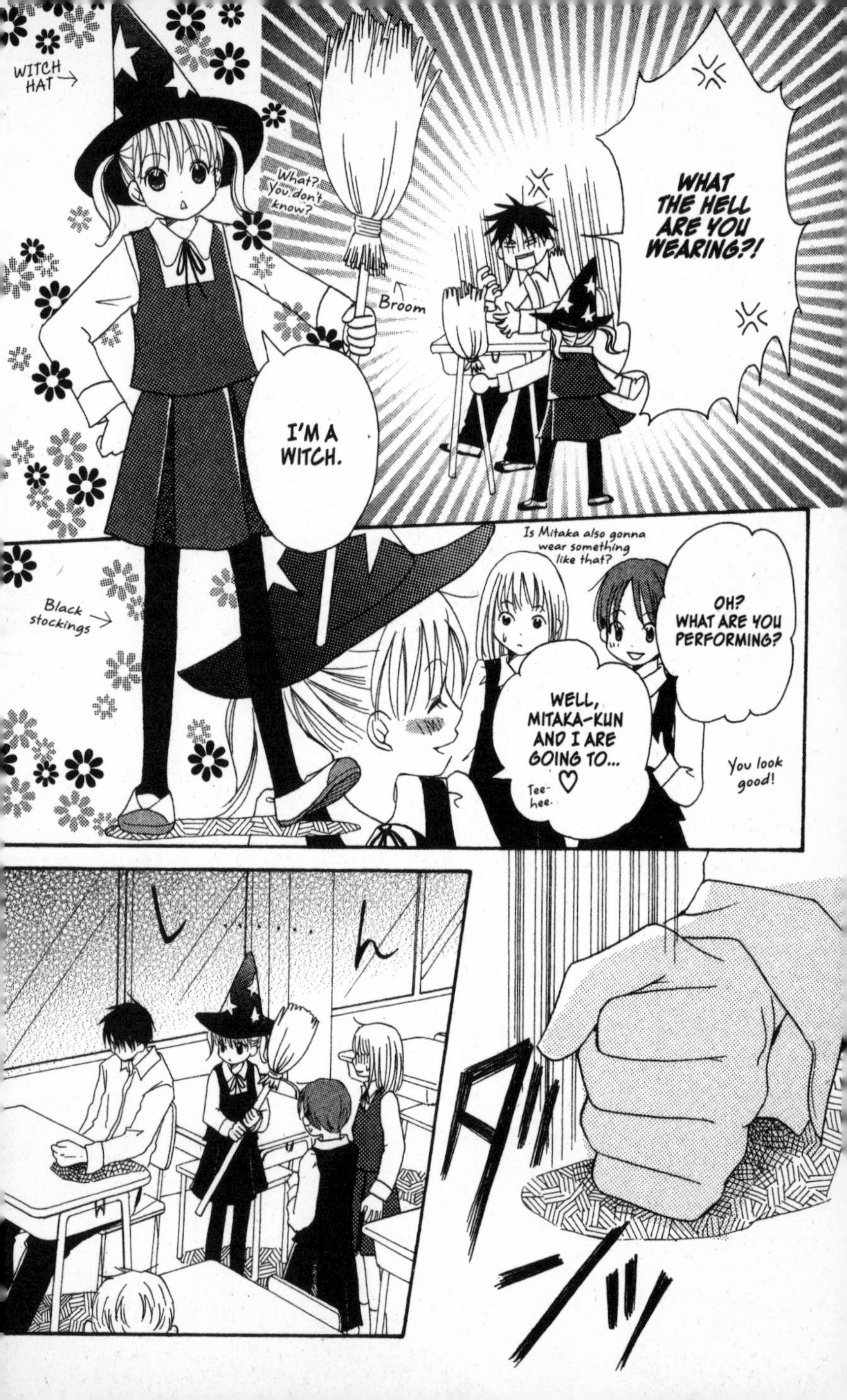
WHAT THE HELL ARE YOU WEARING?!
Is Mitaka also gonna wear something like that?
OH? WHAT ARE YOU PERFORMING?
You look good!
WELL, MITAKA-KUN AND I ARE GOING TO... ♡
Tee-hee.
What? You don't know?
WITCH HAT
Broom
I'M A WITCH.
Black stockings
し......ん

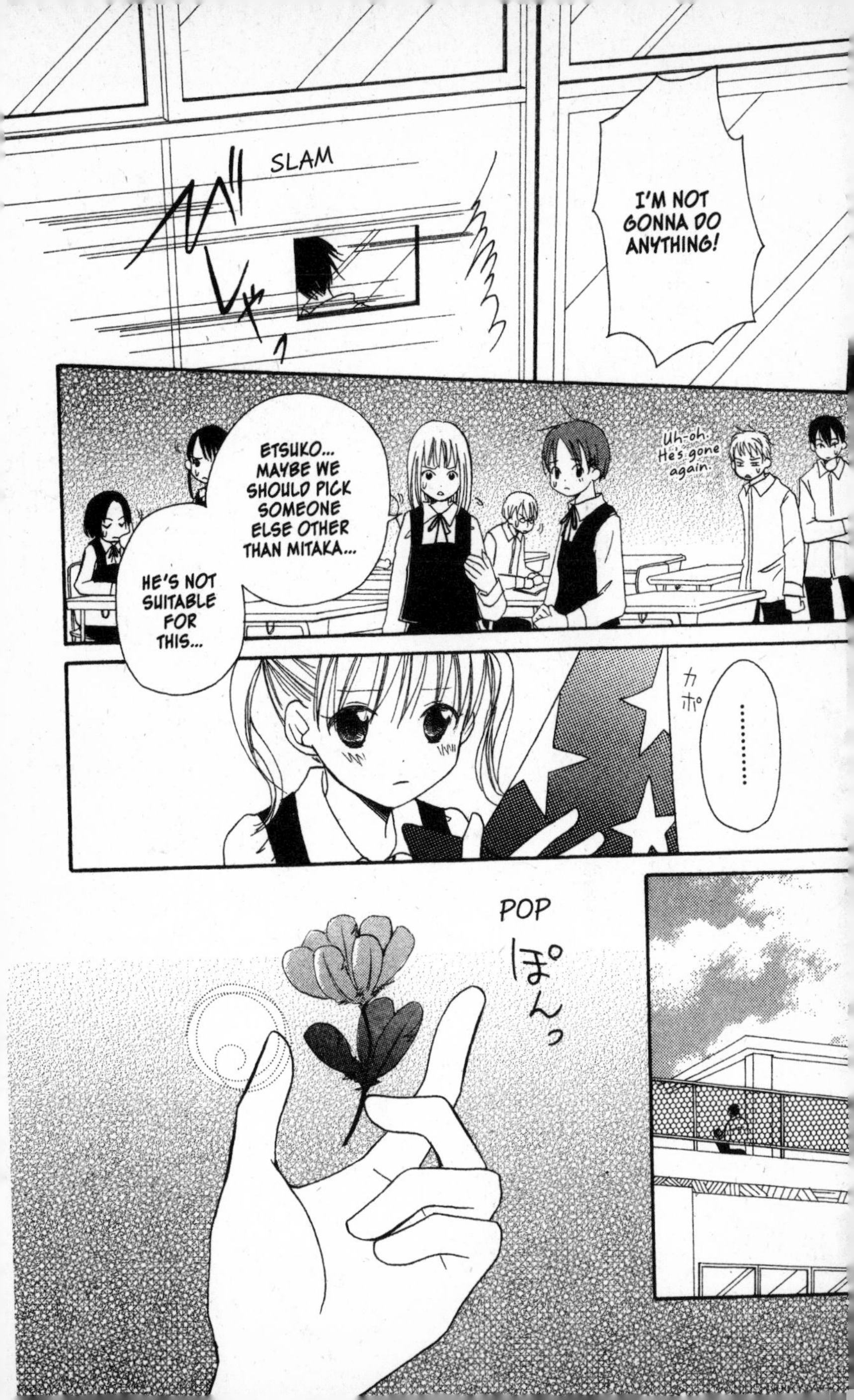
I'M NOT GONNA DO ANYTHING!
SLAM
Uh-oh. He's gone again.
ETSUKO... MAYBE WE SHOULD PICK SOMEONE ELSE OTHER THAN MITAKA...
HE'S NOT SUITABLE FOR THIS...
....
カポ
POP
ぽんっ

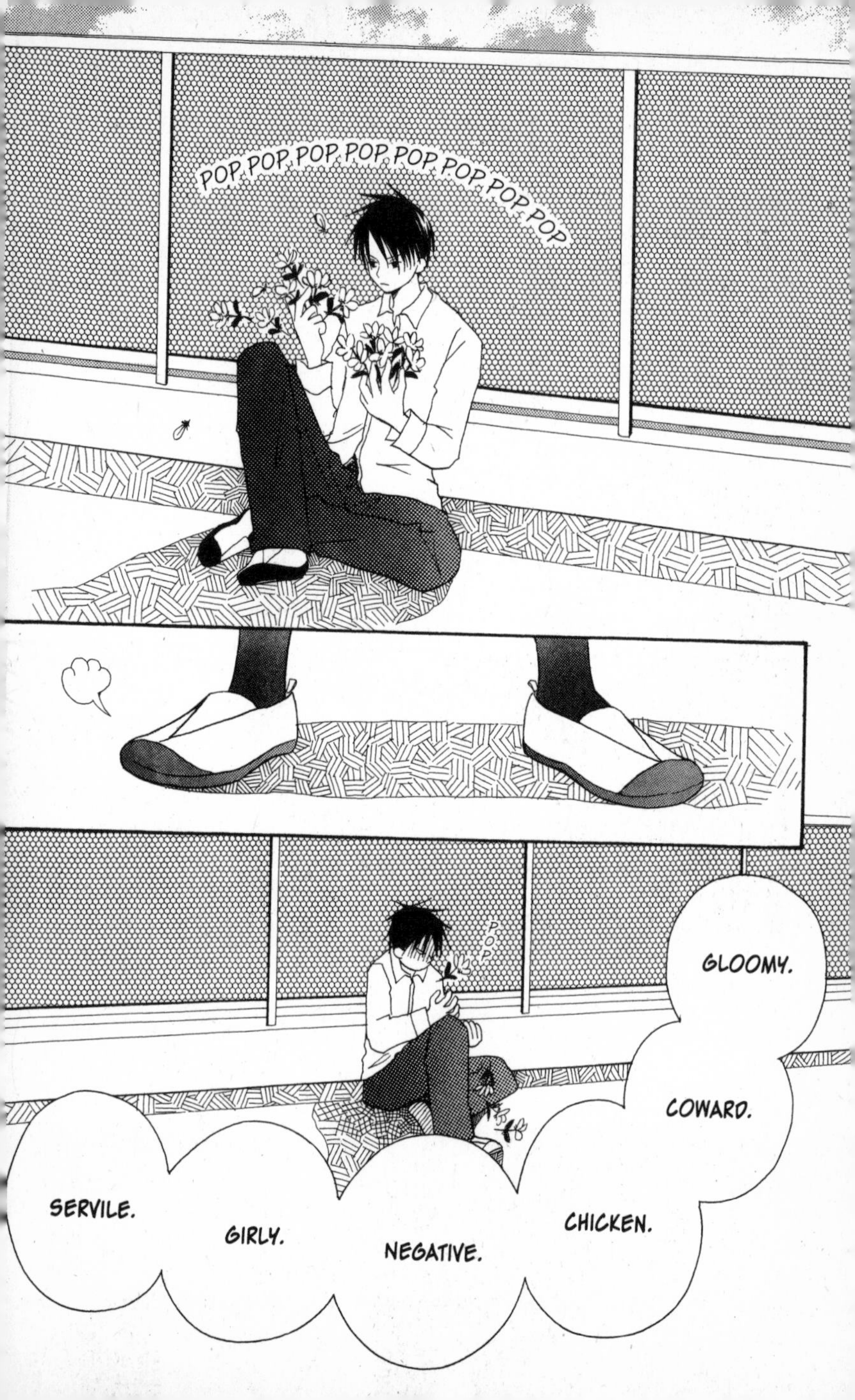
POP POP POP POP POP POP POP POP POP
POP
GLOOMY.
COWARD.
CHICKEN.
NEGATIVE.
GIRLY.
SERVILE.

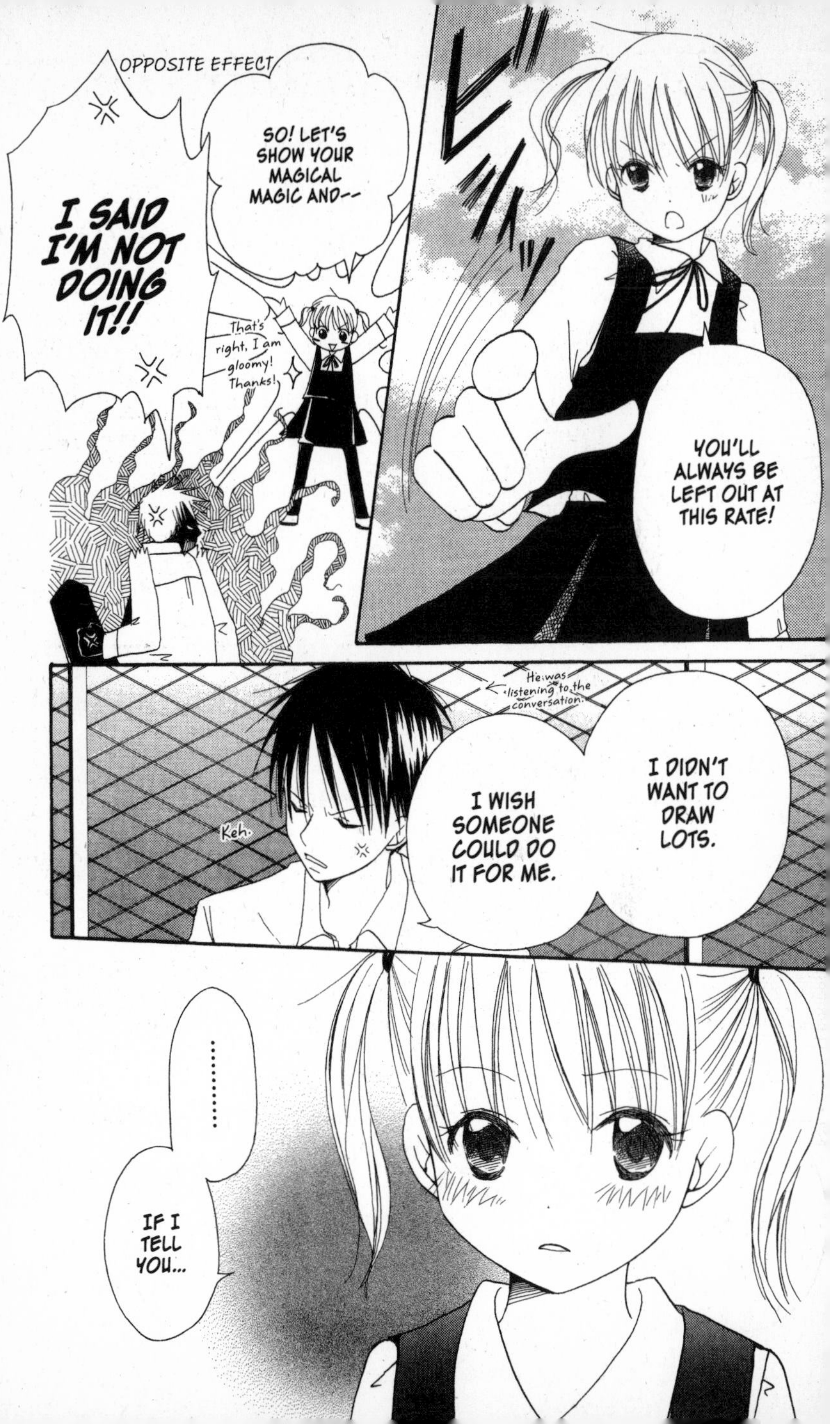
YOU'LL ALWAYS BE LEFT OUT AT THIS RATE!
OPPOSITE EFFECT
SO! LET'S SHOW YOUR MAGICAL MAGIC AND--
I SAID I'M NOT DOING IT!!
That's right, I am gloomy! Thanks!
He was listening to the conversation.
I DIDN'T WANT TO DRAW LOTS.
I WISH SOMEONE COULD DO IT FOR ME.
Keh.
......
IF I TELL YOU...

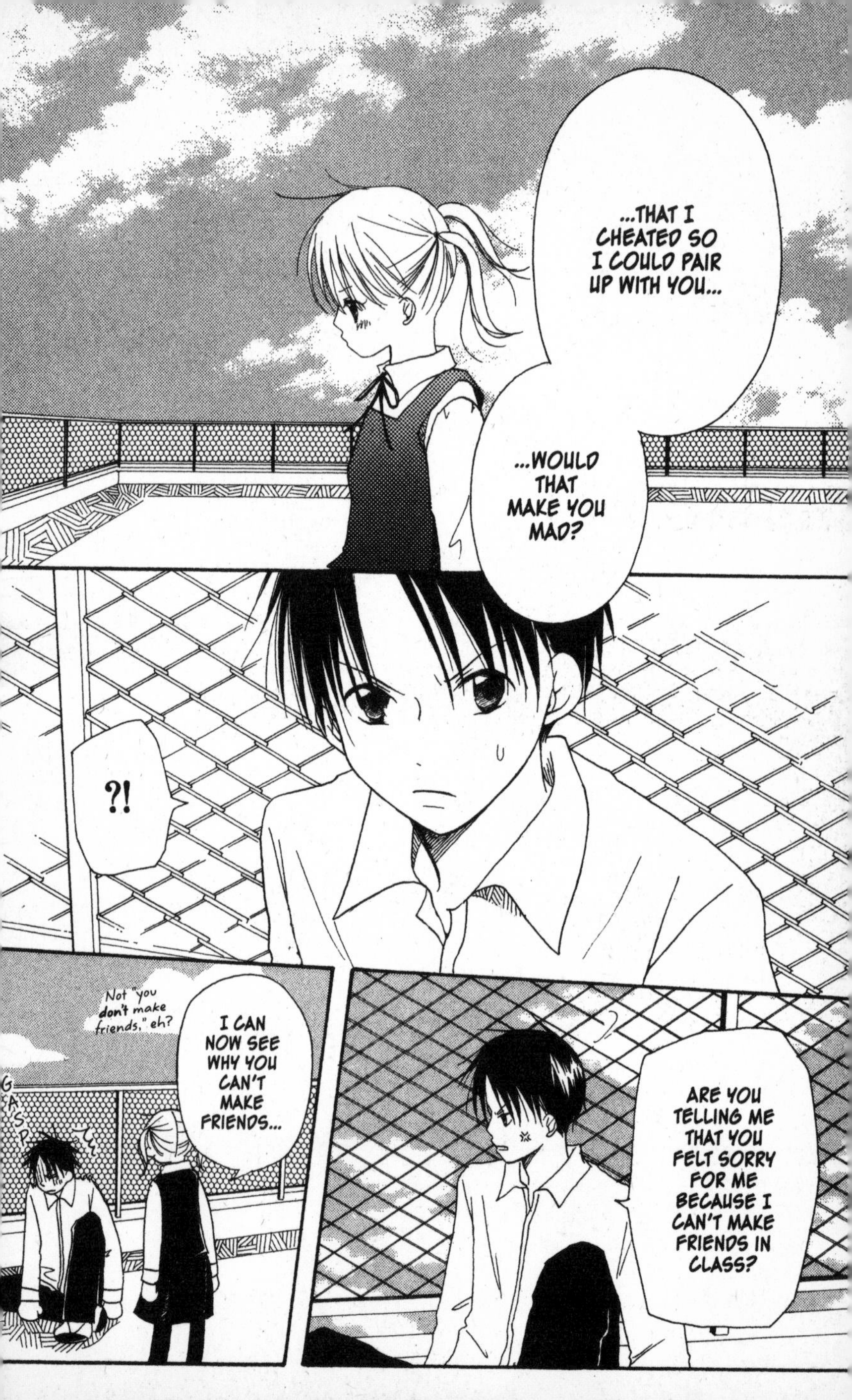
...THAT I CHEATED SO I COULD PAIR UP WITH YOU...
...WOULD THAT MAKE YOU MAD?
?!
ARE YOU TELLING ME THAT YOU FELT SORRY FOR ME BECAUSE I CAN'T MAKE FRIENDS IN CLASS?
I CAN NOW SEE WHY YOU CAN'T MAKE FRIENDS...
Not "you **don't** make friends," eh?
GASP

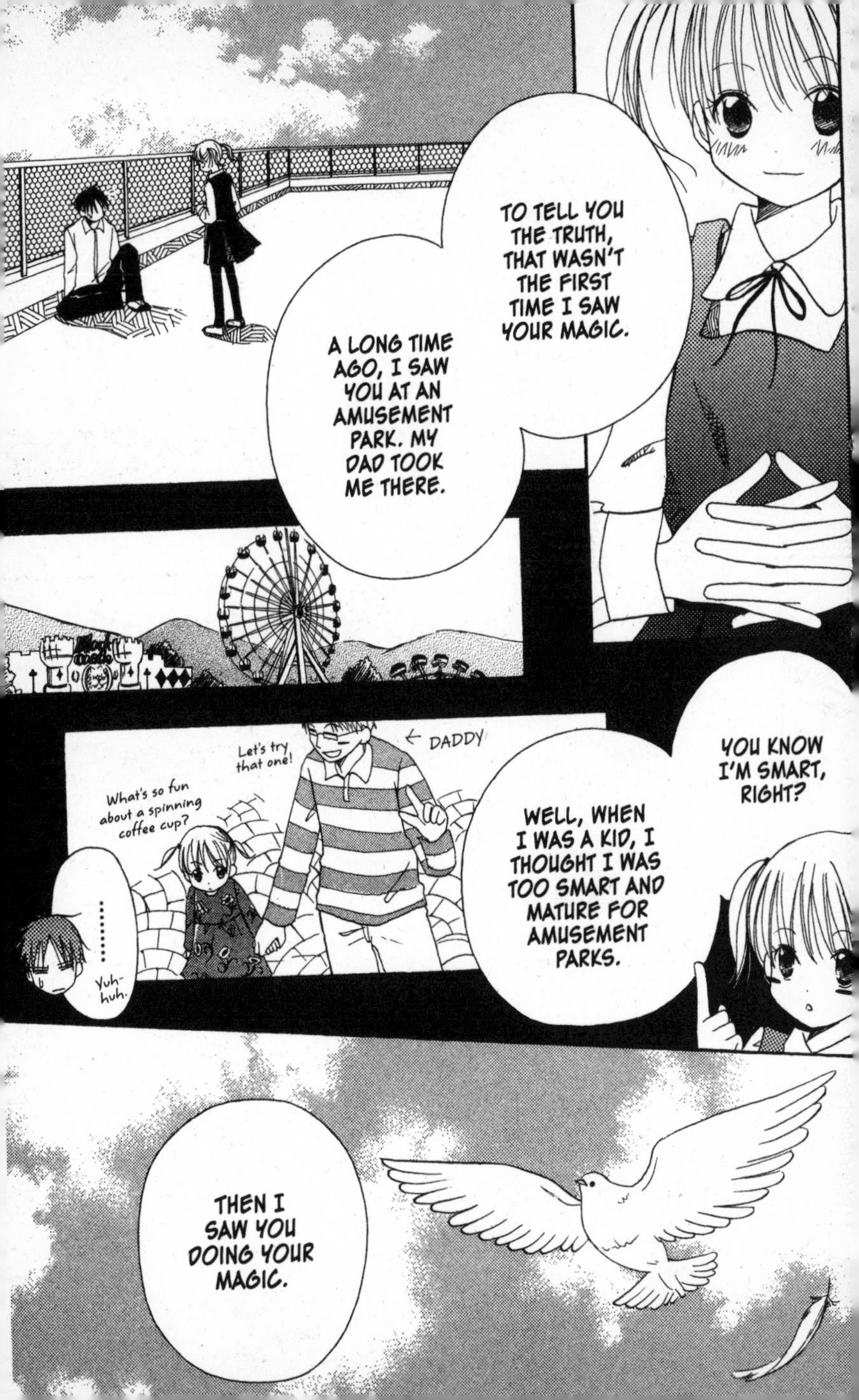
TO TELL YOU THE TRUTH, THAT WASN'T THE FIRST TIME I SAW YOUR MAGIC.
A LONG TIME AGO, I SAW YOU AT AN AMUSEMENT PARK. MY DAD TOOK ME THERE.
YOU KNOW I'M SMART, RIGHT?
WELL, WHEN I WAS A KID, I THOUGHT I WAS TOO SMART AND MATURE FOR AMUSEMENT PARKS.
← DADDY
Let's try that one!
What's so fun about a spinning coffee cup?
....
Yuh-huh.
THEN I SAW YOU DOING YOUR MAGIC.

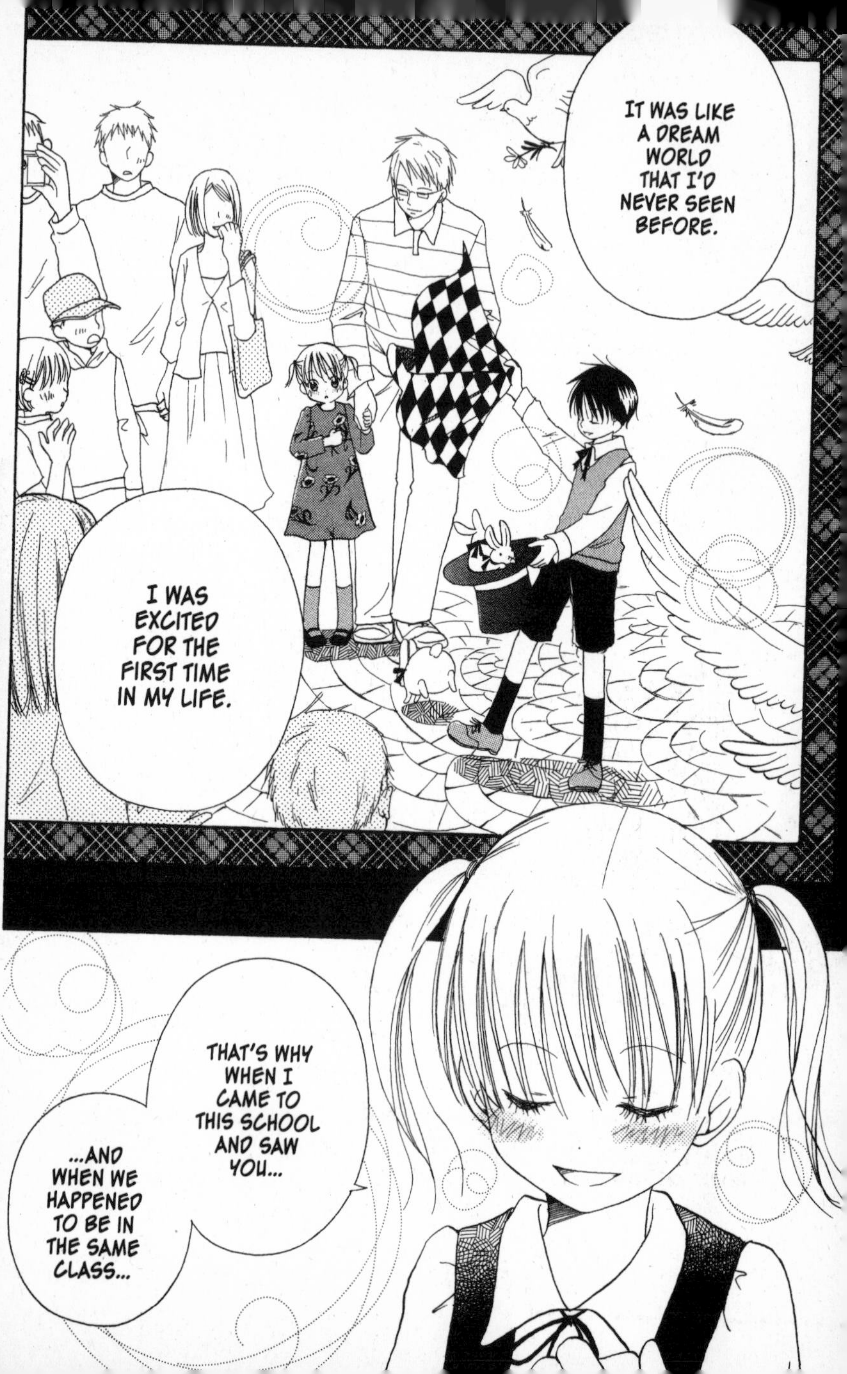
IT WAS LIKE A DREAM WORLD THAT I'D NEVER SEEN BEFORE.
I WAS EXCITED FOR THE FIRST TIME IN MY LIFE.
THAT'S WHY WHEN I CAME TO THIS SCHOOL AND SAW YOU...
...AND WHEN WE HAPPENED TO BE IN THE SAME CLASS...

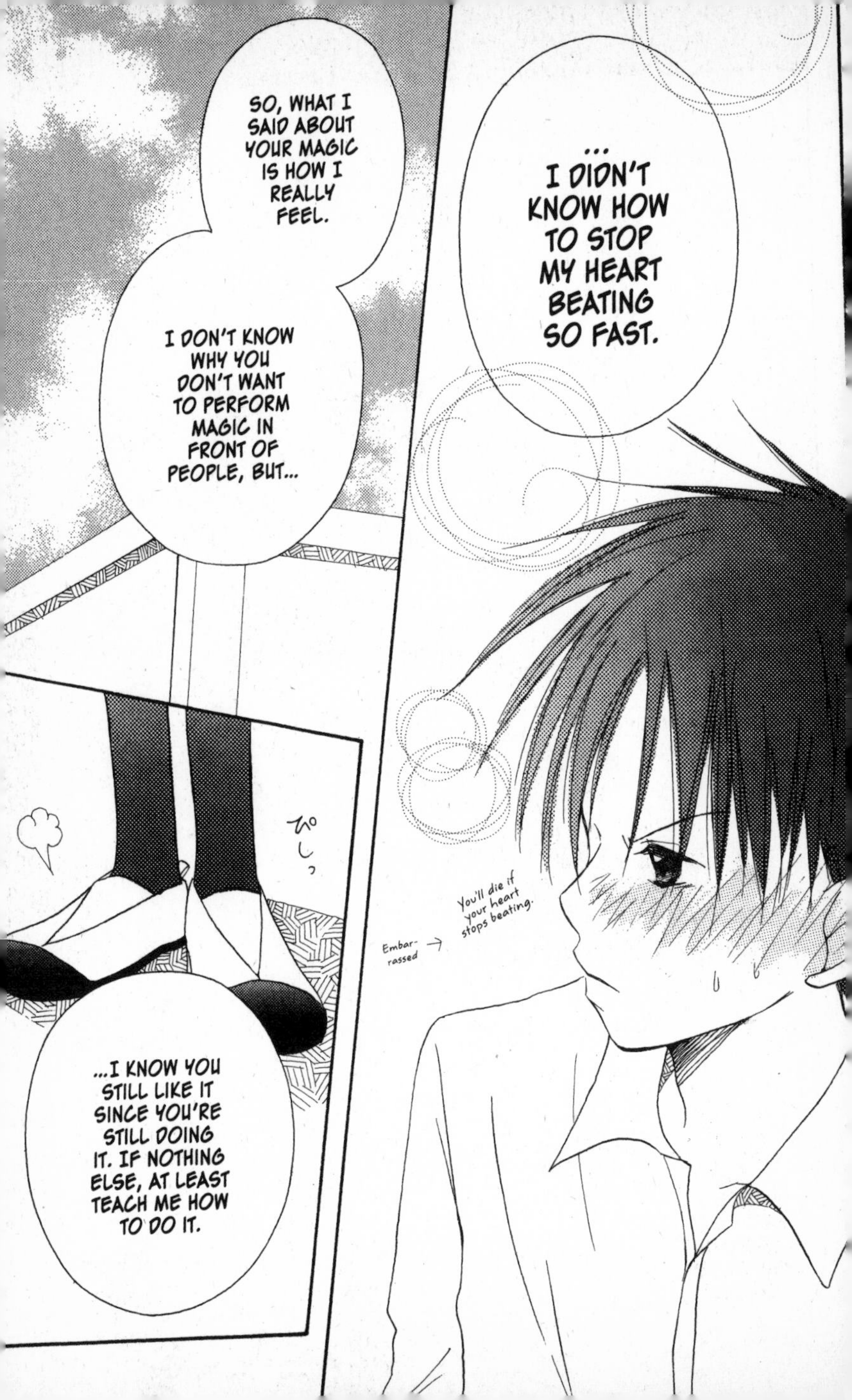

... I DIDN'T KNOW HOW TO STOP MY HEART BEATING SO FAST.
You'll die if your heart stops beating.
Embar-rassed →
SO, WHAT I SAID ABOUT YOUR MAGIC IS HOW I REALLY FEEL.
I DON'T KNOW WHY YOU DON'T WANT TO PERFORM MAGIC IN FRONT OF PEOPLE, BUT...
ぴしっ
...I KNOW YOU STILL LIKE IT SINCE YOU'RE STILL DOING IT. IF NOTHING ELSE, AT LEAST TEACH ME HOW TO DO IT.

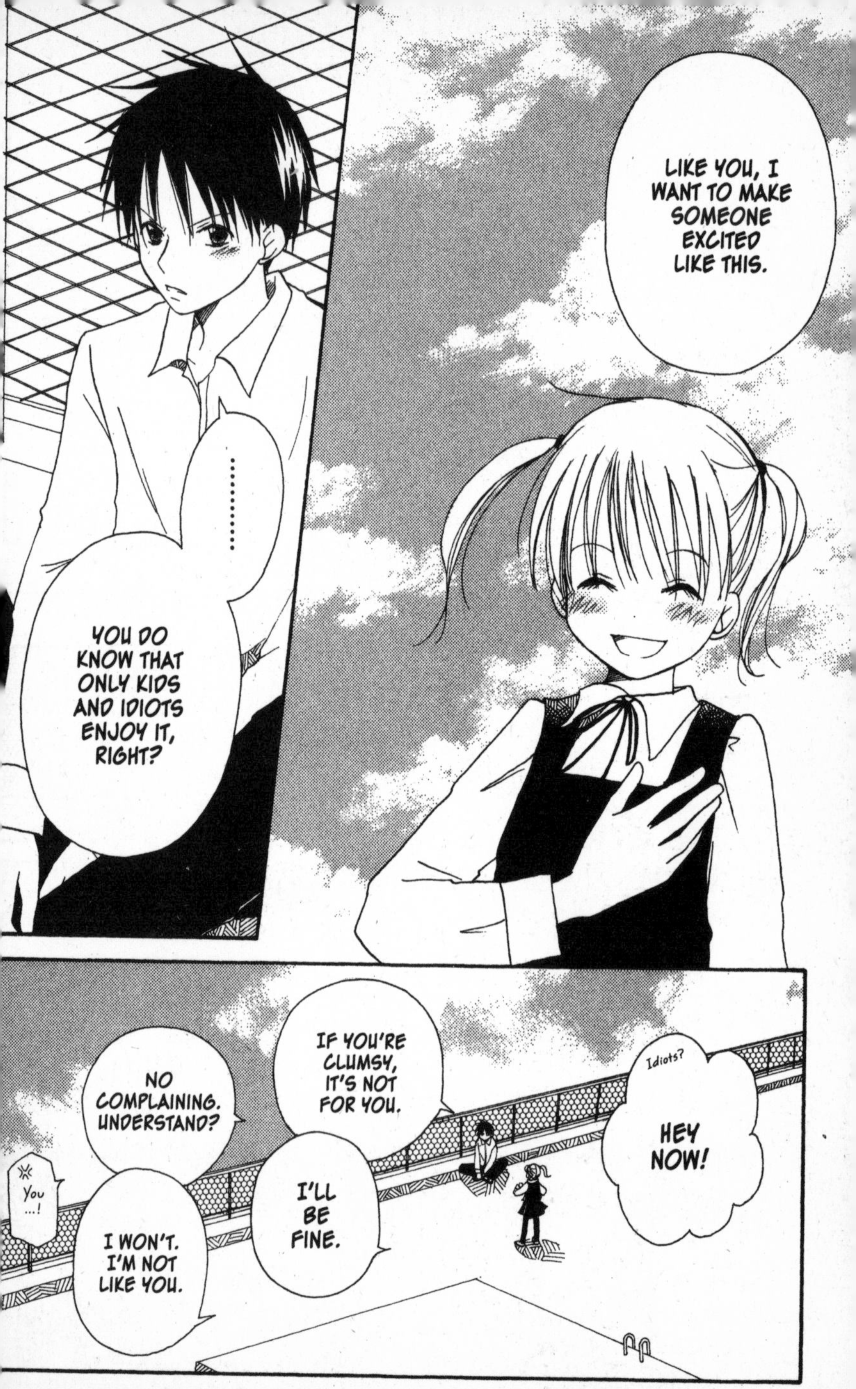
LIKE YOU, I WANT TO MAKE SOMEONE EXCITED LIKE THIS.
....
YOU DO KNOW THAT ONLY KIDS AND IDIOTS ENJOY IT, RIGHT?
Idiots?
HEY NOW!
IF YOU'RE CLUMSY, IT'S NOT FOR YOU.
I'LL BE FINE.
NO COMPLAINING. UNDERSTAND?
※ You ...!
I WON'T. I'M NOT LIKE YOU.

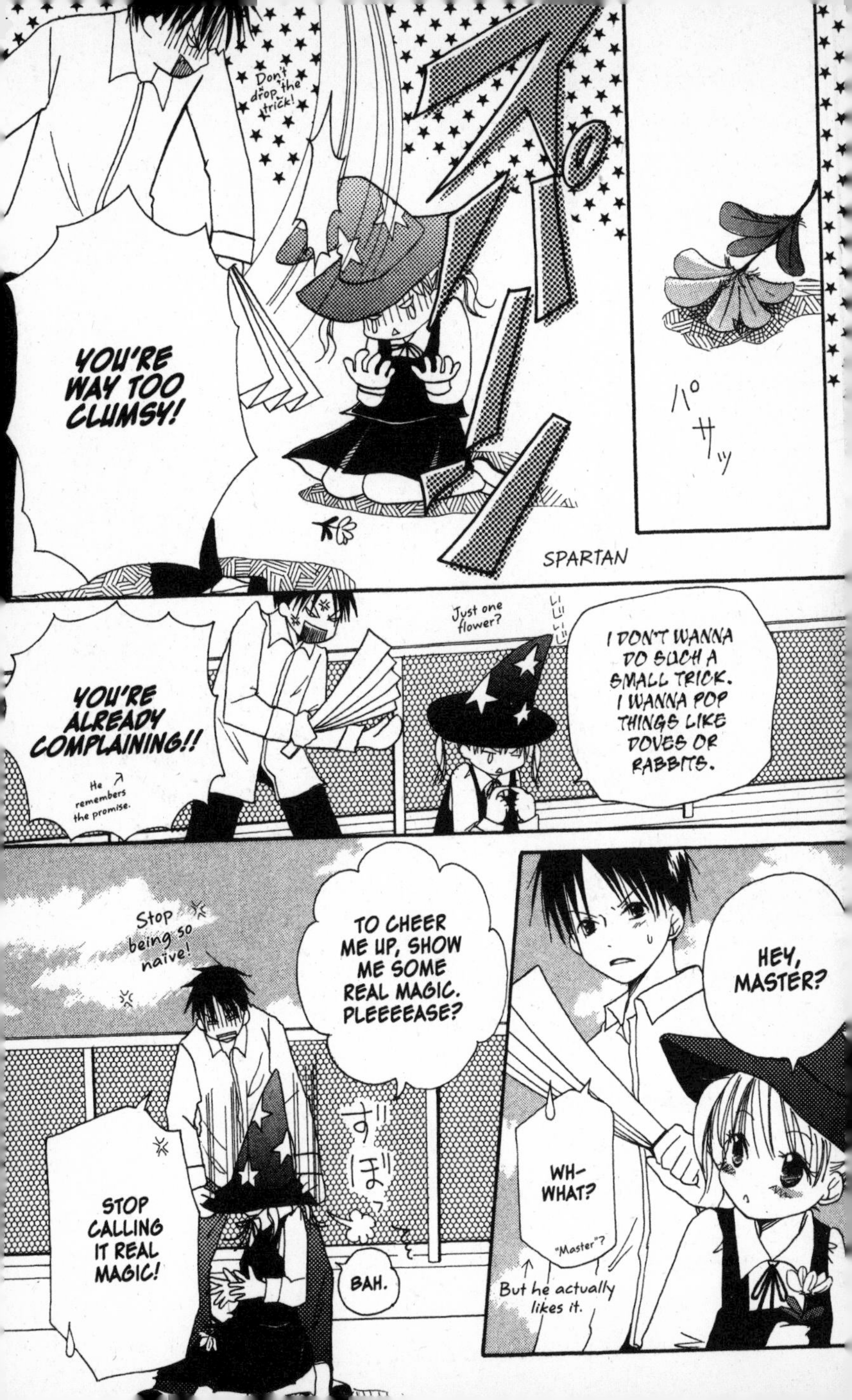
パサッ
Don't drop the trick!
YOU'RE WAY TOO CLUMSY!
SPARTAN
I DON'T WANNA DO SUCH A SMALL TRICK. I WANNA POP THINGS LIKE DOVES OR RABBITS.
いじいじ
Just one flower?
YOU'RE ALREADY COMPLAINING!!
He remembers the promise.
HEY, MASTER?
WH-WHAT?
"Master"?
But he actually likes it.
TO CHEER ME UP, SHOW ME SOME REAL MAGIC. PLEEEEASE?
Stop being so naïve!
ずぼっ
BAH.
STOP CALLING IT REAL MAGIC!

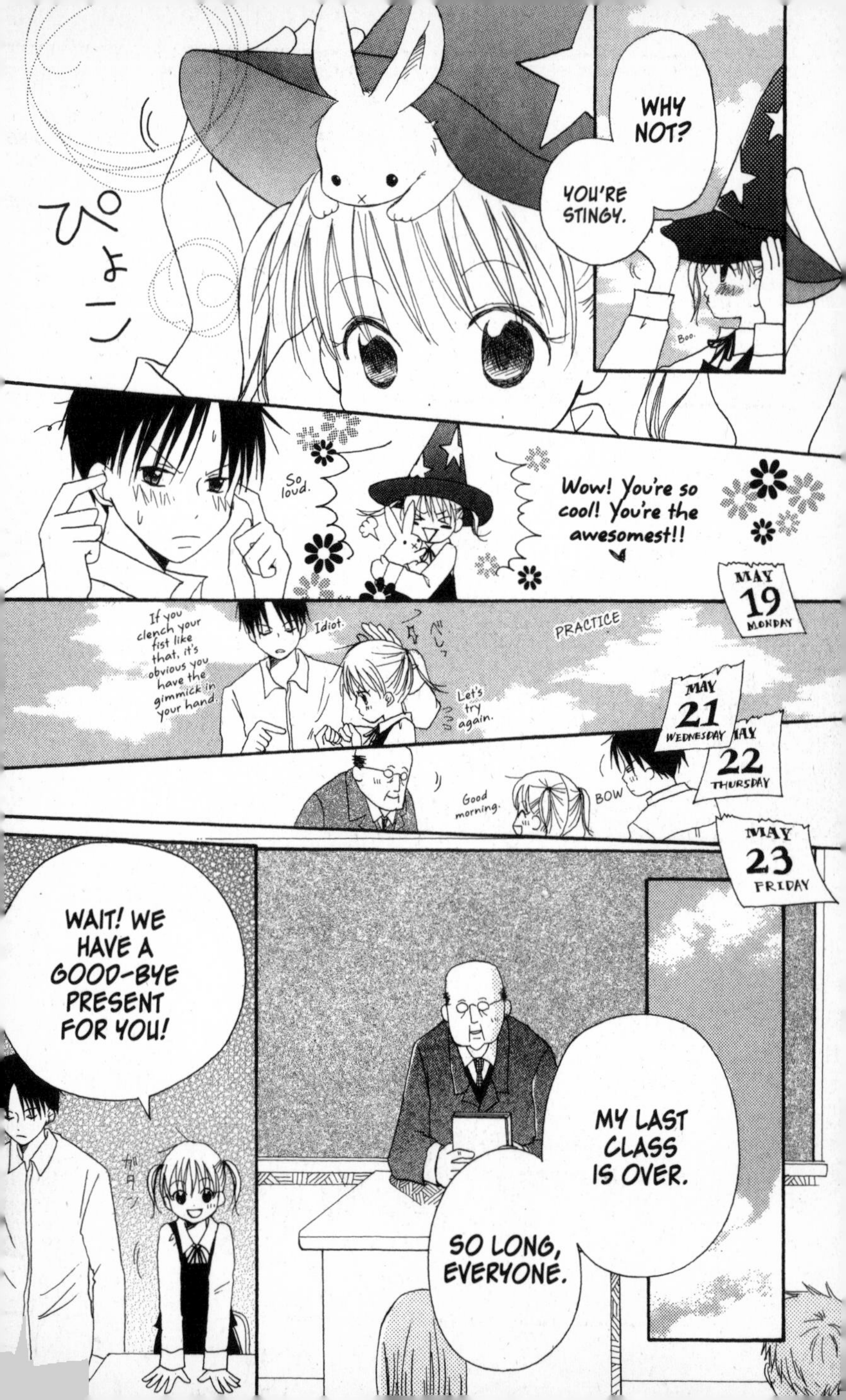
WHY NOT?
YOU'RE STINGY.
Boo.
ぴょこン
Wow! You're so cool! You're the awesomest!!
So loud.
MAY 19 MONDAY
PRACTICE
Let's try again.
べしっ
Idiot.
If you clench your fist like that, it's obvious you have the gimmick in your hand.
MAY 21 WEDNESDAY
22 THURSDAY
BOW
Good morning.
MAY 23 FRIDAY
MY LAST CLASS IS OVER.
SO LONG, EVERYONE.
WAIT! WE HAVE A GOOD-BYE PRESENT FOR YOU!
ガタン

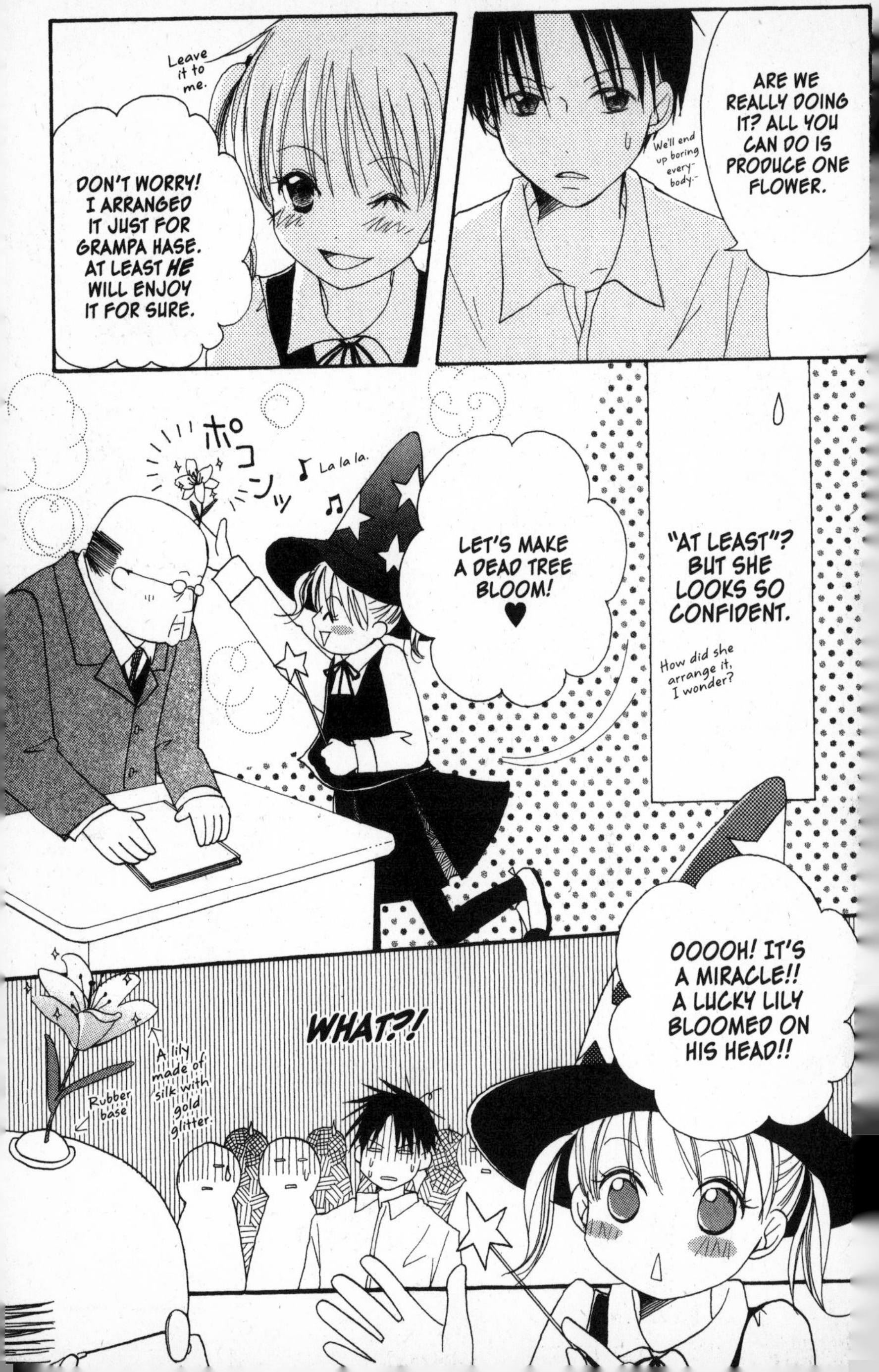
ARE WE REALLY DOING IT? ALL YOU CAN DO IS PRODUCE ONE FLOWER.
We'll end up boring every-body.
Leave it to me.
DON'T WORRY! I ARRANGED IT JUST FOR GRAMPA HASE. AT LEAST HE WILL ENJOY IT FOR SURE.
"AT LEAST"? BUT SHE LOOKS SO CONFIDENT.
How did she arrange it, I wonder?
LET'S MAKE A DEAD TREE BLOOM! ♥
La la la.
ポコンッ
OOOOH! IT'S A MIRACLE!! A LUCKY LILY BLOOMED ON HIS HEAD!!
WHAT?!
A lily made of silk with gold glitter.
Rubber base

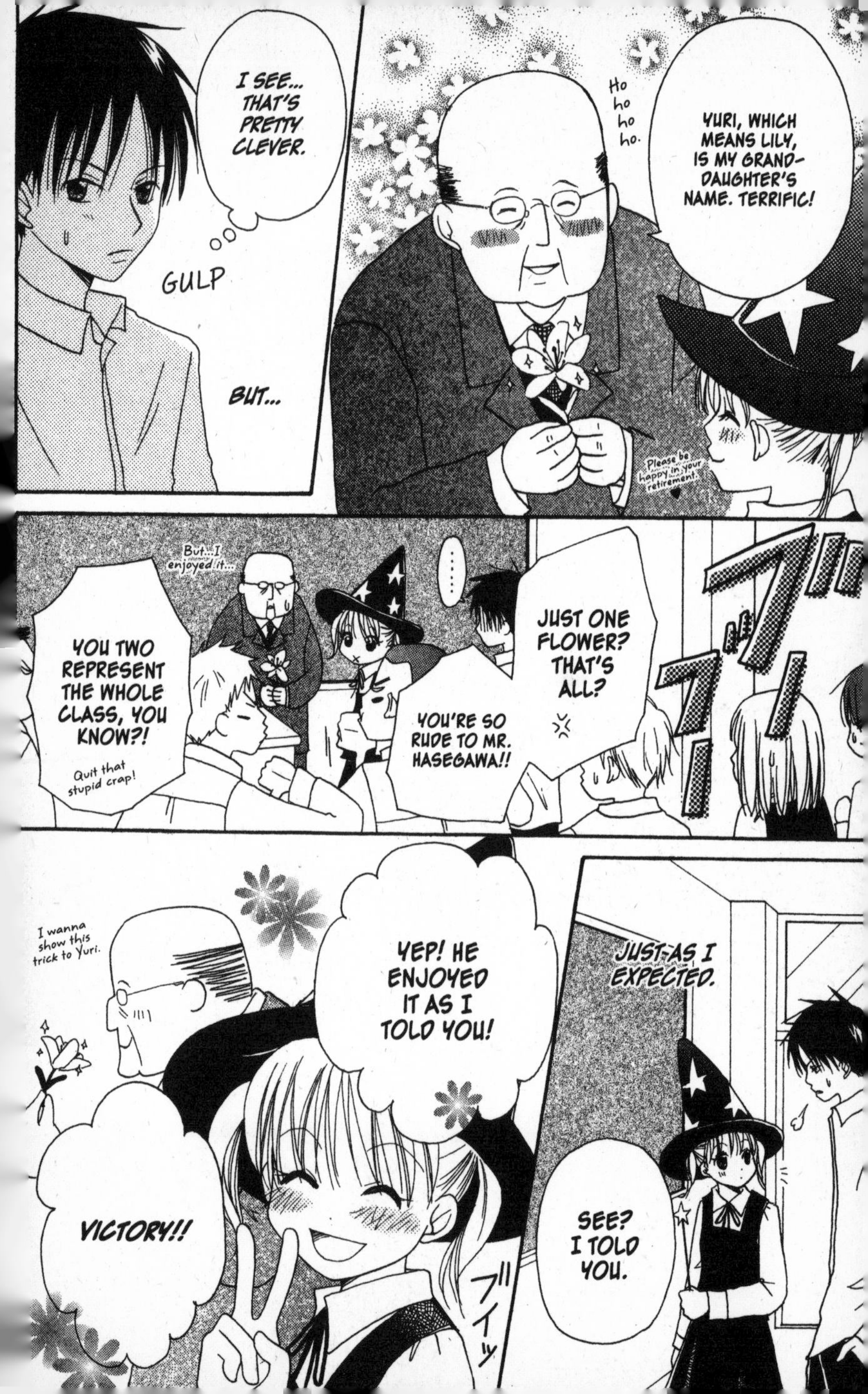
Ho ho ho ho.
YURI, WHICH MEANS LILY, IS MY GRAND-DAUGHTER'S NAME. TERRIFIC!
Please be happy in your retirement.
I SEE... THAT'S PRETTY CLEVER.
GULP
BUT...
......
JUST ONE FLOWER? THAT'S ALL?
YOU'RE SO RUDE TO MR. HASEGAWA!!
YOU TWO REPRESENT THE WHOLE CLASS, YOU KNOW?!
Quit that stupid crap!
But...I enjoyed it...
JUST AS I EXPECTED.
SEE? I TOLD YOU.
YEP! HE ENJOYED IT AS I TOLD YOU!
I wanna show this trick to Yuri.
VICTORY!!

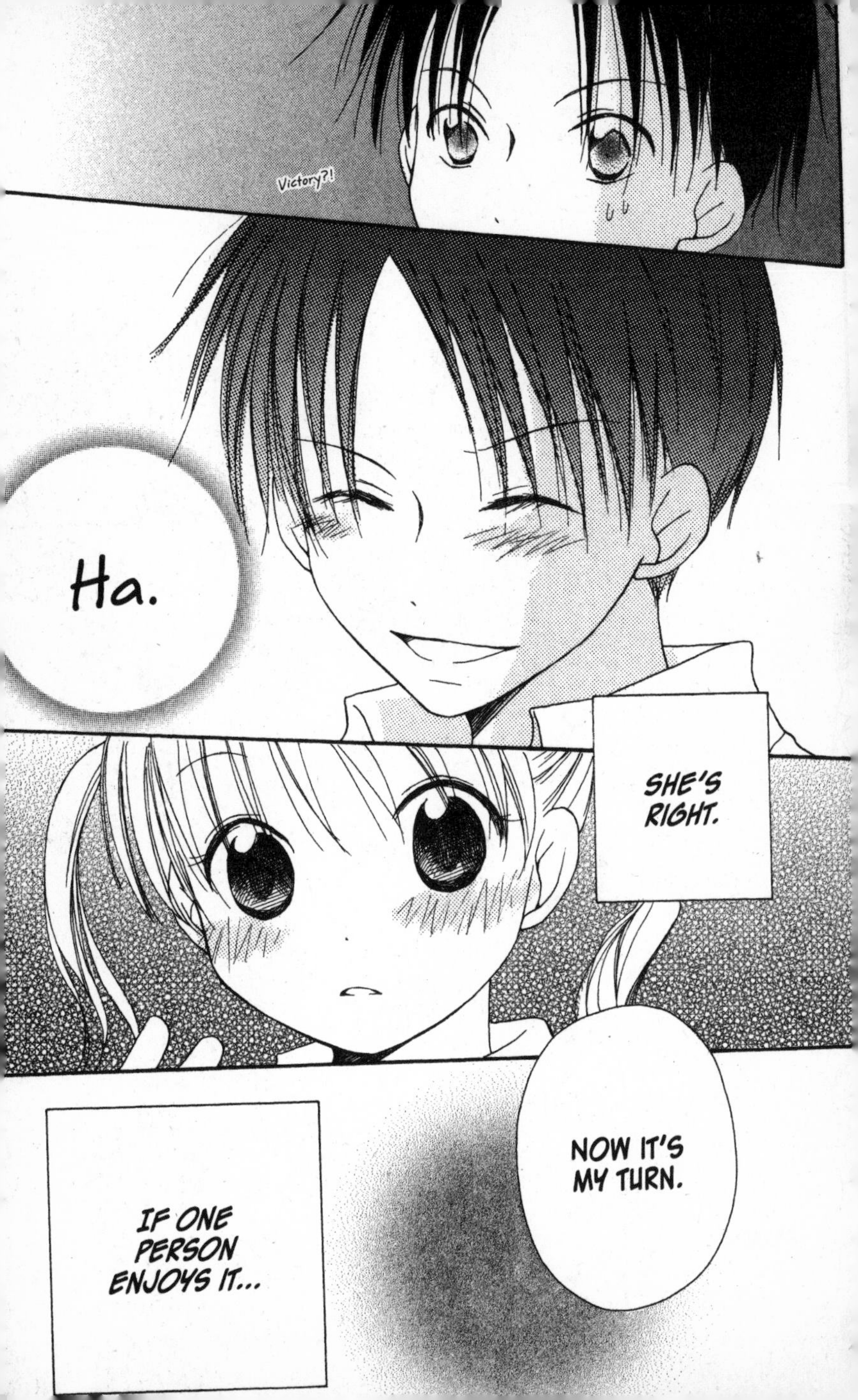
Victory?!
Ha.
SHE'S RIGHT.
NOW IT'S MY TURN.
IF ONE PERSON ENJOYS IT...

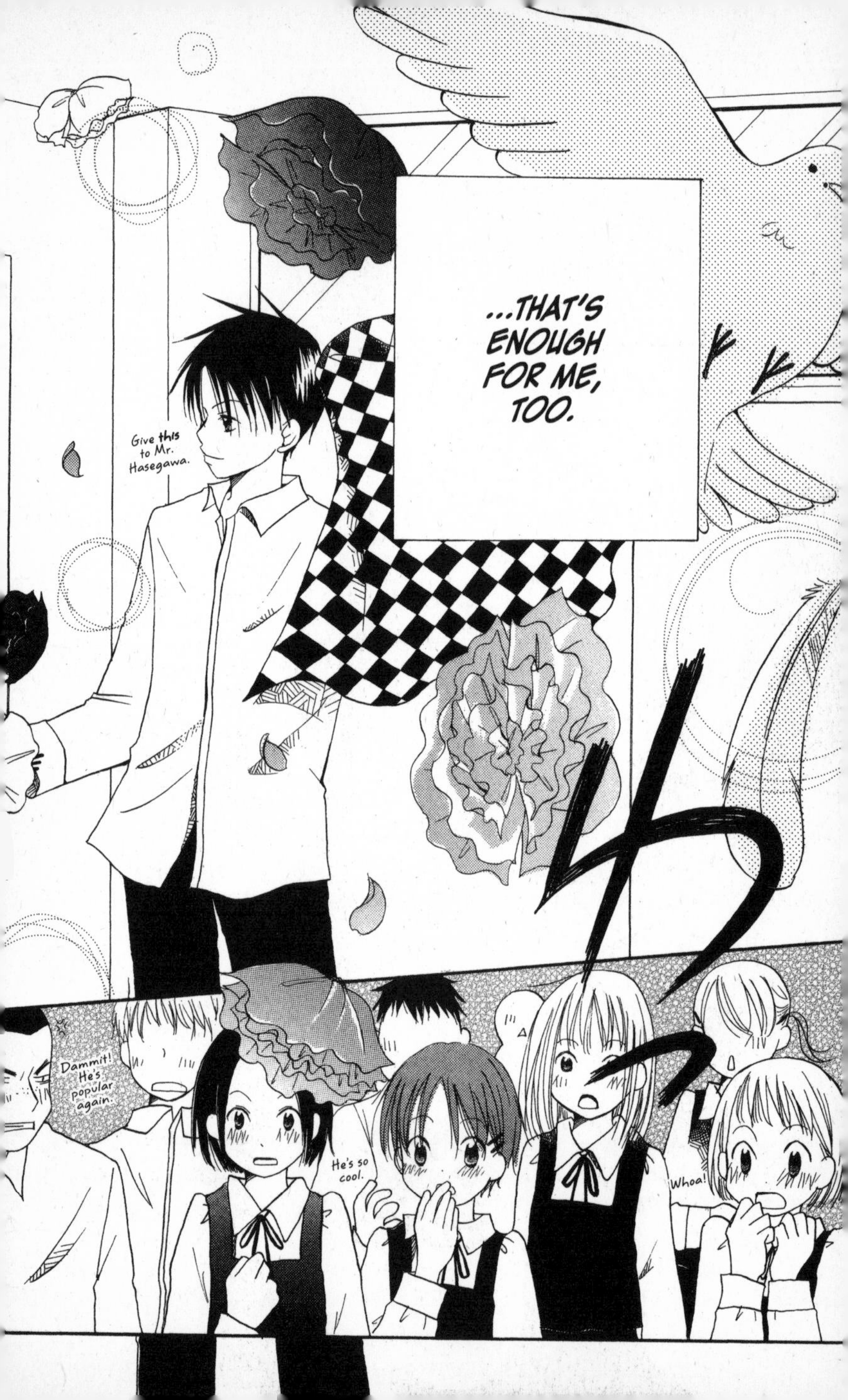
...THAT'S ENOUGH FOR ME, TOO.
Give this to Mr. Hasegawa.
Whoa!
He's so cool.
Dammit! He's popular again.

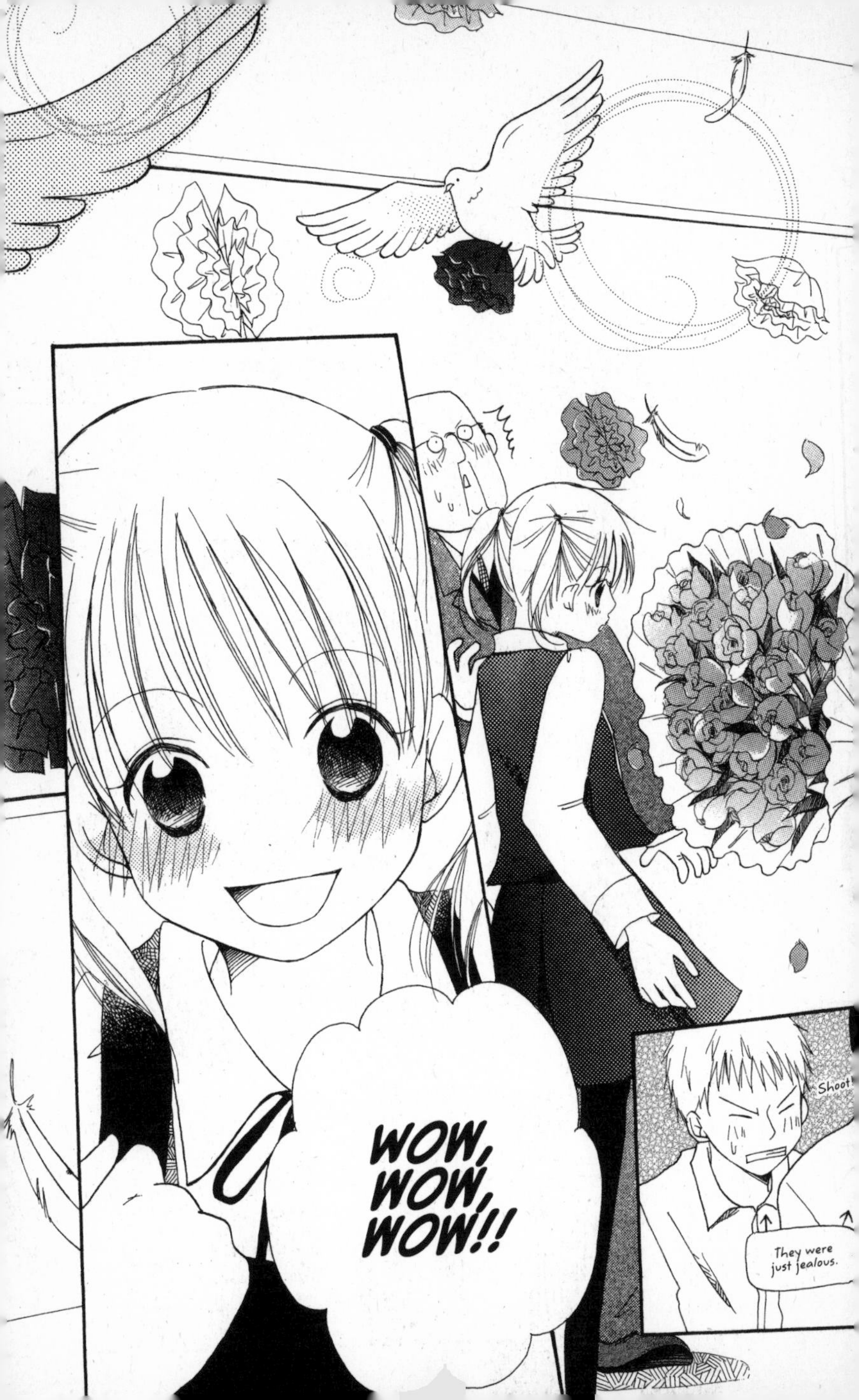
WOW, WOW, WOW!!
Shoot
They were just jealous.

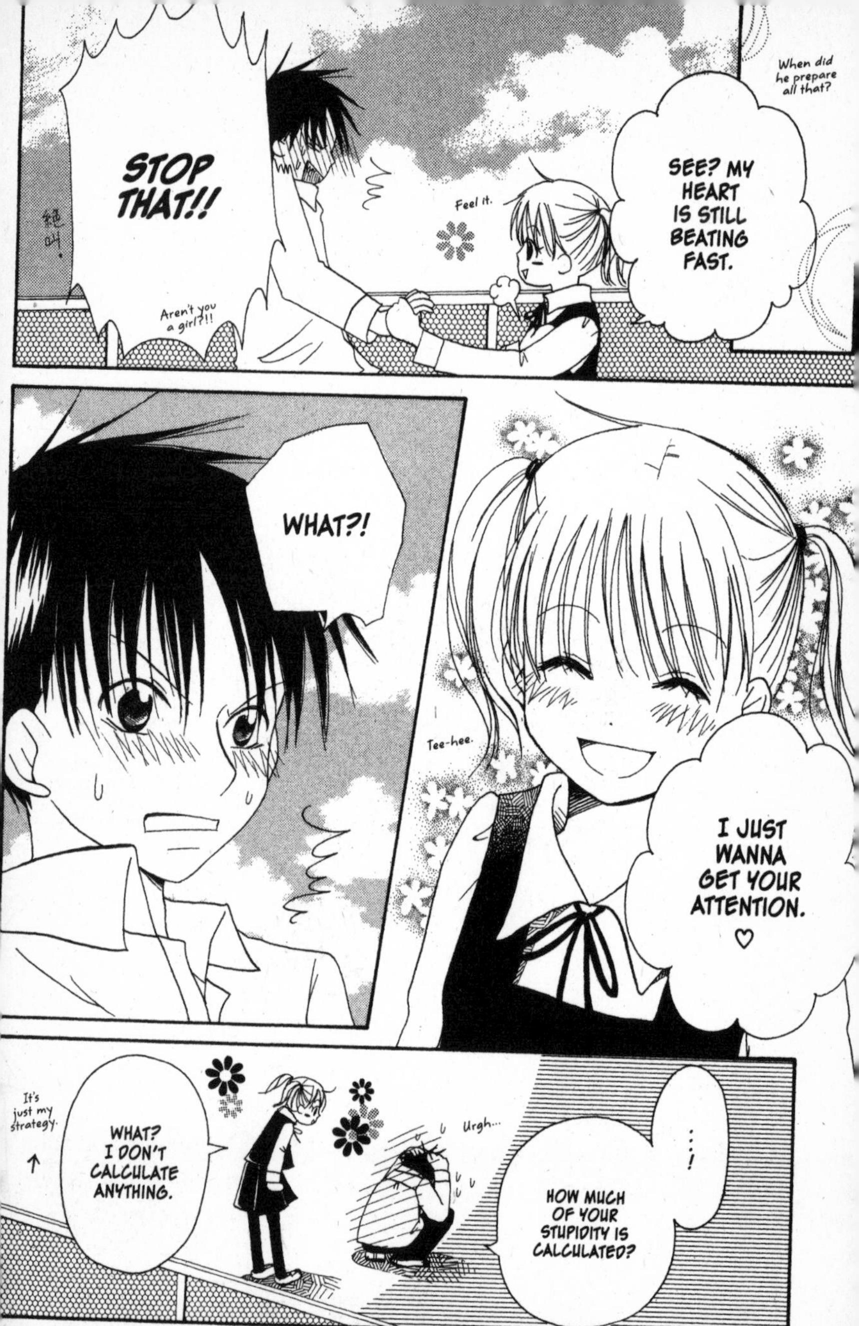
When did he prepare all that?
SEE? MY HEART IS STILL BEATING FAST.
Feel it.
STOP THAT!!
絶叫
Aren't you a girl?!!
I JUST WANNA GET YOUR ATTENTION. ♡
Tee-hee.
WHAT?!
...!
HOW MUCH OF YOUR STUPIDITY IS CALCULATED?
Urgh...
WHAT? I DON'T CALCULATE ANYTHING.
It's just my strategy. ↑

How to use Magic / End

Me & My Brothers

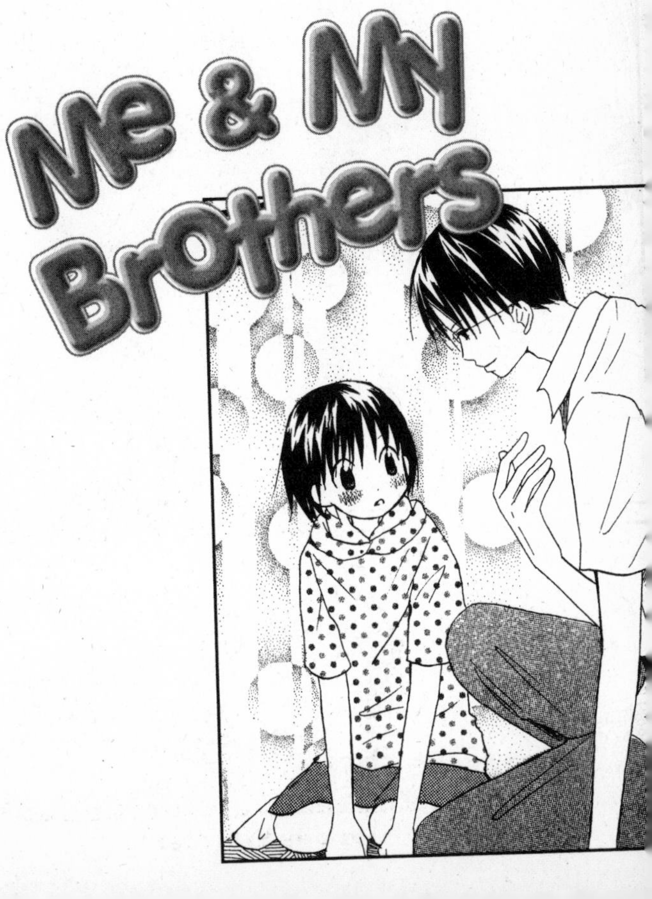

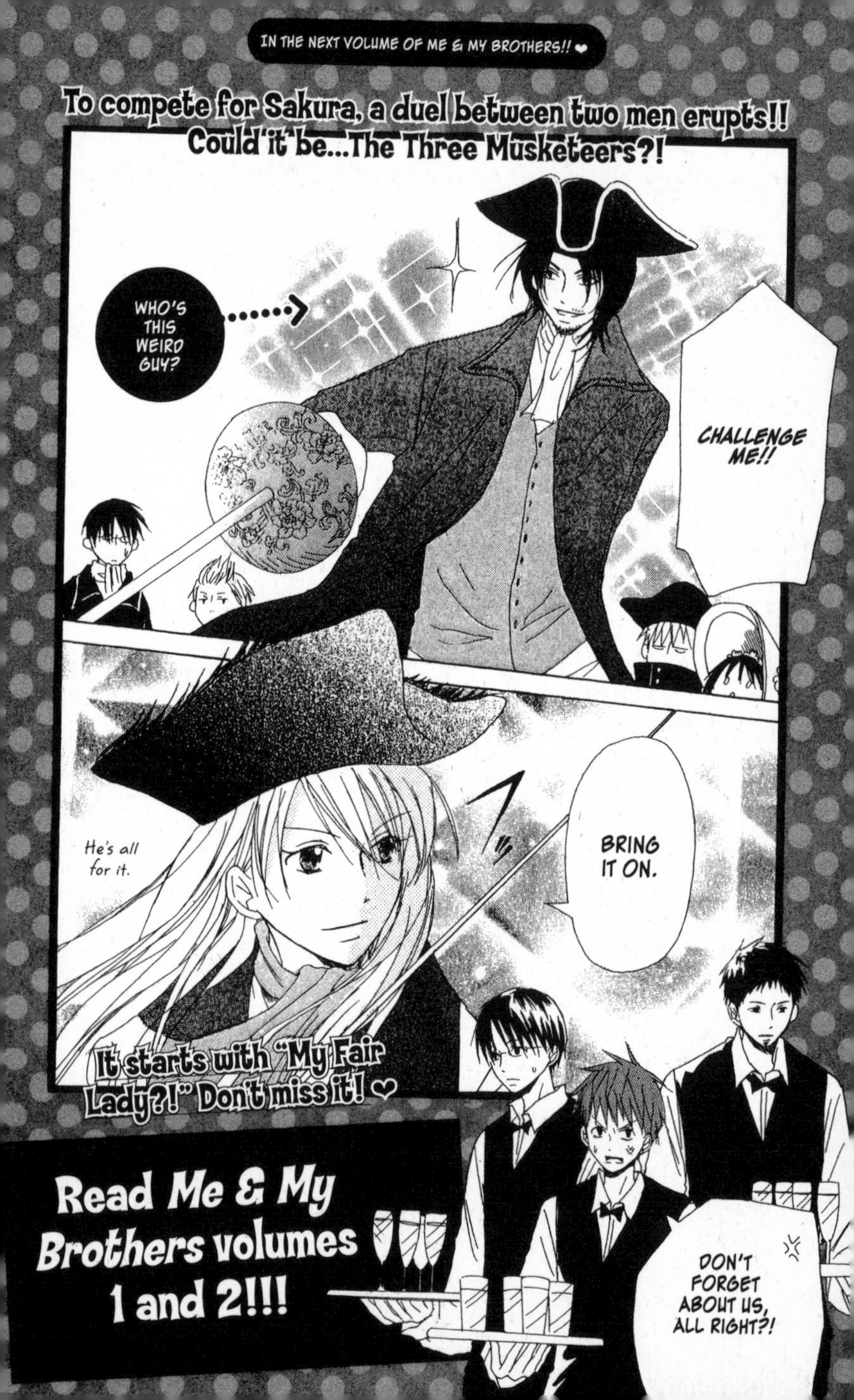
IN THE NEXT VOLUME OF ME & MY BROTHERS!! ❤
To compete for Sakura, a duel between two men erupts!!
Could it be...The Three Musketeers?!
CHALLENGE ME!!
WHO'S THIS WEIRD GUY?
BRING IT ON.
He's all for it.
It starts with "My Fair Lady?!" Don't miss it! ❤
DON'T FORGET ABOUT US, ALL RIGHT?!
Read Me & My Brothers volumes 1 and 2!!!

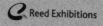